Live from Dar es Salaam

 **Ethnomusicology Multimedia**

Ethnomusicology Multimedia (EM) is a collaborative publishing program, developed with funding from the Andrew W. Mellon Foundation, to identify and publish first books in ethnomusicology, accompanied by supplemental audiovisual materials online at www.ethnomultimedia.org.

A collaboration of the presses at Indiana, Kent State, and Temple universities, EM is an innovative, entrepreneurial, and cooperative effort to expand publishing opportunities for emerging scholars in ethnomusicology and to increase audience reach by using common resources available to the three presses through support from the Andrew W. Mellon Foundation. Each press acquires and develops EM books according to its own profile and editorial criteria.

EM's most innovative features are its dual web-based components, the first of which is a password-protected Annotation Management System (AMS) where authors can upload peer-reviewed audio, video, and static image content for editing and annotation and key the selections to corresponding references in their texts. Second is a public site for viewing the web content, www.ethnomultimedia.org, with links to publishers' websites for information about the accompanying books. The AMS and website were designed and built by the Institute for Digital Arts and Humanities at Indiana University. The Indiana University Digital Library Program (DLP) hosts the website and the Indiana University Archives of Traditional Music (ATM) provides archiving and preservation services for the EM online content.

# Live from Dar es Salaam

POPULAR MUSIC AND TANZANIA'S
MUSIC ECONOMY

*Alex Perullo*

INDIANA UNIVERSITY PRESS

*Bloomington and Indianapolis*

Indiana University Press
601 North Morton Street
Bloomington, Indiana 47404-3797 USA

iupress.indiana.edu

*Telephone orders*    800-842-6796
*Fax orders*            812-855-7931
*Orders by e-mail*    iuporder@indiana.edu

♾ The paper used in this publication
meets the minimum requirements of the
American National Standard for Information Sciences—Permanence of Paper
for Printed Library Materials, ANSI
Z39.48-1992.

Manufactured in the United States of
America

Library of Congress Cataloging-in-
Publication Data

Perullo, Alex.
  Live from Dar es Salaam : popular music
and Tanzania's music economy / Alex
Perullo.
    p. cm. — (African expressive cultures)
  Includes bibliographical references and
index.
  ISBN 978-0-253-35605-5 (cloth : alk.
paper) — ISBN 978-0-253-22292-3 (pbk. :
alk. paper) 1. Popular music—Tanzania
—Dar es Salaam—History and criticism.
2. Music trade—Tanzania—Dar es
Salaam—History. I. Title.
  ML3503.T348P43 2011
  781.6309678—dc22

                              2011004798

1  2  3  4  5  16  15  14  13  12  11

FOR
*Joan, Noah, and Zachary*

# Contents

# Preface

Music is research into the essence of things.

—REMMY ONGALA

On a warm July afternoon in 2005, I walked with friends in a neighborhood on the outskirts of Dar es Salaam, Tanzania. As we neared the center of the neighborhood, we heard drumming and singing coming from a sandy field where local children play soccer throughout the day. It was unusual to hear music in the middle of the afternoon, particularly on a workday. After a few minutes, we found a crowd of a hundred people encircling a group of traditional *ngoma* musicians and dancers engaged in performance. The group used cylindrical, hand made drums and sang but also added a whistle in the style of the popular Congolese rumba artists that perform in the city's nightclubs. The songs were about health issues, and the male singer gave advice on ways to take care of oneself. During a break in the singing, a mixed group of men and women in matching outfits began to dance. Their steps were based on a traditional ngoma called *mdundiko* with many added variations drawn from contemporary dance routines. The crowd watched with great interest as the dancers took turns showing off their moves before returning into choreographed patterns that followed the drum rhythms. For an afternoon, it was a wonderfully entertaining and educational break in the day.

Given the unusual time and setting of the event, I asked about the performance. Why would a group perform for free in front of a large audience in the middle of a weekday afternoon? There are so many pressures to make a living in the city that it was odd to see a free concert where no money was exchanged between audience and performers. I came to learn that a local non-governmental organization (NGO) had hired the ngoma group to perform in certain areas of Dar es Salaam where health concerns were gravest. The group's job was to compose songs that would teach listeners about certain diseases and then use entertainment to keep their attention while they sung about either prevention or remedies. Drawn to the free concert, people eagerly stopped their afternoon tasks to watch and learn. No money needed to be exchanged since the NGO covered the costs of composing the songs and performing them in the city.

Similar to other events that take place in urban areas, the music of the ngoma troupe was both a form of entertainment and commerce. The music inspired people to gather because it was aesthetically pleasing and rhythmically interesting. The performers sang about issues that resonated with the audience, and listeners talked frequently during the event about the lyrics and their meaning. The music was also part of a business transaction. The musicians would not have composed the songs and played them around the city without being paid for their work. There needed to be financial incentive, a trade of money and creativity, in order for the event to take place.

Social science scholarship on music often analyzes songs as works of art that provide insight into people's daily lives. Songs are treated as texts, categorized into genres, and defined according to their most salient characteristics. These studies are vitally important to comprehending the arts as forms of expression that are unique to humanity. Of equal importance is analyzing music that exists in an economy of exchange and value. In societies driven by market economies, art forms become consumer goods that move through social networks of exchange and trade. There are so many ways to earn a living from music, whether in live performances, sound recordings, song compositions, or textual writing that it is difficult not to recognize the economic value placed on music in contemporary societies.

In this ethnography, I examine popular music in Dar es Salaam through analyzing music as both a cultural and economic resource. The focus is on presenting music as a *work* that people create, enjoy, and celebrate, and as a *commodity* that moves through an economy geared toward profiting from its social importance. The term work conveys the notion that there is something unique and irreplaceable being produced by artists, while commodity emphasizes the social life of music as a resource of economic potential (Lefebvre 1991: 70). Where one idea celebrates creativity in cultural forms of expression, the other provides a means to analyze music as distinct from mere products, goods, and artifacts (Appadurai 1986: 6). Combined, the notions of work and commodity provide a means to discuss the potential of music as a resource of human creativity and financial gain.

In analyzing music as both a work and commodity, I argue that one can attain a stronger sense of the contemporary place of music in urban African societies. The different ways that people relate to music provides a means for deciphering their interactions and relationships with cultural forms (Ginsburg 1997). Musicians rearrange notes, chords, harmonies, textures, and words to arrive at new and potentially influential material. As the music flows from artists to audience, it impacts people's worldviews and relations to each other. It influences emotions and allows people to escape into a world of meaning conveyed through lyrics and sounds. Moving from its source, people find ways to make music profitable. Profit, in this case, does not always mean monetary gains. It can also refer to improving status, social mobility, and power within different communities. This study is a means to conduct research, as Ongala states in the epigraph above, into the essence of things that are associated with living with and through music.

My focus on music as both a work and a commodity is meant to draw attention to broader shifts taking place in urban areas of Africa. Music is increasingly becoming an economic resource in countries undergoing social and economic transitions brought on by neoliberal reforms. Neoliberalism refers to movements away from state regulations toward permitting markets to operate unimpeded. In this deregulation, the focus has turned toward allowing individuals and businesses to operate without state intervention or restrictions. In Tanzania, the impacts of deregulation are significant. It has allowed for dramatic expansions of independent radio and television stations; expanded the commercialization of recorded music; and promoted efforts to claim ownership in songs. It has also brought many new struggles to earn a living in urban areas. Cities have always been challenging places to live. However, changes brought on by neoliberal reforms have made them even more difficult as people conceptualize success in new ways, even as their opportunities for social mobility often remain unchanged.

In response to the pressures of living in cities, people need to be more creative and self-reliant. Dar es Salaam is one of the largest urban areas in eastern Africa with 4 million residents. There are skyscrapers and vibrant commercial areas that provide evidence of affluence from neoliberal reforms, yet there are also higher rates of poverty, social insecurity, and marginalization than at any other time since independence. There are frequent cuts to utilities, water, and other resources. Corruption is endemic to most bureaucratic interactions, and health care systems are frequently near collapse. To make ends meet or to find success, people living in Dar es Salaam need to employ creative strategies that allow them to deal with the uncertainties that mark urban life. Creativity may be the "ultimate economic resource" (Florida 2002: xiii), as people innovatively apply skills and forms of knowledge to increasingly difficult situations. Getting by in Dar es Salaam, as in other cities in Africa, requires innovative strategies that can be used to overcome the lack of state support and increased attention to capitalist processes that position the individual as the source of economic production.

In this ethnography, I refer to people's innovative strategies as *creative practices.* The term creative practice encompasses both legal and illegal schemes that people use to find economic and social opportunities. It includes strategies, such as networking, positioning, branding, payola, bribery, and belief in the occult. Many popular songs in Tanzania reflect the growing need for creative practices. The African Stars song "Fainali Uzeeni" (The Final is in Old Age), for instance, refers to the need to use intelligence in order to live until old age (PURL P.1).

| | |
|---|---|
| Maisha ni mechi isiyo na sare, | Life is a match that cannot end in a tie, |
| Uyashinde au yakushinde, | You win or are beaten, |
| Hivyo unavyocheza mchezo huu, | So, as you play this game, |
| Lazima uwe makini, | You must be careful, |
| Unatakiwa utumie akili, | You need to use your intelligence, |
| Busara pia uwe mvumilivu. | Use your wisdom and also be a patient person [in order to overcome obstacles in life]. |

Dar es Salaam (2002) in the midst of rapid development in the downtown area. Several new office buildings were recently built or were being constructed at this time. *Photo by author.*

Numerous other songs, such as Tanzania One Theatre (TOT) Band's "Mtaji wa Maskini" (The Capital of the Poor), which became an anthem for the urban poor in the early 2000s, also reference the need to use individual skills to survive. The chorus states, "Mtaji wa Maskini ni nguvu zake mwenyewe" (The capital of the poor is their own strength). The use of the word *mtaji* (capital), meaning financial wealth, is emblematic of the move toward understanding social issues that are based on capitalist ideologies. In his lyrics, Banza Stone, who also composed the song, mocks the notion of free markets, since there is nothing free about them. Too many outside forces, such as foreign governments, international institutions, and companies, can control the economic capital of the country. This leaves many residents of urban areas struggling to find opportunities in an increasingly competitive environment. Strength and intelligence are their only assets, their only capital.

In analyzing creative practices within the popular music scene, I do not focus on a single musical genre. Rather, I am interested in aspects of music as a work and product that are interwoven within all genres of music. In Tanzania, there are eight genres that are central to popular music: *muziki wa kwaya* (choral music), *muziki wa injili* (gospel music), *dansi* (dance music), bongo flava (rap, ragga, and r&b), *taarab* (sung Swahili poetry), *ngoma*, reggae, and *mchiriku* (urban *ngoma*) (see appendix A for descriptions of these genres). Each of these genres has unique histories, musicians, and performance techniques that provide insight into the importance of the popular music in Tanzanian society. In this ethnography, my interest is in making connections between genres to show that all performers use similar creative practices to get their songs to air on the radio; find reliable distributors; interpret the meaning of fame and celebrity; or learn to perform music on stage. Wherever possible, I also make distinctions that are unique to a specific genre or that set it apart from others. More often, however, the following chapters focus on individuals who live and work within popular music. My interest is in the musicians, producers, distributors, radio announcers, and copyright officials who creatively discover strategies to survive or find success in Tanzania's music economy.

It is important to take a moment to understand the components involved in a music industry and why I have chosen to use the term music economy instead. The term music industry refers to all areas of manufacturing, distribution, and performance of music. It encompasses record companies that search for talent, chart the sales of songs, produce records, and market those records to interested audiences. It includes radio promotion companies that assist artists in attaining prominent radio airplay, as well as distributors that ship records to stores nationally or internationally. There are booking agents, managers, publicists, producers, and promoters, as well as lawyers and accountants. A music industry also includes music publishing, copyright laws, music videos, performance licenses, music schools, and places of performance. Of course, there are also bands, artists, roadies, sound engineers, composers, technicians, and others. All these components exist for the purpose of benefiting, financially or socially, from music. Even though music may be considered an object of aesthetic beauty, as it moves through a music industry it becomes a commodity that can generate income, fame, and prestige. Music is an expressive art form that carries tremendous potential within a system amenable to turning profits on sources of enjoyment.

But what happens when there are no record companies, radio promoters, or publicists? What if there is no person to chart record sales or handle music publishing? And what if there are no lawyers involved in music? Is it still a music industry? There is a tendency to want to see the music business in Africa through the same paradigm used in the West. That is, to understand the way music is being produced, sold, and purchased is to look for record companies, performing rights organizations, and large numbers of albums sold. Music economies in any country, however, are a reflection of the resources, capabilities, and interests of local populations. To comprehend the way they function and the overall interests of local stakeholders means to investigate peoples' relationships with music. Tanzania may lack many of the components of other music industries, but music is still a source of commercialization where many different people attempt to profit from its production and distribution. As this ethnography shows, the rapid expansion in the commercialization of music emphasizes the interest that many Tanzanians have in treating music as works of art and sources of income. The term *music economy* usefully captures this commercialization of music without relying on preconceptions and customs associated with a music industry. → JUST LIKE TAYLOR.

My use of the term music economy is also meant to avoid some of the disparaging comparisons that are often made in looking at economies of African music. In June 2001, for instance, the World Bank formed a task force to examine African music industries. Several members of the workshop commented that it would be difficult to create a successful music industry since African economies "aren't the best-managed economies in the world."[1] There is extensive piracy of musical recordings and a lack of copyright enforcement. Gerard Seligman, Senior Director of Hemisphere and Special Projects for EMI, added, "What makes this situation [for African music industries] even worse is the plethora of dishonest producers and corrupt or incompetent managers. Because there is no professional music business in most of Africa, there are few professional managers." The recommendation at the end of the meeting was to use the dramatic rise of Nashville's music scene as a model for developing industries on the African continent. The argument was that "Nashville went from being dirt-poor before 1940, to an affluent center" and something similar could be done in Africa.[2]

The beleaguering comments made during the workshop are not unique to this one meeting and are often supported with numerous statistics. The International Federation of the Phonographic Industry (IFPI) analyzes music economies around the world in a yearly report entitled *Recording Industry in Numbers: The Definitive Source of Global Music Market Information*. In the 2007 report, IFPI showed that while all music industries amassed $19.6 billion in recorded music sales, Africa barely registered at 0.008 percent, all of which was generated by South Africa. The authors of *The Global Music Industry* write that the "minute" sale of recorded music in Africa makes it "crystal clear why it is virtually impossible for African musicians to survive on the income from sales on the continent" (Bernstein, Sekine, and Weissman 2007: 101–03). The minimal profits are often coupled with statistics on the high rates of piracy in local music economies, which can range from 25 percent to 80 percent of a given economy depending on the country and author of the statistic. Overwhelmingly, the data and analysis demonstrate the failure in the commodification of music on the continent.

These statistics and ways of comprehending African economies do not take into account local forms of music making and commercialization. This tendency to limit perspective is common in many popular forums that deal with the African continent and fail to comprehend the "full spectrum of meanings and implications that other places and other human experiences enjoy, provoke, and inhabit" (Mbembe and Nuttall 2004: 348). In the case of music industries, available statistics focus on key issues that evidence success in Western economies. The IFPI statistics compile data, including figures on global sales, retail sales, and performance rights incomes. Many statistics come from recording industry associations, such as the Recording Industry Association of America (RIAA) and from record companies who are members of the IFPI.[3] Problematically, most African countries do not have record industry associations, music publishing firms, or record companies, which creates a vacuum for statistical information.

The lack of official statistics, however, does not mean that a music infrastructure does not exist. Funkazi Koroye-Crooks, a consultant for the World Intellectual Property Organization (WIPO), points out that in countries where there is a banderole program—a program that places holographic stickers on every cassette sold, making it difficult for people to pirate cassettes and compact discs and also allows one to track how many local albums are sold—the number of albums sold is considerable in comparison to extant statistics.[4] In the year 2000, the Copyright Society of Malawi (COSOMA) recorded 1.4 million albums sold with four artists selling over 80,000 albums each. In Ghana, 6.2 million albums were sold, 3.5 million of which were captured by gospel groups.[5] In Nigeria, more than 12 million albums were sold. Of course, these are only the officially recorded statistics based on the banderole program; actual sales could be much higher.

Other countries without banderole programs are also selling cassettes, but accurate numbers do not exist. In my own estimates, Tanzanian artists sold around 8 million original cassettes in the year 2007 but most likely sold more than 12.5 million pirated and original cassettes of music.[6] Further, the figures listed above are only for local cassettes. For foreign cassettes, Ghana sold 25.4 million in 1998 and Zimbabwe 12.4 million in 1999, and I imagine Tanzania is currently above the figure for Ghana. Considering the statistics provided by banderole programs and ethnographic research, African countries are selling and profiting from music. These statistics, however, do not appear in publications due to the extensive differences in the way music is commodified in various markets. These countries are, therefore, easily left out and ignored by international business communities. → KEY!

More important for this ethnography, privileging statistics presumes analogous forms of cultural relations to music. Western music businesses frequently depend on quantifying music in terms of album sales, concert revenue, and the frequency of radio airplay. There is some level of this numeric relation to music in Tanzania, but it is minimal at best. Instead, music depends on networks of personal relations, ideas, and communities that form and reform through constant negotiations of success, popularity, and cultural importance. Those who are concerned with the commodification of music remain close to its production: deejays play music on the radio for listening audiences; distributors sell music through working with artists; musicians perform for audiences; and producers record music by working with artists. There is little distance between anyone working with music and the actual music. Music as work and as commodity remains closely entangled, related, and engaged. Of course, statistics are not the only means to interact with music in other parts of the world. Many of my descriptions of Tanzania's music economy apply to those that exist elsewhere. The difference is that there is no upper-level management in Tanzania that quantifies music in terms of its business acumen. There are no executives, lawyers, or advertising specialists who may only have a cursory relation to the production of music but who significantly impact its presence in society. This may come with time in Tanzania. In the current environment, the creators and beneficiaries of music remain close to its circulation in the music economy.

In addition, ownership of businesses related to music remains in the hands of Tanzanians. Development of African economies, particularly in the decentralization of formerly socialist countries, frequently creates opportunities for international corporations to purchase or become significant investors in local enterprises. This has not occurred with music, and Tanzanians, for the most part, control the ownership in key areas of the music economy. This is not to suggest that outside influences do not impact local-level decision making or that international laws and regulations do not shift people's approaches to the music economy. Rather, control over bands, broadcasting stations, copyright law, recording studios, and educational facilities remains in the hands of local populations. This is a significant reason for the success of the country's music economy. Through empowering people to control and profit from their own cultural resources, there is far greater interest, investment, and zeal to find opportunities where none may have existed before. In the event that outside investors begin to control aspects of Tanzania's music economy, it would likely undermine many of the personal and creative efforts currently centered on music.

To conduct research on creative practices in Tanzania's music economy, I carried out ethnographic research using interviews, surveys, and participant observation. Beginning in 1998, I conducted interviews with members of the music community, including radio presenters, deejays, producers, copyright officials, government officials, and musicians. I recorded the majority of these interviews, and often reinterviewed some of the same people in subsequent trips to see the ways that creative practices may have changed over time. I also worked at radio stations and for newspapers and music magazines and became affiliated with various copyright efforts. By 2005, I had acquired an invaluable recorded history of music in Tanzania. What was missing, however, were in-depth discussions of creative practices. Putting away my recording equipment, I continued my research in Tanzania and talked to people informally about music, daily life, and Tanzanian society. Not surprisingly, people were more willing to discuss both legal and illegal strategies used in the music business without being formally questioned. Visiting people's homes on return trips, and calling and emailing once I was back in the United States, provided a tremendous assistance to deciphering innovative approaches people used to make a living on a daily basis. The last informal interviews I conducted were in July 2010, which helped cap a useful longitudinal study of the country's music economy (over the course of this research, I lived in Dar es Salaam for over three years).

In the span of just sixteen years (1994–2010), Tanzanian musicians, deejays, producers, promoters, and others created one of the strongest music economies in all of Africa.[7] Considering the amount of knowledge needed to make music commercially successful, the transition from state control to the proliferation of independent institutions in such a short amount of time is impressive. For all the discussions in popular media that Africa is in peril and in need of being "saved," this ethnography demonstrates something quite different. It presents examples of opportunities, successes, and ingenuity juxtaposed with difficult economic circumstances, disappointments, and failures. Ultimately, this book suggests that more attention should be directed at finding and exploring narratives that evidence achievements in African contexts, since so many exist and yet few appear in scholarly and popular texts.

Each chapter of this book interprets the formation and content of the Tanzanian music economy. I begin by discussing the most dominant themes that not only run through the ethnography but also shape people's relationship with music. From creative practices to post-socialism and neoliberalism to globalization, chapter 1 defines the contexts and policies that fostered the emergence of a prominent and successful music economy. I also discuss the role of youth, the most dominant social category in shaping the neoliberal music economy. Subsequent chapters provide specific details about the music economy historically (chapter 2) and in the contemporary period, including performance (chapter 3), musical learning and study (chapter 4), radio broadcasting (chapter 5), recording

studios (chapter 6), and music distribution and piracy (chapter 7). The
chapters that deal with the contemporary period focus on specific people
involved in music, including musicians, radio announcers, promoters,
distributors, and the state. In most chapters, I also pay particular attention
to the innovative strategies that people use to learn their craft despite the
lack of educational institutions that cater to people working in the music
economy.

In the final chapter (chapter 8), I present future directions in the
commercialization of Tanzanian music. Often in interviews and discussions, members of the music economy discuss their apprehensions for
the future. There is a sense among many that the prosperity of the first
sixteen years will not be repeated given the stiff competition that exists
in music, the dominance of media monopolies, and increases in internet
piracy. Even if these apprehensions prove to be unfounded, they illustrate
people's stance toward the future. It gives insight into the insecurities
people experience in the current economy as they continue to search for
ways to benefit from Tanzanian popular music.

# Acknowledgments

Many people were involved with this project from the early stages of research to the final touches on the manuscript. I am indebted to all the musicians, producers, radio deejays, promoters, managers, and distributors for talking about and explaining the local music scene. In particular, I would like to thank members of Kilimanjaro Band, DDC Mlilmani Park Orchestra, Msondo Ngoma, Tanzania One Theatre, All Star Modern Taarab, Mambo Poa, African Stars, and Wagosi wa Kaya, as well as the staff of the radio stations Clouds FM, Radio Tanzania Dar es Salaam, Times FM, and Radio Tumaini. Other members of the music community who assisted me in innumerable ways include Waziri Ally, Ally Chocky, Shaban Dede, Ahmed Dola, Joseph Haule, Ally Jamwaka, Hamza Kalala, Shem Karenga, King Kiki, Joachim Kimario, John Kitime, Ramesh Kothari, Taji Liundi, Sebastian Maganga, Gaudens Makunja, Fredrick Mariki, Charles Mateso, Joseph Mbilinyi, Muhidin Issa Michuzi, Ruge Mutahaba, Remmy Ongala, and John Peter Pentelakis.

My thanks to King Kinya, Said Mdoe, Ibrahim Washokera, and Adam Lutta for allowing me to use their artistic works in this publication. E. Shogholo Challi, Angelo Luhala, Ruyembe Mulimba, and the staff at BASATA always welcomed me into their offices to talk about music. I am very grateful for their support. Stephan Mtetewaunga and the current staff of COSOTA, E.E. Mahingila of BRELA, and Daniel Ndagala formerly of the Ministry of Culture and Education provided me with invaluable insight into the political side of Tanzania's music economy. Werner Graebner and Douglas Paterson were exceedingly generous in providing me with information about record labels, companies, and artists that greatly informed my research. My thanks also to John Lukuwi, who helped me comb through the national press archives looking for historic photographs of Tanzanian music.

Academically, I benefited greatly from the advice of many people. I want to especially thank Ruth Stone for her guidance over the years. Kelly Askew, Richard Bauman, Alan Burdette, Eric Charry, John Hanson, Clara Henderson, John Fenn, and Daniel Reed each provided critical commentary either on my research or writing. Scholars of Tanzania who enlightened me on many aspects of the country's history and culture include Kelly Askew, Greg Barz, Ned Bertz, James Brennan, Andrew Burton, Thomas Gesthuizen, Frank Gunderson, Stephen Hill, Heather Hoag, Andrew Ivaska, Loren Landau, Dodie McDow, Harrison Mwakyembe, and Elias Songoyi. I am particularly grateful to Amandina Lihamba and Frowin Nyoni at the Fine and Performing Arts Department of the University of Dar es Salaam for generously talking with me about my research ideas. Finally, I owe a great deal of gratitude to Deo Ngonyani and Ray Mwasha for providing insight into the subtle meaning of Swahili words, and assisting with my translations of songs and other critical texts that appear in this ethnography.

The Bryant University research librarians, including Jenifer Bond, Maura Keating, Laura Kohl, Trish Schultz, and Cheryl Richardson, were wonderfully helpful and kind in finding research materials for me and fact-checking my references. I also received comments and support from my colleagues Andrea Boggio, Bill Graves, Terri Hasseler, Rich Holtzman, Mary Prescott, and David Lux.

The staff at Indiana University Press has been very supportive of this project. I am particularly grateful to Dee Mortensen, Peter Froehlich, and Brian Herrmann for being so accommodating with my requests and providing valuable advice on my work. The reviewers of this manuscript should also be thanked for their clear and concise comments on an earlier draft.

I am grateful for the generous support provided by the Fulbright-Hays Doctoral Dissertation Research Abroad Fellowship, the Laura Boulton Senior Fellowship, and Bryant University Research Grants. Thank you, as well, to the Tanzania Commission for Science and Technology (COSTECH) for granting me research clearance on each of my fieldwork trips.

James Browne Nindi, a Tanzanian journalist and scholar, has assisted me over the years in interpreting and understanding Tanzanian society. James helped me with interviews, surveys, and transcriptions during my fieldwork. Most important, his friendship over the past twelve years has been one of the greatest benefits of living and conducting research in Tanzania.

I am grateful to Diane Perullo for taking the time to read each chapter of this book and comment on my writing, and to Paul Perullo for his support over the years (even when I tell him I am traveling to Tanzania, to which he replies "not again"). Many other family members encouraged my research and took part in spirited sessions to come up with a title for this book. It has been a blessing to have such a supportive family.

Last, I am indebted to Joan, Noah, and Zachary for their love and patience. Joan read and commented on this manuscript and always had kind suggestions. Her willingness to travel with me to Tanzania and spend late nights sitting in clubs just to hear "one more great song" shows how fortunate I am. Our sons provided the playful humor that filled my time away from researching and writing with laughter and amusement. It never ceases to amaze me how they wake up each day as if it is the best day in the world. That has profoundly influenced me and led to a stronger ethnography than I would have otherwise been able to produce.

# Note on Names and Interviews

For those who read materials from Tanzania, several people's names in this book may appear to be misspelled. In many Tanzanian newspapers, the name of the Double Extra singer is written as "Ali Choki," "Ally Chokey," or "Ali Chockey." The singer himself spells his name "Ally Chocky." Many other people's names in Tanzanian newspapers are spelled differently from how they themselves write them. Kasongo Mpinda Clayton's first name is often written with two 's's. Luizer Mbutu's name is often misspelled even by the people in charge of managing her career (she is also commonly referred to as Luiza, which further complicates finding a commonly accepted spelling for her name). In some circumstances, the misspelled names are actually used by the artist or band. Lady Jay Dee's name is written as Lady JD and Lady Jaydee, all of which appear in various official publications by her and all of which appear appropriate to use. Many times the changes are due to the Swahilization of words, which adds a vowel to the end of names (Said becomes Saidi or Hassan becomes Hassani). The famed dansi singer Marijani Rajab's last name is often written as Rajabu. The wide variety of spellings proved challenging in writing this book. I began to wonder what spelling was best to use: the one that the artist uses or the one that is commonly used in publications and on sound recordings? Many people know Kanku Kelly's surname as Tubajike even though it is actually Kashamatubajike. In writing about him, is it better to use the more familiar or the more proper name?

For this book, I have usually chosen the way the individual spells his or her name rather than the media spelling. Using proper spellings, however, only proved effective in situations where I knew, interviewed, or at least met the individual. Given the size of the local music economy, I could not learn the spelling of everyone who appears in this book, particularly in historical materials about an artist who had passed away. Therefore, in these cases, I have relied on my research in the media to arrive at the most common spelling of a name even though this might not concur with the individual's own spelling of his or her name. I also depended on registries of artists provided to me by various organizations in Tanzania to see how artists signed their names on official documents.

With few exceptions, all interviews for this book were done in Swahili. Most of these interviews, in their entirety, are archived in the Archives of Traditional Music in Bloomington, Indiana, under accession number 07-007-F/B/C. In the translations of the interviews that appear in this ethnography, I have attempted to capture the meaning of people's comments, but I also recognize that speech does not always translate well in print. In these cases, I have edited people's statements to arrive at more readable texts.

All quoted individuals that appear in this ethnography had an opportunity to look at their quotes as they appear in this book. This provided a useful means to fact-check details and allowed me a chance to ask new questions and expand on details from initial interviews. Only one individual asked that I change some of the wording in my translation of his words, but the editing only proved more informative rather than altering the original quotations. Finally, James Nindi and Ray Mwasha checked many of the transcriptions and translations for accuracy. I am grateful for their assistance in improving the quality of these texts. All errors and omissions are my own.

# Video Clips on the Ethnomusicology Multimedia Website

A selection of video recordings I made during fieldwork in Dar es Salaam between 2000 and 2002 can be accessed on the Ethnomusicology Multimedia website, www.ethnomultimedia.org. Keyed to specific passages in *Live from Dar es Salaam*, each example listed below has been assigned a unique persistent uniform resource identifier, or PURL. Within the text of the book, a PURL number in parentheses functions as a citation and immediately follows the text to which it refers, for example, (PURL 3.1). The numbers following the word "PURL" indicate the initial chapter in which the media example is found and the order in which the PURL first appears in that chapter.

There are two ways for readers of the print edition of this book to access and play back a specific media example. The first is to type in a web browser the full address of the PURL associated with a specific media example, as indicated in the list below. Readers will be taken to a web page displaying that media example as well as a playlist of all of the media examples related to this book. Once readers have navigated to the Ethnomusicology Multimedia website, the second way to access media examples is by typing into the search field the unique six-digit PURL identifier located at the end of the full PURL address. Readers of the electronic edition of this book will simply click on the PURL address for each media example; this live link will take them directly to the media example on the Ethnomusicology Multimedia website. Readers will be required to electronically sign an end-users license agreement (EULA) the first time they attempt to access a media example.

The list below, organized by chapter, includes the PURL number, the title of the video segment, and the full PURL with the six-digit unique identifier.

In addition to the recordings linked to this book, twelve hours of my fieldwork video from Dar es Salaam, along with detailed annotations that describe and analyze Tanzanian popular music, is accessible through the EVIA Digital Archive Project website (www.eviada.org). The EVIADA Project is a collaborative endeavor to create a digital archive of ethnographic field video for use by scholars and instructions. Funded from 2001 to 2009 by the Andrew W. Mellon Foundation with significant contributions from Indiana University and the University of Michigan, the Project was developed through the joint efforts of ethnographic scholars, archivists, librarians, technologists, and legal experts. On the EVIA website, readers should search for the collection "Generations of Sound: Popular Music, Genre, and Performance in Tanzania." Users of the EVIA website will need to create an account by clicking on "enter the archive" and then clicking on the login button. This will take you to a page where you can "create an account" to register with the Project. Other fieldwork videos that I recorded between 2005 and 2010 can be accessed at the Indiana University Archives of Traditional Music under accession number 07-007-F/C.

## PREFACE

PURL P.1 | Performance: African Stars, "Fainali Uzeeni"
 (The Final is in Old Age)
http://purl.dlib.indiana.edu/iudl/em/Perullo/900001

## CHAPTER 1

PURL 1.1 | Performance: Mabaga Fresh, freestyle
http://purl.dlib.indiana.edu/iudl/em/Perullo/900002
PURL 1.2 | Performance: Mabaga Fresh "Tupo Kamili" (We are Able)
http://purl.dlib.indiana.edu/iudl/em/Perullo/900003
PURL 1.3 | Performance: Mabaga Fresh "Hakuna Noma" (No Problem)
http://purl.dlib.indiana.edu/iudl/em/Perullo/900004
PURL 1.4 | Performance: TOT Taarab "Mambo ya Fedha"
 (Matters of Money)
http://purl.dlib.indiana.edu/iudl/em/Perullo/900005

PURL 1.5 | Performance: Mr. II, "Mambo ya Fedha" (Matters of Money)
http://purl.dlib.indiana.edu/iudl/em/Perullo/900006
PURL 1.6 | Performance: King Kiki, "Pesa Yetu" (Our Money)
http://purl.dlib.indiana.edu/iudl/em/Perullo/900007
PURL 1.7 | Performance: Mr. II, "Dar es Salaam."
http://purl.dlib.indiana.edu/iudl/em/Perullo/900008

CHAPTER 2

PURL 2.1 | Classic dansi performance, King Kiki "Songo"
http://purl.dlib.indiana.edu/iudl/em/Perullo/900009
PURL 2.2 | Performance: Simba Theatre, "Ngoma ya Moto"
    (Dance with Fire)
http://purl.dlib.indiana.edu/iudl/em/Perullo/900010
PURL 2.3 | Performance: Hamza Kalala, "Tanzania Yetu"
    (Our Tanzania)
http://purl.dlib.indiana.edu/iudl/em/Perullo/900011
PURL 2.4 | Performance: TOT Kwaya "Which Way to Go"
http://purl.dlib.indiana.edu/iudl/em/Perullo/900012

CHAPTER 3

PURL 3.1 | Audience Interaction, African Starts, piga bao (score a goal)
http://purl.dlib.indiana.edu/iudl/em/Perullo/900013
PURL 3.2 | Performance: African Stars, praising Dar es Salaam
    and the videographer
http://purl.dlib.indiana.edu/iudl/em/Perullo/900014
PURL 3.3 | Performance: TOT Taarab performs "Kinyang'unya"
    (Old Hag)
http://purl.dlib.indiana.edu/iudl/em/Perullo/900015
PURL 3.4 | Performance: TOT Kwaya sings a song for
    Mwalimu Nyerere
http://purl.dlib.indiana.edu/iudl/em/Perullo/900016
PURL 3.5 | Performance: TOT Band "Jahazi" (Dhow)
http://purl.dlib.indiana.edu/iudl/em/Perullo/900017
PURL 3.6 | Performance: Gangwe Mobb and Inspekta Haroun
    freestyle
http://purl.dlib.indiana.edu/iudl/em/Perullo/900018

PURL 3.7 | Dance to Kilimanjaro Band's song "Boko" by the
    dance group Chocolate
http://purl.dlib.indiana.edu/iudl/em/Perullo/900019
PURL 3.8 | Performance: Banner waving at concert
http://purl.dlib.indiana.edu/iudl/em/Perullo/900020
PURL 3.9 | Interview: Ndala Kasheba and "Kadi ya Njano"
    (Yellow Card)
http://purl.dlib.indiana.edu/iudl/em/Perullo/900021
PURL 3.10 | Performance: Ndala Kasheba, "Kadi ya Njano"
    (Yellow Card)
http://purl.dlib.indiana.edu/iudl/em/Perullo/900022

## CHAPTER 5

PURL 5.1 | Performance: "Sérieux ya Mukoko" performed by
    Kasongo
Mpinda Clayton and Nguza Viking [originally performed by
    Orchestra Maquis du Zaire]
http://purl.dlib.indiana.edu/iudl/em/Perullo/900023
PURL 5.2 | Performance: New Millennium Band, "Amina"
http://purl.dlib.indiana.edu/iudl/em/Perullo/900024
PURL 5.3 | Interview: Kasongo and old is gold Part 1
http://purl.dlib.indiana.edu/iudl/em/Perullo/900025
PURL 5.4 | Interview: Kasongo and old is gold Part 2
http://purl.dlib.indiana.edu/iudl/em/Perullo/900026
PURL 5.5 | Performance: Hamza Kalala, interview and performance,
    "Kitimoto" (Pork) Part 1
http://purl.dlib.indiana.edu/iudl/em/Perullo/900027
PURL 5.6 | Performance: Hamza Kalala, interview and performance,
    "Kitimoto" (Pork) Part 2
http://purl.dlib.indiana.edu/iudl/em/Perullo/900028
PURL 5.7 | Performance: Muungano Cultural Troupe, "Sanamu la
    Michelini" (Symbol of the Michelin Man)
http://purl.dlib.indiana.edu/iudl/em/Perullo/900029
PURL 5.8 | Performance: Lady Jay Dee, "Machozi" (Tears)
http://purl.dlib.indiana.edu/iudl/em/Perullo/900030

CHAPTER 6

PURL 6.1 | Performance: Ndala Kasheba performing the OSS song,
　　"Bagama" (Witch)
http://purl.dlib.indiana.edu/iudl/em/Perullo/900031

CHAPTER 7

PURL 7.1 | Performance: Simba Theatre, "Sindimba"
http://purl.dlib.indiana.edu/iudl/em/Perullo/900032
PURL 7.2 | Performance: Mambo Poa performs "Mimi sio Mwizi"
　　(I am not a Thief)
http://purl.dlib.indiana.edu/iudl/em/Perullo/900033

CHAPTER 8

PURL 8.1 | Interview and Performance: Ndala Kasheba,
　　"Dunia Msongamano" (The World is Harsh)
http://purl.dlib.indiana.edu/iudl/em/Perullo/900034
PURL 8.2 | Interview: Ndala Kasheba and the music industry
http://purl.dlib.indiana.edu/iudl/em/Perullo/900035
PURL 8.3 | Interview: Kasheba and the music business
http://purl.dlib.indiana.edu/iudl/em/Perullo/900036
PURL 8.4 | Mambo Poa at Mambo Club
http://purl.dlib.indiana.edu/iudl/em/Perullo/900037
PURL 8.5 | Performance: Mvita Dancing Troupe, "Haiwezekani"
　　(It's Not Possible)
http://purl.dlib.indiana.edu/iudl/em/Perullo/900038

APPENDIX A

The following video segments are full-length events or songs that correspond to a particular genre of music. The genre name is listed in parentheses after the event name.
PURL A.1 | Concert: Mr. II album release concert (bongo flava,
　　rap and r&b)
http://purl.dlib.indiana.edu/iudl/em/Perullo/900039

PURL A.2 | Concert: Hamza Kalala Interview and Performance (dansi)
http://purl.dlib.indiana.edu/iudl/em/Perullo/900040

PURL A.3 | Concert: Classic dansi music performed by Ndala Kasheba,
   Nguza Viking, and King Kiki (dansi)
http://purl.dlib.indiana.edu/iudl/em/Perullo/900041

PURL A.4 | Concert: African Stars Performance in Mnazi Mmoja (dansi)
http://purl.dlib.indiana.edu/iudl/em/Perullo/900042

PURL A.5 | Concert: Mvita Dancing Troupe (mchriku)
http://purl.dlib.indiana.edu/iudl/em/Perullo/900043

PURL A.6 | Concert: St. Joseph's Choir, downtown Dar es Salaam
   (kwaya)
http://purl.dlib.indiana.edu/iudl/em/Perullo/900044

PURL A.7 | Concert: Simba Theater performing at Nyumba ya Sanaa
   (ngoma)
http://purl.dlib.indiana.edu/iudl/em/Perullo/900045

PURL A.8 | Performance: TOT Taarab, "Huyu ni Wangu" (That Person
   is Mine) (taarab)
http://purl.dlib.indiana.edu/iudl/em/Perullo/900046

PURL A.9 | Performance: Muungano Cultural Troupe, "Huna Lako"
   (Mind Your Own Business) (taarab)
http://purl.dlib.indiana.edu/iudl/em/Perullo/900047

*Live from Dar es Salaam*

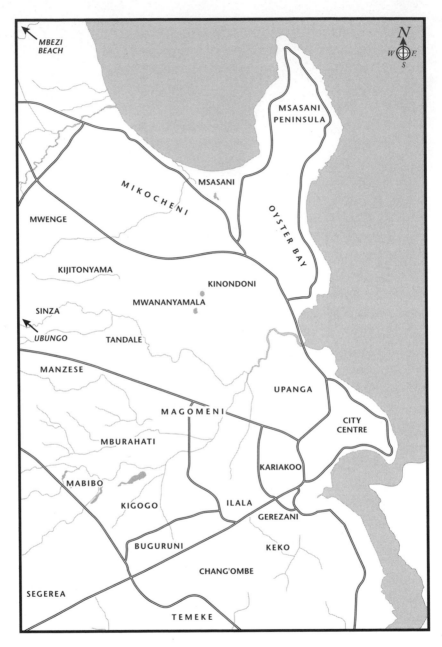

Map of Dar es Salaam.

# ONE

# Kumekucha (It Is Daylight / Times Have Changed)

You need to be smart to live in the city . . .
Everyone lives by their own intelligence,
To live in the city depends on your ingenuity,
Finish your plans before the end of the day,
Don't fail to return home.

—EXTRA BONGO "Mjini Mipango" (In the City Is Planning)

*1961 Independence*

In 1963, members of the band Western Jazz entered the recording studio of the Tanganyika Broadcasting Corporation (TBC), a semi-independent radio station informally controlled by the government. The TBC was the only recording facility in the country and an important resource for local artists wanting to publicize their music and concerts. After the ten members of Western Jazz set up their instruments in the cramped studio and did a sound check with the recording engineer, they began to record their music for the first time. During several hours in the studio, the group performed a number of popular songs, including "Mpenzi Wangu Shida" (My Lover Shida), "Wamenisingizia Kifo" (They Wrongly Proclaimed My Death), and "Fitina za Dunia" (Intrigue of the World).[1] The songs, which brought together traditional Tanzanian music with American soul and jazz, Congolese dance music, and Latin rhythms, were powerful and important for a nation that had become independent only two years earlier. Though the band was paid a minimal few hundred shillings for their songs, they received constant airplay by the radio station for the next several decades. The airplay helped solidify the group as one of the most important in Tanzania's popular music history.

Almost forty years later, I sat in a small, crowded room with five of the original Western Jazz band members and Joseph Kisandu, the head of a copyright association in Tanzania.[2] It was early evening and, though most of the city was returning home after a day of work, a dispute needed to be settled within the group. Kisandu, who led the discussion, gave each band member a chance to speak, beginning, as is customary in Tanzania, with the eldest musician. Mzee Juma told about his life in music, the hardships he faced, and how he ended up in Western Jazz as an instrumentalist and a composer. The story, like many told by elder Tanzanian musicians, touched on the struggles of living in independent Tanzania, working under a socialist government, recording at the government radio station, and fighting through the country's long depression after its war with the former Ugandan dictator Idi Amin.

After a short time, the elder brought us to the point of the meeting: to discuss the sale of Western Jazz recordings by a local Asian storeowner.[3] Mzee Juma accused the former band leader, Rashid Mafumbo, of selling the rights to Western Jazz recordings, including those recorded at the TBC forty years ago. This was done, according to Juma, without providing compensation to any of the other band members. Mafumbo sat still, defiant, with his eyes staring absently at his hands. The elder proceeded to tell how Mafumbo signed a contract and received 300,000 Tanzanian shillings (Tsh), equivalent to US$300, for giving the rights of twenty Western Jazz songs to the local storeowner. The contract gave the storeowner the right to sell the recordings for two years with a chance to renew the contract after that point. The elder emphasized the amount Mafumbo was paid, Tsh 300,000, and repeated that none of the other living band members had received a single shilling.

When the elder finished, each of the other three band members told similar stories. All accused Mafumbo of the same wrongdoing and looked as if they were on the verge of physically lashing out at him. Kisandu tried to keep the situation diplomatic, but the band members' fury at not getting their share of the royalties was difficult to contain. Finally, Mafumbo was given his chance to speak. His few words were clumsy but defiant. He tried to state that he received only Tsh 30,000 ($30) in the deal, not the larger amount for which he stood accused. Kisandu quickly pulled out a copy of the contract Mafumbo had signed with the Asian storeowner. The contract, accompanied by several receipts, showed the total amount of the royalties paid to Mafumbo: Tsh 300,000.

Still defiant, Mafumbo said, "Fine, if you have a problem, take me to court." In one sentence, he had shown the inherent flaw with the group's anger at him. In the urban environment in which they lived, the band members could do nothing to retrieve their share of the money: the police would never arrest Mafumbo without a significant bribe, a court case could take years, and each of these would cost far more money than it was worth. Kisandu quickly dismissed the threat of a court case and said that the problem needed to be solved internally. But Mafumbo gained some confidence from his threat, as idle as it was. For the next half hour, he continually repeated himself, sounding like a broken record, but silencing the criticism against him.

Toward dark, the mood in the room began to change. The band members had vented their anger at Mafumbo and realized they were never going to get their money. As they said, Mafumbo "has already eaten it." They even began to feel sorry for him. Sorry, they said, that Mafumbo had been forced into signing a contract in English, a language which he apparently did not understand. The blame now shifted from Mafumbo to the storeowner. Kisandu saw his moment and proposed a united front to get the storeowner to pay each member a share of the royalties. He agreed to write a letter on behalf of the group demanding that the store pay each member separately, a part of which would go to Kisandu. Now, ironically united, the band agreed to sign the letter and attempt to receive their shares of the royalties.

The storeowner was someone I often spoke with, and a few days after the meeting with Western Jazz and Kisandu, I went to see him. He had already received Kisandu's letter, which he showed to me. Typed on an old, electric typewriter with official stationary, the letter accused the storeowner of stealing from poor musicians and tricking Mafumbo with a contract written and signed in English. The owner was shocked at the offensive language, both derogatory and inflammatory. He was hurt by the accusations and told me, "I paid Mafumbo the royalties; I have a contract here. I did not know there were any other [living] band members." Unfortunately, the owner could not know that other members were still alive since no system or resource exists to find people who performed in a band in a particular period. The storeowner had to, or wanted to, trust Mafumbo, who told him that everyone else in the band had passed away.

The letter that the storeowner received was typical of Kisandu's negotiation procedures. Kisandu was well known for scaring people, through either letters or personal visits, until they paid him money. The storeowner knew this about Kisandu and was worried that something might happen. Would he be arrested for not searching out all the members of Western Jazz? Would he be taken to court? Would other musicians not sign a contract with him after hearing about the Western Jazz debacle? In the end, the storeowner continued to sell the cassettes because the contract and the royalties had been dealt with as legally as possible. And, though Kisandu and Western Jazz continued to fight the storeowner, they were unable to do anything until the contract expired two years later.

## AN ECONOMY OF MUSIC

Most people in Dar es Salaam do not envision themselves as being part of a music industry per se. In fact, the term for music industry, *tasnia ya muziki*, is rarely used in daily conversation. Instead, people describe music and the social spaces that surround it (studios, clubs, radio stations, etc.) as an opportunity for employment and an outlet for furthering their own aspirations, opportunities, and affiliations. Those aspirations may include musical competency as a songwriter, composer, or producer. It may include attaining recognition as a strong radio presenter. Or, it may mean running a successful bar in downtown Dar es Salaam that can compete with other establishments in the city. But individual aspirations within the local music scene always include making the most of the limited resources that exist. It is a means of establishing a better position within society by creating opportunities in a highly competitive environment. Tanzania's music economy is an arrangement of creative human activities and practices intended to produce, distribute, perform, and consume various facets of music.

The Western Jazz narrative illustrates this economy of music well. All the parties involved—Mafumbo, Kisandu, the members of Western Jazz, and the storeowner—sought to transform a few recorded songs from the 1960s into profitable commodities. These songs were technically the property of Radio Tanzania Dar es Salaam (RTD), which took over the rights in the TBC recordings. Mafumbo, however, was able to sign a contract with an independent storeowner, since no guidelines or effective enforcement existed on legal contracts. There could be no lawsuits or efficient means for other members of Western Jazz to sue or dispute Mafumbo's actions due to the costs involved in hiring lawyers and in the inherent problems of the country's legal system. Nor would RTD make a case against Kisandu for illegally selling their recordings since the original contract between RTD and Western Jazz stipulated that the station could only use the song for broadcasts, even though they had long been selling them for profit. Further, Kisandu's music organization had no legal jurisprudence but pursued copyright matters with such zeal that local businesses became intimidated by his forcefulness and knowledge of legal matters. The meeting between Western Jazz and Kisandu was therefore an opportunity, a creative endeavor for everyone involved to find new avenues of profiting from a few post-independence recordings that remained popular. The interaction between them was a strategy for finding social and economic benefits where none had existed before.

Mainly located in Dar es Salaam, the country's largest city, the Tanzanian music economy consists of people from various economic and social backgrounds, who attempt to find innovative strategies to establish a living from music. These strategies are a part of any person's interaction and highlight the resourceful ways individuals make the most of a given situation in their attempts to attain power, status, and/or social mobility. People act creatively in order to compete with or outdo others vying for the same thing. Competition and the increasing influence of capitalism in the neoliberal period play a role in the use of creative practices. Yet the struggle that many people encounter in areas of Tanzania, such as Dar es Salaam, make creative practices more compulsory and forceful. There is urgency in the strategies people use since few options are available for financial or social wealth. Certainly, all the people involved in reselling classic songs of Western Jazz looked for an opportunity to profit from songs that were, for years, not thought to have economic value.

Discussing creative practices provides a means to analyze the formation of the contemporary music economy as one of the most successful and prosperous on the African continent. Between 1994 and 2009, Tanzania moved from having one state-controlled radio station and two recording studios to fifty-two radio stations, twenty-seven television stations, and over a hundred recording studios (see appendix B; a list of studios can be found in chapter 6). In 2005, there were 350 registered newspaper and magazine publications in Tanzania, with one-third regularly making it to press. The number of producers, radio deejays, music distributors, and music journalists increased at the same exponential rate, as did the sale and distribution of recorded albums. There were also awards ceremonies, local fashion lines that catered to the music scene, and sponsors from Tanzania, South Africa, Kenya, and elsewhere who began hosting large concerts. International artists, such as Kofi Olomide, Miriam Makeba, Sean Paul, and Jay Z, all made stops in Dar es Salaam to perform their music. Although Kenya's music economy rebounded to some extent in the early 2000s, no other country in eastern Africa offered the same array of options and skills that Tanzania did. How did this happen? How did a formerly state-controlled music economy with limited means grow into the most successful in eastern Africa within such a short period? How did people, such as artists, deejays, producers, managers, and distributors, fill the gaps in knowledge that came with such a rapid expansion of musical commerce? And what occurred within Dar es Salaam's urban society that allowed for such significant movement toward the commodification and commercialization of music?

*ARGUMENT* —→  The next several sections examine these questions by analyzing the formation of the Tanzanian music economy and the basis for my use of the term creative practices. The sections move out in concentric circles, beginning with ideologies that gave rise to creative practices, and progress through national and international issues, including post-socialism, neoliberalization, and globalization that greatly influence the economic conditions of Tanzania. These historical and theoretical ideas overlap and connect together to illustrate processes that position Dar es Salaam as a hub for the commodification of music in eastern Africa. It is not by any form of planning that a prosperous music economy emerged in Tanzania but rather through the confluences of disparate modes of so-cial action that had rich implications for the performance, production, distribution, and protection of music. The remainder of this chapter takes apart those confluences in order to provide a necessary means to interpret the Tanzanian music economy as it is lived and experienced on a daily basis.

## NATIONAL CULTURE AND LOCAL PHILOSOPHIES

Creative practices are not a new phenomenon in Tanzania. There are numerous historical examples of people using innovative strategies to overcome obstacles, which form critical points in documenting and describing the country's history. For instance, in conflicts against colonialism, scholarly narratives of the country frequently focus on key individuals who used ingenious means to move people to collectively resist colonial occupation. In the early twentieth century, during the German occupation of the country, Kinjikitile Ngwale convinced his followers to take medicine that he said would turn German bullets into water. The strategy empowered many to fight the Germans in violent conflicts that became known as the Maji Maji Rebellion. In the 1950s, this time under British rule, when the county was called the Tanganyika Territory, Bibi Titi Mohammed and other activists used dance associations to mobilize women to attend meetings and join the Tanganyika African National Union (TANU). In drawing people to join TANU, Mohammed would give speeches that were effective in mobilizing productive resistance against British colonial rule (Geiger 1997: 58). Numerous other examples exist in Tanzanian history, particularly as people struggled against various forms of repression. In many ways, it is difficult not to find examples of innovative strategies, whether successful (Mohammed) or not (Kinjikitile).

In this ethnography, I focus on individuals who demonstrate creative practices, as well as on broader narratives of people's abilities to make opportunities emerge in difficult economic and social situations. I am interested both in exploring the formation of creative practices in response to particular circumstances and the impact of those practices on the music economy more generally. When there are few places to learn music, what does a young artist do? How does a music producer find ways to outcompete the hundreds of other people recording music in Dar es Salaam? And how do radio deejays use their social popularity to earn higher salaries? The answers provide insight into the strategies that people use on a daily basis, as well as to the ways music is being lived in Tanzania. Music exists as a central component to many areas of Tanzanian society: from live performance to media; distribution to recording studios; law to education; advertising to entertainment. There are few other cultural forms that connect with a diversity of employment opportunities in the way that music does. Following the movement of music from work to commodity provides a glimpse into people's relationship with songs and into the creative strategies used to earn a living in urban areas of eastern Africa.

The basis for my use of the concept of creative practices comes from two autochthonous philosophies—*bongo* (wisdom/ingenuity) and *ku-jitegemea* (self-reliance)—that are used in Tanzania to represent local views and interpretations of the transition from socialism toward neo-liberalism. Bongo literally means "wisdom" or "brains" but is slang for "survival of the fittest" or "doing anything to survive." During my field-work, I spent a great deal of time talking to people about bongo because it is so commonly used to explain the country's current economic and political condition. Dar es Salaam is called "Bongoland," a term more recently applied to the country of Tanzania as a whole. Musicians speak of a bongo philosophy or a bongo mentality that they must maintain in order to survive in an economically impoverished country. There is bongo music, essentially any music written and performed in Dar es Salaam, but also a music developed through "blood, sweat, and tears," as Professor Jay, a Tanzanian rapper, told me. As a concept, it is central to Tanzanians' relationship with their country and pervades the fabric of everyday life, not just in music but in most daily socioeconomic experiences and practices.

The bongo ideology took shape during the country's socialist period. Though many people initially viewed socialism positively, the collapse of the Tanzanian economy during the 1970s and 1980s, particularly after the war with Uganda (1978–1979), led to a sense of frustration and anger with the government's communalist proposals.[4] Lack of food, salt, clothes, medicine, and other amenities developed into mistrust for the government as people searched for ways to make a living for themselves and their families. The linguist Deo Ngonyani explains that this frustration led to the development of bongo ideology and practice:

> In the early eighties, not only was food scarce, but also stores were empty of other basic supplies. Rice, sugar, soap, cloth, etc. were in acute short-age. Their prices shot to astronomical levels. Suddenly, the salaries people were getting were not enough to take them through the month. Now, if you knew somebody who sold rice, sugar, soap, etc. then you had a good chance

of getting the supplies. If you worked in a state company such as a Regional Trading Company (RTC) that had the retail monopoly, you had thousands of people adoring you asking for favors. If you did not have money but you had access to the supplies ... use your brains, man! That is what you would be told. ... Everybody, use your brains now. Find some supplier of stuff stolen from the harbor, warehouse, factory, office, employer, anything, to make a few more shillings. You just have to use your brains; otherwise, you perish. That is how Dar came to change its name to Bongo. It became the unsafe city, filthy, unfriendly to some extent, except when you had the brains to help you survive. It is always prestigious to say you lived in Bongo because then you exude the wit, cleverness, and trendiness of Dar.[5]

*— its like la vivere criolla*

Bongo was an ideological and practical necessity for a majority of Tanzanians, particularly those living in urban areas. Just over one million people lived in Dar es Salaam in the mid-1980s and many, particularly those who worked in music, relied on the government in some way. The government controlled and owned bands, social halls, and clubs, along with the recording studios and the sole radio station. When government salaries, decent health care, and an honest police force disappeared, ingenuity took over as the dominant form of social welfare. Under socialism, people were supposed to eschew two jobs, extra incomes, or other "unfaithful" activities. Given the economic state of the country in the 1980s, these practices became commonplace as people struggled in an increasingly caustic environment (Tripp 1997).

The ideology embodied in the term bongo is not unique to Tanzania. In fact, there is a strong connection between economic liberalization of the 1980s and the creative practices embodied in urban, African daily life. In Zambia, the creative practices are referred to as "Getting by just like that" (*gwaya gwaya bubwena obo*) (Cliggett 2005); in Kenya the concept is presented as people toiling in the "hot sun" (*jua kali*) (King 1996); and in Mali people state, "If you don't eat them, they'll eat you" (*N'i m'u dun, u b'i dun*) (Skinner 2009). The formal economies in these countries are unable to produce adequate and sufficient prospects for jobs, social mobility, and financial success. In order to get by in these economies, people take on additional jobs (secondary employment), work in illegal and often unhealthy situations (informal economy), and depend increasingly on social and kin-based networks to navigate through pitfalls encountered in daily interactions. There is, in short, a need for "improvisational adaptability" to find success on a daily basis (Freeman 2007: 254).

Bongo has historical connections to another important term of individual initiative in Tanzania: kujitegemea. During the 1960s and 1970s, kujitegemea or self-reliance was an important concept for defining the way that individuals could help the nation achieve socialist ideals (Ikoku 1980). To be self-reliant meant working hard to help yourself and those around you in order to strengthen the nation. President Julius Nyerere, who was the first president of post-independent Tanzania, states:

> Self-reliance is not some vague political slogan. It has meaning for every citizen, for every group, and for the nation as a whole. A self-reliant individual is one who co-operates with others, who is willing to help others and be helped by them, but who does not depend on anyone else for his food, clothing or shelter. He lives on what he earns, whether this be big or small, so that he is truly a free person beholden to no one. This is the position of the vast majority of our people now; it must be the position of all of us. (Nyerere 1971: 151–52)

Through self-reliance, the state created a value system of hard work ("the root of development"), intelligence, and cooperation. The individual had to learn the merits of labor and the shortcomings of drunkenness and idleness (TANU 1967: 17–18). It was only through these efforts that a nation such as Tanzania could be successfully independent and have a prosperous populace.

One of the impetuses for developing self-reliance was to show that neither the state nor its citizens needed to rely on foreign governments for support. It was a do-it-yourself mentality meant to build a strong society and foster a period of national pride. This mentality began to change, however, when Ali Hasssan Mwinyi became president in 1985. Almost immediately, Mwinyi accepted loans from the World Bank and the International Monetary Fund. These loans came with drastic Structural Adjustment Policies (SAPs) that made Tanzania more dependent on the recommendations and funding of other countries. No longer could the state successfully argue self-sufficiency when it was relying on outside institutions for both economic and political support. The sociologist Joe Lugalla (1995, 1997) states that the loans were meant to open the country to free markets and provide a means to expand economically and democratically. The conditionalities that came with these loans, however, created many more problems than they solved and, in Lugalla's words, made living conditions for most Tanzanians far worse. Even an internal report by the World Bank found that the institution's projects in Tanzania were poorly managed, featured "unrealistic or overly ambitious project design," and had "little appreciation for the time required to carry out major reforms" (2007: 43, 41).[6] Combined with the Tanzanian government's own fallibilities, foreign loans did not produce their intended results.[7]

The relaxation of national forms of self-reliance trickled down to the level of individuals. Mwinyi allowed people to pursue entrepreneurial activities that had previously been restricted or banned during the socialist period. Mwinyi did not formally announce laissez-faire policies but signaled reforms through his hands-off approach to people's lives. Mwinyi became known as *Mzee Ruksa* or *Rais Ruksa* (President Permissive), and people quickly recognized the new opportunities emerging from a government willing to allow them to pursue any means for survival. The result was a dramatic rise in imported goods, new technologies, and small enterprises, all of which helped fill a vacuum created by the country's recession. New forms of employment emerged, and people openly sold goods without permits, bribed officials, or traded in merchandise that was forbidden in the socialist period, such as televisions, recording equipment, and foreign music. Due to this relative economic freedom compared to the past, a derivative version of self-reliance emerged, emphasizing individual aspirations and creative practices. It was a shift from hard work to build a nation to hard work to support oneself.

Both bongo and kujitegemea are used in this book to connote the means by which individuals in Tanzania overcome difficult economic and political situations. The two terms present Tanzanians not as a collective mass, thinking and acting in the same way, but as individuals with diverse interests, motivations, and worldviews. They are not passive observers or intrinsically "determined by external influences" that shape their identities (Giddens 1991: 2). Nor are they able to shape the world in any way they desire, for individuals are also the recipients of other people's choices and actions. The constant attempts to discover opportunities in society reflect a broader competition between individuals creatively situating themselves in contemporary urban landscapes. Competition becomes a means to recognize human agency and the "capacity of social beings to interpret and morally evaluate their situation" (Ortner 1995: 185). Certainly, the terms bongo and kujitegemea are local philosophies

*[handwritten margin note:]* This is an interesting concept because ideologies are being formed by economy, then these ideologies make it into music which is part of economy

that provide insight into people's actions as they evaluate their economic and political struggles.

In Tanzania, people's awareness and ability to talk about bongo and kujitegemea also reflect the centrality of self-evaluation. Self-evaluation, which a person continually engages in, consciously or not, reflects a person's ability to make sense of actions, interactions, desires, and motivations. Charles Taylor states that the capacity to "evaluate desires is bound up with our power of self-evaluation, which in turn is an essential feature of the mode of agency we recognize as human" (1985: 16). Within the framework of urban African societies, self-evaluation takes on important meanings within the context of social relations. It illustrates a connected history to innovative strategies that people employ to deal with adversity or achieve some form of success. Strategies are embodied in the cultural formulations of life in Tanzania that become a part of socialization processes. Children grow up watching family members creating opportunities for their survival or success and become indoctrinated in those actions. Stories constantly circulate in Dar es Salaam about approaches people take or have taken to deal with their economic and social situations. Even simply acknowledging the long history of popular song that encourages people to use ingenuity and wisdom to survive in the country gives a glimpse into the cultural importance of creative practices. The cultural framework of bongo and kujitegemea provides a means for individuals to interpret their position in society and evaluate their prospects and potential outcomes.

## POST-SOCIALISM AND CULTURE

Creative practices are a part of any economy, yet they are particularly prevalent in formerly socialist countries undergoing neoliberal reforms. In Africa, thirty-five countries practiced some form of socialism, and the transition toward capitalism significantly impacted people's ability to make a living on a daily basis. Similar to other formerly socialist countries, such as those in the former Soviet sphere, the transition toward free market economies brought sometimes drastic changes to employment, salaries, and basic necessities as the state no longer supported local industries. The movement away from state control forced populations to rely on their own resources, knowledge, and skills to survive, which deflected

*× conflict b/w economic interests & values →*

demands on the state (Bridger and Pine 1998; Burawoy et al. 2000: 46; Tripp 1997: 11). The movement away from socialism further left populations struggling to interpret notions of commodities, entrepreneurialism, and markets even as they continued to be connected to socialist values, ideologies, and memories (Pitcher and Askew 2006: 2).

To better comprehend post-socialism in Tanzania, it is useful to separate economic and political developments. Economically, Tanzania has steadily deregulated local industries and withdrawn government involvement in many businesses. The privatization of major companies, such as Air Tanzania Corporation, Southern Paper Mills, and Metal and Engineering Companies, has been coupled with the emergence of numerous foreign banks, mining companies, and non-governmental organizations. There is a Dar es Salaam stock exchange, which began operation in 1998, and several foreign investment companies that work in the country. There is also intense competition by foreign interests in the cell phone industry, which may be the fastest growing sector of the economy since the early 2000s. These economic movements require Tanzanian citizens to depend less on the state and rely more on their own ingenuity to navigate competition between local, regional, and foreign interests.

Politically, the government has moved more pragmatically in maintaining its influence over certain areas of society. Several political changes have been instituted, such as the introduction of multi-party democratic elections at all levels of government. Yet many policies and laws continue to rely on a socialist ethos in affecting and influencing the relation between the state and citizens. Considering the hierarchies of administrative power, the maintenance of socialist rhetoric and practice is not surprising. Some of the same people who worked for the state during socialism continue to hold prominent jobs. Others were educated by those who closely followed socialist ideologies. Even into the 1990s, the state continued to hold on to a communalist vision of society. On a government radio broadcast on January 1, 1990, for instance, President Mwinyi urged the country to devote the year to the implementation of the national policy of socialism and self-reliance.[8] This was four years after accepting foreign loans that required changes to socialist political and economic policies.

Given the uneven confluence of socialist and capitalist ideologies, post-socialism cannot be articulated in any direct or singular way. It

means many different things depending on context and individual interests. For the Tanzanian music economy, the importance of post-socialism
rests both in the economic changes, which provided opportunities for
the increased commodification of music, and attempts to maintain state
involvement in national culture. The privatization of radio stations, the
introduction of copyright law, and the importation of new recording studio technologies are examples of changes that ushered in new ways to
produce and profit from music. The government's attempts to remain
relevant in cultural industries, including shaping the content of radio
broadcasts and popular music, reveals a continued maintenance of so-
cialist-influenced political policies.

Due to the significance of these policies on Tanzania's music economy, it is important to briefly examine the connections between culture and socialism. Here, I do not wish to provide an in-depth analysis
of state formulations of culture in the post-independence period. For
instance, noticeably absent in my discussion is the state's role in re-con-
ceptualizing the performance and repertories of local genres of music.
I address that topic in more depth in chapter 2. Instead, my intention in
the remainder of this section is to draw attention to socialist approaches
toward culture that continue to influence people's relations to popular
music.

Tanzania's movement toward socialism began soon after independence from British rule in 1961. Among newly elected leaders, there was a
concern in rebuilding an African national culture in the wake of colonial
rule. Independence signified the ability to revitalize and rediscover indigenous traditions and build a more unified society. *Utamaduni* (culture)
became a primary interest to the new government, as Ruyembe Mulimba,
an Arts Officer at the National Arts Council (BASATA) in Tanzania,
explains:

> After independence, President Nyerere saw the importance in starting a
> Ministry of Culture.[9] So, in 1962, he started the Ministry of Culture and said
> that he was organizing this Ministry to help restore and assure the progress
> of our culture, which is our heritage. The Ministry was very broad—because
> if you look at culture it touches many things—there were games, clothing,
> customs, traditions, language. In order to improve the implementation
> of these things, they saw the need for a new Ministry.

The formation of a ministry was viewed as an important step toward focusing attention on African traditions and in unifying populations across the country. It was an effort to select traditions among Tanzania's cultural groups that best suited the formation of a newly independent, post-colonial state. In Nyerere's words, "I want [the new ministry] to seek out the best of the traditions and customs of all the tribes and make them part of our national culture."[10]

Officially, Tanzanian socialism began with the Arusha Declaration (Azimio la Arusha), a policy document presented by TANU on February 5, 1967, which Julius Nyerere (1971) argued "reaffirmed" that Tanzanians were free to develop on their own. For Nyerere, socialism was an attitude of mind that promoted notions of egalitarianism, collectivism, unity, and dignity. All humans were equal, integral to the nation, and part of an extended family. Unity was necessary to "break the grip of colonialism," while the notion of the extended family was part of a precolonial past that provided security and belonging. To achieve this attitude of mind, Nyerere and the TANU government emphasized education for all citizens, focused attention on hard work, and constructed *ujamaa* villages that encouraged or forcibly moved populations into rural cooperatives. Rural agrarianism was seen as beneficial to the development of the country, while urban spaces were viewed as morally corrupt and "wasted in gossip, dancing, and drinking" (TANU 1967: 15). Commercialization, capitalism, and money were all labeled as offenses to the development of the country. → key for commodification of music

Even though the focus on culture lost momentum in the late 1960s, it again became central to socialist state policy in the mid-1970s.[11] Under the Ministry of National Education and Culture, the focus returned to reviving indigenous traditions, preserving the country's heritage, and forming a unified national culture that could contribute to development (Askew 2002: 179). In discussing the role of the arts in a socialist society, Louis Mbughuni and Gabriel Ruhumbika write, "In a socialist society all art is seen as a servant of society. A tool to help man better understand and shape his society according to his collective needs. Divorcing art or the artist from society is another sin of the decadent bourgeoisie society, inseparable from the commercialisation of art, which all socialist societies have to fight" (1974: 280).[12] Numerous councils, including the National

Arts Council (BASATA), were created to support and strengthen national artistic forms.[13] The national radio station, Radio Tanzania Dar es Salaam, also increased efforts to record and document traditional music while attempting to restrict or remove foreign cultural forms.

By the late 1970s, many of the most popular and successful bands in the country were affiliated with government agencies, such as JKT (National Service Army), Urafiki Jazz Band (Urafiki Textile Mill), Orchestra BIMA Lee (National Insurance Corporation), and DDC Mlimani Park (Dar es Salaam Development Corporation). The agencies paid bands salaries, and, in some cases, their pensions, health care, and transportation. Social halls were also built as centers for entertainment and, more important, community organization. The artist and scholar Mgunga Mwa-Mnenyelwa explains, "During that time, the arts were not a commodity to be sold. It was a time when art was talked about as belonging to the people, belonging to society so there was no free market. The employment of all artists depended on the government." Some artists were well taken care of during the socialist period and the music infrastructure that was built provided a critical foundation for the contemporary music scene. Nonetheless, for musicians and other members of the music community, the socialist period did not have a lasting benefit for their financial well being, which became increasingly apparent during the 1980s recession.

Even after the implementation of neoliberal reforms, the government continues to influence cultural development in the country. Perhaps the most important legacy of the socialist period is the role of the state in monitoring and managing the arts in Tanzania. At the highest level of government is the Ministry of Information, Culture, and Sports (MISC), which generates cultural policies and coordinates their implementation with the Ministry of Regional Administration and Local Government. Under MISC are several organizations, such as the Tanzania Broadcasting Corporation (TBC), National Swahili Council (BAKITA), Tanzania Standard Newspapers, Film and Stage Plays Board, and the Tanzania Culture Trust Fund (TCTF). In all these organizations, there is continued focus on educating citizens in traditional knowledge and preserving cultural heritage.

More important are the connections being made within the government between culture and economic development. In the Cultural

Development Master Plan for Tanzania, a policy document produced in 2001, the authors draw from the language and ideas of socialist policies but reframe them to articulate a new position on culture:

> Culture constitutes the foundation of our progress and creativity. Economic development, in its honest meaning, is part of people's culture. Development divorced from its human or cultural context is growth without a soul. This view of culture is not very much accepted. Nonetheless the prime goal of this and any other cultural policy is not only to enable our people access to goods and services, but also provide them with the opportunity to choose a full, satisfying, valuable and appreciable way of living together and attain the flourishing of human existence in all its diverse forms as a whole.... Culture's role is not that of a servant of ends but is the social justification of the ends themselves.
>
> Governments do not determine people's culture: certainly they are partly determined by it. But they are in a position to influence culture, for better or for worse, thus affecting the path of development. Respect of all subcultures whose values are tolerant of others that subscribe to national unity should be the fundamental principle. Policy makers can hardly legislate respect nor can they force people to behave respectfully. They can stipulate cultural freedom as one of the pillars on which the state is built.[14]

Many of the statements made in this passage and in other areas of the Master Plan borrow directly from socialist cultural policy. There are connections between culture and national development; the importance of culture for mankind; and interest in the preservation of cultural heritage and the revival of traditional culture. There are guidelines for managing cultural policies in curriculum, supporting national arts competitions, and continuing to push Swahili as the language of instruction at all levels of education. The above passage, however, also illustrates a more post-socialist vision. The notion that culture is *not* a servant to society and that the government should respect subcultures is a significant reformulation of past policies. The Master Plan is far more conciliatory of diversity, ethnic pluralism, and cultural freedoms, and has specific language for promoting the voices of women, youth, and those who are marginalized in society.

The post-socialist position evidenced by the Master Plan emerges in many relations between the state and music. Parliamentary Debates frequently center on proposals or attempts to promote indigenous music and hinder artists from copying foreign genres.[15] There are efforts to use traditional music to promote the country globally and attract tourists to Tanzania.[16] State-sponsored competitions, such as MASHIBOTA and the Tanzanian Music Awards, require popular dance bands to perform traditional songs.[17] Efforts continue to fund, document, and preserve the country's traditional culture. There are also policy recommendations that require or encourage popular music bands and broadcast media to produce content in the interests of Tanzanian values and ideals. These approaches maintain many of the prescriptions of a socialist vision for music, history, and traditional culture within the local music economy.

Nonetheless, the state also accommodates cultural pluralism through allowing many groups to record, broadcast, and perform in ways they were not permitted in the past. Music is far more commercially oriented now than it was during the socialist period, which is in part due to the state's acceptance of the economic value of music. There is a new copyright law, which allows individuals and bands to protect rights held in music. Ownership in music or any form of traditional culture was not possible in the past, since culture was conceptualized as communal and shared by everyone. The fact that youths are not hindered from performing and producing foreign genres of music signals the hands-off approach that the government has taken to popular culture. Artists are even able to speak openly about controversial and politically sensitive issues, though, as I explore in chapter 5, there are boundaries to this freedom of speech.

It is important here to acknowledge an additional legacy of the socialist period that continues to function within the local music economy. The government-run National Arts Council (BASATA) works with all forms of arts and crafts in the country, from theater to acrobatics to music.[18] The organization conducts research into production, marketing, and management of arts, is a partner in music awards ceremonies, and promotes local artists abroad. The organization also regulates the production of any cultural form that occurs in public spaces. The Cultural Development Master Plan summarizes BASATA's post-socialist role as follows: "Anything which is done against the generally accepted Tanzanian fine art, music or theatre arts is easily noted by the people, so the council has to be aware all the time that national cultural values are maintained."[19] Part of BASATA's mandate is to monitor and reprimand inappropriate cultural displays that counter national values as defined by the government.

Since music is the most public and popular of the arts, members of the music economy are frequent recipients of BASATA's attention.

In order to keep track of and maintain some control over musicians in Tanzania, BASATA requires groups to register with them and other local organizations. In 2010, BASATA updated the requirements and fees of registration, in part to comply with provisions set out in the Master Plan. Every band and solo artist must have a constitution, passport pictures of the group leaders, and a completed BASATA registration form. Groups must attach a statement signed by all band members and leaders which states that everyone has read and understood the constitution of the group. This form is critically important since so many conflicts have emerged between band owners and musicians in the terms of contracts and constitutions (see chapter 4). To provide added assurance that the signatures of band members are not forged, bandleaders must also present a written statement explaining the agenda of meetings between band members, owners, and leaders. All forms must then be brought to the office of the regional cultural officer for approval. Finally, once approved, the band or artist needs to pay for a permit, as well as registration and other fees, which totals $75 for one year.

Before the update to the BASATA requirements, artists needed to consult with independent associations that focused on each of the major genres of music. Ruyembe Mulimba explains:

> The form and constitution must pass the association of that genre of music; if it is the genre of muziki wa dansi then the musicians must go to CHAMUDATA; if it is rap, they must go to the Tanzania Rap Music Association (TRMA); if it is taarab, then they must pass the Tanzania Taarab Association (TTA). Once the forms are endorsed, they return to BASATA and receive a certificate [permit] that allows them to continue with their business for one year. It is like a license that allows them to legally work in this country.

The associations acted as unions that helped artists and bands in their musical genre attain the necessary clearances so that they could play music. Problematically, many of these associations had difficulty remaining effective with shaky leadership and claims of dishonest management. As a result, in the update to the registration process, regional cultural officers, who are included in the Cultural Master Plan and who are appointed by the government, replaced associations in permitting bands and artists to perform music in the country. The loss of independent associations to handle the rights of artists further concentrated control of public performances into government organizations.

In addition to registering bands, BASATA plays a central role in maintaining culturally appropriate values in the arts. In times when there is public uproar over a perceived cultural offense, journalists, members of Parliament, and others ask BASATA to step in to correct the inappropriate presentation of culture. In 2008, for instance, BASATA enforced a ban on improper forms of dress at dansi concerts, since scantily clad dancers were considered "bait to attract customers" and not morally appropriate.[20] In 2009, BASATA worked with musicians to encourage them to avoid copying aspects of other artists' music. And, on several occasions, BASATA has been called upon to deal with problematic musicians and songs, several of which are discussed in this ethnography.

Other branches of the Tanzanian government monitor programming on radio and television, and often censor songs deemed to be socially inappropriate. The result of these initiatives is that many bands and artists compose songs that connect to post-socialist values within a neoliberal framework. There is awareness in the music community of the boundaries of acceptability with the performance of songs in public spaces. Members of the artistic community explore the bounds of acceptability but also need to anticipate the broader impact of their actions. To avoid conflicting with social and political policies, they censor their words, actions, and practices. Or, they compose music with hidden meanings and double entendres to obfuscate their intentions. Of course, most societies have some level of anticipatory self-censorship as people create expressive art forms that accommodate the parameters of radio, television, or other outlets. Media organizations are run by professionals who can share ideologies or "dominant codes" of the nation-state, which encourages artists to compose materials for the acceptance of those professionals and, by default, the government (Abu-Lughod 2005: 12–13). In Tanzania, however, the state plays a more active role in the decisions being made in the media, performance spaces, and in musical groups. While there is freedom to compose and perform a wide variety of music ideas, there are still guidelines that present restrictions in the directness of people's criticisms toward the government, political leaders, or public policies.

## NEOLIBERAL TRANSITIONS

Neoliberalism refers to a movement away from collective structures, such as centralized governments, toward strong market economies where there is emphasis on private property and free trade. The concept of neoliberalism is often linked to privatization, deregulation, and decentralization, whereby governments restrict their involvement in economic activities in order to provide individuals and companies opportunities to freely benefit from markets. According to proponents of this ideology, a strong market economy is better able to serve the interests of local populations by allowing competition, ingenuity, and risk to thrive relatively unimpeded. Critics, however, lambast the unevenness at which neoliberalism occurs since it creates stronger social and economic divisions between populations and tends to benefit the same institutions that promoted it in the first place. Both proponents and detractors seem to agree that the processes embodied in neoliberalism have wrought a strong emphasis on an "individuated sense of personhood" that stresses competition, possessiveness, and self-responsibility (Comaroff and Comaroff 2001: 15; see also Ong 2006; Peters 1999).

One of the defining characteristics of neoliberal reforms is that it encourages individuals to be innovative in situations where the state is rationalizing itself according to free markets (Coe and Nastasi 2006: 193; Gregory 2007: 30). Innovation is a means of creatively using available resources and knowledge to provoke strategies for economic success or survival. It is a means to outcompete those who vie for the same financial opportunities by establishing strategies to best maneuver in a specific context. Marketing one's music or branding the name of a recording studio requires ingenuity in order to make them stand apart from others competing for the same audience. Although innovation often has a positive connotation, it can also refer to strategies used to manipulate economic and social circumstances for individual rather than community benefit. Finding loopholes around tax laws, evading paying royalties on contracts, or forcing musicians to pay in order to air their music on the radio are all potentially unethical practices that can be regarded as innovative strategies within the reforms taking place in African countries. In addition to innovation, neoliberalism also encourages flexibility of social action. Since many people are vying for similar opportunities, there needs to be a willingness to improvise and adapt to new information, experiences, and knowledge in order to make the most of any given situation. Pierre Bourdieu refers to neoliberalism as an "absolute reign of flexibility" and Carla Freeman writes, "Few if any spheres of life appear exempt from the neoliberal demands for flexibility, from the structures of economic markets to the nuances of individuals' subjectivities as citizens, producers, consumers, migrants, tourists, members of families, and so on" (quoted in Freeman 2007: 253). Contemporary social environments, particularly in many African countries, require people to consider many options, to remain flexible, in order to find opportunities in circumstances that emerge unexpectedly or haphazardly. It is a necessary adaptation to environments where economic stability and success depend on a person's skill or capacity to find opportunities within the challenges of market forces.

Central to the ideas of innovation and flexibility, as well as to neoliberalism, is an emphasis on the individual. There is a belief that anyone who is creative, resourceful, organized, and willing to take risks can take advantage of newly available opportunities. The globe is imagined in terms of "private property, free trade, and the entrepreneurial spirit" (Tsing 2005: 106). This conceptualization disproportionately privileges individual agency and implies that any obstacle can be overcome through strategies dependent solely on an individual's innovative capabilities. If survival is simply a matter of strategy more than resources, than people who use appropriate strategies would be able to overcome any obstacles that they encounter, be it loss of job or limited education (Clarke 2002: 194). Survival is more than simply strategies or entrepreneurial spirit that one uses to get by on a daily basis. It requires resources, including education, capital, connections, and status, which are frequently difficult and at times impossible to attain depending on social and economic situations.

Nonetheless, while individual agency does not guarantee success, lack of resources also does not predict failure. There is the possibility for success or failure in future outcomes even despite adverse circumstances (Weiss 2009: 235). Many people in urban areas of eastern Africa find ingenious ways of turning insurmountable obstacles into useful opportunities. One of the more popular Tanzanian hip-hop groups, for instance, consists of two handicapped rappers from the poorest district in Dar es

Salaam. Being handicapped and poor in Tanzania can make finding work extremely difficult. Yet the duo, who call themselves Mabaga Fresh, are successful because they embrace the potential of their disadvantage and present a unique style within popular music (PURL 1.1, PURL 1.2, and PURL 1.3). Their physical and economic condition does not limit their potential within the local music scene but becomes their distinct advantage. Creativity involves innovative use of available resources, including turning perceived adversities into opportunities.

In addition to innovation, flexibility, and attention to the individual, neoliberal reforms and global economic markets have encouraged interest in the commodification and competition of cultural forms. The notion of commodification refers to turning elements of social life into objects that can be bought, sold, traded, or protected. Cultural and economic worlds are becoming more intertwined as people turn anything into a resource for financial and personal mobility. There is a proliferation of strategic calculations being made to draw on the possibilities of objects, services, relations, and beliefs that occur in people's daily lives. Different contexts emerge that transform and legitimize commodities as they become socially accepted objects of consumption. Everything from organs, human bodies, water, and even identities are recognized as being or becoming commodified in global economies (Castile 1996; Curtis 2004; Scheper-Hughes 2000; Wilk 2006).

Music shares in these commodity prospects. In African contexts, there is an increasing potential for songs to become property, whether in tangible (phonograms) or intangible forms (broadcast or performed live). Artists are being encouraged within the music economy to protect their property through promoting authorship and ownership in music and lyrics of songs. Even rhythms, which typically cannot be protected in Western industries, are being debated as something that can be owned and controlled among music producers. These transformations expand the economic importance of music and make it part of a commodity chain where different people benefit financially. A song can still be regarded as a form of entertainment, education, ritual, or the basis for conjuring memories and emotions as it has in the past. Additionally, it becomes a commodity that circulates through the Tanzanian economy, coming into contact with numerous individuals interested in treating it as a form of property that can be owned, bought, sold, protected, and pirated.

*But is copyright not a way of controlling creations + one way a gov't can retain control?*

The commodification of music points to a broader trend occurring globally of consumers replacing citizens (Foster 2002: 4; Thomas 1997). Rather than people being centered or united on the goals of the nation, there is an increasing emphasis on being connected to broader markets of consumption. People desire the things they see in print and on television and hear about in songs on the radio. They want to be included in media displays of success, power, and fame. In Tanzania, displays of a more consumer-oriented society are easily seen. There is an increasing array of fashion shows, films, advertising, boutiques, spas, and modeling agencies aimed at a generation interested in global desires of success and power. Videos show artists holding glasses of champagne and driving fancy cars. Magazines glorify symbols of wealth and feature photographs of prominent Tanzanians in the United States, Europe, and South Africa. There are new words in Swahili to refer to money, such as *mshiko, mapeni, mkwanja, ngawira, dau,* and *faranga*. Referencing a lack of money or being broke also produces an equally impressive list of slang terms: *kapuku, kafulia, chacha, chali, kachoka, kapinda, mchacho, tee,* and *ukapa*. There are phrases to refer to foreign forms of wealth, such as *ameoga vizuri* (literally to shower well, but slang for dressed in nice, often Western, clothes) and *mambo ya isidingo* (referring to the wealth and prosperity shown on the South African soap opera *Isidingo*). Numerous songs address issues of money or wealth in the new economy (PURL 1.4, PURL 1.5, and PURL 1.6). The movement toward consumerism in urban areas of Tanzania articulates new forms of desire that focus on individual wealth, happiness, and success.

*PSYCHOLOGICAL EFFECTS of DESIRE / NEO-LIBERALISM*

Central to the commodification of music is that it creates desires to pursue careers associated with the increasing financial value of songs. As local and international artists present images of wealth and prestige, people imagine a musical career as an opportunity to attain these social statuses. Even the notion of fame, relatively absent in the past, is now a sought-after ambition. The Tanzanian artist Balozi Dola explains: "A lot of young kids that have talents were being discouraged by parents at first when they wanted to indulge in the arts or music. The parents saw it as a profession for people that couldn't get good grades in school, and it was seen as a Western lifestyle that was being imposed on young Tanzanian youth." He continues, "Only when money and fame come into play do parents became more supportive." Once the economic value of music becomes evident, it overturned previous social apprehensions by those who cast doubts on the viability of a career in music. This, in turn, forcefully established music as an opportunity for achieving consumer-oriented desires and led to new roles of music in society.

Increased interest in the economic value of songs has also intensified competition between people vying to secure opportunities for their economic well-being. Since economic value in a commodity is subjectively determined, there are benefits to those who can quickly and convincingly secure control over a resource. To be competitive means to outwit others into establishing power over objects that have economic value. A rivalry between two bands—a relatively common occurrence in Tanzanian popular music—benefits both in terms of being able to create musical recordings, art, clothing lines, and marketable images that can be used to promote the careers of band members. Played out on stage, in newspapers, and on radio, rivalry rewards each group's ability to promote themselves to a broader public for economic and social gain. Paying off journalists, talking to researchers, and creating specific symbols (dances/drawing/signs) that make the group more economically viable in the local music scene are part of the formulation of strategies that define creative practices. *[handwritten: before post-socialist reforms?]*

[handwritten margin note: CONTROL (GRAMSCI)]

Competition has long been a prevalent aspect to East African music. In *Mashindano!*, Frank Gunderson describes competition in ritual ngoma as a great social equalizer: "Competitions are communicative arenas where differences are made public and defended, and where difference as 'norm' is contested, equalized, and subverted in ways that would be difficult to resolve in everyday life" (2000a: 11). Numerous other scholars in the same collection identify the roles of prestige, power, and community in both traditional and popular music competition.[21] The importance of these studies, as well as other historical studies on traditional music in Tanzania, is that they provide a means to conceptualize a long-running narrative in the use of music as a means to garner social mobility. While notions of wealth and fame were not as implicated in traditional musical forms, the role of competition as a means to contest or claim success, power, and prestige reveals antecedents to the music economy discussed in this ethnography.

This difference between previous and contemporary forms of competition is in the value of songs. In the past, the focus was on aspects

of competition centered on the creativity and cultural significance of a
work. Songs communicated forms of identity, power, and prestige: they
had an edifying influence and symbolic importance. These cultural relations to music remain prominent in contemporary popular music, but
the increased attention to songs as commodities alters interests in competitions. Whether performed, broadcast, recorded, or copyrighted, each
situation offers alternative means to interpret the economic importance
of music. Competitions emerge as people negotiate rights and control
over artistic forms. Which radio station is able to perform a popular song
first? What band can outperform their rivals? Which producer can create
a bigger hit? These forms of competition create tensions in people's relations to popular music both as a work and a commodity.

Whereas the previous section emphasized the continued interest in
socialist ideologies, this section emphasized capitalist movements taking
place in Tanzania. The mixture of socialist and capitalist orientations in
Tanzania is common in many post-socialist countries. In writing about
Russia, Jennifer Patico describes some people as having a greater desire
for "expensive consumer commodities from the West," while others have
a historically oriented sense of value rooted in socialist and Soviet-norms
of propriety that are used to "critique post-Soviet class developments
and crass nouveau riche materialism" (2005: 480). These divergent forms
of relating to consumer commodities present a useful framework to examine contemporary issues of value in the arts. In Tanzania, there is a
consistent tension between those who believe in the ideas and behaviors
of the socialist period that articulate an effort to build a strong, united
nation, while others become consumed by the wealth, status, and ways
of life imagined in the West. Increasingly, however, these two perspectives are blurred, and it is not uncommon to find people articulating both.
A popular song, for instance, can present vivid images of socialist ideology while being composed explicitly for financial gain.

## NATIONALISM AND GLOBALIZATION

In his book *Let the People Speak,* Issa Shivji writes about the path that
Tanzania took toward neoliberalism. He writes about nationalist policies
of the country's first president, Julius Nyerere, who pushed for unity, nationalism, and prosperity, even as he ushered in more controversial ideas,

such as *ujamaa* villages, which encouraged people to work in collectives for the benefit of community and country. By the early 1980s, Nyerere and his policies had become unpopular and, under the presidency of Ali Hassan Mwinyi, *mageuzi* (changes/reforms) were introduced that allowed for multiple political parties, privatization, and unfettered imports from abroad. Benjamin Mkapa, the third president, maintained the language of Julius Nyerere's administration—unity, solidarity, good policies, and good leadership—but, according to Shivji, added another concept: capital. The concept of capital reshaped the other terms to mean something different. Under Mkapa, good policies became those policies that enabled an environment for capital; good leadership was one that attracted capitalists; and unity meant providing labor for capital growth.

In his analysis of Tanzanian politics, Shivji strongly criticizes the movement from nationalism to globalization through neoliberal reforms. Globalization, according to Shivji, is a new form of imperialism that has reduced people to consumer statistics and denied them their independence (2006: 178). His comments are important as they reflect perceptions of many people living in Tanzania who have become fearful and angry over the changes taking place under the rubric of globalization. Rumors continually emerge throughout Tanzania that warn of the problems brought on by free trade. Songs, such as Irene Sanga's "Tandawazi" (Globalization), lament the influence of foreign cultures on local ways of thinking. Newspapers decry the loss of companies to foreign investors. One opinion writer titles her piece in the newspaper *Tanzania Daima*: "Miaka 45 ya uhuru; utandawazi umeleta ukoloni mpya" ([After] 45 Years of Freedom; Globalization Brings a New Colonialism).[22] Playwrights, such as Vicensia Shule (2009), have characters who decry the problems brought by foreigners trying to set up development projects. Tanzanian bloggers comment on the impact of global trends on their country. In an essay on globalization, Hafiz M. Juma writes, "Its [sic] funny how words that should have positive connotations are now feared by the masses; development is a monster, liberalization its secret weapon."[23] Politicians have even chimed in to present their view of globalization. In a 2004 speech, President Mkapa said, "Globalisation has increased our interdependence, and there is no hope of disentangling ourselves. But it has also brought into sharp distinction the imbalances that exist in our world. And the closer we get to one another the more we see and experience the unfairness of the system, exacerbating underlying political, social, economic and cultural frustrations, uncertainties and in some instances outright anger."[24] More recently, economic development experts, civil society representatives, and government officials from Tanzania and elsewhere met in Dar es Salaam and agreed that "neoliberal Washington-backed policies are a cause of trouble rather than a solution to the problems of developing countries."[25]

The mounting trepidation over globalization stems from many significant changes that have occurred in Tanzania. Most state-owned businesses, such as tanneries, textile mills, and shoe factories, have collapsed under liberalization. Many of the most significant companies, such as the leading cell phone company (Vodacom) and the major mining companies, are now owned and operated by South Africans. The national phone company, Tanzania Telecommunications Company Limited (TTCL), is managed by the Canadian firm SaskTel International. The Presidential Parastatal Sector Reform Commission (PPSRC) administers the effort to sell, lease, or transfer ownership of Tanzania's publicly owned institutions and businesses. The commission, formed in 1992, is an effort to "drive the process of privatization."[26] Considering that many people viewed nationalization as a government effort to take care of it citizens, retain power over local industries, and promote pride in African ownership, privatization has led to a sense of abandonment where nationalist programs and ideologies were sold to the highest bidder.

One result of this sense of abandonment is nostalgia for the socialist past and for the parental-like approach that the state took toward its citizens. Even Mwinyi's liberating policies are often admired more than the tactics taken by the country's most recent presidents. In his 2005 inaugural speech, the current president of Tanzania, Jakaya Kikwete, states, "First, they [critics of globalization] must realise that in today's world of globalisation, they will not be competitive if they are not more aggressive and more innovative, or if they do not unite and form stronger, professionally-managed, indigenous companies and investments. . . . There is no turning back."[27] The comment "there is no turning back" admonishes the desire to return to the past, to nationalism and socialist ideals. For Kikwete, the country has moved on and an individual's only hope for success is to be more aggressive, competitive, and innovative. His statement reflects one of the central tenets of Tanzania's contemporary economy, where the focus moves away from the state toward individual responsibility and creative practices.

Despite many people's disillusionment with neoliberalism, <u>the Tanzanian music economy is seen by many as a successful example of priva</u>tization. The businesses associated with music have thrived and, more important, <u>retained local ownership.</u> With the exception of religiously based radio stations and recording studios, almost all the companies associated with the music economy are owned, operated, and financed by Tanzanians. Further, the government still has a stake in the music economy and continues to operate Tanzania Broadcasting Corporation (TBC) and Radio Uhuru, which is the radio station for the country's main political party, Chama cha Mapinduzi (Revolutionary Party).

Nevertheless, the success of the music economy is seen as an anomaly given more dramatic failures, particularly of foreign-owned or foreign-controlled businesses located in Tanzania. In 2003, for example, the Tanzanian government leased the Dar es Salaam Water and Sewerage Authority (DAWASA), which provides water to Dar es Salaam residents, to City Water, a consortium of the three firms, Biwater (British), Gauff (German), and STD ( Tanzanian). The Tanzanian government was required to lease DAWASA in order to receive debt relief from the World Bank's program known as The Enhanced Heavily Indebted Poor Countries Initiative (HIPC).[28] Within the first year of the lease, Dar es Salaam residents experienced higher water prices, disconnections to poor areas of the city, and other problems that created extensive frustration (Greenhill and Wekiya 2004). The anger over these problems led many citizens to stage protests against City Water, and a coalition of NGOs, including the Tanzania Gender Networking Programme and The Tanzania Association of Non Governmental Organizations (TANGO), held forums where people spoke about the lack of water in their homes and neighborhoods. For many citizens, the privatization of DAWASA illustrated the ills of globalization, manifested in the government and international businesses working in their own interests rather than for the people. Even after the government broke its agreement with City Water, another mismanaged deal was struck in which DAWASA was leased to a company that did not really exist. After internal investigations and extensive claims of corruption, DAWASA remains worse off and operates under greater debt than it had under state control.

Before the collapse of the City Water deal, the privatization of DA-WASA was held up by the international community as a model for neoliberal development.[29] For residents of Dar es Salaam, however, the City Water narrative represents one of the more grating results of large business deals made in the interest of free market economics. The dramatic failure of several other privatization efforts has led to a sense of cultural and economic loss and suspicion of the government's ability to provide for the country's people. Shivji's equation of globalization with imperialism reflects an uneasiness that many Tanzanian citizens have even as they desire commodities that exemplify neoliberalism.

The conflicting ideologies of nationalism and neoliberalism, as well as tensions over successes (the music economy) and failures (the water supply) of privatization, give shape to lived experiences in Dar es Salaam. In interpreting creative practices or the way people approach daily life in Tanzania, I analyze the tensions over these competing ideologies and the ways individuals gain inclusion into the local economy or find themselves being excluded. Even though the music economy is thought of as a successful area of reform, members of the music community still live with the other realities occurring in Dar es Salaam and the rest of Tanzania. They embody their awareness and wariness of these large neoliberal reforms in their music and everyday actions. This ethnography, therefore, explores the notions that neoliberalism can be both a form of economic imperialism and a benefit to individual entrepreneurial freedoms in the economic situations that people live with on a daily basis.

STANCE .-
NEOLIBERALISM

## YOUTH AND *KIZAZI KIPYA* (NEW GENERATION)

No other age group has been tied to the dramatic rise of the contemporary music economy more than youth. The generation born in the late 1970s to the 1990s, referred to as the new generation or *kizazi kipya*, embraced transformations occurring in Tanzanian society, including economic reforms away from socialism and increasing interest in global cultural movements, such as hip hop. This generation had less affinity toward creating united African identities since they were born well after colonialism—thereby not connected to struggles for independence—and into a time of period of economic turmoil. They experienced the meaning of the terms bongo and kujitegemea firsthand, given food and

Job insecurities that existed during their early childhood. Once economic liberalization took place, during their formative teenage years, many took an avid interest in music, concerts, radio, and technologies associated with the production of sound. In conjunction with several entrepreneurial businessmen, youth played a vital role in Tanzania's music economy. They established new job opportunities as radio announcers, music producers, engineers, promoters, managers, music critics, and deejays, all of which encouraged and promoted the commercialization of popular music among people living in Dar es Salaam and other urban areas.

There is a tendency in scholarship and popular culture to treat African youth as a unified group that shares common goals, beliefs, and ways of being. The word youth is for many a static category bounded between certain age groups (children and adult) and levels of maturity, where there is checklist of defined characteristics. Often this checklist features a well-worn inventory of terms that stereotype young people as "alienated, embittered, ill-educated, prone to violence, socially and economically marginalized, politically radical, etc." (Van Zyl Slabbert et al. 1994: 18). Susan Wright describes this static, bounded, and unchanging view as "old culture" in which there is a tendency to authoritatively describe populations as containing homogenous groups of individuals (1998: 8).

Scholars who examine youth as a homogenous population often miss oppositional characteristics of similar aged individuals who can be studious, hardworking, reliable, and socially influential (Perullo 2005). Certainly some youth commit crimes or become involved in illicit activities, but there are many others who create opportunities where none existed before and become influential in supporting social development relevant to specific cities and places. Further, arguing that youth are marginalized is to suggest that people of other age groups are not. In any area of Tanzania, poverty, level of education, sexual orientation, and physical characteristics can be cause for marginalization, and there is nothing to suggest that people who fall into the category of youth are somehow more marginalized than others. Certainly, individuals who reach teenage years undergo numerous obstacles in the transition from childhood to adulthood, yet this transition is culturally constructed and variable across cultures and times (Durham 2004: 591). To imagine youth as a monolithic group is to deny them agency and individual consciousness.

Part of the contestation over youth identites is due to public perception of youth as being jobless and lazy. In Dar es Salaam, so many young
people are without employment that they often gather in specific areas
referred to as *kijiweni*. Abel G.M. Ishumi refers to these spots as "jobless
corners." In his book on the urban joblessness in eastern Africa, he writes,
"The spots [jobless corners] began as points of convergence for youths
of approximately same age levels, same urban backgrounds and, more
important, similar job-hunting experiences, with similar tales of their
reconnaissance efforts and failures. They have grown to be popular places
of resort, of physical and emotional recoupment, or 'fresh' thinking and
'new' strategies, of plans translated into action" (Ishumi 1984: 76–77).
Due to the visibility of kijiweni, many citizens have come to associate
youth who gather on street corners as lazy, unimaginative, dirty, and
parasitic. The government has only encouraged this association through
attacking, arresting, and deporting youth who loiter in common areas
(see chapter 7). The public image of youth in kijiweni establishes a disparaging perception where young people become equated with laziness
and incompetence.

Less visible, however, are the many influential positions in society
that youth occupy. In the music economy, youth are prominent in radio
and television, working as announcers, deejays, technicians, managers,
and, in a few cases, owners. Youth own and operate the majority of the
recording and video studios, which means that they create a large portion of the content heard and viewed on public airwaves that deal with
music. They are the primary performers in bongo flava, which is thriving
in Tanzania and other areas of eastern Africa. They work as promoters,
writers, photographers, and filmmakers. Further, it is not just the jobs in
which they are employed but also the resources and energy they bring to
the production of culture that position them to benefit from the expansion of the music economy. Many youth are passionately knowledgeable
about music, its history, and the importance of the arts in Tanzanian
society.

This is not to deny that other people are not also influential in the music scene. Adults and elders have a significant impact on the commercialization of popular music: they manage and organize most independent
radio stations; educate younger artists about music, instrumentation,
and other facets of the country's music economy; represent musicians on

copyright societies; and administer the majority of the music organizations in the country. These positions provide a significant framework in
the production and consumption of popular music nationally and regionally. However, in terms of the volume of people working in radio stations,
recordings studios, or other areas of the music economy, the majority are
young.

Part of the reason why so many people working with music are young
is due to timing. Beginning in 1994, the music economy expanded rapidly,
which favored those not already in other forms of employment or career
paths. Hundreds of jobs and opportunities became available in the first
decade, and there was a need for a tremendous influx of energetic people
willing to work for little or no money for long periods of time. Many of the
first radio deejays and recording studio producers worked without pay
for several years. When these businesses became profitable, these deejays
and producers began to earn steady salaries. These circumstances favored
youth who could wait to earn a salary while they learned a new skill. This
gave them a significant advantage over other people in the economy once
music became profitable.

In this discussion of the term youth, there is one issue that remains
unsettled. Who is considered a youth in Tanzania? The term *kijana* means
youth in Swahili and technically refers to someone who is between fifteen
and thirty-five years of age. Marriage and children, however, complicate
the definition of youth in Tanzania since someone who is married with
children is often considered an adult, while someone who is over thirty-
five without being married can still be considered a youth. In a humorous story in the newspaper *Raia,* the author Hidaya writes a letter to the
Ministry of Arrogance and Pompousness in which she debates the issues
of youth. Understanding that one needs to be married with children in
order to be considered an adult, she asks her partner: "Is it truly possible
that a person old enough to be a grandfather and grandmother can still
be considered a youth? I have verification that if I reach the age of 35 and,
God willing, we have children, I will be seen completely as an adult and
even you would be praised like an elder of the village."[30] The story pokes
humor at the categories of youth, lamenting the fact that childhood is
technically shorter than youth, while also recognizing that it would be
possible for both mother and daughter to be youth if they are between
fifteen and thirty-five.

Part of the humor in the category of youth is that it is frequently dependent on numerous factors, such as social status, class, gender, age, and marital status. It makes any clear distinctions difficult. Many people I have worked with in Tanzania consider themselves youth even when they are forty years of age simply because they do not have children and/or are not married. Others feel that they are youth even at older ages with children because they identify with the ideas, practices, and beliefs of other *vijana* (the plural of kijana). The term *kizazi kipya* (new generation) helps to overcome some of the vagueness and problems that permeate definitions of youth. Kizazi kipya refers to a generation of youth who generally came of age during neoliberal reforms of the 1990s. It refers to people's interest in being active participants in international movements of music, fashion, and identities that have become prominent in the past two decades. The grouping based on generation allows for more flexibility in understanding populations, particularly those who most influence the Tanzanian music economy, as well as many other cultural industries across Africa.

A significant element of the new generation is the allure of cities. Cities are cosmopolitan, offering youth a chance to be a part of worldly ideas, aesthetics, beliefs, and characteristics. Dar es Salaam has a particular draw for youth in eastern Africa. Even though it is not the capital of Tanzania, it is considered the center of the country's cultural industries. There is a vibrant nightlife, diverse forms of employment, and a shipping port that receives goods from all over the world. The city is celebrated in films, newspapers, songs, and in cartoons (Lewinson 2003). Mr. II's song "Dar es Salaam" declares that everything in the city is amazing (PURL 1.7). Professor Jay's "Bongo Dar es Salaam" opens with the line "Ndani ya bongo mambo super hapana uwongo" (Inside Dar es Salaam everything is super, it's not a lie). The majority of the stories in the country's newspapers and magazines focus on life in the city. Popular radio and television stations are based in the city, as is the country's music economy. It would be difficult to be young and not be drawn to some element of life in Dar es Salaam.

The attraction of youth to Dar es Salaam is not new. In the 1920s and 1930s, youth migrated into the city to escape family, customs, and traditions, and to find employment. Reports from this period note the high volume of youth drifting into the city and searching for work (Burton

2005: 71–73). Youth moved to the city because it was both the commercial
and administrative capital of the country. (Dar es Salaam was the capital
of the country until 1974.) In a letter sent in response to a 1956 survey, an
African resident writes an account of the reasons people move to Dar es
Salaam. In one part, the text reads, "What, you live in a village without
electricity? No Cinema? No dance hall? No bands? What a dump!" (Leslie 1963: 24).

In the contemporary music economy, youth have been active participants in the formation of radio stations, recording studios, and bands
that make up the country's popular music scene. By some accounts, over
two-thirds of the Tanzanian music economy is run, at some level, by individuals categorized as the new generation. Despite limited educational
and employment opportunities in other areas of society, youth push the
local music economy into becoming one of the most influential in East
Africa. Youth embrace economic changes in the country in ways that
recognize their adaptability to emergent ideas, systems, and contexts.
Conceptualizing the range of possibilities in a post-socialist context is not
always easy. There is a sense of starting from scratch in forming institutions that allow for the commodification of music. The myriad of choices
and actions that originate in the new generation illustrates their self-determination to overcome obstacles in the formation of a prosperous music
economy. It provides a sense of aspirations needed to create something
reflective of their diverse interests, ideas, and beliefs in relation to music
as art and music as commodity.

*are these dissen youth considered as dissent?*

### AND NOW . . .

The choices and decisions made in Tanzanian's music economy reflect a
broader understanding of music's social and economic potential. A song
moves from composition to recording studio to radio stations to distribution in a flow that is reflective of broader struggles for survival and
success. To be able to move music into this commodity flow requires an
understanding of post-socialist state expectations, neoliberal interests in
the commodification of the arts, and conceptions of global trends in arts,
business, and daily life. Creative practices emerge in response to people's
attempts to benefit from the potential of the arts in the music economy.
For a radio deejay to profit from songs that he or she did not compose or

record, there must be imagination for the potential value in songs. For a distributor to sell music that he did not create, he must apply innovative strategies to overcome limitations on the consumption of music. For artists to perform successful concerts there needs to be an understanding of desire and cultural knowledge in performance spaces. Creative practices rely on context (places where interaction and power manifest), resources (the flows of goods, money, labor, transport and communication systems, markets, and so on), and the politics of daily life (motivations and desires that inform individual interaction with contexts and resources).

There is a wealth of scholarship that examines the commercialization of music.[31] This ethnography builds on these previous studies, particularly approaches toward analyzing the importance of historical narratives in understanding the contemporary state of Tanzania's music economy. To that end, the next chapter provides a historical analysis of the formation of the music economy from 1920 to 1984. The music economy emerged from a plurality of voices contesting, supporting, and struggling over the meaning of music in the colonial and post-independence periods. Although there is a great deal that could be covered in this chapter given the expanse of time discussed, I focus on three areas that most directly impacted the music scene: demand for local and foreign sound recordings, attempts to control music in the post independence period, and the formation of social halls and broadcasting networks. In its entirety, chapter 2 provides a means to evaluate a musical infrastructure created around popular music and which significantly impacted social and economic choices in the commodification of sound in the contemporary music scene.

# Shall We Mdundiko or Tango? Tanzania's Music Economy, 1920-1984

If you love me, take me to see doctors,
For our marriage, you will come to marry me later,
To quit rumba music, I cannot accept it,
I cannot give up rumba for you.

—VIJANA WA MBEYA (MBEYA YOUTH), "Siwezi Kuiacha Rumba"
(I Cannot Give Up Rumba), recorded in 1950

In the March 1954 issue of *Mambo Leo* (Current Affairs)—a Tanganyikan educational, monthly magazine operated by the British colonial government—there appeared the results of an essay competition. The magazine's 50,000 readers had been invited to discuss the importance of "tribal" dances. Though few people entered the competition, the essays were unanimous in proclaiming these dances as one of Tanganyika's greatest heritages. But the editor questioned the dearth of entries and wondered if the "educated African" was actually ashamed of the country's traditional culture: "Perhaps he [the educated African] really does feel, but is afraid to say, that [tribal dances] are barbaric and out of line with what he feels is Western civilisation." In his commentary, the editor was concerned with how Tanganyikan people perceived traditional culture and the colonial culture they were taught to emulate. He worried that traditional culture—rooted in the history of Tanzanian society—was losing out to a foreign one.

The winner of the essay competition, Francis Nicholas, who worked for the Dar es Salaam Broadcasting Station, agreed with the editor in recognizing the importance of traditional music. Nicholas said that many colonial influences were beneficial, but, as he stated, "When it comes to our tribal dances, I think, it is our duty to maintain them, and never take ourselves to ballroom dances."[1] To Nicholas, ballroom dancing was a custom meant for foreigners and could only create unwise actions, including people wasting their money on expensive clothes and high entrance fees. Maintaining tribal dancing was a priority, according to Nicholas, for it was only through this means that the Tanganyikan people could remain "properly civilized."

Despite the agreement between Nicholas and the editor, their reasons for embracing traditional music were vastly different. From the editor's perspective, promoting traditional music meant that the British colonial administration would have an easier time maintaining racial and political barriers between Africans and British peoples. After the British Mandate of 1922, which established the Tanganyika Territory, colonial officials enforced laws designed to safeguard traditional culture and the "moral well-being" of Africans.[2] By the 1950s, a system of multi-racialism emerged that provided political representation for Africans, Asians, and Europeans. The historian John Iliffe notes that multi-racialism was not multiculturalism (1979: 481), and divisions remained stark between each of the racial groups in the administration of the country. The editor's desire for Africans to preserve their cultural forms was an effort to make differences more visible, thereby establishing barriers between populations that were far easier to manage.

For many African elites, however, traditional music represented a means to counter colonial influences. Through embracing African values and ideas as embodied or imagined in traditional music, elites were signaling their desires to strengthen pride in African cultures and find ways to potentially undermine the control of colonial administrators. Only a few months after the March *Mambo Leo* competition, the Tanganyika African National Union (TANU) formed in Dar es Salaam. Organized mostly by elite and intellectual Africans, TANU was a nationalist party aimed at establishing freedom and equality through removing colonial rule in the country. One approach used by TANU was to promote African cultural forms, such as language, traditional values, and music. The support for traditional music, particularly in urban areas, became a means to promote African national pride and foster collective resistance against colonial rule.

The two opposing views of the same musical form highlight variations in meaning that emerge through people's engagement with songs.

In this chapter, I argue that songs become grounds to support or contest different ideologies that form around interpretations of musical meaning. The context of performance, the relation of the listeners to the performers, and the cultural knowledge of dance, music, lyrics, gestures, and so on provide numerous points of distinction between people listening to the same music. Attempts are made to control and shape these meanings in order to cultivate support for particular ideological perspectives. Music holds influence over populations and gives power to those who can control its shape, its outcome, its performance, and its reception. A music economy is not simply the use of music as a commercial entity, but also the ability of songs to circulate through records, radio broadcasts, and government policies to an array of listeners. In this circulation, those who can best manage the production and consumption of songs attain some ability to shape their outcomes. This accords authority to those who record, broadcast, and permit the performance of music in public cultures. Yet this power is far from absolute and, given the multiplicity of meanings found in music, frequently elusive.

Given the expanse of time covered in this chapter (1920–1984), I focus on the policies and practices of colonial officials and Tanzania's African elite in relation to popular music, leisure activities, and broadcasting. It is these two populations, more than any other, which provided the foundation for the contemporary music economy. Their political influences in building social halls, radio stations, and recording studios created a movement toward the commercialization of the arts able to support the professionalization of music.

Nevertheless, these two populations only illustrate a part of the range of ideologies that emerged around popular music. Particularly through the popularity of the gramophone and radio broadcasting, the urban landscape was far more musically and socially expansive than evidenced by these two groups. Many Africans living in cities attempted to show their separation from the villages and the towns they had left by appropriating sounds and ideas from other parts of the world. Unlike the *Mambo Leo* editor or Nicholas, who argued that foreign music was detrimental for Africans peoples, many Africans living in Tanzania found foreign music exciting and sonically alluring. Cosmopolitanism in urban areas of Africa signaled a desire and a "willingness to engage" with "divergent cultural experiences" (Hannerz 1990: 239). One's level of incorporation in and engagement with city life could be shown through knowledge of foreign cultural forms, whether ballroom dance from England, *son* from Cuba, or the tango from Argentina. Occasionally, interest in separating from traditional musical forms led to more extreme forms of conflict, such as one incident where youth in Dar es Salaam threw rocks at ngoma musicians to get them to stop playing.[3] More often, foreign music was a means, particularly for youth, to attain familiarity with something compelling and create some measure of distinction between themselves and other members of society.

The desire by some Africans to connect with foreign cultural forms, however, did not mean an abandonment of African traditions. Mamadou Diouf states that cosmopolitanism is "too often perceived as incorporation into Western universality and the abandonment of one's own traditions" (2000: 683). In Tanzania, many musicians and audiences simultaneously looked toward foreign and regional musics to create popular forms that resonated with the urban African experience. It was a means to "know the foreign" as part of the local landscape (Caldwell 2008). Song compositions drew from multiple forms of music so long as they represented the experiences and ideologies of performers and participants. One did not have to choose between *mdundiko,* a traditional dance, and the tango since they could be incorporated into an altogether new musical form.[4]

In addition to African interests in cosmopolitan forms, expatriates also promoted Western instruments and music as a means to regulate and discipline urban society, or simply to foster bands that could entertain white audiences. Missionaries and military officials in particular encouraged Africans to learn foreign musical instruments, including wind instruments, military style drums, piano, and guitar. Through controlling leisure activities, some colonialists proposed that African populations could "imbibe European values and coexist in a non-threatening manner with white society" (Martin 1995: 96). In addition, music could discipline populations by encouraging them to refrain from performing music and dance that could promote unsophisticated beliefs (Ranger 1975: 10–11).

The views presented thus far reveal different interpretations of traditional and foreign forms of music. Both local and foreign forms were supported, contested and merged together in one way or another by Africans and colonialists in the pre-independence period. Many Tanzanian musicians who performed during the 1940s and 1950s, however, argue that the conceptualization of music as bimodal—featuring two separate orientations—oversimplifies the way that music is continually integrated and reformulated in each iteration of sound. According to this argument, colonial administrations created the categories of music as native and non-native, foreign and local in order to achieve distinct separations between African and colonial populations. Ally Sykes, who performed with several post–World War II bands, explains:

> Bantu ethnic groups really like music. This is something that is centuries old and not something new. Even if you look at music performed, let's say, in America or South America, the origins of that music are here [in Africa]. Rumba, conga, *chakacha,* and all of these musical forms came from the culture of the Bantu ethnic groups starting in the south and moving up. For instance, in the south, the rhythms are like jazz music. There is no difference between [American jazz artists] and those that perform in South Africa, such as Miriam Makeba. The rhythm of rumba, if you look in the distant past here [in eastern Africa], you will see the same rhythm. Even in America they know this. The origins of this music are here in Africa.

To substantiate connections between foreign and local musical forms, Sykes points out that the musicians the British hired to perform in ballroom style dance bands were from ethnic groups that shared similar aesthetic styles to the British: "The ngoma of the Wanyamwezi and Wasukuma, they sing very well, they harmonize, and have orchestration. For this reason, the British took musicians from the Nyamwezi and Sukuma ethnic groups to play in the police and military bands because of their background in music." Although some of Sykes's language should be acknowledged as legitimization of Tanzanian popular music as being African in origin, which thereby supports historical nationalization efforts of the post-independence period, many ballroom styles of music do have African origins. The choreography, rhythm, and/or sound of rumba and tango, for instance, have antecedents in the music and dance of Africans living in the Americas (Chasteen 2000: 46; Daniel 1995: 18). Other genres of music that became popular in Tanzania, such as Cuban *son* and American rhythm and blues, further emphasize the connections between rhythm, movement, and sound in these various musical forms. Categorization of local and foreign, in other words, creates an imaginary division that hides the many commonalities between them. Or, more

*Do songs serve better to make these distinctions?*

problematically, the emphasis on the foreign dominating local musical forms diminishes the importance of East African music globally.

My intention in this opening narrative is not to support one view over another, but rather to argue that music in urban areas is polysemous and generates "an infinite range of meanings" (Hebdige 1979: 117). Traditional music can be both a means to strengthen colonial and anti-colonial ideologies; foreign music can be used to civilize population or promote cosmopolitanism; or the categories of music as either local or foreign miss the historical relation between all musical forms. These different ways of engaging with music mirror diverse experiences with urban music in contemporary Tanzania.

The next sections of this chapter use the notion that music is an expressive art form that is flexibly and socially constructed to create a historical narrative about the formation of a popular music scene in Tanzania. It is an archaeology of the most cogent factors influencing the formation of the contemporary music economy particularly relating to the commercialization and nationalization of sound that took place in the colonial and post-independence periods. In the next section, I look at the influence of records in the formation of popular music in Tanzania, particularly the configuration of cosmopolitan publics interested in distancing themselves from local traditions and identifying with international trends in music. This is followed by an examination of the nationalization of music during the 1960s and 1970s, which sought to promote Tanzanian culture in urban musical forms and forbid any forms of dress, sound, or language deemed inappropriate in the evocation of Tanzanian culture. The final two sections analyze nationalization of many of the country's social halls and only radio station, Radio Tanzania Dar es Salaam (RTD). Collectively, these sections illustrate the formation of the Tanzanian music economy through the entanglement of interests in controlling and shaping the performance of popular songs.

## RECORDS AND THE INFLUENCE
## OF NON-TANZANIAN MUSIC

Starting in the 1920s gramophone records became central to the creation of an urban popular culture in Tanzania. Records encapsulated the urban experience: they were modern, both musically and technologically; embraced by Europeans, a population influential with many educated and upwardly mobile Africans; and they brought in sounds and musical ideas that gave migrants an opportunity to celebrate their arrival in an urban environment. Other items of Western material culture aided in urban transformations, such as magazines, fashion, and cinema. But records, more than anything else, influenced the musical identity of urban Tanganyika. They helped strengthen (and alter) certain genres, particularly dansi, as musicians and bands imitated or improvised on the sounds coming from gramophones.[5] Records, as well as radio, also created a larger audience for popular music and formed a perceived separation between the performer and listener, making performance more presentational than participatory (Racy 1978: 55).

Gramophones first appeared in East Africa at the turn of the twentieth century. Intended for European settlers, records featured popular and classical music from Western Europe and the United States. Since no disc pressing plants existed in East Africa at the time, records were only imported and sold in stores to expatriates. By the mid-1920s, however, an African and Asian middle class emerged that could afford gramophones. Like other items of prestige, gramophones became symbols of success and wealth and were bought to emphasize a person's social class. But records were far more than a social symbol. They were novel talking machines that brought music and speech from another part of the world close to home. Teachers, families, and business people purchased records to listen to and learn about other cultures. As this new group of listeners steadily expanded, records of diverse music, such as African American spirituals, church music, Indian music (imported from India), Arab music (particularly the 78 rpm discs of the Egyptian singer Umm Kulthum), and early recordings of big band music from the United States became popular (Harrev 1989: 103; Suleiman 1969: 87).

Local populations of Africans and Asians first heard records either at social gatherings or Asian shops, where music was often used to entice customers to enter local stores (Kubik 1981: 90; Ewens 1992: 160). After hearing records around town, customers would often try to purchase them, as a 1939 advertisement shows:

"Hello friend."

"Hello, how is your day?"

"Good. Today I heard a record, it was so good, but I do not know which store I can find it in. Oh! For Swahili records, Jim Rodgers, and South African Bantu records, go to Shah Kalyanji Bhanji, Indian [sic] Street, Dar es Salaam, P.O. Box 37."[6]

Other stores opened during the 1930s and 1940s, including Dusara's Music House, the first commercial music shop in Dar es Salaam. These stores offered townspeople a chance to hear new sounds, if they passed close to the store, and purchase new records.

Due to the commercialization of music in Tanzania, demand rose by Africans for African music. Foreign companies searched for artists to record in hopes of capturing this burgeoning market. The first recorded album of East African music intended for commercial distribution was of the Zanzibar-based taarab singer Siti binti Saad. In 1928, His Master's Voice (HMV) flew Saad and her band to its branch in Bombay, India. The thirty-one songs that Saad recorded became celebrated throughout the Swahili-speaking world of Kenya, Tanganyika, the Belgian Congo, the Comoros, and Somalia (Harrev 1989: 104). By 1931, Saad had sold over 23,000 copies of these initial recordings with a meager advertising budget.[7] Given the demand for her music, Saad recorded an additional one hundred songs that sold over 40,000 copies (Graebner 2004: 173). Other musicians recorded in this period, but Saad was the first East African star. This was due to her ability to interpret a foreign genre into themes and contexts relevant to the people living in eastern Africa.

In 1930, Colombia[7] Gramophone Company set up studios on both Zanzibar and Dar es Salaam. The studios consisted of at least two rooms where the windows and doors could be sealed for acoustic insulation. One of the rooms held a recording machine, while the other had a microphone for artists. Due to the delicacy of recording with needles, wax, and portable batteries, as well as the time needed to teach artists how to sing properly into microphones, recording projects often took several days. In Dar es Salaam, during twelve days in June 1931, Columbia Gramophone Company recorded children's, military, religious, and ngoma songs. Each of the wax recordings was then sent to Europe to be pressed into a steel master recording, which was then used to make copies. The copies were then shipped back to East Africa for sale.[8]

After the Second World War, other recording tours took place that were released on the Trek and Gallotone labels, which were under the South African Gallo Record Company. These recordings featured a variety of sides of popular music from Tanganyika, such as Dar es Salaam Jazz Band, Chipukizi Rumba, Rhythms Expert Band, and the taarab groups Egyptian and Al-Watan Musical Clubs. The recordings emphasize the influence of foreign recordings on early popular music in Tanganyika. Dar es Salaam Jazz Band, which formed in 1932, recorded a song titled "Hayo Siyakweli" (That's Not True). The song was a rendition of the Cuban *son* song "Lamento Esclavo" (Slave's Lament), recorded by Rico's Creole Band in Paris, and released on the His Master's Voice GV series around 1932. The 78 rpm disc found its way to Africa around 1933.[9] In the notes for the Dar es Salaam Jazz Band recordings, Hugh Tracey writes, "This band does not play from music at all—but has picked up its tunes from records or from other similar bands." On another recording, "Sikilizeni Masaibu" (Listen to Stories of Calamity) by Atomic Jazz Band, based in Iringa, Tracey notes, "The playing of a kind of jazz or European dance music, learnt from records is to be found in most towns. The players take it very seriously."[10] Most other popular music bands, including the taarab groups, used records to build a repertoire of songs and playing techniques that they could perform in Tanganyika. Imitation was a popular form of musical learning.

As records became commonplace, European instruments, such as guitars, banjos, mandolins, violins, accordions, and even pianos were imported into East Africa. The inexpensive Gallotone acoustic guitar, manufactured by the South African Gallo Record Company, was one of the most popularly purchased items. There was also a steady stream of Asian and Arab instruments, such as the *dumbak* (double-headed drum), *rika* (tambourine), and *oud* (a plucked lute with no frets). Of the few musicians I interviewed who were able to remember this period (1930s-1950s), all commented on the availability of these instruments and their importance for building an indigenous form of popular music that could be performed in the social halls of urban areas. Several pointed out that it was easy to learn these foreign instruments because they resembled indigenous ones: the guitar resembled the *zeze* of the Wagogo peoples (though the zeze is bowed like a violin), while the clarinet resembled the coastal *zumari*.

Records also became an important means to instruct artists on the ways to entertain foreigners. Since better salaries could be had performing for expatriates, top musical groups would attempt to learn and master music from commercially available recordings. Ally Sykes led some of the top bands, including the Ally Sykes Band and the Merry Blackbirds, which played tangos, foxtrots, and quicksteps for colonialists at the Dar es Salaam Club, Gymkhana Club, The New Africa Hotel, and the Hotel Internationale. During the late 1940s, Sykes's groups would receive 100 shillings for a performance, which was a considerable amount at the time (as Sykes pointed out, a kilo of rice cost 6 shillings at that time). When Sykes joined Peter Colmore in Nairobi to form the Ally Sykes Band, the band primarily relied on records to find hits to play for the mostly white audiences in urban areas. Sykes explains, "Colmore used to record the American Top Ten from the Voice of America . . . and the band would practice these songs and play them to their audiences. In this way, American pop songs found their way into the dance halls of Nairobi soon after they were released in New York, Los Angeles, and London. The quality of our music was excellent" (Mwakikagile 2006: 325). In 1947, the Ally Sykes band recorded a series of records with Guy Johnson in Kenya at East African Studios for Jambo Records (Said 1998).

When Ally Sykes became leader of the Merry Blackbirds in 1948, he performed jazz and ballroom dance for foreigners and ngoma-influenced music for local audiences. The back-and-forth between ballroom style dance, traditional music, and other popular musical genres created the formative sounds of the dansi genre, which remains the most popular form of live entertainment in Dar es Salaam. Other dansi bands, such as Dar es Salaam Jazz Band, Western Jazz, and Kilwa Jazz Band, also performed in the pre-independence period. Zibe Kidasi, a former Brigadier-General in a beni ngoma group, led a brass band for weddings.[11] There were several taarab groups, such as Al-Watan and Egyptian Musical Clubs. For all these groups, imported records became an important means to keep up with hit songs, styles, and ideas, which would then be incorporated into each group's repertoire. The recording of their songs also became a means to promote regional forms of popular music that increased people's interest in records as a commercial commodity.

The Merry Black Birds Orchestra, Dar es Salaam,
Tanganyika, 1950. Ally Sykes stands on the right
with the saxophone. *Photo courtesy of Ally Sykes.*

By the late 1940s, numerous companies manufactured or imported
records and record players to East Africa. Foreign companies, such as
Gallo of South Africa (Gallotone, Tropic, and Trek labels), Philips (HIT
label), Columbia (YE), and HMV (JP series), imported their products,
mainly to Kenya, which were then distributed further to major towns
in East Africa. Many of the local record labels that formed at this time
pressed their recordings at the East African Records plant in Nairobi,
which, in 1953, manufactured 12,000 discs per month for the African
market (Graham 1992: 148). Philips Electronics Ltd., based in Arusha,
Tanganyika, manufactured record players, radio receivers, and later tape
recorders.[12] In the late 1950s, ASL released albums of Congolese artists
such as Franco and O.K. Jazz (Harrev 1989: 109). These Congolese recordings, as well as imports of records on the Ngoma label from the Congo,
encouraged the long preoccupation of Tanzanian artists with Congolese
music (for an example of Congolese artists and songs popular in Tanzania

in the 1960s and 1970s, see PURL 2.1). The efforts to manufacture and import objects related to popular music created significant enthusiasm for recorded sound throughout eastern Africa and encouraged people's interest in pursuing musical careers in genres that appeared on sound recordings.

To realize how records influenced artists before independence, it is useful to look at the life of one of Tanganyika's most popular artists, Salum Abdallah Yazide. Abdallah was born on May 5, 1928, to an Arab father and an African mother in the town of Morogoro, which is roughly 200 kilometers west of Dar es Salaam. From the time he was eleven, Abdallah would finish his Qur'anic studies each day and then head to a neighbor's house to listen to records. These records—particularly the Latin American and Cuban songs on the GV label—made such an impression on Abdallah that he would often neglect his responsibilities at home.[13] After a failed attempt to travel to Latin America to find the popular music he heard on records, Abdallah returned home to work in his father's hotel, earning a meager wage but enough to purchase a legitimate guitar. However, the hotel business was slow and did not allow him to earn enough money to buy the other musical instruments he needed. In order to generate sufficient finances to fulfill his dream of becoming a musician, Abdallah secretly sold one of his father's houses. From the sale of the house, Abdallah made enough money to purchase a full set of instruments, like those of Dar es Salaam Jazz Band, which was the band he admired in Dar es Salaam.

In 1947, he and some friends formed the group La Paloma.[14] In 1952, Abdallah changed the name of the group to Cuban Marimba Band and recorded with the Mzuri label in Mombasa, Kenya. Over the next thirteen years, Cuban Marimba Band and Salum Abdallah became famous in East Africa for their unique, guitar-based music. His voice emulated the nasal intonations of coastal taarab singers, but also the rhythmic inflections of Cuban *son* he had heard as a youth on the GV records. Lyrically, Abdallah's songs captured the social and political climate of Tanganyika. In the song "Beberu" (Imperialist), he celebrates the Tanganyika African National Union (TANU), the party that led the country to independence, by joyfully singing, "Thank you TANU, let us work together in Africa / To kick the imperialist out of Southern Africa / The

Portuguese out of Mozambique and the racists out of Rhodesia." Accompanied by repeating bass and guitar lines, elements of ngoma music and Latin American percussion (including maracas and the *guiro*), Abdallah wrote upbeat music that would become, along with Dar es Salaam Jazz Band, the precursor to the Tanzanian dansi movement: a movement born partially out of records of foreign music and partially out of local music traditions.[15]

The life of Abdallah illuminates some of the salient features of popular music before independence. Records offered people a chance to hear and learn about diverse music from around the world, particularly since the performance of foreign popular musicians rarely took place in Tanganyika.[16] All over the country, in towns such as Tabora, Mwanza, Songea, Iringa, Arusha, Tanga, and Dar es Salaam, musicians like Abdallah created music that captured the ideas they heard on records and combined it with local conceptions of rhythm, harmony, and music making. By the 1950s, as Abdallah began to make his name, many groups throughout the country formed and toured in Dar es Salaam, making the city the center of the country's growing music scene. Bands such as Nyamwezi Jazz Band, which became Jamhuri Jazz (1955), Atomic Jazz Band (1954), Kilwa Jazz Band (1958), and Moro Jazz Band (1954), established a new period of Tanganyikan popular music that captured the country's drive for independence, its connection with foreign music, and its foundation in local music traditions.[17]

Even after independence, with a national radio station that aired local music and had a recording studio, records of foreign music were still extremely popular, far more so than any music produced in East Africa. In particular, residents of Dar es Salaam, Arusha, and other East African cities identified with African Americans such as Aretha Franklin (who was referred to as the "black queen of soul"), James Brown, and Otis Redding, whose lives and music were promoted not only on records but also in local magazines, such as *Nyota Afrika* and *Nchi Yetu*.[18] Country artists, made popular by American western movies, popular rock groups from America and Europe, and Hindi film stars also received attention. Due to the diversity of music available in East Africa, Agehananda Bharati found record collections among Asian households in the 1960s extremely varied:

In all houses, rich and poor, there lurks a phonograph, and many many H.M.V. and Columbia 78 rpm shellacs made in Dum Dum, India. I browsed through well over a hundred collections in all the three countries [Kenya, Uganda, Tanganyika] and found a total of ten classical or semi-classical records at various places; the rest were *filmi*. . . . Now a good percentage of the wealthier adolescents, boys and girls, are both admirers and performers of such alien imports as the Twist, the Frug, and Rock n' Roll: it takes an American choreographic creation less than a year to get firmly established in East Africa. (Bharati 1972: 251, 253)

The reference to "choreographic creation" emphasizes the speed with which popular music and their associated dances could become firmly rooted in Tanzanian popular music performance.

The interest in foreign music resulted in the formation of numerous cover bands or bands that sounded just like the music on records. One example was a group that became popular in the 1960s, the Flaming Stars. Started in 1965, their songs were, according to an article in *Nyota Afrika*, the "shake and twist variety," and heavily influenced by American and European icons: the lead singer sounded like Elvis Presley, the drummer was named Ringo, the lead guitarist was named Rock, and Peko and Jet played bass and rhythm guitar. The entire band wore white "soul" suits with striped shirts and, in pictures, stood together like American rock "soulsters."[19] Music of local groups was more popular than "copyright" bands—bands that imitated other groups or played cover songs—but foreign music dominated the local record market, partially due to its availability and partially due to its connection to people, ideas, and places outside of Tanzania. Records and music more generally became a means to establish one's cosmopolitanism to other people in the city.

The freedom of Tanzanian bands into the 1960s led to considerable diversity in the performance and composition of music. It was, perhaps, the most active and influential period in Tanzania's music history, for it brought disparate genres from around the world and reoriented them toward traditional conceptions of music. Urban leisure was epitomized by the bands that flooded the local market, each with its own take on the sounds and styles of post-independence Tanzania.

In response to the growth and interest in local bands, numerous small record labels emerged in Kenya that recorded Tanzanian artists. Assanand & Sons in Mombasa had a production wing run by M. J. Shah as early as 1939 that recorded for Columbia. In the 1950s, Shah established the Mzuri label to record a variety of groups, including Kiko Kids and Lucky Star Musical Club (Graebner 2004: 184). African Gramophone Stores in Nairobi created the AGS label. A.I.T. records in Nairobi recorded Atomic Jazz, Western Jazz, Vijana Jazz, Afro 70, and numerous other popular Tanzanian dance bands on the Moto Moto and Africa/79 record labels. A.P. Chandarana operated the Saba Saba label, which was an outlet for many of the bands already listed, as well as Orchestra Safari Trippers, Urafiki Jazz Band, and Mwenge Jazz Band.

By the late 1960s, efforts toward nationalization created stricter limitations on the meaning and use of music: non-African records and popular magazines received heavy criticism and censor; the use of pseudonyms drawn from American and European culture declined as people were encouraged to embrace traditional terminology; local papers featured fewer articles on non-African artists and, instead, covered Congolese and South African groups; and popular music became forcefully rooted in the political and cultural movements of Tanzania's socialist/nationalist identity. The entire country was called upon to remove cultural trends that were deemed non-African and, more important, non-Tanzanian. Art became the servant of society (see chapter 1). Andrew Ivaska writes, "As state-sponsored campaigns were launched in the late sixties and early seventies targeting mini-skirts, soul music, wigs, cosmetics, 'Afro' hairstyles, beauty contests and Maasai 'traditional' dress, the national cultural question became a terrain upon which some of the capital's most pressing social struggles of the time were fought out" (2003: 2–3; see also Ivaska 2002). Music was undergoing increasing pressures to become Tanzanian in the image of the independent government even though much of the music heard in Tanzania, such as dansi, taarab, and kwaya, were influenced by foreign cultures. Similar efforts occurred in the Congo/Zaire, where Mobutu Sese Seko ushered in notions of *authenticité* and Zaïrianization, and in Zambia where Kenneth Kaunda brought in Zambianization (Perullo 2008b).

In these efforts to nationalize local industries and, at the same time, to become more African or promote Africanness, records and instruments became more difficult to purchase (even Zaire's tremendous output of records plummeted during this time due to the nationalization of local industries and sudden rise in costs for vinyl). For Tanzania, the inability to purchase records, even those from Zaire, meant that people needed to rely more on Radio Tanzania Dar es Salaam (RTD), the government-controlled radio station, for news, music, and ideas about their country and the rest of the world.[20] The promotion of indigenous genres of music, however, became problematic since little of what was promoted, even in traditional ngoma music, had anything to do with precolonial notions of music. Rather, the choices made by government administrators, musicians, and others on acceptable music were based on reactions to colonization, Cold War opportunities, and an assertion of assumed notions of what was more African in light of independence ideologies.

## CREATING NATIONALIST MUSIC

In 1959 and 1960, TANU won decisive victories in the country's general elections, and on December 9, 1961, the country became fully independent. Julius Nyerere, as prime minister and then as the country's first president, wasted no time in trying to build a national cultural identity (Ntiro 1975: 113). In a 1962 speech, often cited in scholarship on the arts in Tanzania, Nyerere addressed Parliament:

> I believe that culture is the essence and spirit of any nation. A country which lacks its own culture is no more than a collection of people without the spirit which makes them a nation. Of all the crimes of colonialism there is none worse than the attempt to make us believe we had no indigenous culture of our own; or that what we did have was worthless—something of which we should be ashamed, instead of being a source of pride. (Nyerere 1967: 186)

The speech marked the beginning of the newly independent government's initiative to promote indigenous culture over foreign influences. While acknowledging the importance of foreign culture—as Nyerere phrases it, "A nation which refuses to learn from foreign culture is nothing but a nation of idiots and lunatics" (Nyerere 1967: 187)—Nyerere also wanted to ensure that Tanganyikans would learn and perform the country's traditional music and dance. In 1969, he told a gathering of ambassadors, "It is not that Tanzanians claim that their culture is better than everyone else's. They claim that their culture deserves, like the cultures of other people, to be placed within their history and current development. Every one of us should try to develop our culture by following its basic principles without carelessly imitating the principles of other people."[21]

In the immediate years after independence, an explicit effort was made within the government's cultural policy to promote indigenous genres over foreign ones. Ngoma, in particular, was recognized for its Tanzanian qualities. It existed throughout the country, long before colonialism, and was considered authentic in comparison to the more popular, foreign-based genres of music that were thought to have emerged mainly in urban areas. In recognizing ngoma as a proto-African musical form, there was also an essentialization of traditional cultures as a reflection of an unchanging history. The unchanging nature of traditional songs was heavily promoted by Western researchers and colonizers who regarded certain forms of traditional music as untainted forms of expressive culture that provided windows into the origins of human cultures (Perullo 2008a). Many of the Tanzanian political elite viewed ngoma similarly: it was a form of music that could return the country to the values and ideals of African societies before the tainting of local cultures through colonial rule. Certain forms of traditional music, in other words, were static entities that encapsulated the ideologies of the community of people who composed them.[22]

After Nyerere's inaugural speech, the government established the Wizara ya Utamaduni wa Taifa na Vijana (Ministry of National Culture and Youth), which promoted music and dance, arts and crafts, drama and theater arts, as well as the country's national language, Swahili. By 1963, the government had created a National Dance Troupe, featuring forty-nine dancers and musicians from all over the country.[23] The troupe traveled to Algeria, Somalia, Ethiopia, and Japan and sent members to Guinea to train in other African music. Ngoma was also used in primary and secondary schools to teach students about local traditions and customs. Competitions were also held between local ngoma groups to encourage performers to practice and sharpen their skills (Ntiro 1975: 113; Ballanga 1992).

By 1967, under the announcement of the Arusha Declaration, the government continued to push its interest in ngoma but in new and different ways. Ngoma, once touted as the music of Tanzanian people, began to be acknowledged for its "innate" socialist qualities. Kelly Askew explains, "Cultural officers, state-sponsored musicians, and teachers at the National College of Arts began altering *ngoma* performance to better fulfill, embody, and enact socialist objectives" (Askew 2002: 278). To better comply with socialist objectives, ngoma groups sang only in Swahili rather than the country's other languages. This impacted the sound of ngoma as artists needed to shift the rhythms and melodies of songs to accommodate the Swahili language. At public performances, groups were encouraged to perform songs from more than one area of Tanzania, thereby creating unity between the country's many ethnicities.[24] And ngoma groups were expected to sing political and social themes, dropping songs used in traditional ceremonies. In its modified form, ngoma carried with it notions of unity and equality, ideal principles of Tanzania's socialist objectives but principles that may not have existed in the initial intentions of traditional music.

Despite the government's promotion of traditional arts during the 1960s, ngoma did not receive wide acceptance or support in cities, such as Dar es Salaam. The National Dance Troupe, based in Dar es Salaam, shrank to only nine members. Though the government tried to sustain the Troupe by hiring more ngoma experts, raising its numbers to twenty-five, it never possessed the vigor of its early days.[25] Similarly, ngoma competitions and education in schools dwindled as the country became more preoccupied with socialism. The Music Conservatoire of Tanzania, Limited, which was formed in 1967 to rediscover and develop Tanzania's indigenous musical heritage, lost most of its funding (Mbunga 1968: 53–54).[26] Dar es Salaam also lacked performers and elders to administer dances, and many youth became more interested in modern aspects of city life rather than in traditional arts (Leslie 1963: 54–55).

Part of the reason for the lack of enthusiasm for traditional music and dance can be found in the colonial period. In cities such as Dar es Salaam, people of the same ethnic group did not necessarily live together. J.A.K. Leslie, who carried out a survey of Dar es Salaam from 1956 to 1957 writes, "This ... has had its effect in reducing the influence of tribe on the lives of the immigrants, of diluting the feeling of being surrounded by one's own, and increasing the interest in those of others" (1963: 38). Leslie continues by pointing out that young people relied more on their close kin and on themselves than on associations with specific ethnic groups.

E. C. Baker noticed similar trends in Dar es Salaam over twenty years earlier: "The young men sometimes dance in the ngomas of tribes other than their own and the dance tends to regroup society into guilds rather than tribes, as when the transport drivers clubbed together and held their annual ball which was modeled on European lines and was in no respect tribal" (1931: 73). Young men also avoided ethnic associations since they did not want the extra burden of giving money for weddings, funerals, or other traditional ceremonies. As more people made acquaintances at work, clubs, and sporting events, the dominance of ethnic groupings became more limited. People interested in keeping their families involved in traditional customs often had to send children back to rural areas.[27]

The reorganization of ngoma into mixed-member guilds rather than by ethnic group altered the social importance of traditional music. Music that was once tied to traditional customs became oriented toward urban lifestyles, movements, and sounds. Often, the original intention of songs was lost or altered to accommodate a diverse, urban audience. Perhaps more important, ngoma became drawn into public shows with other genres of music. It was common, for instance, to attend performances of ngoma, dansi, taarab, or kwaya music since sharp divisions did not exist between musical genres. For this reason, articles that reference music in Dar es Salaam before independence often refer to music as "band," "club," or "entertainment" rather than strictly dansi, taarab, or ngoma. A band could have ngoma drummers with a rumba-style guitarist (Chiume 1975: 17), a club could have musicians from all varieties of music, or the term ngoma could just refer to a dance featuring dansi or taarab music.

After independence, musical genres underwent stricter delineations as the state encouraged artists to refine their music and promote appropriate cultural forms. There were debates and discussions, particularly among government officials assigned to deal with the arts, about the formation of the country's musical genres. Even though dansi and taarab musicians assisted in the independence effort by drawing audiences to hear nationalist speeches and attend meetings, many people considered these genres of music foreign and, therefore, potentially not acceptable in post-independence reconstruction.[28] In criticizing dansi, referred to here as jazz, the choral composer Stephen Mbunga writes:

> Fortunately a number of attempts to readjust the nation musically are tak-
> ing place these days, but I am afraid that a great many of them proceed in a
> wrong direction and achieve undesirable results. Many of our young people
> believe that the problem is solved by the inferior Tanzanian jazz bands,
> which are mostly sentimental, and imported forms of, say, cha cha cha,
> twist, rock, rumba, shake, and highlife. All this is, in fact, a musical neo-
> colonialism, a blend between Western and African forms based upon cheap
> means of getting excitement from rhythms and chords at a superficial level.
> We should all support the critics who want to see something better than un-
> varied presentations of jazz. (1968: 48–49)

Mbunga regarded dansi as an essentially European-derived music and
one that should not be promoted within the nationalist movement (ironically, he was a choral composer, a music that could be argued to be more
replete with Western melodies, rhythms, and aesthetics, which may have
been his impetus for criticizing dansi and taking the focus away from
choral music). In urban areas, even among politicians, dansi was by far
the most popular music. To ban it or restrict it might bode poorly for the
government efforts to use music as a tool to promote nationalist ideas. The
question that emerged during the 1960s was this: What genres should be
promoted as African and which sounds, ideas, and aesthetics should be
discouraged from the local music scene?

In Dar es Salaam, dansi brought a desired air of sophistication, mod-
ernism, and cosmopolitanism to the city. Many migrants imagined the
city to be a magnificent place, connected to other parts of the world, and
ahead of other areas of Tanzania. Though the government continued
to promote traditional arts, Dar es Salaam and other cities and towns
in Tanzania became a refuge for dansi. Due to the popularity of dansi
within urban areas, the Tanzanian government realized its importance
within the nationalist framework. Starting in the mid-1960s, companies
and departments of Tanzania's government formed bands to advertise
themselves and entertain their employees. In 1964, the National Union
of Tanzanian Workers started the group NUTA Jazz Band. Following
NUTA Jazz, other government departments formed groups, including
Vijana Jazz Band (the TANU/CCM youth league),[29] Urafiki Jazz Band
(Urafiki Textile Department), UDA Jazz Band (Public Transportation
Department), Tancut Almasi Jazz Band (Diamond Mining Department), Police Jazz Band (under the Police Department), and JKT Jazz

Band (the military band). All the members of these groups were workers of the organization for which they played. They therefore received salaries, healthcare, and housing like any other employee. Several groups, such as DDC (Dar es Salaam Development Corporation) Mlimani Park Orchestra, were even given transportation to and from their homes to practice venues and concert engagements.[30] Many of these bands thrived under the employ of the government, since they could concentrate on their music and not worry about salaries or other issues that plagued private artists.

The government also had a national band, which was chosen from preexisting bands and which changed each year. Abdallah Liochi, a member of the 1967 national band Kilwa Jazz, noted: "I was here in Dar es Salaam since 1967. The government at that time had a Minister of Culture who promoted bands and there was a national band—in 1967, it was Kilwa Jazz. Dar es Salaam Jazz followed. And because at that time there were not many bands, the cycle continued. The Minister . . . promoted bands that praised Tanzania." Competitions were also held among dansi groups, as they were with ngoma. The competitions offered dansi bands a chance to compete with one another, and, depending on the year, win money or other honors. Although the government was still interested in promoting ngoma, many politicians enjoyed dansi more than ngoma. The irony was not lost on numerous musicians, who commented that many political leaders would spend their evenings at dansi concerts and then promote ngoma as the national music during the day.

Despite the interest in dansi music, it was not accepted immediately or completely into the government fold. In order to become a part of the nationalist and later socialist movements, dansi musicians and bands had to shed musical elements considered foreign and strengthen those that were traditional. A reflection of this new push can be found in the opinions of popular musicians during the 1960s and 1970s. Michael Enoch, then leader of the popular dance band Dar es Salaam Jazz Band, stated, "We are tired of imitating styles of other people and now it is our time to stop imitating all together and start Tanzanian styles."[31] Former bandleader Joseph Bagabuje of Jamhuri Jazz was asked in 1970 about his take on soul music: "Jamhuri Jazz or any band in Tanzania can play 'soul.' But, our objective is to write and perform music ourselves, with-

out imitating [anyone else]."[32] Many bands eliminated musical elements
that sounded foreign, such as soul chord progressions or funk rhythms.
Lyrically, bands wrote songs praising the efforts and policies of the government. As Shaaban Dede explains, it was not that the government
pushed dansi groups to make these changes; they did it because they
wanted to show support for independence: "It's not just that the government wanted it [nationalist songs], Tanzanians themselves wanted to
hear it because they were excited about independence. So, bands wanted
to sing political songs and people liked to hear them. It wasn't like the
government said, 'Sing this. Or do this and this.'" Tanzanian bands and
artists were proud of their government and country, and therefore wrote
songs of praise.

Due to these nationalist movements, bands that performed foreign
music, such as soul and r&b, lost some popularity. Records of foreign pop
artists became rare in Tanzania by the 1970s and were mainly the preoccupation of the urban elite. There were even efforts to ban soul outright
(Ivaska 2003). Nevertheless, groups such as the Flaming Stars and the
Comets continued to play the music of James Brown, Otis Redding, and
Harry Belafonte.[33] The government encouraged the use of some foreign
artistic forms that coincided with state interests: given Tanzanian support for South Africa's struggle against apartheid, Tanzania's national
anthem was based on "Nkosi Sikelel' iAfrika," a song of resistance among
black South Africans. The National Dance Troupe featured acrobatics
learned in China, since that country gave generously to Tanzania (PURL
2.2). And the national arts competition included kwaya that drew heavily
on Christian hymns (Askew 2002: 277).

Possibly due to the popularity of dansi and efforts to legitimize it
as a nationalist music, it came to be regarded as an offshoot of ngoma.
One dansi musician stated in 1968, "We play traditional music but we
use modern instruments instead of traditional instruments."[34] Dansi
came to epitomize, both within the government and among the public,
the balance between maintaining a popular music scene and promoting
traditional culture. D. K. Mswanyama's poem "Ngoma ya Kitamaduni-
Kiko" (Traditional Ngoma-Kiko) is a good example of this balance.[35] In
writing about the band Kiko Kids, from Tabora, Tanzania, he explains
how the band plays traditional ngoma, supports the government, and still
performs dansi.

1. Dwana, Mtengenezaji, tengeneza gazetini
   Naomba usinihoji, kunitia kikapuni,
   Mziki wenye kipaji, kuusiifu natamani
   Densi la kitamaduni, Kiko Kidisi [sic] pongezi

2. Ni bora kuziachia, kizitupa jalalani
   Tungo zinazoanzia, Yuropa na Kisangani
   Tungo za Kitanzania, zafaa kuwa safuni,
   Densi la kitamaduni, Kiko Kidisi pongezi

3. Kiko mziki wa sasa, ngoma ya Kitamaduni
   Kueleza yanipasa, wala sifanyi utani
   Tungo zake za kuasa, hazisifii wahuni,
   Densi la kitamaduni, Kiko Kidisi pongezi

4. Kiko husifu TAIFA, uchumi wa mashambani,
   Kiko pia ana sifa, Mawaziri rekodini,
   Kiko hutunga kashifa, udhalimu kuulani,
   Densi la kitamaduni, Kiko Kidisi pongezi

5. Kiko Kidisi hususa, kuigiza majirani,
   Kiko huzika anasa, utungaji wa kigeni,
   Kiko hupiga siasa, na mafumbo yenye shani
   Densi la kitamaduni, Kiko Kidisi pongezi

6. Mafundi ninawataja wa huo Utamaduni,
   Huishi hapa pamoja, Tabora si Kiloleni,
   Tungo zao zina haja, warembo ni
   mashakani
   Densi la kitamaduni, Kiko Kidisi pongezi.

1. Sir, producer, put this in your newspaper
   Please do not doubt me, lest you put me in the trash bin
   Music that is a natural gift, I hope to praise
   Traditional dance, congratulations Kiko Kids

2. It is better to let go, to throw away compositions
   that start in Europe and Kisangani [Congo]
   Tanzanian compositions are good enough
   Traditional dance, congratulations Kiko Kids

3. There is modern music, Traditional ngoma
   I am obliged to explain without jest
   Their songs educate, they do not praise misfits
   Traditional dance, congratulations Kiko Kids

4. Kiko praises the nation and its farm economy,
   Kiko also praises, Ministers on records
   Kiko exposes slander, condemns oppression
   Traditional dance, congratulations Kiko Kids

5. Kiko Kids refuses to imitate their neighbors
   Kiko buries the pleasures of foreign songs
   Kiko has political lyrics with curious puzzles
   Traditional dance, congratulations Kiko Kids

6. The artists that I want to mention of this culture,
   Live here together in Tabora and not Kiloleni,
   Their songs have meaning, there is no doubting
   their beauty
   Traditional dance, congratulations Kiko Kids.

The poem continues for seven more verses praising each member of the band. In the first six verses, however, Mswanyama clearly sets out to explain the virtues of Kiko Kids as both a modern and traditional group. More important, perhaps, he does so by explaining how Kiko Kids dismisses compositions written in Europe and the Congo (verse two) and does not imitate Tanzania's neighbors (verse five). Instead, Kiko Kids praises the nation and the policies of the government (verse four), using modern and traditional elements (verse three) and burying the pleasure of foreign music. According to Mswanyama, the debate over whether to promote traditional or foreign music is easily settled when listening to the music of dansi bands, such as Kiko Kids. Mswanyama and others argued that, in urban areas, one could have both the modern and the traditional.

Many other groups also combined traditional and foreign music in a way that was acceptable to the nationalistic music scene. Stephen Martin explains how NUTA Jazz, the band of the National Union of Tanganyika Workers, merged local and foreign music while still garnering acceptance as a national dance band:

> The band [NUTA Jazz] is able to play at such events as a local night club dance competition, being required to play music which is very local in character, i.e. derived from the traditional music forms of many of the Dar es Salaam residents—Zaramo, Nyamwezi, Makonde, etc. On the other hand, NUTA Jazz is capable of assimilating some of the more international styles which give the group its cosmopolitan quality. For example, NUTA Jazz will occasionally perform music in a variety of Western popular styles—rock and roll, soul, even country and western—as well as in the Congolese and South African veins. (1980: 71)[36]

In listening to NUTA Jazz's recordings from the 1970s, the melding of traditional and foreign elements is immediately apparent. Take the song "Azimio la Arusha" (Arusha Declaration), which NUTA Jazz recorded sometime in the mid-1970s. The vocal melody and harmony parts sound like contemporaries of late 1960s soul and r&b singers. The lead singer has a smooth, clear tone and delivers the lyrics in a register typical of many soul singers. The lyrics, however, are about Nyerere's five-year plan to improve the country: "The five year declaration / That was passed in 1974 / For liberation / Has succeeded." Further, the underlying rhythm and the interplay of instruments incorporates traditional concepts of music with a Congolese feel. Earlier NUTA Jazz recordings, such as "Mpenzi Ninakukanya" (Lover, I Warn You), which was released in 1973, had even stronger American music influences and perhaps highlights how the group was trying to make its sound more Tanzanian throughout the 1970s, especially as other bands that competed with NUTA Jazz were favoring Congolese and traditional musics over foreign, particularly Western, ones.

Although many bands were created in Tanzania's government departments during the 1960s and 1970s, private bands also existed. The most popular musician throughout the 1970s, who only played in private bands, was Mbaraka Mwinshehe and his groups Morogoro Jazz Band (1964–1973) and Orchestra Super Volcano (1973–1979). Mwinshehe is sometimes referred to as one of the greatest East African composers, singers, and guitarists. Mostly because of Mwinshehe's musical talent, his bands were able to tour all over East Africa and represent Tanzania at the Osaka Expo 1970 exposition in Japan.[37] In May 1970, his group Morogoro Jazz defeated NUTA Jazz in a competition sponsored by the TANU Youth League at Diamond Jubilee Hall in Dar es Salaam.[38] Though Mwinshehe and his groups were not affiliated with a government department, they were able to draw popular support from both government officials and the public because their music was lively and danceable, and Mwinshehe's lyrics were in line with Tanzania's socialist stance.

The song that won Mwinshehe and Morogoro Jazz the 1970 contest against NUTA Jazz was "TANU Yajenga Nchi" (TANU Builds the Nation). Other songs, "Kifo cha Pesa" (Death by Money), "Miaka 10 ya Uhuru" (Ten Years of Independence), and "Mwongozo wa TANU" (The Guidance of TANU), also supported Nyerere and the TANU government's vision for the country. One of Mwinshehe's most famous compositions, "Mama Chakula Bora" (Mama Healthy Food), is another example of the educational purpose that bands in Tanzania were expected to have in the 1970s:

| | |
|---|---|
| Kutokana na maradhi mbali mbali | Due to various diseases |
| Lazima tufuate kanuni za afya (x2) | We must follow healthy standards |
| Mtu ni afya kwa kila binadamu | A person's health helps every human being |
| Ni lazima kula chakula bora | It is necessary to eat better food |
| Aina za chakula ziko tatu | There are three types of food |
| Cha kwanza ni kile kinachotia nguvu | The first gives strength |
| Cha pili ni kile kinacho jenga mwili | The second builds the body |
| Cha tatu ni hasa kinacholinda mwili | The third protects the body |
| Vyakula nyenyewe sasa ninavitaja | Foods that I should mention |
| Nyama na maharage na mayai | Meat and beans and eggs |
| Maziwa samaki na matunda mengi | Milk, fish, and a lot of fruit |
| Ni vyakula bora kina mama | Is better food for every mother |
| Tule chakula bora | Let us eat better food |

What sounds like a commercial for a health food organization was actually a popular song throughout Tanzania, effective in educating people about healthy eating habits. "Mama chakula Bora" along with many of Mwinshehe's songs fit attempts by the Tanzanian government to unify and assist the nation. Yet Mwinshehe's music was the product of an independent band, not one owned by a government department.

Morogoro Jazz Band at a party for the African Cup competition between Tanzania and Mauritius. The photograph was taken in front of the Dar es Salaam Club in September 1966. Mbaraka Mwinshehe stands second from the right. *Photo courtesy of the National Press Archives.*

After Mwinshehe died on January 8, 1979, Tanzania's music economy lost not only an important musician but a successful independent band. News reports, editorials, and statements broadcast regularly on the radio and appeared in local newspapers to mourn the loss of the country's most influential artist. The National Music Council wrote, "Mbaraka's death is a major blow to the development of music" (BAMUTA n.d.: 48). Bands and musicians from all over the country wrote memorial songs for Mwinshehe to commemorate his life. Even more significant, Mwinshehe and Super Volcano represented the regional success of an independent band during the country's socialist period. While several independent groups did continue to perform, form cooperatives, or find other ways to make a living through music, most struggled in the period after Mwinshehe's death (Perullo 2008b). Even though the struggles of private bands were due more to the economic crises of the 1980s, Mwinshehe's death symbolically marked the decline in popular and independent musical groups. Not until the mid-1990s, when privatization and neoliberal policies ushered in new ways of profiting from music, did a new and stronger influx of private bands emerge.

Aside from dansi, other popular music also underwent nationalist transformations. Several kwaya and taarab songs were written in a style that veered from the typical lyrics of the genres to those that promoted the government and its ideologies. Black Star, one of the most famous taarab groups of the 1960s, wrote several songs promoting TANU (and later CCM), Nyerere, and socialism. One of the more popular, "Chama cha Mapinduzi Juu" (The Revolutionary Party on Top), was recorded around 1977 by the Tanzanian Film Company and sounds like a characteristic Black Star song with a chakacha rhythm, interplay between the accordion and lead guitar, and typical poetic and vocal nuances. Yet the lead singer presents straightforward, pro-government lyrics that are uncharacteristic of taarab.

| | | |
|---|---|---|
| *verse 1* | Karibu mgeni wetu | Welcome our guest |
| | Mapinduzi wa heshima | Respect our honored revolution |
| | | |
| *chorus* | Ni wajibu wa kila mtu | It is everyone's responsibility |
| | Kukaa kwa tahadhima | To come together in appreciation |
| | Kupokea chama chetu | To welcome our party |
| | Hukuna kurudi nyuma | Without going backwards |
| | Chama cha Mapinduzi Juu | Chama cha Mapinduzi on top |
| | Mwalimu Nyerere Juu | Mwalimu Nyerere on top |
| | Aboudi Jumbe Juu | Aboud Jumbe on top |
| | Ndugu Kawawa Juu | Comrade Kawawa on top[39] |
| | Siasa ni kilimo | Politics is agriculture |
| | Na lengo ni Ujamaa | And the goal is *Ujamaa*. |

Black Star also wrote numerous songs, such as "Sononeka" (To Grieve), "Umefanya Inda" (You Are Hostile), and "Mimi na Wewe Basi" (This Is the End of Our Relationship), more characteristic of popular taarab music of the 1960s and 1970s, with themes of love or social commentary hidden under double entendres and metaphors. Yet to be able to find work within the socialist music economy, record at the government radio sta-

NEGOTIATION

tion, and easily register with the National Music Council (BAMUTA), Black Star needed to compose songs that praised the political and social policies of the government.

The post-independence period—with initiatives to create a nationalist identity and establish institutions to monitor and control the arts—set the tone for the country's future music economy. Within these nationalizing efforts, music was entertainment, but it had another function: to promote and safeguard the ideologies of the state. As the back of *Tudumishe Utama-duni na... Siasa Yetu*. Azimio (AZLP-001), one of the first records released by the Tanzania Film Company stated, "Enjoyable music. Educational music." The two attachments to music were interwoven into a national-ist and, later, a socialist agenda. Each aspect of the music economy, from radio to band performance, was geared toward unifying the country and rejecting, as Nyerere stated, "the capitalist attitude of mind which colo-nialism brought into Africa" (1967: 166). Music was a form of enjoyment that needed to escape the oppressiveness of capitalism to re-educate popu-lations about the importance of community and social development.

Thirty-five years later, the interweaving of music with nationalist ide-als continues: newspaper articles lament the destruction of traditional culture in urban centers;[40] the *Baraza la Sanaa la Taifa* (National Arts Council, BASATA), a department of the government, continues to reg-ister, monitor, and educate bands; and various forms of censorship occur around controversial songs. Artists are also encouraged to write socially meaningful lyrics that address issues of Tanzanian politics and society (for an historic example of socially meaningful lyrics, see PURL 2.3; for a more contemporary example, see PURL 2.4). It is this nationalist interest in the arts—started immediately after independence—that guided the early growth of Tanzania's music economy and remains influential to this day. The formation of distinct genres, ways of profiting from music, and connections between music as entertainment and education continue to inform the commercialization of music in Tanzania.

## SOCIALIZING SOCIAL HALLS

The importance of using bands and music to support state initiatives par-allels the formation of social halls in Tanzania. Social halls were places where people gathered to listen to music, dance, drink, and enjoy them-

*Popular culture as the dumbing down of the masses! ADORNO*

selves. In areas where other forms of entertainment did not exist, performance spaces represented an influential means to foster social development: people exchanged ideas, information, and opinions about politics and society; they engaged in managed forms of music and dance; and they were diverted from other activities that might be more destructive. Social halls became spaces of social engineering, whereby music and dance could be managed to produce a particular outcome.

The British colonial authorities built several social halls in Dar es Salaam during the 1950s, due in part to worries over the activities of African populations after the Second World War. African men returning from war were frustrated by their oppression under colonial rule and sought ways to overcome their situation (Geiger 1997: 28). There were demands by civil servants for higher salaries, housing allowances, and other needs (Iliffe 1979: 267). The 1947 dockworkers strike paralyzed Dar es Salaam for over a week (Brennan and Burton 2007: 39). Race riots, including one in January 1950, resulted in looting of homes and the death of a police officer (Burton 2005: 182–183). The African population was also growing significantly in this period reaching 77,330 in 1952, more than twice that of the decade before (Burton 2005: 282). This caused a shortage of consumer goods, as well as housing and jobs. Mau Mau was also emerging in Kenya, causing additional fears that Africans in Tanganyika would create more disturbance. Social halls became one tactic to try to maintain some form of calm and order among populations. Susan Geiger writes, "Since African men were considered most likely to cause trouble, social development efforts were primarily designed to channel their energies into 'appropriate' activities" (1997: 27). Women were also included in these social engineering efforts and were given special "ladies nights."

The colonial administration used social halls as a means to contain populations by giving them leisure activities that would distract them from other problems occurring in the country. In December 1952, Arnautoglu Community Centre (ACC) opened in Mnazi Mmoja, Dar es Salaam.[41] The ACC provided space for multiracial leisure activities, such as cinema, dancing, and drinking.[42] The ACC was an important place for women's entertainment and, by 1954, at least forty associations used the Centre for their activities (Geiger 1997: 67). Egyptian and Al-Watan Musical Clubs, for instance, used the ACC during this time period. Nevertheless, the restrictions placed on the performances at the ACC may have limited both those who attended and those who performed. In 1952, for instance, rent-free accommodation was offered to The Red Cross Society, the Royal Society for Prevention of Cruelty to Animals, and other groups, but advice from the advisory committee was sought before granting accommodation to the Egyptian Musical Club. Public dances were controlled with "high standards," and the ACC could not be rented for public dances given that the "standards of behavior at dances would deteriorate."[43] The restrictions on granting accommodation and hiring the dance space limited the types of performance heard at the ACC. The tactics represent a form of control intended to shape and engineer racial identities in the colonial period (Bertz 2008: 245).

Other social halls emerged, including the Ilala Social Club and Alexandra Hall, both maintained by the Social Welfare Department. There were also clubs only for Europeans, such as the Dar es Salaam Club, which formed as the Klub Dar-es-Salâm during German occupation and remained a Europeans-only club under the British (Anthony 1983: 155; Weidmann 1955). Frequently, Indian conductors would lead mixed-race bands at these exclusive clubs. For instance, in June 1950, The Tanganyika Police Band, conducted by Gulab Singh, performed at the British Legion Club; the Tanganyika Swingtette played at the European Railway Club; and the G.M.O.S. Band at the Au Perroquet.[44] There were African style clubs, such as the New Generations Club, that featured ballroom dance performance with an occasional women's ngoma (Iliffe 1979: 392). There were also clubs that formed to support taarab, ngoma, and dansi bands. Dar es Salaam Jazz Band had a club in Kariakoo. Club members paid a fee and the money earned from playing concerts helped to pay rent and instrument upkeep (Graebner 2007: 187). In the song "Chama Nikiingia" (If I Join the Club), the band sings, "If I join this club [the Dar es Salaam Jazz Band club], I shall never miss rumba."

After independence, the Tanzanian government took an expressed interest in using social halls to promote national interests. Many of the social halls used by the British were taken over by the independence government. The Dar es Salaam Club featured local popular music, while the Ilala Club remained a government run social hall. Others, however, were constructed by the government including one of the most famous, DDC Social Hall in Kariakoo, Dar es Salaam. The Mwananchi Engineering Construction Company (MECCO) built the DDC Social Hall

Rufiji Jazz Band performing at the Tanzanian Legion in Dar es Salaam, August 21, 1968. *Photo courtesy of the National Press Archives.*

between 1969 and 1971. According to Shaaban Mafumbi, who works as the personnel and administrative officer for the DDC, after the Arusha Declaration, the government decided to build social halls and cinemas (DDC Social Hall was originally a cinema) to help the country's people find places of entertainment and strengthen local community initiatives. Social halls were thought to be important meeting points for people to gather, enjoy themselves, and assist in establishing united neighborhoods within urban centers. The DDC was responsible for the development of at least three social halls during the late 1960s and into the 1970s in the Keko, Magomeni, and Mlimani areas of Dar es Salaam.[45]

Other departments of the government also funded and sponsored entertainment centers in Dar es Salaam, such as Vijana Social Hall, Amana Social Hall, and Silent Inn, as well as a number of hotels, such as the Kilimanjaro Hotel in City Centre, that featured live music. Several of the remaining clubs in Dar es Salaam were privately run but publicly supported, given the interest by the government in fostering community programs that could help to strengthen notions of collective responsibility and unity among populations. Many clubs had a house band that played several nights of the week, a tradition that continues today. The Gateways, for instance, which was home to Ndala Kasheba's group Safari Trippers and the Tanzanian Legion, an establishment built for war veterans during the colonial period, remained home to Dar es Salaam Jazz Band. Each band also circulated throughout the city and played at other establishments but would generally play one or two nights a week at their home base.

The colonial and post-independent formation of social halls had a long-term impact on the Tanzanian music economy. Through the formation of specific spaces for listening to live music, there was an implicit acknowledgment of the importance of performance, entertainment, and concerts within urban areas. Social halls may have been imagined as efforts to control, monitor, and influence local populations, but they also had practical implications on the development of popular music. They helped foster musical professionalism given the authority and legitimacy generated by well-established performance spaces. Even during the socialist period, Tanzanian social halls legitimized the importance and commercial potential of popular music.

*Doesn't dwell on the top-down control by gov't but focuses on importance of agency of musicians. I LIKE THIS despite the s[...]tion.*

## THE ONLY RADIO IN TOWN

On the second floor of the National Museum in Dar es Salaam is a large, rectangular metal box covered in knobs, buttons, and meters. The box represents a significant part of Tanzania's history, for it was the first transmitter purchased by the British colonial government to begin a radio station, Sauti ya Dar es Salaam (Dar es Salaam Broadcasting Station).[46] The 400 watt Hallicrafter transmitter was purchased in 1951 for £70, supposedly from the American military, with funds from the British Colonial Development and Welfare Fund. The project was put forth by Thormy Craft, an official of the British Broadcasting Corporation, as a means to disseminate information and entertainment to the public. The studio was situated at house number 64 on Kichwele Street, which is now Uhuru

Street, in Dar es Salaam. In its original configuration, the studio had two microphones, one turntable, a mixer made from an old sound amplifier, and aerials slung between coconut trees (Mytton 1976: 171). The station broadcast on a low power, short-wave signal, allowing for good reception in town and some outlying areas, with intermittent reception all around the territory. By July 1951, the station and its now historic transmitter were operating with a regular program schedule: one hour, three days a week.

Despite its meager beginnings and its rather late start compared to neighboring countries, the station quickly grew.[47] Initially located under the colonial government's Social Development Department, on July 1, 1956, the station set out to establish more independence for itself and raise funds through advertising and licensing. The new station was modeled after the British Broadcasting Corporation (BBC); the new name, the Tanganyika Broadcasting Corporation (TBC), reflected this. More important for the success of the station, people in Tanganyika began purchasing radio receivers. During the station's first year, there were only one thousand radio receivers in the country. But between 1954 and 1955, 40,000 sets were imported and, by 1960, according to a TBC-commissioned survey, about 210,000 radio receivers were in use.[48]

A mere fifty people worked at the TBC in the early years. They were young, mostly Tanganyikan, and were given strict guidelines by the British who ran the station. All the employees had to dress well and could not smoke or drink anywhere near the studio. Each staff member had a specific job: librarians handled phonograms; technicians fixed the voice and controlled the broadcast levels; newsroom staff wrote segments on current affairs; and radio announcers, which often consisted of more women than men, talked to the audiences about music, politics, and education. As the former broadcasting officer of the TBC stated, "Until now, women have shown that it is easier to have a good voice."[49] The salaries for employees were quite high by colonial and post-independence standards. In 1958, a technician would receive Tsh 120 (US$17) each month. Gaudens Makunja, a technician at the TBC, explained that Tsh 1 was enough to buy milk and bread and have enough money for a coffee.

In 1958, Tom Chalmers, a former employee of the BBC, joined the TBC for four years. In that time, he split the station into two networks, the *Idhaa ya Kiswahili* (The Swahili Service), with programs only in Swahili and the English Service network. Both networks aimed to educate and inform the public in a manner that conveyed "a wide variety of thought and action in Tanganyika" (Mytton 1976: 178). More significant, Chalmers pushed for the station's independence and tried to base its financial support on radio licenses and advertisements. At that time, licenses were required to own and operate a radio receiver. Though the license fee was small, Tsh 5 (75 cents), there were enough receivers in the country to help support the station.[50] There was even a committee whose responsibility it was to find people who had radio receivers and collect the license fee from them. Even though the station would always rely on government subvention, Chalmers's efforts made the station more financially independent than it had been in the past.

Due to this moderate financial independence, the TBC aired content, such as weekly commentary on current events, where broadcasters attempted to give a balanced view of controversial subjects. TANU and its leaders were treated with some respect, allowing the country to learn about its future leaders without overt criticism and slander that could have existed. Though the TBC did not favor TANU, they were less critical of the organization than the British administration, which attempted to destabilize the organization through various efforts, such as sending several founding members of TANU to areas far from Dar es Salaam as punishment for being part of an anti-British organization (Said 1998: 150–51).

One of the principal African deejays to work at the TBC, Godfrey Mngodo, explained that a significant amount of East African and southern African music was broadcast on the radio by the time he joined the company in 1959. At that time, people conceived of local music as an East African phenomenon rather than a Tanganyikan one. The borders between Kenya, Uganda, and Tanganyika were fluid, and people easily traveled between the three countries. TBC was also purchasing records from Nairobi to play on the air. A representative of a Kenyan record company would bring samples of their catalogue to an executive of the station. Depending on TBC's needs, albums were purchased for airplay. Similar to operations at the BBC in London, any time a deejay played a song on the air, he or she kept a detailed log, including song title, composer, performer, recorder, and performing rights society. Based on the play lists, the station would then pay royalties to the appropriate performing rights

A radio advertisement for portable transistor radios, which were popular in eastern Africa. The advertisement plays on the purported strength of the radio to receive broadcasts from Kampala, Dar es Salaam, Nairobi, London, and the Congo. *Published* Nyota Afrika, *January 1964.*

societies, which, according to Mngodo, was a concession never made to local Tanganyikan musicians.

At the time of independence, television or locally produced films did not exist. Print media was less effective given high rates of illiteracy. Reaching mass audiences in the country was only possible through radio broadcasts. Due to the importance of radio, programming strongly impacted the listening public's interpretation of news, music, and local issues. The influence of radio made political leaders increasingly wary about the types of information being broadcast. Radio was too powerful a medium, and the new government became increasingly concerned over the autonomy of such as powerful medium. On February 15, 1961, only months before independence, Lawi Sijaona , who became the first minister of the Ministry of National Culture and Youth, stated:

> A broadcasting system is a very powerful instrument and it can be a very
> dangerous instrument if those who are responsible for running it happen
> to hold different views from those of the Government. . . . It is my view . . .
> that to avoid this powerful instrument being used by people who may not
> have the interests of the country at heart, this instrument should be taken
> over by the Ministry of Information Services and run as the Government
> Departments.[51]

For the next several years, members of the government, and even some
members of the TBC board, stressed the importance of a state-run radio
station for disseminating the government's information and activities
(Mytton 1976: 186). In 1964, the same year that mainland Tanganyika and
the Zanzibar archipelago became the union state Tanzania, the government established the Ministry of Information and Tourism, with a new
minister, Idris Wakil.[52] Although the ministry did not take immediate
control of the TBC, it did use its power to ensure that the station broadcast sufficient news and information on the development of the nation.
The TBC was required to produce news on political speeches and activities of the president, ministers, and parliamentary services. Pressured by
the government, TBC officials and staff altered the station's format to
accommodate the increased coverage of politics and politicians. The TBC
became a voice of the Tanzanian state with allegiance to government policies and personnel even as it remained financially semi-autonomous.

Given the political climate of post-independence Tanzania, the push
to make the TBC more responsible to the nation made sense. The government was trying to remove much of the colonial influence in the country
and to promote its own national identity.[53] Many members of Parliament,
however, felt that it was still dangerous to have a radio station that was
not completely controlled by the government. Although from the debates
it appears as if Wakil was content to leave the station under its own control, in March 1965 the nominal independence of the TBC was abolished
under the TBC Dissolution Bill. The TBC became Radio Tanzania Dar
es Salaam (RTD) and was placed as a department under the Ministry
of Information, Broadcasting, and Tourism.

The nationalization of the sole radio network within Tanzania had
profound impacts on popular music. The post-independence music economy can effectively be traced to the development of this one radio station,
which operated the only successful recording studio in the country prior

key!

to liberalization. Most radio deejays on RTD preferred muziki wa dansi over other genres, even traditional ngoma, which made this genre far more dominant both in the recording studio and in the playlists of the station (Mytton 1976: 117; see also Malm and Wallis 1992: 116). Even though taarab, kwaya, and especially ngoma music appeared on the radio with regularity, according to former deejays and technicians at the station, the most investment was in dansi. This impacted the shape and sound of popular music in the country and strongly supported efforts by other parastatals (state-owned institutions) to use dansi bands to promote their interests.

The nationalization of broadcasting also had a profound impact on radio staff. As new employees of a government-controlled station, staff lost their pensions and became civil servants. When I asked Gaudens Makunja about this, he responded: "Even I did not receive my pension. . . . We disputed the decision, but there was no way for us to do anything. So we agreed. I remember that one person served as our representative, Suleiman Hegga, but he was unable to do anything." Many staff resigned because of the lost pensions. Those who remained faced a frustrating battle against the government's ignorance of the radio business. Changes were made to staff responsibilities, as well as the content of programs, scripts, and news. Instead of basing their broadcasts on their listening audience, the radio personnel had to follow the requests and desires of the state. Many announcers and producers worked twelve- to fifteen-hour stretches, destroying the broadcasting professionalism that existed before the government took control of the station. The results of the changes were predictable: people worked in fear and had no motivation (Kabalimu 1996: 58). "There was no sweetness in the station's broadcasts," explained Makunja. "RTD was only a political section. Many people, especially in production, did not like it very much."

More changes came after the introduction of the Arusha Declaration. The Declaration was a move toward socialism and self-reliance, ideologies that the TANU government thought better reflected an African world-view than the systems that were remnants of colonialism. For RTD, the Arusha Declaration meant there was even more broadcasting aimed at developing and educating the country's people. "Since the Arusha Declaration radio programs have an increasing amount of political content," wrote Graham Mytton. "No distinction is made any longer between teaching farmers to better their production and encouraging them to adopt *ujamaa*. Ideologically the one complements the other" (1976: 369). Members of Parliament called for less entertainment on the radio and more coverage of political issues. The RTD newsroom was pressured not to take initiatives in gathering news but rather to broadcast content believed to be in the interests of national development, such as government-mediated speeches, news, and educational materials. The slogan of the radio station, repeated throughout the day, was *ujamaa ni utu / ubepari ni unyama* (socialism is humanity / capitalism is cruel). Fearing an attack, the station was even kept under strict guard, a practice that remains in place today.

To better spread the message of the Arusha Declaration, RTD increased its size to six radio services: (1) the National Program, formerly the Swahili Service, broadcast for most of the day, 6 A.M. to 11 P.M., with a four-hour morning break during the week; (2) the English Service became the External Service and was on the air for forty-nine hours per week; it also shared transmitters with (3) *Idhaa ya Maarifa*, the adult education service; (4) the Commercial Service, in Swahili, broadcast seventy hours per week; (5) during school terms, seventeen hours were allotted to primary and secondary schools; and finally, (6) the External Service broadcast to Mozambique, Rhodesia, South Africa, and Namibia in both European and African languages. By the time all the services were up and running, the RTD staff had increased to 350 people spread throughout the country.[54]

Due to the Tanzanian government's desire to use radio to promote its own initiatives, entertainment broadcast on the radio often emphasized political themes. Music, plays, stories, and poems became pro-socialist and pro-Tanzanian. Other songs, particularly love songs, also appeared, and in this way artists were free to write about many different themes. Yet most artists had a repertoire of songs, poems, or plays that could be used on the radio to promote the government's ideology. Bands were encouraged to produce these songs and many did so in order to gain airtime and show their support for the country. Many of the most popular bands, such as Western Jazz, Dar es Salaam Jazz, Morogoro Jazz, Kiko Kids Jazz, NUTA Jazz, and Black Star Taarab, wrote songs that discussed Nyerere's social and political policies. Kilwa Jazz Band's song "Mwalimu Kasema" (Teacher [Nyerere] Said), recorded at RTD, is one example:

| | |
|---|---|
| Haya shime watu wote, tusikize ya viongozi | Hail everyone, let us pay attention to the leaders, |
| Mwalimu katwelezea maendeleo ya miaka mitano | The teacher has set a five-year plan, |
| It can be done, play your part, | It can be done, play your part, |
| It can be done, mwalimu kasema, play your part. | It can be done, teacher said, play your part. |

Sung by a chorus of voices led by the famous dansi singer Juma Mrisho, the entire song contains only four lines of text, yet highlights key aspects of socialism and Nyerere's ideology. Though many of these songs did not have a lasting influence politically, they were important for helping to broadcast the country's transformation to a socialist state and promoting the leaders' ideologies.

Much of the Tanzanian music heard on RTD from independence onward was recorded at the station. Significant changes took place once socialist initiatives were underway in the government, as Gaudens Makunja explains:

> There was a department that ran a seminar for people who worked in sections of the government. I did not know who did the seminar. But, later, there was a change in available programs. There were changes from what we learned. And, for example, I can say, when bands came to record there—in the past they came to record love songs, education songs, etc.—they were required to record songs that related to politics. For instance, *ujamaa* villages, what is culture? Is this a radio station or a political program? So, a little bit it was like this. But, I thought this was fine since every country has a plan for its workers. So, I thought it was ordinary. I worked without any problems.

Even before independence, the station made efforts to record local music, particularly traditional ngoma in rural areas, and released a few records on the Twiga label (Harrev 1989: 109). By the early 1960s, the station increased its efforts to record traditional and popular music. Using a Land Rover, a team of recording engineers toured Tanzania to find ngoma groups. Makunja says:

> I was one of the people who went around the country recording ngoma. We went with a Land Rover and a recording machine. We traveled outside of Dar and recorded traditional ngoma, such as ngoma *za Wapogoro*, ngoma *za Wandaba*, ngoma *za Wasukuma*, ngoma *za Wakonde*. We toured like this. But, after a while, a man from Sweden came. It was 1971. The Swedish came to teach about recording and how to use a broadcast van. I remember the

first time we went in the broadcasting van to record and to make a direct
transmission from the van, straight to the radio station. After every two or
three months we would go out to record all over the country.

Many trips, however, were cut short or abandoned because the station
was still understaffed and underfinanced. Further, staff needed to record
popular music since the government wanted to limit foreign music on the
air and continue to attract radio listeners who were more interested in the
contemporary hits than in traditional music.

Most music that aired on the station was recorded at the station. The
two-track recording facility at RTD was, despite its poor storage and
care for master tapes, run extremely well. The principal sound engineers
in the 1960s and 1970s were John Ndumbalo, James Mhilu, and Gaudens
Makunja. The process to record a song took considerable time. First the
band had to write a letter asking for a chance to record. The technicians
would then attend a performance by the band to hear them play the
song. This was done without the band's knowledge. Then the technicians interviewed the band members. Once a date was set to record the
songs, the band came into the studio and rehearsed for thirty minutes.
Makunja explained that just as the band was about to "hit," meaning
come together musically, the technicians would start recording. Each
technician would take turns recording different songs and rarely would a
single engineer work alone. Recordings were made both in the morning
and the evening, and bands were paid around Tsh 20 per song, typically
recording five or six songs. The band also signed contracts with RTD,
which gave the recording rights to the radio station solely for broadcast
purposes.

Each year, a band would enter the studio once or twice to record. The
station established conditions for songs planned for recording and had the
artists submit their lyrics before recording to ensure they fit the station's
requirements (Mbega 2001). Shaaban Dede explained this process:

> First, you write a letter asking to record at RTD. Then they say, "Ok, let's
> arrange a date." So, a letter arrives in July: "On September 10, you will have
> a chance to record. In August, we want the lyrics to your songs." You write
> down the lyrics. They read them and [motions with hand over paper] they
> change them. "Get rid of this, change this, add this." They remove the
> meaning of certain lyrics that are too heavy. For example, in the Hassani
> Bitchuka composition "My Sister" (Dada Yangu):

*[handwritten margin note: Shows how lyrics were censored]*

| | |
|---|---|
| Dada yangu | My sister |
| Eh Sauda | Eh Sauda |
| Nilipata barua kutoka kwa shemeji | I received a letter from my in-law |
| Ya Sema | It said |
| Mume yuko Jamaica | Your husband is in Jamaica |
| Anataraji kurudi | And he is preparing to return |
| Kweli, oh? | It is true, oh? |
| Jambo ninalokusihi hivi sasa | I am asking you |
| Ni uja uzito ulionao, oh | about the pregnancy, oh. |
| Utafanyaji Sauda? | What will you do, Sauda?[55] |

The RTD staff said, do not say, "It is your pregnancy." Instead, they told us to say:

| | |
|---|---|
| Jambo ninalokusihi hivi sasa | What I am asking you right now, |
| Ni huyo mzigo ulionao. | The responsibility you have. |
| Utafanya nini, Sauda? | What will you do, Sauda? |

Don't say "pregnancy," say "mzigo" (package). But, in Swahili, the way that comes [in the song], mzigo is something that you can open and take things out of. Or, it is something that can be gotten rid of.

While Dede points out changes made to the song, he also emphasizes the ironies in RTD's corrections. The change from pregnancy to *mzigo* implies the notion of responsibility, since mzigo can mean "burden." In the context of the song, mzigo is heard as both burden and its literal sense package. Package thereby becomes a metaphor for pregnancy and implies that the "package" could be opened (give birth to a child) or gotten rid of (aborted). In some ways the change provided far more profound and complicated interpretations of the song, which the RTD staff that corrected the original version did not likely intend.

In other songs, however, the RTD staff altered words that did not allow the musicians to present their intentions. Dede sings another song:

| | |
|---|---|
| Samaki baharini | The fish in the sea |
| Huishi vipi? | How do they live? |
| Wadudu mapangoni | Insects in caves |
| Wanyama waporini. | Animals in the wilderness |
| Masikini walemavu | The poor with disabilities |

The RTD staff said, "Ah, don't say 'the poor with disabilities.' Say, "na wasioji-weza huishi vipi (those who are not capable)." Even the way that it came out, I was talking about "walemavu" (disabilities). I didn't say "those who are not capable."

Here the change in wording created frustration within the band since it really did not state the intentions of the lyricists. To refer to someone who is not capable glosses over the issue of disability, which to the group was important for addressing issues of poverty.

Though RTD emphasized social and educational programming, the recording and airing of local music was arguably its most important contribution to Tanzanian culture. If RTD had not made the thousands of recordings of dansi, ngoma, and taarab, much of the early Tanzanian music would have gone unrecorded and unappreciated. It would have also created a weaker music economy, since the exposure that bands received from their recordings came from the radio, which helped draw audiences to concerts and encouraged artists to compose and record new songs. For instance, the ethnomusicologist Stephen Martin writes about NUTA Jazz, who composed the song "Instrumental No. 6." The song aired on RTD in 1976 and became so successful that the band's concerts sold out as audiences crowded local venues to hear the new hit (1980: 82). For many bands, RTD became a quick and easy way to gain popular support, which is also the reason so many groups were willing to write songs that encapsulated a nationalist vision.

RTD staff also relied on music more than any other medium to connect with their audience. In writing about the radio station in the mid-1980s, Bakilana C.M. Magayane found that "music contributes 58.5% of the total output of Radio Tanzania's broadcasting. Radio Tanzania airs music that ranges from those which show love between male and female, music that teaches on good behavior, music that emphasizes the importance of work and discourages laziness etc." (1988: 100).[56] According to Magayane, over sixty percent of the music that RTD aired was love songs. The rest were songs that promoted social responsibility and development of the country.[57] Several announcers also explained to me that if the entertainment of RTD, including the music, ever became too educational and political, there was a fear that the station would lose its listening audience.

In the 1980s, the effectiveness of the RTD recording studio, the poor economic conditions in Tanzania, and the popularity of dansi music led to theft from the RTD music library. Numerous master tapes or copies of the master tapes were taken from the station and sold to distributors in other parts of eastern African, particularly Kenya. Werner Graebner,

The guitar section of NUTA Jazz Band at the New Dar es Salaam Club on October 3, 1970. From left to right are Abel Balthazar (solo guitar), Kiza Hussein (second solo guitar), and Ahmed Omar (rhythm guitar). *Photo courtesy of the National Press Archives.*

who lived in Dar es Salaam during the 1980s, explains: "There were always people hawking Radio Tanzania stuff in Nairobi, either the employees of RTD or the musicians themselves. Or somebody from their organization would go to the radio station, pay someone to make them a copy, they would have the reel to reel, and then they would go to Nairobi and license them to anybody, Polygram, CBS, whoever was there. Then these tapes would filter back into Tanzania and be copied." Several Kenyan record labels released music originally recorded at RTD. In a majority of these situations, the person who brought the recordings to the label received a lump-sum payment or a royalty payment for the recordings. Given that the original RTD contract only stipulated that the music could be broadcast on the air, the majority of agreements were technically not legal. Yet since radio staff, musicians, and others were all involved in the pilfering of the RTD library, few actions were ever taken to limit this practice. By the mid-1990s, RTD even set up a store in downtown Dar es Salaam and a kiosk at the Saba Saba grounds to sell the music directly to the public. Royalties were never paid to musicians in these situations.

What is most important for Tanzania's post-socialist music economy is that the trends, practices, and programming promoted by RTD for three and a half decades influenced the development of new stations. Even though RTD lost its listening audiences in urban areas to independent stations, many of the established mechanisms it put in place acted as models for newer radio stations. Staff who worked at RTD left to earn better wages in the new stations and took their concept of radio with them. RTD staff worked at the Tanzanian Broadcasting Commission, which dictated their ideas about appropriate content and programming to private stations. Even though workers at private stations would find success by escaping RTD, conventions of government radio would nonetheless permeate their operations and broadcasts.

Due to a significant decrease in listeners, RTD underwent several changes in the mid-2000s. More youthful announcers were hired; programs remained educational but were less politically motivated; alternative genres of music, such as bongo flava, were added to playlists; call-in programs were incorporated into daily schedules; and the content of shows resembled that of private stations. To reflect these programming and content changes, in 2007 the station dropped RTD as its name and once again became the TBC (though now Tanzania rather than Tanganyika). In news reports on national television, the name change was heralded as a move to become more "self-reliant."[58] The notion of self-reliance references the contemporary meaning of the term in Tanzanian society as self-sufficient and self-sustaining. Moving away from complete state control, the station is trying to establish some level of autonomy even as it continues to follow and support many state guidelines. There were similar policies in the original TBC station, though, and in many ways both the current and former TBC reflects an interest in following the design of the British Broadcasting Corporation (BBC). The current TBC is responding to numerous changes in broadcasting that diminish politically focused radio services in favor of ones that are more responsive to the interests and concerns of listeners.

## PAST POLICY TODAY

After independence, the Tanzanian government established a direct role in the development of the country's music economy. It took control of the country's radio station, recording facilities, and many performance venues. It helped form the distinct separations between musical genres and create government-run dance bands that removed many of the hardships associated with forming and maintaining a music group. This helped transform music from a pastime, carried out on weekends by people who also had other careers, into a professional enterprise where musicians could earn a living from playing or composing music. During the country's movement toward privatization under the second president Ali Hassan Mwinyi (1985–1995), many socialist economic systems were razed, yet the ideologies pertaining to social and culture policies remained strong. The former Tanzanian Commissioner of Culture, Daniel Ndagala, explains that the policies developed in the 1960s are vitally important to current national cultural policy. When asked if every president has a different vision in regards to culture, he states:

> No, our country has had consistent leadership. So, ideas do not change just
> because of the president. Mwalimu Nyerere's opinions have continued to
> be upheld concerning culture. And, cultural policy concretizes Mwalimu
> Nyerere's opinions so that they can be implemented through various activi-
> ties. In short, the government has remained the same as far as its views and
> visions are concerned. The problem is with a few senior officials who are not
> aware of the meaning of culture as it is. They have a narrow understanding
> of some things—maybe of ngoma—but otherwise do not know much about
> culture. But this is not unique to Tanzania, it is all over the world. So, I do
> not think that there have been changes.

Despite the country's liberalization and government efforts to revitalize the economy, according to Ndagala, the country's leadership has remained steadfast in its conception of and relationship to Tanzanian music and culture. Nyerere's ideas on culture, embraced by Mwinyi, Benjamin Mkapa, and the current president, Jakaya Kikwete, have continued to grow and take shape as the country undergoes socioeconomic changes. Ndagala explains:

> The government maintained that to move forward was not to forget our culture. Our culture must continue. So, the government has a big obligation to give direction, to explain that we still need to promote our culture. We will still receive things from the outside, but the main content remains Tanzanian. And musicians do not stop playing Tanzania music. . . . So, in the present time, the government's job is to show the path—like with ngoma groups—so people know what is important.

Ndagala's switches in tense here—from past to present to future—highlights the continuum within which his ministry and other areas of government place music and culture. Since independence, the government has been responsible for educating people about traditional music and encouraging them to continue to perform. Although I would argue that many of the concepts and ideologies associated with music and culture have changed since the 1960s, the underlying impetus of the government has remained to promote those things that are identifiably Tanzanian even if the notion of "Tanzania" has shifted significantly.

Appointed Commissioner of Culture in the Ministry of Education and Culture, Ndagala has a tremendous understanding of the problems and issues facing the music community, and he realizes that, despite government efforts and desire to maintain the country's traditions, changes have taken place within the post-socialist period:

> When you have an economy that depends on help from outside [foreign aid], those that give aid are able to insist on certain conditions, rather than if you were to do them yourself. This is because, when you receive foreign aid, the aid is not aimed at cultural things. We try to explain that, on the side of investment, culture and music are important avenues. People should come and build modern buildings for music, build music recording studios, put up factories to make CDs, etc. In that way, our music can get a market and our musicians can have a better life. So, I do not think that there are differences—the trust is the same—but our ability has changed because our economy is not strong; it depends on assistance.

Ndagala describes a complex situation: there is a desire for a strong national identity relating to the music and arts of Tanzanian culture. On the other hand, the government is forced to comply with many foreign donors who are bolstering the local economy. The dilemma results in a government that still has socialist tendencies (maintaining control of certain areas of the country's arts) but with free market practices (complying with the wishes of donors and aid agencies). Similar to the conflict between traditional and foreign forms of dance that helped create the local music economy during socialism, the neoliberal era is marked by a conflict between local and foreign ways of relating to music. The current Tanzanian music economy can be articulated as an assemblage of socialist and capitalist ideologies that are employed is many different ways, in different contexts. The movement toward capitalizing on the commodification of music creates a flow of creative practices that make use of the various modes of conceptualizing the local music economy. Flows between local and foreign, socialist and capitalist, and education and profitability are continually experimented with in order to find socially and politically acceptable means of profiting from performed or recorded sound. This dynamic interplay underlies the remaining chapters, which explore the contemporary music economy in Tanzania from music performance to education, recording to radio, and piracy to copyright law.

→ I like how Perullo does not get caught up
in the top-down; he recognizes the control
of the gov't, but demonstrates how, creatively,
the industries adopted & hence changed the
government &

# THREE

# Live in Bongoland

I go to the best clubs in civilized Bongo
Slipway, Blue Palm or Mambo Club
If you are not used to them you can break your neck
Very upscale life, people with cell phones in their hands
    Nokia ringtone . . .
Everyone glitters like a European, my friend.

—PROFESSOR JAY "Bongo Dar es Salaam"

The four million inhabitants of Dar es Salaam live in a two-hundred-square-mile area, roughly equivalent in size to New Orleans. During the working week, many of the city's residents flood the downtown areas, particularly City Centre and Kariakoo, to work, buy goods, or take care of personal matters. It is during these periods that the downtown area actually feels like a city: densely populated with intense activity. As the sun begins to set, which is around 6:30 PM all year round, everyone who has entered the city returns home, taking the minivan-style buses (called *daladala*), taxis, or private cars. By 9:00 PM, the city's roads are nearly empty, and the dust and diesel fumes settle over the coastal landscape. Except for a few areas, such as Kariakoo and Manzese, where activity rarely ceases, the city is eerily calm, making it appear more like a small town than the most heavily populated area in Tanzania.

The calmness of the city has fooled many visitors into believing that nightlife does not exist. Even long-time expatriate residents of the city asked me how I could study popular music when there were no concerts or dances to attend. To them, the city died at night and the only activity occurred in the few restaurants and bars that dotted the wealthier areas of town, and occasionally featured live music. Considering that they often live removed from heavily populated areas of the city, their view of the city's nightlife makes sense. They drive through the main streets, see few people walking, experience little commotion, and figure that everyone must be indoors watching television, listening to the radio, or eating evening meals. But tucked into all areas of the city, often hidden from the main roads, are small clubs, bars, and social halls that offer people a night out of their homes and a chance to hear live music, drink with friends, and dance.

In Dar es Salaam, as in many other areas of Africa, music represents the main nightly form of entertainment outside of the home. Attending a musical performance offers people the opportunity to enjoy themselves, forget about their problems, and be among other like-minded people. As one fan put it, musical performance "consoles, teaches, entertains, and relaxes me, and it 'pulls' at my feelings."[1] It also offers performers a chance to earn a living from their creative talents, promote their music and themselves, and connect to an enthusiastic audience. Live performances remain a critical form of entertainment for fans of local music and the main source of income for most groups. For this reason, most musical activity revolves around performances: tapes are made to draw audiences to shows; radio shows talk to musicians and play their music to inspire people to see them live; and local businesses use live bands to promote their products, especially beer and cigarettes. In some other parts of the world, the sale of songs or albums takes precedence over performance, since it is more profitable. In Tanzania, musical performance is the reason for a music economy and creates the need for other activities.[2]

Given the importance of musical performance, bands and solo musicians need to consistently stage well-attended shows. To generate enough earnings to be considered successful, top bands perform three or more times per week and close to two hundred shows per year. The challenge in maintaining such a rigorous performance schedule is finding ways to continually entice people to concerts. Competition is intense among hundreds of groups vying for places to perform, and audiences are often fastidious in their evaluation of music. How do artists stage concerts that will both keep audiences and club owners satisfied? How do they ward off competitors who are more than willing to take over their positions in bands or at clubs? And how do they generate enough support among club owners, journalists, and the public to establish a viable career in music?

I argue that musicians use two strategies to find success in live performance: direct and indirect engagement. Direct engagement refers to close

KEY!

interaction with audiences during performances or in other social situations. It requires using an artistic understanding of symbols, rules, and cultural cues that characterize genres of music, performance spaces, and audience expectations. Inspiring people to dance is the most important visual cue to an audience's acceptance of a band and their performances. Equally important is identifying with the concerns and desires of the audience and fostering a collective sense of healing. In the first three sections, I examine approaches used by musicians to perform concerts and relate to audience members during live events. My intention here is not to provide an in-depth analysis of music performance, but rather to focus on strategies used by artists to remain competitive in the local music economy.

In the second half of this chapter, I analyze forms of indirect engagement through discussing correlations between a performer's career and marketing, celebrity, and tabloids. Indirect engagement involves strategies that musicians use to create marketable identities. The music economy has increasingly become a focal point of many other businesses in Tanzania, including the press, radio, television, and advertising. An artist's movement toward popularity requires them to be able to negotiate their public persona in these forms of media and, more broadly, in public cultures. Popularity and economic success in music frequently favor those who are able to build a marketable image that can easily be interpreted and consumed by audiences and a broader public. Celebrity, fame, and identity increasingly matter in the ability of artists to generate audiences at concerts and a broader fan base within Tanzanian society.

In the final section, I combine the issues of direct and indirect engagement to comprehend the position of women in the music economy. Much of the attention of this ethnography is on men: they hold most of the primary decision making positions within the music economy and occupy many of the jobs that focus on the production of music. Women do fill prominent roles as stage performers in every genre of music but frequently have to overcome obstacles in order to attain credibility as artists. Through looking at ways that women become performers, this section provides a means to interpret both direct and indirect engagement in relation to a largely patriarchal music economy. It demonstrates that popular music is a flexible and dynamic artistic form that allows artists to push against socially accepted customs to influence people's understanding of gender roles and interpersonal relationships.

## PERFORMANCE STRATEGIES

Live music can be heard in over a hundred establishments throughout Dar es Salaam from Tuesday through Sunday (see appendix C for a list of these clubs). Concert venues range from small clubs that cater to forty people to those that can fit over a thousand. Smaller clubs, particularly those in areas outside downtown, entertain residential audiences who live nearby. People are often familiar with one another inside these clubs, and it is not uncommon to see the same audience members sit in the same seats each night as if they had bought season tickets. Clubs recognized as "hip" establishments have the most popular live performances. To be seen at these clubs is often a sign of being young, cosmopolitan, and part of the social elite. While not active every weekend, the largest concert halls in Dar es Salaam provide opportunities for Tanzanians to see and hear music of regional and international superstars.[3]

Most clubs in Tanzania are open-air, meaning that they do not have a roof over a portion of the establishment. Since it is often cool in the evening, the open-air venues allow the heat of the day to escape the clubs and keep the audience and the band comfortable. Only a few clubs in Dar es Salaam, such as Billicanas, Mambo Club, and California Dreamer, are fully enclosed and have air conditioning, though the latter does not offer live music. Most clubs have a simple, covered stage with a few electrical outlets and weak fluorescent lights that illuminate the faces of the singers. The dance floor is typically in front of the stage, which fills with people during a show (unless the show is a competition, in which case people sit and watch). Beer and konyagi (a locally made gin), as well as sodas, juices, and fried food, flow freely through these clubs. The entrance fees to local shows range from Tsh 500 to 10,000 (50 cents to $10.00) and are paid at the door upon arrival. Shows, even though they are often advertised to start at eight or nine at night, begin later and run until early in the morning.

Performance, as I am using it here, is communication that occurs among and between performers, audiences, and club employees. It is a dialogue shaped by the context of events and the people who take part in the presentation of music. Part of this form of communication involves various forms of expression, such as gesture, dance, speech, and music, which are used to influence the outcome of performance. For instance, listeners dance, celebrate, react, tip, and sing according to the actions

of musicians and other audience members. Musicians respond to the audience by increasing song tempos, adding dynamic solos, praising members of the audience, doing call-and-response, and engaging in other interactive forms of entertaining. Even on nights where the same audience
members attend a show of the same band, the communication fluctuates
based on the individual and collective responses that audiences and musicians make toward one another. This emergent quality to performance
provides excitement and anticipation that is central to popular music. Yet
it also provides the potential for dramatic failure in cases where audiences
and performers do not appear to be in dialogue with one another.

To create and sustain effective dialogue in musical events, musicians
rely on a variety of strategies. First, performers need a strong knowledge
of musical aesthetics. To draw audiences into a performance, musicians
incorporate and innovate on timbres, tempos, dynamics, harmonies,
musical phrases, rhythms, and other sonic cues to effectively communicate compositions to listeners. They must be aware of the sounds that
people associate with certain styles or genres of music. They need to be
cognizant of the emotional and physiological impacts that certain musical effects can have on people. Repetition, for instance, is an important
element in most Tanzanian popular music. Performers frequently sing
the same line several times before moving to the next. Musicians also
repeat different phrases, musical cues, and rhythms through the duration
of songs. These forms of repetition create pleasure among audiences who
enjoy accompanying the performer, "in going over a passage that has now
become familiar" (Okpewho 1992: 71).

A second means for creating effective dialogue in performance is
corporal communication. Movement, gesture, and facial expressions are
critical to live performance and provide a distinct separation between
listening to recorded music and attending a performance. Performing
theatrically involves treating the body as an instrument that can be as
effective in communicating musical meanings of lyrics or music (Seeger
1987: 78). The guitarist and composer Commando Hamza Kalala always
receives cheers when he takes his guitar, like a machine gun, and blasts
his audience with a fury of fast, high energy notes. The movement shows
power, force, and musical skill. It is not viewed as violent since the weapon
(the guitar) is not aiming to harm people, but hit them with a flurry of enjoyable musical notes. Movement also becomes important as performers

act out the subtleties of songs through gestures, signals, and gyrations. Clothing further adds to this dramatization of meaning. In all these strategies, the body becomes an effective means to communicate with audiences during a musical event.

③ Fostering emotional and psychological responses is another means to establish rapport with audiences. Individual members of bands or solo artists need to fulfill expectations of audiences, while simultaneously creating moments of intense emotional connection and pleasure. Pleasure is an important feature of popular music that is often overlooked in scholarly studies (Mahon 2000: 479). Music is something that can be deeply felt and experienced as it resonates with conscious and unconscious parts of the mind. It is also the most difficult area of musical performance to understand. Sentiment and pleasure vary by performance and individual listener, and there are often fewer visual cues to a person's emotional state. Nonetheless, performers must be able to somehow read the emotions of the audience in order to create moments of pleasure. Effective performances do not just emerge through playing the right notes or referencing the proper cultural cues. It is a dialogue that creates an emotional impact on the experience of listeners.

④ To further engage audiences in performance, many artists also reference shared forms of cultural meaning. Band leaders or lead singers often tell stories before performing a song. Digressions are common as artists use events as a means to discuss political or social issues. Humor is an effective connection between audience and performers. There are also common expressions that generate responses among audiences. Yelling "mikono juu" (hands up) gets people to raise their arms and dance while united in gesture. The phrase "piga bao wawili wawili" is another commonly used phrase. Piga bao is vernacular for scoring a goal in football (soccer), but it is used in popular music to tell audience members to slap hands. "Wawili" means two people. In other words, the expression tells people to slap hands with someone else in the audience (PURL 3.1). These interactive forms of communication are useful for energizing concertgoers when other strategies are not working.

⑤ Another form of interactive communication is praise singing. Praise singing is intended to gain favor among those with financial, political, or social power. Performers, for instance, occasionally mentioned my own name because they wanted me to write something positive about their music (PURL 3.2). They routinely call out the names of fan clubs in order to continue to emphasize their importance in live shows. Visiting politicians, however, receive the most accolades. The art of praising requires a skillful use of language and an effective knowledge of key people in positions of social, economic, and political power.

Finally, there is musical competence: the ability to compose, sing, or play an instrument well is central to popular music performance. Among audiences and within music communities, talented artists are often discussed and described by their level of musical skill. The ability to artfully layer together difficult conceptual ideas within concise rhymes is admired among listeners. A dansi singer's ability to imbue lyrics with meaning by varying vocal timbres and dynamics is a sign of musical competence. And a drummer's ability to incorporate various traditional and popular musical styles into a performance is highly valued. Competence is obviously connected to knowledge of musical aesthetics. Yet competence involves more than just routine familiarity with notes, chords, timbres, and rhythms. It involves an understanding of the meaning and cultural impact of these aesthetics on listeners' expectations.

Many authors who write about folklore, storytelling, and music explore similar strategies as those discussed here (see, for example, Askew 2002; Bauman and Briggs 1990; Belcher 1999; Edmondson 2007; Erlmann 1996; Ojaide 2001; Okpewho 1992; Reichl 2000). My interest in drawing attention to these musical and cultural strategies in Tanzania is to emphasize their importance in performance events. Performers combine, merge, and reformulate these strategies in order to interact with audiences and stage successful shows. Maintaining a large audience ensures that performers remain commercially viable as entertainers. Creativity emerges in the abilities of performers to draw from a musical and cultural body of knowledge to entice an audience to dance, sing, tip, and become involved in performance space. The success of a performer or band can often be determined by their knowledge of musical history, audience dynamics, and strategies for direct engagement.

In the next three sections, I provide a means to interpret direct forms of engagement in the performance strategies of popular artists. I begin by discussing part of a song performed in a popular social hall in Dar es Salaam. My intention in focusing closely on one song is to dissect performance strategies as they occur during an event. This helps to illustrate the presence of multiple strategies simultaneously produced and altered over time. The multifaceted means with which artists interact with audiences gives a stronger sense to the creative practices that they use to attain success. The subsequent two sections explore strategies that performers use to incorporate emotional and contextual meanings into events. Combined, these sections provide a means to interpret the possibilities of popular music performance and the requirements of performers within the local music economy.

### THE MAIN EVENT — Performance Strategies

On Christmas Day 2000, I filmed Tanzania One Theatre (TOT) Taarab performing a concert to a packed audience at the Vijana Social Hall in Kinondoni, Dar es Salaam (PURL 3.3). TOT Taarab is one of the more popular taarab groups in Tanzania, and this performance took place at the height of their success. In taarab music, a lead singer stands at the front of the stage and backup singers sit directly behind. Some groups have only a handful of backup singers, but TOT Taarab employs as many as fifteen. TOT's singers usually wear matching outfits—in this case, a short-sleeve, full-length dress of shiny red satin—and sit for the duration of the performance making hand gestures and facial expressions throughout the song. There are several lead singers who rotate performing songs, and it is customary for the most prominent singer to perform later in a musical program. Songs are long, lasting twenty or more minutes, and bands typically feature two keyboardists, two guitarists, a bassist, and a drummer.

In watching the film of TOT Taarab, the popularity of the group is apparent in the rush of people who move to the dance floor when the band takes the stage. Other groups do not receive the same attention in their performances, particularly in venues where groups rarely perform. TOT Taarab, however, is able to rely on their rapport with their fan base to encourage the audience to participate. As one of the better funded popular music organizations in Tanzania (Edmondson 2007), TOT Taarab can hire the best composers, musicians, and singers; they can record at the best studios using quality instruments; and they can influence the amount of airtime their songs receive on the radio. Such advantages in the music economy lead to significant benefits on the dance floor at performances.

Toward the latter half of TOT Taarab's performance, Khadija Kopa takes the stage to sing the song "Kinyang'unya." Kopa is the group's principal singer, referred to as the Queen of Modern Taarab. Her presence on stage brings tremendous excitement to the throngs of people who crowd the stage. Among music journalists, radio presenters, and taarab aficionados, Kopa is recognized as one of the more talented singers in Tanzania who has a keen understanding of the subtleties and meanings found in taarab music. Her performances are highly anticipated during TOT concerts, and her commanding presence on stage gives a sense to her popularity and celebrity within the music scene. Even the outfits she wears—in this case, a bright yellow and brown Swahili-style dress—helps her to stand out from everyone else around her.

During her performance of "Kinyang'unya," audience members walk up to Kopa and place tips in her hands and on her forehead. Tipping is common in Tanzanian popular music as a means of showing respect. Usually, tips are given after a few verses of singing to show appreciation for the choice of song or for the quality of musicianship. In Kopa's case, she receives tips from many people after only one verse. Part of the reason to tip Kopa is to be close to her. Several people put their arms around her, and one person gets Kopa to pose for a picture while the singer is in the middle of a verse. Kopa takes each of these situations in stride, smiling and allowing people to slide off her as she turns back to the audience to sing. She moves slowly and subtly, and yet she appears to have no difficulty dealing with the many people crowding the stage.

Many performers in Tanzania have trouble with the overt affection of audience members on stage. Particularly when drunkards approach singers, there are struggles to convince the inebriated to maintain common codes of courtesy. In such cases, bouncers for the band usher the person off the stage. Kopa, however, handles everyone on her own. People approach her and dance, carrying a child, a bottle of beer, a cassette tape of music, a camera, money; in each situation she smiles and gracefully allows them to approach her. Children stand at the corner of the stage for the duration of the song singing along with Kopa. Young women also stand on the stage acting out the meaning of songs. Perhaps they requested the song and perhaps they are aiming the confrontational lyrics at someone in the audience. In any case, they have a chance to stand on the stage for a short time, after tipping Kopa, to sing the words.

There is skill involved in this form of social interaction. A more conservative performer would not allow so many people a chance to stand on stage. Kopa recognizes the importance of participation in the event, as well as the popularity of her identity among those in attendance. By allowing them to approach her and become part of the show, she is giving them a chance to share the stage and establish a sense of belonging. This also reflects her confidence as a performer, knowing that she can handle any of the people and still maintain control over the performance.

On stage, performers create particular connections with audiences based on the establishment of consumable identities. Performers can supersede audiences through notions of superiority and greatness. They can transform themselves to become an entirely new character that is unique from their everyday lives. Or they can become a model for audiences and present an image with which people want to aspire. The "imaginative manipulations" of bodily practices, musical aesthetics, and cultural codes fosters a means for performers to connect to audiences in different ways, depending on intentions and desired outcomes of their public images (Waterman 2002: 33). For Kopa, her confidence on stage presents a model for audiences. The words she sings evidence struggles that people deal with on a routine basis, but her self-assured presentation of those words demonstrate an ideal that people desire to replicate in their everyday lives. Creating the persona of a role model, particularly through confidence and poise, establishes charisma needed for her to succeed on stage.

The main focus of the performance is on the words and message of the song. Kopa opens her song with the following lines: "Nasikia wewe nasikia / nasikia wewe wajitapa" (I hear you / I hear you boasting). She repeats the line with a smile and a suggestive dance that almost appears flirtatious. People respond to the repetitions of each line by joining in the singing. The song proceeds with repetition of each of the main phrases. This provides some sense as to why people quickly learn TOT Taarab's songs. "Kinyang'unya" was only released a few months prior to the event, and yet everyone from little kids to adults sings parts of the song.

After the opening line, Kopa sings the next stanza, "Watu ukiwaju-lisha wewe ukiwajulisha / Eti n'nakuogopa nakuogopa wataka kuniko-mesha" (You inform people, yes you inform people / That I am afraid of you since you want to thwart me). Kopa sings the words with great care, stretching the final word of each line. Her timbre is warm and open but also conversational. The effect of these aesthetic choices makes it appear as if she is speaking to someone attending the event. The words have resonance and meaning because they theatrically present the songs as if it were happening right then. "Yes you inform people" is directed out into the room. It does not matter who the "you" is. Rather, the feel of the song as conversation makes it appear as if the conversation is not a composed song. It is happening live and in the moment.

Watching some of the backup singers mouth the words provides a stronger sense to the meaning of the lyrics. The word *komesha* means to abolish, stop, or punish. Here "thwart" is more accurate since it conveys the notion of another person trying to bring down or hinder the success of someone else. One of the backup singers sings the words with disdain and uses her hand to gesture the idea of being taken advantage of. Kopa, however, sings in a calm, conversational tone suggesting that she is not affected by the actions of this other person. It is as if the backup singers represent the emotions that most people would feel from being thwarted by someone else, while Kopa has a more self-assured and confident demeanor. She is less concerned with the problems of this other person.

During the chorus of the song, the roles between the backup singers and Kopa switch. The singers are responsible for the lyrics while Kopa mouths them, even though the mannerisms of both remain the same:

| | |
|---|---|
| Kinyang'unya usitake ya watu kinyang'unya, | You old hag, do not imitate other people, you old hag, |
| Kinyang'unya yako yanakushinda kinyang'unya, | You old hag, you cannot even manage your own affairs, you old hag, |
| Kinyang'unya usitake ya watu kinyang'unya, | You old hag, do not imitate other people, you old hag, |
| Kinyang'unya kumbe hujaboya si bure umerogwa. | You old hag, you haven't yet exhausted what you are capable of doing; it is not by accident, you must have been bewitched. |

The Swahili lyrics are succinct and to the point. It provides a sense of the importance of taarab as a poetic form where the directness and confrontational manner of songs is in the spirit of modern taarab. Kopa takes center stage to act as if she were speaking the lyrics to someone. She is joyful in her gestures except once when she looks with pity to

say that the only reason someone would act this way is if they were
possedssed.  *means musicians must be versatile*
*& have a large knowledge of repetoire*

At taarab performances, audience members use lyrics as a means
to speak to other people. If a song is requested, the band may perform
it but the person who requested it is really using it as her voice. If a song
comments about a woman stealing the husband of another woman, then
the person who requested the song may center herself on the dance floor,
dramatize the lyrics, and then look at the woman on the dance floor
whom she believes to be cheating with her husband. The lyrics act as the
woman's voice in alluding to that which cannot be said in normal conversation. The variations in applications of taarab songs among participants,
such as it being used to *kumpasha mtu* (send a message to someone),
*kumwimbia mtu* (sing about/to someone), or *kumaanisha* (imbue with
meaning), provide audiences opportunities to proclaim their social and
moral stances on a variety of issues. Song lyrics provide a resource for
negotiating, "social relations Swahili-style" (Askew 2002: 128–29). The
performer's job is to sing the song well so that the person who requested
the song can make her ideas, feelings, or complaints known. The performer is always rewarded in these circumstances with tips and audience
appreciation.

At this event, it does not appear as if anyone requested the song to
lodge a critique against another person who is in the room. (It is, after
all, a holiday show.) At other events, however, "Kinyang'unya" becomes a
powerful vehicle to address social disagreements. Kopa's conversational
tone and confident mannerisms become a means for other people in the
audience to partake in a critique against another person. They can get up
on stage, look at someone in the audience, and sing, "You old hag, you
cannot even manage your own affairs, you old hag." This is a powerful
and deeply emotional form of dialogue. Fights occur on occasion, but
more commonly a critical social conflict is being addressed. The song
acts as a means to emotionally address a personal problem. The lyrics
become the voice of the person lodging the complaint, while the event is
a therapeutic means to overcome personal conflicts. At one point in the
song, Kopa raises her head and laughs and the audience laughs with her.
It is an engaging moment of audience interaction and healing through
music.

*Kopa's strategies ① confidence ② well persona of people ③ control ④ playing requested songs*

*want more n healing*

## MUSICAL HEALING

Cities in Tanzania, such as Dar es Salaam, have become extraordinarily stressful places to live. Wages rarely cover expenses of everyday life; parenting in urban areas is routinely challenging and often exhausting; electricity and water supplies are sporadic and unreliable; health problems are common; and the intense competition for resources, jobs, and social security causes conflict among many populations. For many audience members, their purpose in attending a concert is to find relief from these issues and undergo a sense of healing even if this healing only emerges from the possibility to forget or ignore the world outside of the club. To produce this outcome, it is the responsibility of performers to be aware of the problems that occur in everyday life, directly or indirectly comment on those problems, and then move people to overcome them in ways that they would be unable to do on their own. The challenge for the performer is to achieve this using music, dance, and their understanding of the issues facing those who attend their concerts.

The death of the country's first president, Julius Nyerere, altered performances for months after his funeral due to audience members' connection with both the post-independence period and the role Nyerere played as a vital leader to the country. Since it is customary to mourn the loss of a loved one for months after his or her death, the public bereavement that transpired within many clubs around the country made the experiences of individual attendees more unified, communal, and socially aware. Band leaders continually reminded the audiences of the importance of Nyerere in the country's history. Pro-Tanzania and pro-Nyerere songs were prevalent at performances (Askew 2006; PURL 3.4). And frequently, band members would hang their heads in sadness as they sang Nyerere's name. On these nights, the performance space was continually used to reaffirm people's connection to the country and its past. Regardless of the differences among audience members' backgrounds, the club became a central space for addressing loss and reaffirming communal connections.

Similar senses of community and loss emerged in New York after September 11, 2001. In New York City at that time, people's initial forays into performance halls were accompanied with a sense of guilt and fear. But in the spaces themselves, New Yorkers connected together in their

DDC Mlimani Park Orchestra performing songs in memory of the country's first president Julius Nyerere. Their shirts have a picture of Nyerere with the statement, "Tutakuenzi Daima" (We will glorify you forever). *Photo by author.*

*left field?*

sorrow in ways that rarely occurred in other, everyday performances. At these events, there was a palatable sense of belonging to a group, of sharing a traumatic memory, and sensing the need to connect together to overcome grief. Songs reflected people's emotions in ways that can only occur in live performance through mirroring emotionality and memory, trauma and grief, with belonging and healing. Similarly, the performances after Nyerere's death captured a sense of belonging and healing. The loss of the country's first leader—a person often revered for ushering in independence and for unifying the country—also meant that many people sensed a loss of someone who kept the country together, who kept the country whole. Performance, as well as other events and experiences around the country, served to unify audiences into a sense of purpose and continuity even after the passing of one of the country's most revered leaders.

The adverse events that occur in Tanzania mean that performances frequently embody some form of shared, traumatic memory: the embassy bombings that occurred in 1998; the 2002 train accident that killed over 200 people; the difficulties of day-to-day life that emerge with the rationing of electricity; and even the death of the 26-year-old activist and member of Parliament Amina Chifupa are events that are collectively dealt with in social halls and clubs. Certainly, these events are also debated and discussed in newspapers, television shows, and daily conversations at the work place and in people's homes. However, performance spaces in Tanzania, whether for music, theater, or some other occasion, are central for showing a sense of community that allow people's emotions to be reflected in the band's performance and refracted on the dance floor and other spaces in a club. In this dialogue of dance and song, a sense of healing emerges that is never consistent or predictable but reflects the issues unfolding outside the walls of the social hall.

On other nights, audiences and performers fall into more predictable routines. Discussions about the work week, sports teams, and relationships are common. There is an ever-present courting of companionship and the heavy imbibing of liquor that steals from the week's paycheck. Even in these settings, however, there is a sense of healing that takes place given the everyday struggles that people encounter in Dar es Salaam. On Saturday nights, for instance, the band All-Star Taarab plays at a club called Max Bar in the Ilala district.[4] Since it is close to downtown, a diverse audience of Arabs, Indians, and Africans attend. Once the music starts, the audience dances, sings, and dramatizes their favorite songs. Although the band is playing and the audience is listening, the dancers are mainly watching each other, as are the people sitting at the tables. The dancers' movements are subtle—a shuffle of the feet, swaying of the hips, and swinging at the arms, bent at the elbow. According to Mzee Muchacho, who is the leader of All-Star Taarab, the responsibility of the band is to learn about the people attending a performance and select songs with lyrics that are likely to move people to dance, and thus find social connections.

In popular music, dancing acts as a form of performative healing that allows audiences to both participate and engage with music. Other authors note the connection between dance and healing particularly in trance ceremonies that occur in eastern and southern Africa (Friedson 1996; Gilman 2009). Popular music does not produce trance in the same way, but dancing at events has a similar effect. Interaction with performers and other audience members produces deep psychological and emotional pleasure. There is a cathartic release that is almost immediately experienced when entering a dance floor. The dim lighting of many clubs further fosters a sort of meditative state where the mind and body connect to the music. The interrelationship between participations builds a sense of community that is both desired and therapeutic. *→ Not convinced here.*

In addition to dancing, song compositions are also influential in providing forms of therapeutic healing. Good composers find ways to use the combination of music and lyrics to foster a broad sense of cultural resonance among listeners. Given the frequency with which audience members quote and discuss lyrics, they obviously pay close attention the meaning of songs. In dansi music, audience members sit and listen to the main lyrics of the songs before getting up to dance. In bongo flava, fans frequently sing along with songs. And, as illustrated already, there is strong tradition of theatrically acting out the meaning of taarab lyrics. Each of these situations creates intense moments of communication and identification. The lyrics represent a common connection between performers and listeners, which creates a collective sense of understanding. *But what about double entendre. Critique*

In these moments, healing also becomes part of the connection between music and participants. Songs become a means for artists to directly engage audiences in common life experiences while also providing a level of healing through these shared moments. Just as certain songs contain melodies and rhythms that can alter our emotions—from happiness to sadness—so too can lyrics provide a deeper realization of people's connections to each other and to life's experiences. The appropriately composed song can provide a sense of belonging, which in itself is a form of healing. *where is the ethnographic data here?*

Songs that tend to be the most therapeutic are those that address social issues relevant to everyone in attendance. They contain lessons within the lyrics that provide the potential for personal connection. Compositions by TOT Band, for instance, frequently deal with themes common to many people. "Jahazi" (Dhow), composed by Banza Stone, addresses conflicts that emerge between people and that can result in instability and even death (PURL 3.5). The context of the song is rather vague and could be sung in a variety of situations where people in a family, community, or nation quarrel.

| | |
|---|---|
| Sisi sote ni wasafiri ndani ya jahazi moja, | We are all travelers in one dhow, |
| Haina haja ya malumbano. | There is no need for arguing. |
| Tunakotoka ni kina kifupi cha maji, | We leave from shallow water, |
| Hapa tulipo sasa ni kina kirefu cha maji. | We are in deep water now. |
| Sisi sote ni wasafiri ndani ya jahazi moja, | We are all travelers in one dhow, |
| Haina haja ya malumbano. | There is no need for arguing. |
| Malumbano ngoma kinoma noma ooh | Arguing in good music is dangerous, oh |
| 'Bavon' | Bavon. |
| Tunapoleta malumbano ndani ya jahazi | When we argue in our dhow, it is |
| letu ni hatari. | dangerous, |
| Kwani jahazi likizama nani atakayeokoka? | Since, if the dhow sinks, who will rescue you? |
| Tuache malumbano ndani jahazi letu, | Let's stop arguing in our dhow, |
| Tuache malumbano ili tufike salaama. | Let's stop arguing so that we can safely arrive. |
| Tuache malumbano ndani jahazi letu, | Let's stop arguing in our dhow, |
| Tuache malumbano ili tufike salaama. | Let's stop arguing so that we can safely arrive. |

USE IN CRITIQUE
AS FOIL to OTHER PAGE!

The potential to read into these lyrics allows audiences to create their own interpretations of the song's meanings. Vagueness and timelessness help to allow listeners to conjure their own memories and experiences. It is like a Rorschach test but with song. The words also contain cultural referents that make them more evocative to Tanzanians. Dhow refers to a sailing vessel used in Dar es Salaam and other coastal areas of the country. Hearing this word provides a measure of cultural association that establishes more significance for the participants of local shows. Further, in following Stone's narrative, listeners can attain a level of healing through arriving at the conclusion of the song, which suggests that any conflict should be set aside so that the journey can go on.

In addition to song lyrics, digressions are a necessary means of fostering a sense of community and healing. Digressions are a means for the performer to speak directly to the audience without using formally composed song or speech. Instead, they improvise on some issues that are pertinent to their audience and the context of performance. In a major album release for Mr. II at the Kilimanjaro Hotel, for instance, the rap duo Gangwe Mobb took the stage to sing a few of their best-known hits. One of the members of the group, Inspekta Haroun, stopped the music after it had just begun and spoke directly to his audience. Piecing

together parts of their songs with some freestyle, he energized the crowd
with his social commentary about "real life." The crowd applauded loudly
when Haroun imitated the voice and speech patterns of former president
Nyerere. In describing the problems with life in Tanzania, Haroun made
the crowd laugh and cheer with this line: "It is better to be born a dog or
a cat in Europe—at least you'll get milk." He became their voice, and his
digression successfully moved them to acknowledge his ability to both
recognize the issues that they endure while providing a sense that he was
there to help them through these forms of inequality (PURL 3.6).

    Regardless of the setting, musicians must be well aware of the over-
all circumstances that surround their performances. Their song choices,
compositions, digressions, and other techniques must fit the context
of their presentation. Directly engaging the audience is, therefore, more
than a form of communication or a means to establish a sense of community within a club or social hall. Performance is also a consciousness
about cultural, political, and economic issues that surround those in attendance. Performers must be able to interpret an audiences' mood and
desires and create an environment in which audiences deal with events
occurring around them and establish strategies to resolve fears, tensions,
or concerns. The field of music therapy has long discussed the curative
role that music can have in a performance setting. It can build self-esteem,
establish emotional awareness, and promote physical healing. Researchers even acknowledge the way that creativity may be an adaptive form
of survival, since it promotes healthy expressions of emotions that may
be beneficial to the body and establishes brain wave shifts that improve
overall health (Crowe 2004: 225). For popular music, generating curative healing is a significant part of being a performer in urban popular
music.

## CONTEXTUAL MEANINGS

A third means of attaining direct engagement is context dependent.
Due to competition over bookings at local venues, bands must ensure
that audiences celebrate, dance, drink, and enjoy themselves at each
performance. All the strategies discussed thus far aim to achieve this
goal. There is an added challenge in that performance halls frequently
embody the meaning of previous events. In the same way that songs

can conjure up memories, so too can social halls, bars, and clubs remind people of previous experiences. Everything from lighting, sound system, walls, chairs, and staff elicit responses from those in attendance. Dancing occurs far more naturally at establishments where there are positive contextual memories of the space than at social halls that are new to the audience or the band. Given the proliferation of new bands and social halls, there is a frequent lack of contextual engagement at shows, which often results in lackluster performances and audiences sitting for the duration of events. A sitting audience reflects an unpopular or failed performance.

Amana Social Hall is a central institution in Tanzanian popular culture. Since the 1960s, the club has been the home to Msondo Ngoma, formerly OTTU Jazz and, before that, Juwata Jazz. Given its long history, people often have past personal and cultural experiences of the concert space (Stone 1982: 8). The limited amount of light in the hall, the open-air coolness, and the presence of the aging speakers remind people of earlier experiences with the dance floor, stage, and even the staff. Rather than being unfamiliar with the dance floor or unsure of how to behave or act, most are already aware of the band's musical and visual cues, the meaning of songs, and their place within the event. While people's individual engagement with the space always undergoes transformations, those who sit through at least one performance become well aware of forms of behavior and action that occur in the hall.

The first night I attended a performance at Amana Social Hall, I sat with three friends at the back of the dance floor. As Muhiddin Maalim Gurumo, the 60-year-old patriarch of the band, took the microphone, all heads focused on the stage as he sang the opening verse of one of his famous compositions. After a few minutes, the band launched into the *sebene* or *chemko*, the fast-paced instrumental section of the song. The audience responded by shuffling onto the dance floor, where many would remain until late in the night. I turned to my left and the cook, who had been standing over a wok of grease, continually feeding it strips of potatoes, was also dancing. His head was bowed, his arms were in the air, and a smile was on his face. The other cooks behind the counter were doing the same. Only a few other people sat at tables watching the dancers, and it was obvious that we were out of place at the event. We were not participating, which was the main reason most people attended. After a few minutes of watching, we also entered the dance floor. No one questioned our presence or made some gesture to acknowledge us. We quickly learned the sonic cues, the movements, and the body language of other dancers. By dancing, we were joining a community of regulars and feeding off the cycle of tunes that played every weekend. In fact, every time I returned to Amana, all the cues were the same and my previous knowledge quickly informed me of what I should do. I had been socialized into the context of the performance space.

Msondo Ngoma used their music and long performance history in the hall to quickly move the audience to dance. It was up to the band to perform songs that reconnected listeners to the performance space and that reminded them of the historical associations within the social hall. "Social and spatial relationships are dialectically inter-reactive," writes Edward Soja, and the "social relations of production are both space-forming and space contingent" (1989: 81). In the dance halls of Tanzania, the space between performers and audiences needs to be bridged in order for there to be a successful performance. Social halls with long histories help produce a mood for the audience entering to see a show. The space itself becomes part of the performance and can assist performers in entertaining an audience. But what do bands do in new spaces when people are not familiar with them or the dance space?

In June 2005, I sat with members of the band Double Extra at the Leaders Club in Dar es Salaam. It was late afternoon and another band, Mchinga Generation, was playing underneath a large tree that provided shade to both the band and audience. About a hundred people had gathered to hear an early set of live music before the bands shifted to their evening performances elsewhere in town. The band worked energetically to engage the audience: the band's dancers performed choreographed, high-energy routines in hopes of drawing audiences into the show; the musicians worked to make the songs more meaningful through their aesthetic choices; and the lead singers praised people in the audience to provide a sense of belonging. Despite these efforts, Mchinga Generation was not entertaining the audience into active participation. Attendees sat motionless in chairs or stood on the outskirts of the performance space. The expressions on their faces was one of passive viewing—as if they were watching television—while the musicians and dancers were sweating profusely.

When Double Extra started their set, the audience gave the same initial response. The show appeared to be a flop, but Ally Chocky, who was then the band's leader, appeared unfazed. His expression mirrored that of the audience, as if he were watching them as they watched him, both with little interest. The space between Double Extra and the audience remained contested, an area that could only be entered after something occurred. But what? What had to happen for the audience to become moved by the performance? What needed to occur for people to connect to the outdoor space that did not hold regular concerts? And how could Chocky, a seasoned musician, appear as if he did not care about the lack of excitement by the audience? He was in a new band that needed to succeed in small venues. Up to that point in the show, they were failing.

Although Leaders Club had been used prior to 2005, the performance space itself continually shifted. Occasionally there was a stage set in a grassy field on the far end of the outdoor club. On other occasions bands simply set up their instruments on the ground and had audiences define the space for dancing and watching. Rarely was there any period of a single band or musician performing on a regular basis. In 2001, for instance, I attended a festival at Leaders Club that featured numerous popular groups from various genres of music. As with Double Extra event, the musicians appeared to have little ability to get people up and dance. Even some of the best performers in the country failed to move anyone to rise out of their chairs. The tension on the dance floor was finally broken when two men entered the dance space and began to provoke the audience with their movements. Dancing by themselves and then with each other, they moved the viewers to become participants both in their excitement and displeasure.[5] Still, aside from a handful of other people, the audience never participated in the show. By all accounts, it was a mediocre event.

At the Double Extra show, the conclusion was heading for the same result. The band played most of its set without anyone moving to the dance floor. An inebriated woman began dancing to the taunts of the audience (public displays of drunkenness are not always welcome in these settings). After she left, the open dirt dance floor again became a void. In the penultimate song, the band's fan club finally moved in front of the audience and began to cheer, dance, and sing along to the songs. They

During the early part of the Double Extra show at
Leader's Club on June 4, 2005. *Photo by author.*

had a somewhat choreographed routine as they gathered in a circle and
touched their hands together forming an arch before retreating again.
These movements entertained the audience but were seen simply as part
of the performance. They did not engage the audience in ways that made
viewers consider themselves included in the event.

After a few minutes, one of the lead singers of Double Extra, Khalid
Chokora, took his wireless microphone and began running through the
audience to get them excited. He sang and danced in front of various
audience members and then was picked up by the fan club and carried
throughout the club while he continued to sing. In other words, Chokora
took action by moving the performance to the audience rather than waiting for them to move toward the band. He punctured the barrier between

the band and the audience. Pleased by the effort, the audience applauded appreciatively at the end of the song. In the final song, many members of the audience stood up and danced for the first time. Even though it took nearly two hours and two bands to get the audience to dance, the performance was not considered a wasted effort, since people were moved enough to enter the dance floor and participate in the music. But why did it take so long?

A significant issue for the Double Extra audience was lack of familiarity with Leaders Club. "Performance in many ways brings a renewal of shared knowledge and experience," writes J. H. Kwabena Nketia; "the contextual approach enables one to observe how this experience unfolds both in the musical processes and in the interaction of those present" (Nketia 1990: 80). Although Nketia is describing a means for scholars to examine a performance event, the contextual approach applies to how audience members engage with performances as well. Those who attend a performance make judgments about their role in the performance. The more unfamiliar the space, the less able the audience member is to determine his or her actions. At Leaders Club, there was no shared knowledge, memories, or experiences that the audience could use to interpret the context of performance.

The contextual engagement of performance includes the ways that performers use their music, stage show techniques, and knowledge about a social hall to find ways for people to enjoy themselves. The band management also tries to influence the interest of some audience through offering raffles, awards, and other perks to audience members. The creation of fan clubs has been a popular strategy to guarantee a welcoming and highly enthusiastic audience at shows. Members of fan clubs are frequently given privileges over other audience members. The fan club members follow the band everywhere they perform and even work as roadies, moving the band's equipment. As they did with Double Extra, fan clubs also employ various strategies to guarantee the band's success and, in essence, repay the band for giving them privileges. Despite these strategies, however, even the most talented and well financed bands in Tanzania do not succeed on stage unless they create strategies for directly engaging their audiences. For Double Extra, that meant sending a lead singer into the audience to stir up the audience. But even that approach does not always work.

In 2010, I returned to Leaders Club to watch a double-bill show of dansi bands. As in previous years, the audiences remained motionless during the performance, neither clapping nor dancing. I went to speak with some of the band members before they went on stage and asked about the lack of celebration during the club's concerts. They explained that, over the past decade, since the club opened, the audience had learned to be more passive in their participation at shows. With few exceptions, artists had failed to encourage audience engagement. Though greatly frustrated by the lack of enthusiasm, bands had also learned to begrudgingly accept the lack of audience animation through working harder to entertain them. The African Stars singer Luizer Mbutu explained that the dancers and singers choreograph stronger dance routines and more elaborate interaction between the people on stage in order to entice and entertain listeners. These efforts continue to generate large audiences but never alter the interactions between those who attend. The space in the club had become fixed in the memories of attendees to be one of passive viewing rather than active engagement.

## INTERMISSION

Being able to communicate directly with audiences in different social spaces is a valued performance skill. To remain active in music and continue to entice audiences, however, artists need to do more than just perform songs in ways that directly engage audiences. Performers also need to shape their public identities and deal with celebrity and fame. The strategies involved in creating and marketing an identity have become increasingly important in Tanzania's music economy. It is in these indirect forms of engagement that the most significant shifts have taken place within popular music. In the next several sections, I analyze indirect engagement by exploring the identities of performers on and off the stage.

## IDENTITY MARKETING

In February 2004, the r&b singer Mr. Nice performed a few opening songs for the album release concert of *Gere* (Jealousy) by Kilimanjaro Band. The show was at the austere Diamond Jubilee Hall, a landmark of large-scale musical performances since the 1970s. During one of Mr.

Nice's songs, the rap artist Dudubaya walked on stage unannounced, strolled over to Mr. Nice, and punched him. Mr. Nice fell to the ground with wounds to the head and ribs. The event staff pulled Dudubaya away from Mr. Nice and an ambulance came to take the wounded artist to the hospital. Over the next several weeks, journalists, radio stations hosts, and even the prime minister's office deliberated over the disturbing, violent conflict between the two musicians. The media questioned Dudubaya's sanity and the well-known journalist Fred Ogot called Dudubaya a "sick person" in need of psychiatric help. He also blamed the National Arts Council (BASATA) for not upholding professional standards in the local music scene.[6] Several major local radio stations banned Dudubaya's music from their airwaves. Even the judge who heard the case appeared to be swept up in the furor as he refused to grant Dudubaya bail, since "the public had the right to live in peace."[7] An additional factor was that Dudubaya had previously attacked Mr. Nice and was already on bail.

In the months that followed the 2004 attack, Dudubaya became a household name in many areas of mainstream Tanzania. His third album, *Papo na Papo* (Right at This Moment), sold 25,000 copies in the first week, a significant number compared to his previous record sales. Despite being banned from the radio, more people demanded that his music be broadcast because they were enticed by this rogue figure in the music scene. Of course, simply hitting Mr. Nice was not the reason that Dudubaya became so popular. Rather, he worked to build an image of himself as a tough, reckless person and used many American rappers, such as 50 Cent, as role models for his success. Unlike most other Tanzanian rappers, Dudubaya is heavily muscled and tattooed. During the attack on Mr. Nice, he wore his pants well below the waist, as often seen in videos from the United States, and he appeared to flash gang signs as the event staff pulled him off stage. What's more, "Dudubaya" means "bad bug."

Even though unprovoked violence is not culturally appropriate in Tanzania—the country is better known for the relaxed, non-confrontational approach of its people—Dudubaya's image as a tough, uncontrollable person helped garner him a large community of fans. Part of the reason is that his actions, dress, and demeanor are atypical and made him stand out as a performer and entertainer. Yet his actions are only unusual within Tanzania's music scene. International videos, movies, and news broadcast in the country often feature the same rogue-toughness embodied by Dudubaya's persona. In essence, his identity localizes people's perceptions and interpretations of other music cultures. By being physically tough, Dudubaya is better able to position himself as a local purveyor of foreign practices and market himself and his music as something unique. On the Young African website, a Tanzanian argues, "As an artist, you have to have an identity and it seems to me a kwamba [that] the lad [Dudubaya] has chosen u-bad boy as his identity. And remember, in a musical genre dominated by the adulation of violence, being an ex-inmate offers a credibility no marketing consultant can create."[8] ⟶ *key!*

Marketing oneself using various strategies to construct a popular, consumable image has become increasingly important in the Tanzanian music economy. Though Dudubaya's case is extreme, the need for artists and bands to establish identities that audiences connect to is a central part of making music profitable to an increasingly selective Dar es Salaam audience. Drawing on various areas of popular culture, the contemporary performer uses dress, attitude, and style to attract listeners to their concerts. There is increased value in a performer's actions outside of the performance space that audiences expect to see at live concerts. This marketing of the self is necessary to outcompete other performers who want to attract a similar audience to shows. When there are many talented stage performers, identity becomes an increasingly useful tool to better situate the self within popular culture.

One of the earliest purveyors of identity marketing in Tanzania was the musician Remmy Ongala. As an independent artist during the 1980s, Ongala could not depend on government funding to support his career. He had to rely on his ability to compose songs that attracted audiences interested in music with strong social messages meant to both support and critique the socialist government. It is important to remember that Tanzanians were suffering due to the economic problems that plagued the country in the 1980s. Ongala was one of the few artists who used his music as an overt form of respectful social protest. He always argued that he was a strong supporter of the national party, but his music frequently pointed out the problems wrought by the government. Ongala told the music journalist James Nindi, "Many bands here in this country [Tanzania] insist on singing love songs. . . . I cannot sing love songs. I want songs that have powerful lessons that are direct and do not hide anything."[9] His music became a means to address the concerns within a populist framework. Whereas many other bands, particularly those who worked for the government, composed songs reverential of state policies, Ongala, even as an immigrant to Tanzania, was willing to risk the ire of the state to market himself as a spokesperson for the poor. He became known as the voice of the voiceless.

Ongala's witty, socially conscious lyrics about the rights of every person (such as "Kilio cha Samaki" [Cries of the Fish]) and the ironic lack of rights for the poor who can "only lean on God" ("Mnyonge Hana Haki" [Feeble/Poor Person Has No Rights]) helped to create his identity as a fighter for the poor. His songs dealt with life, death, low incomes, corruption, and other issues relevant to the lives of the urban poor, and were particularly well received by male and jobless youths who referred to Ongala as "Doctor Remmy," since he helped heal their problems. His song "Maisha" (Life) embodied his compositional approach to music: "Life / Don't blame yourself because others have got cars / Others have got houses / And you don't / Life." The song was often read as a critique of both the poor economic state of Tanzania during the 1980s and the growing urban desire for attaining more materialist signs of wealth and power. From the viewpoint of the urban poor, it was a simultaneous admonition of socialist and capitalist economic policies, neither of which assisted those who most need support.

Ongala's songs could also bring controversy, such as "Mambo kwa Soksi" (Matters of Socks), where Ongala talks about free distribution of condoms: "No, they [condoms] should not be sold at all / when you buy a bottle of beer/ you should get one free as a present / When you sleep in a guesthouse, you should receive a towel, soap and spare socks [condoms]." He then composed another song to embody the voice of a struggling woman. The song "Nalilia Mwana" (I Am Crying for a Child) is a painful lesson of the difficulties bearing children. Sung from the point of view of a childless woman, Ongala sings, "I am crying and am sad my friends for I have no luck / I have gone to see all the doctors / All for nothing / God, I am asking for this one thing." The song addresses cultural traditions that pressure women to have children, but also the poverty that keeps them from receiving basic healthcare. Even still, Ongala places humor in the middle of the song to suggest that even in these difficult circumstances, life must go on. The woman sings that she wants a child, "even if he is bad like Remmy."

In addition to composing socially relevant and pertinent music, Ongala built an image of himself that became widely recognized in Tanzania. In attracting media attention, Ongala held yearly *sura mbaya* (ugly face) contests, in which he was almost always the winner, and called himself a *mnyonge* (a feeble/poor person) (Graebner 1997). Although he did lose the ugly face contest one year, these forms of physical debasement helped to show his connection to the community that he was trying to represent. Ugliness became a means to show that he was no better than anyone else. It was a symbol of his identity as a popular figure representing the interests of the underprivileged. His dreadlocks were associated not with reggae, but with a sense of unkemptness connected to the struggles of the poor to attain basic necessities. His clothes, which ranged from mismatched outfits to traditional forms of dress, further represented his commitment to the words that he sang.

Ongala also presented long speeches in his songs and during his shows. The speeches allowed him to talk openly about the ills of the city, country, and politics, much to the consternation of local leaders and to the joy of his audiences. Throngs of listeners would pack in close to the stage to hear his emotionally charged messages that conjured joy, laughter, anger, and frustration. In an interview, Ongala explained to me, "Music is like a basic education. It brings changes to society. Don't sing, 'I'll buy you a car,' if you do not have a car yourself. Don't promise that you are going to build them a house while you rent an apartment. It's always better to tell people the truth." The openness of his speeches could have landed him in prison. Instead, the government continually refused Ongala's application for citizenship, which became a means to control Ongala's criticism of political leaders. If Ongala went too far, they could threaten to expel him from the country. (Ongala eventually did receive Tanzanian citizenship in 2001.)

Finally, to draw people to shows, Ongala worked to form a band that could stand on its own and help him create a populist sound. Part of being able to market personal identity and the popularity of a band is to fashion an environment where other musicians are able to participate in a shared sense of identity. Without their participation and collective sensibility,

Remmy Ongala performing in Dar es Salaam during the 1980s.
*Photo courtesy of the National Press Archives.*

there is a lack of cohesiveness needed to convince listeners in the validity and the sustenance of the music. While Christopher Small (1998) argues that artists are only able to perform to the potential of a composition, a song's potential is only realized through the collaboration of musicians capable of performing and imbuing a song with emotion, energy, and expression.

In forming a strong band, Ongala hired many talented artists, including Cosmas Chidumule, who became one of the band's lead vocalists. At that time, Chidumule had left music, frustrated by his lack of prospects:

> In 1986, I left music because I saw that music did not provide benefits for the future of Tanzanian musicians. So, I lost hope in music, and I left and decided to chop wood in the wilderness. I had this idea that if I split wood

I could earn enough money to buy my own instruments and start a band. While I was in the wilderness, I received a message that someone needed to see me in Dar es Salaam. I went and [the person who called me] was Remmy Ongala. He said, "I heard you were chopping wood. But you are an artist. Stay here and let's see what we can do. If we fail, we'll just eat food with our children." I thought it was a good idea and we started playing together. We became so popular here, we shook things up [*lulitikisa*]. I even went to Europe with Remmy to record with Real World. I thank God for the work with Remmy. He instilled such confidence in me that I was able to go all the way to Europe and perform at big festivals and meet musicians from other parts of the world.

Instilling self-assurance in band members and supporting them in their creative talents became a part of Ongala's ability to form a musical movement that drew strength from the problems encountered in Tanzania not just among audience members, but also among musicians whose talents frequently go unnoticed. Even though musicians lament the many problems they have encountered in Ongala's bands, his reputation as a formidable band leader who kept his group united in their musicality was central to promoting songs to audiences.

The combination of song composition, image, dress, digressions, and the organization of committed band members proved important for Ongala to create a populist identity that could be promoted to local audiences. Audiences, particularly the urban poor, took to Ongala as a fighter for their interests. The music scholar Simon Frith writes, "We use pop songs to create for ourselves a particular sort of self-definition, a particular place in society. The pleasure that pop music produces is a pleasure of identification . . . a process of inclusion and exclusion" (2004: 38). Inclusion and exclusion are prominent features of social life where groups and audiences form around common interests and concerns, thereby excluding others who do not fit within those parameters. Popular music functions as a means to express such identity politics by establishing various aesthetics, styles, and codes of acceptability that people quickly identify with and understand. Identity marketing becomes a means to build distinctiveness or foster notions of inclusion/exclusion to attract/exclude listeners. It is a necessary process where performers move their careers into a competitive framework of music and audience engagement.

Recently, after suffering and recovering from a stroke, Ongala dropped all his old songs and transformed his image from a voice of the

*– wow*

poor to a voice of God.]He shaved off his dreadlocks and began performing concerts dressed in brightly colored West African-styled outfits with
embroidery. In one performance, he wore a pink colored *agbada*-like out-
fit unlike the mostly black clothes he had worn in the past. It would have
been like Johnny Cash donning a pink suit. For Ongala, the transformation has been a positive one, presenting a new image of himself as "spiritu-
ally cleansed," sober, and loyal to his family. It also showed that Ongala
was firmly aware of the importance of dress and image in establishing an
identity that could be marketed to audiences who shared similar interests
and ideologies. (Ongala passed away on December 13, 2010, and his popularity brought thousands of people to his wake and funeral, many singing
the song "Kifo" (Death), one of his best known songs. His music aired on
all Tanzanian radio stations for several days after his death, and President
Jakaya Kikwete gave a public radio address stating that Ongala helped to
broadcast Tanzania to the world and that his passing would leave a hole
in Tanzanian popular music.)

Another group that has found success through creating a marketable
identity is Kilimanjaro Band. During the early 2000s, Kilimanjaro Band
was one of the highest paid concert bands in Tanzania. Since the group
members owned their instruments and were self-managed, their ability
to earn money without concern of one member cheating another kept
the group together longer than any other current band. Three members,
Mabrouk Hamisi, Mohammed Mrisho, and Waziri Ally, have played together since 1973 when the band was called the Revolutions. In 1989, the
group moved from Tanga to Dar es Salaam and began playing in high-end
hotels. These hotels were often a distance from populated areas of the
city, forcing people to drive or take taxis to the shows. For many bands,
this alone would have brought financial strain, since it is uncommon to
have concert spaces far removed from well-populated areas given the
cost of owning a car or taking a taxi. The distance from congested areas,
however, appealed to professional Tanzanians, who attended the band's
shows to escape the realities of city life while enjoying a night of music.
Kilimanjaro Band concerts were a means to appear more cosmopolitan,
powerful, and distinctive from the rest of the city.

The real turning point came in the early 1990s when the band traveled
to Europe and Japan. Waziri Ally, the group's keyboardist, explained how
Kilimanjaro Band developed its cosmopolitan approach while living in

Japan from 1992 to 1994: "We were taken and brought to a discothèque club whose clientele were teenagers who liked pop, rap, and techno. We did not know that music, and we had a major problem. So, we had to learn rap music, techno, so we could please this clientele. Then, we went to play in a game park and there we played purely African music. We stayed there for three months. Then we went to a posh club in Tokyo. We played classics, Nat King Cole, Elvis, etc." By being forced to entertain audiences with international hits in multiple genres, the band developed a talent for cover songs by Elton John, Ricky Martin, and Brenda Fassey, while also composing their own material. They cultivated skills in getting audiences to dance and enjoy themselves in a variety of settings. Creativity for the group came in tailoring their music to fit different audiences and contexts.

Kilimanjaro Band's original compositions draw on many genres of music in order to establish a cosmopolitan sensibility to their performances and recordings. In the song "Kinyau-Nyau," which is a style of dance associated with the band, the percussion draws from a traditional ngoma; the keyboards and vocals provide taarab aesthetics; the timbre of the bass line, as well as its harmonic movement, suggest a combination of r&b and reggae; and, in the second half of the song, the bands breaks into a pseudo-sebene, characteristic of Congolese rumba. The song "Tupendane" (We Must Love Each Other) is rather reminiscent of the music by the Cape Verdean singer Cesaria Evora. It includes synthesized violins, airy guitar arpeggios, and more formulaic bass lines than other songs by the band. "Busara" (Wisdom) is an apparent tribute to salsa but with vocals that sound a bit like Jim Croce. "Ndembele," which is a lullaby of the Wanyamwezi people, combines traditional ngoma, highlife music from West Africa, and the sound of the *likembe*. The ability of the band to draw on so many influences in their music is a testament to their talent in using sound to construct sonic spaces that appeal to the interests of more affluent members of society well versed in the music and issues occurring inside and outside Tanzania.

In Tanzania, it is often difficult to perform styles of music that do not approximate or fit closely within defined parameters of musical aesthetics. John Mhutu from the group Tatunane says, "Here there is a lot of pressure to play music only within a specific style. You will find groups that want to play different styles but they know that they are paid a salary to play a specific style of music. Groups have to continue to play the same style of music or they will have more problems." Kilimanjaro Band's ability to remain popular even though they escape any easy categorization is due, in part, to their ability to combine musical aesthetics and performance routines that accommodate the interests of a particular population. There is an expressed effort within the band to not follow the patterns of other groups, but to use sounds from national and international popular music as colors that they can mix and merge into new artistic forms. The difficulty comes in selecting the right colors that appeal to local audiences while remaining connected to their cosmopolitan sensibility.

In addition to band compositions, Kilimanjaro Band uses concert performances as a means to foster relationships with the audience. Through direct forms of engagement, such as the use of dance routines, call and response, and other techniques during shows, audiences gain a sensibility of being indoctrinated into the band's inner circle. Watching the band's shows, audiences form circles or lines or dance on their own at specific times during the performance. Waziri Ally's well-known expression "hello, hello" is always met with enthusiastic responses of the same. This interaction with the audience is more than just having a few hit songs to which people want to dance and respond. It is a means of drawing on the audience's energy and interest in being part of some larger event, of dancing and celebrating with a common cause. It may be a similar sensation that many people attain when they are part of a large crowd doing the electric slide at a wedding. Familiarity with dance and song makes people feel included and part of a larger community. Few other bands in Tanzania create a specific language of dance that is performed by both audiences and performers with such regularity.

The band then uses these live forms of engagement within their offstage marketing. In their music videos, they incorporate footage from concerts and use dance routines from their shows. Sound recordings include many of the verbal banter heard during shows, such as "hello, hello." These indirect forms of engagement build relationships between the band and the audience, helping to market the group to people unfamiliar with the songs (to see Kilimanjaro Band dance routines and the popularity of the band's songs, see PURL 3.7). Kilimanjaro Band's creativity emerges in making people want to be a part of their shows, to be included in the dance and song. Part of this inclusion derives from the band's ability to create an air of sophistication through their place of performance (upscale hotels), their song choices (international and local hits), and their dress (often evening gowns and sometimes suits). There is also an air of secrecy at the clubs (I often met men with their mistresses at Kilimanjaro's shows), and the ability for the upper class to network, show off their wealth, and make themselves visible to a broader public. Creative practices became the means with which the band markets their identity to a more affluent clientele that would enjoy the cosmopolitan approach of the group.

While the examples of Remmy Ongala and Kilimanjaro Band represent established groups in the country, younger artists employ alternative symbols and meanings to form distinguishable identities for themselves. For younger artists, particularly in bongo flava, marketing an image is far more challenging given the profusion of people competing for airtime, performance space, and ultimately people's attention. Artists use a variety of strategies, including creating unusual names, controversial songs, or sensational performance routines that become celebrated in the music community. Dropping down from the rafters into a performance space or emerging from a coffin onstage are examples that have been used in Dar es Salaam performances in the past few years.

One of the more successful strategies used by young artists is to form camps. A camp is a community of artists who share similar worldviews, musical aspirations, and class connections. Two popular camps in Dar es Salaam are East Coast Team, which features many youth who have a hangout in the fairly wealthy Upanga neighborhood, and Wanaume, a group of around fifty youth who gather near a bus stop in Temeke, one of the poorest sections of the city.[10] Both camps establish and foster specific relationships with the communities around them. They gather each day to discuss life, current events, jobs, and music; they also establish their own codes, symbols, and ideologies unique from the other. Wanaume, for instance, creates original dress, such as TMK (Temeke) T-shirts and armbands, and coins new words and phrases, such as *cheuabeiua* (cough up the money). The group uses the axe as its symbol and members make a hand gesture—essentially two fists together with the index fingers crossed into an "X"—to represent the axe and their camp. Modeling themselves after the military, they shout "eh" in unison when one of the group members bellows "Wanaume." East Coast Team uses

East Coast Team (ECT) graffiti near their hangout in Upanga, Dar es Salaam. The GK between the letters "C" and "T" is for the artist King Crazy GK. *Photo by author.*

spray paint around their "home base" to identify key ideas and images associated with the camp, such as the letters ECT (East Coast Team), a marijuana leaf, and various expressions, such as "sela! one." The group also has "East Coast Team" T-shirts, as well as hats that feature the name of one of their friends, Tippo.

Each of the camps offers a means for artists to quickly and easily establish an identity for themselves. An artist who carries the Wanaume or ECT moniker benefits from the support of other people in the camp who help him record an album, establish a performance routine, and refine compositions. The camp name carries weight in the music economy, making it easier for an artist to get into a good studio. One of the camps even operates a cooperative where funds from concerts are pooled together: any time a problem arises for one of the camp members, the money can be used to help him. Fans become intimately involved in camp identities. They attend shows knowing that artists from their camp will perform;

AY, a member of the East Coast Team (ECT), sitting in his car near the ECT home base. *Photo by author.*

they bring banners and signs announcing their support for a particular group; and they call radio stations to request songs from the camp. This builds a sense of community where performing by both artists and fans' provides a sense of power, strength, and popularity. At concerts, for instance, a camp that has a throng of fans waving banners and cheering attains far more recognition than a group that performs to an unenthused crowd (PURL 3.8). Building interest in camps through identity marketing is central to fostering strong ties with fans interested in being part of significant cultural and musical movements.

The examples of identity marketing presented in this section highlight the diversity of creative practices used to commodify music in Tanzania's economy. Market economies construct strong desires for consumption

Members of Wanaume in a performance at the East-West Hip Hop Show at Diamond Jubilee Hall in Dar es Salaam. The synchronized raised feet are one of the camp's signature dances called mapanga dance. The show took place on June 14, 2005, and was (obviously) sponsored by Coca-Cola. On the left are the musicians KR (Rashid Ziada) and Juma Nature. *Photo by author.*

that become reflected in artists and fans presentations of themselves. Artists create symbols, language, dress, bands, and songs to establish meaning and desire in the commodification of music and identity. Consumers not only respond to artists' identities; they also shape and determine which artists become more successful, powerful, and socially relevant. There is a socialization to the economy as people develop an understanding about the identities of artists that aids in the construction of personhood and status (Prestholdt 2008: 35). Considering the increasing attention paid to music in Tanzania—through the proliferation of tabloids, radio, and album distributors—more consumers are using their ability to attend concerts and buy albums as a means to identify a "coherent definition of the self" (Gell 1986: 113). In these situations, music is more than entertainment. It is a social experience used to connect people within marketable and consumable characteristics of themselves.

Performers working in the local music economy have become increasingly aware of the heightened interest in music as a marker of identity, status, and power. There is competition in attracting fans and in outperforming other artists. Artists need to perform and compose quality songs to attract audiences away from other performers. To foster belonging, they need to construct a sense of self with which fans want to participate and engage. Music critics may lament the success of mediocre performers over talented ones. Frequently, however, second-rate musicians rise above their mediocrity through presenting a marketable image that attracts fans. They connect their interests to that of their audience in a dialogue of identity motives, desires, and consumption that moves music from being a form of direct engagement to one of cultural distinctiveness in everyday life. Through developing a commodified identity, they manage to control their most valuable resource: themselves (Bunten 2008: 390).

## CELEBRITY AND THE TABLOIDS

In his article, "The Church of the Cult of the Individual," Eric W. Rothenbuhler uses the work of Durkheim and Goffman to argue that modern life is built around religion of the individual. He writes that as industrial societies move more toward service industries, our social worlds revolve around the individual consumer where the media functions to produce saints, heroes, devils, and ghosts. The way we communicate, educate ourselves, and conceive of politics, churches, and other cultural institutions becomes more like communication industries devoted to the "construction, display, critique, and improvement of selves" (2005: 99). Perhaps Rothenbuhler's most intriguing proposition is one that builds on Durkheim's notion that the cult of the individual is the only value system that can unite a modern society. Modern societies need to be fascinated with the individual to achieve social order, and the celebrity system highlights the importance and order of that society: "The celebrity system would be drawing the attention of the masses to instances and instructions for the operation of the values that work in the present order" (2005: 95). Thus, celebrity is an important expression of social values, and a sign of that society's view of itself (Berger 1971: 133).

Although Rothenbuhler's arguments focus too much on notions of consumption, Christianity, and individualism to directly correlate to the Tanzanian music economy, there is a strong parallel between notions of celebrity that he describes and ones that exist in Dar es Salaam. Neoliberalization has ushered in a far stronger focus on consumer interests, creating industries that cater to individual desires, wants, and needs even as other ideologies remain influential in everyday life. In this focus on individual consumption and a corresponding reliance on Western forms of media, there is a fascination with celebrity, particularly toward African American artists. Celebrities and becoming wealthy are alluring because they emphasize the fantasy of what is possible (Weiss 2009). Throughout urban areas of Tanzania, one can easily see the fascination with foreign celebrities, particularly rappers such as Tupac, Nas, and Jay Z, in numerous hand-painted signs, billboards, shirts, and murals. There has even been discussion among Tanzanian youth that Tupac Shakur and other deceased American rappers are still alive, which builds on Rothenbuhler's notion of the cult of the individual in posthumous celebrity (2005: 97). When foreign stars travel to Tanzania, as many have done over the past decade, they are greeted at the airport, followed by the press, and met with such adoration that even the most esteemed dignitary would be envious. There is certainly a cult of the individual emerging in Tanzanian society, particularly among youth, even though notions of community, familial responsibility, and nationalism continue to play a significant role in people's interactions with each other.

For Tanzanians working in the music economy, celebrity is less all-consuming than in other parts of the world. Most stars are able to walk freely in cities and towns, unencumbered by the press or adoring fans. Though people greet and talk to them, there is a tendency to leave well-known people alone when they are doing everyday tasks, such as riding the bus, buying goods in the market, or attending a religious institution. Nonetheless, fame certainly impacts the lives of these individuals, particularly through media coverage. In a song about the premature announcement of Ndala Kasheba's death, Kasheba sings, "Nimeshazoea / Imekuwa ni kawaida kukicha kusikia / Wana maarufu wana matatizo, eeh / Dunia [ni] maajabu (I am already used to this / It has become common to hear these things daily / Famous people have problems, eeh / The world is strange") (PURL 3.9 and PURL 3.10).

Newspapers and media journalists are important in supporting artist's careers, and musicians willingly talk to journalists about their music, careers, album launches, and other information. Journalists also attend shows and can enter for free with their press badges. Artists frequently remember the first time they appeared in the newspaper. Mkoloni (Frederick Mariki), who along with Dr. John (John Simba) performs in the group Wagosi Wa Kaya, reminisced: "A journalist interviewed me, and then our discussion appeared in the paper with a picture. It was the first time I picked up a newspaper and saw John and myself in a picture [laughs]. 'Ah, here is a newspaper and there I am!' [laughs again]." The journalist became his wife, which also made the story memorable. Since music journalists make very little money in Tanzania, most leave the occupation after only a few years. This forces artists to work harder to attract the attention of newer, inexperienced music critics.

An alternative to music journalists are tabloid writers. Gossip is a fundamental part of establishing celebrity in Tanzania, and the most important originators of gossip are tabloids. Local tabloids are notoriously aggressive originators of hearsay, rumors, and scandals about musicians, radio announcers, and other members of the local music economy. They have prematurely announced the deaths of artists; forced artists to leave bands due to the presentation of fictitious scandals; and caused once-friendly band members to stop speaking to each other. As the Warioba Report on corruption in Tanzania, prepared by Judge Joseph Warioba, stated, "Reporters accept bribes in order to publish or bury information which glorifies or destroys the reputation of certain persons or institutions" (Kilimwiko 2000: 3). Although other areas of Tanzanian society help create and destroy the popularity of an individual, tabloids are influential in impacting the status of people in society.

In Tanzania, the most popular tabloid, *Uwazi*, sells around 150,000 copies for each weekly issue, which is five times higher than the sale of a more typical newspaper.[11] The sale of tabloids does not reveal, however, the number of people who actually read them. Passed from neighbor to neighbor and from town to town, a single issue can fall into the hands of dozens of people before it is tossed out. Aside from radio broadcasters, tabloids have become one of the most vital forms of news about music and musicians in Tanzania. The stories and news bites gathered by these papers tend to come from a variety of sources and are sometimes interesting and accurate. But many times, tabloid articles stretch facts and details to present skewed but sensational stories. They sell papers through creating heroes and villains, an important part of the celebrity system, which helps establish the notion of value through the actions of famous individuals.

One of the more popular musicians within the contemporary dance band music scene is Ally Chocky. As a singer, Chocky has been a part of several highly successful bands, such as African Stars, Double M Sound, Extra Bongo Group, and Double Extra. Due to his popularity, most people are familiar with his name and the tabloids exploit this to tell stories about his life, success, and music. For a time, many newspapers printed his picture on the cover to sell newspapers even though the headlines about him appeared nearly insignificant. His fame and the potential for news about him was enough to sell newspapers. Eventually, stories appeared about Chocky that began to question his status as a celebrity. In commenting on the tabloids, Chocky states:

> It is a big problem here. When a person becomes well known, many things happen. You can be startled to wake up in the morning and find something strange is written in the paper. For instance, right now for me, these papers are basing a lot of news on my family. They use money to get my father to say things that will hurt my name. You see? So, now I find out that there are people who hate me [because of the tabloid news].
>
> Many times, if a journalist does not like you, he will come after you and try to ruin your name, without a reason. Their job is to ruin your career, so that you look bad. In Europe and America there are these papers too—they write about R. Kelly and Bill Clinton, you see? But, there you find things that are checked and found to be true. Here, it is different.

The news story about his family claimed that Chocky did not help his father financially, which created outrage in Dar es Salaam. Many people believed what they read, including quotations attributed to Chocky's father. Despite the singer's protests of innocence, public opinion turned strongly against him.[12] There is a deep social expectation of filial responsibility toward family in Africa: even when an individual has little to offer, society dictates that he must help his family. The responsibility is even greater when a person has achieved success, as in Chocky's case. Although it came out later that the tabloid article was misleading and that the quotations purportedly from his father were of dubious accuracy, Chocky still had to deal with his tarnished reputation. As a commentary on the controversy, he subsequently composed the song "Umbea Hauna Posho" (There Is No Benefit in Gossip).[13]

As he noted, there is a significant difference between tabloids in the United States and Europe and those in Tanzania: fact checking. In the United States, stars are hounded, followed, and harassed and eventually stories emerge about something that they did. These stories are often based on misinterpretation of events or the presentation of material out of context to make a star look good or bad. While several tabloids fabricate information completely, many other celebrity magazines do check stories, issue corrections, call interviewees to assure that they are properly quoted, and conduct other formal journalistic practices. These journalistic practices occur in Tanzanian as well, but the highly competitive environment of newspapers, combined with the impracticality of fact-checking stories, makes accuracy in the press more unpredictable than in the United States or Europe. A writer for the magazine the *Tanzanian Journalist* noted that newspapers are often replete with, "plagiarism, junkets, deception, kowtowing to advertisers and politicians, or rich individuals, carelessness, checkbook journalism, blackmail, intellectual theft, vendetta journalism, outright bias, character assassination and defamation" (Kilimwiko 2000: 3). Even more, there are many journalists who can gain prestige through inventing stories or subverting a celebrity's notoriety in their journalism.

Since nobody sues newspapers for maliciousness or deceptive journalism, only certain institutions, such as the Tanzania Editors Forum, Media Owners Association of Tanzania, Media Council of Tanzania, and Tanzania Media Women Association, have any ability to control or inhibit the practices of local newspapers. Local journalism schools also often work with students on ethical forms of journalism. These local institutions produce an extensive network of dedicated and conscientious writers. Still, nothing prevents a journalist from publishing a defamatory or fabricated story if an editor is willing to publish it. The only entity that can officially close a newspaper due to its publishing practices is the Minister of Information, Sports, and Culture under the 1976 Newspaper Act, which has closed two newspapers in recent years, *Kiu* and *Tanzania Daima,* for publishing nude pictures.[14] Several newspapers, such as *Uwazi* and *Risasi,* and several television stations did the same thing and were either temporarily suspended or given a warning. More recently, on October 14, 2008, the newspaper *Mwanahalisi* had its license suspended for three months for "inciting public hatred" against President Kikwete. No newspaper has ever been shut down for falsifying stories about local celebrities.[15]

In order to deal with the potential problems posed by journalists, Tanzanian musicians use a variety of strategies to remain popular rather than vilified in the press. These creative practices become a compulsory means of attaining admiration, fame, and prestige, and of maintaining focus on one's talent rather than on one's vices and problems, whether real or imagined. In particular, there are four strategies that many well-known figures employ to establish or maintain positive reputations.

The first may be referred to as producing press. Most highly regarded individuals are well aware of the ways that their actions or inactions are documented by journalists. One only has to have an off-the-record comment printed once to be aware of the dangers of speaking openly to a reporter. Using this knowledge, many individuals attempt to stage events, draw journalistic attention to something specific, or shape an interview with a journalist in order to produce a good news story. Here, the artist attempts to preempt any negative stories with more positive, prestigious news. For instance, in 2005, during a concert for the release of a new album by African Stars, Ally Chocky rode into the concert hall on a horse. Horses are rarely if ever seen in Tanzania, and the strategy was effective in drawing the entire audience's attention to Chocky and forcing journalists to write about the event in the next day's paper. Few journalists even addressed the music at the concert and no one covered any negative press about the band or Chocky. All the local newspapers were content to focus on the horse and Chocky, thereby creating praise for him for his ability to entertain an audience and ride an exotic animal.

The strategy of producing an event worthy of the press keeps artists in more control of the stories that emerge for public consumption. It is for this reason that many celebrities in the United States, Europe, and elsewhere have publicists who help maintain positive news stories and control negative ones. Since publicists do not exist in Tanzania, the burden falls on the artists themselves or the band owners to create and maintain positive news.

A second strategy used by artists to control their celebrity in the press is disparagement. Although journalists certainly fabricate narratives for their own gain, artists also provide gossip about other celebrities. By criticizing or condemning the actions of another person, an individual asserts his or her own superiority, and signals a conflict with the recipient of the disparagement. For instance, several bands constantly compete against one another for public attention and approval of their popularity. One of the strategies that these bands use is to criticize members of the other group in concert performances or during interviews with journalists. This public denouncement is often successful at getting people interested in a heated conflict between two individuals or two bands, even if the actual conflict is a public façade meant more to draw attention to both groups rather than offer legitimate criticism or gossip.

(3) The third strategy is diversionary tactics where the artist will precipitate questions about a sensitive topic from a journalist by bringing up other issues. This is a common practice not just in instances of fame, but in many areas of daily life when someone wants to avoid direct criticism or prevent an unwanted conflict. William Goode, for instance, writes about the use of diversionary tactics, as when a boss scolds an employee to forestall some complaint against him or her, or one spouse questions the other's behavior to stop his or her probing (1978: 289). These tactics divert attention from the self and avoid serious inquiry into an issue by placing the burden on someone else. In Tanzania's music scene, well-known musicians use this strategy to avoid direct questioning about topics that they want to keep out of the press, such as use of drugs, bribery, or specific information in contracts.

(4) A fourth strategy used by artists to promote their celebrity status is helping journalists by allowing them to enter shows free, giving them leads on good stories, and inviting them to hang out at special events. By granting certain privileges, artists subtly coerce journalists to writing favorable or positive news stories. Journalists are less likely to dig for a sensational news story if they feel some bond or closeness with the musician. At concerts by many popular bands in Dar es Salaam, there is often a section set aside backstage with beverages for popular music critics.

Although the focus of this section has been on print media, the internet plays an increasingly important role in promoting individual celebrity to a national and international community of Tanzanians interested in the stars of their country. The website Bongo Celebrity, for instance, launched in 2007, is dedicated to covering the lives of famous Tanzanians. The mission statement to the website reads:

> Whether we like it or not, the public is very interested in celebrities. Politicians, musicians, soccer players, comedians, actors, radio announcers, traditional or modern artists, famous announcers of television and radio, unusual

looking people, ambassadors, etc., all of them together have something enticing among the public that cannot be left alone. If we hear their news many
times we want to know more. It is said that society without distinguished,
famous people is like one that does not exist. It does not mean that we don't
have something more important to do, certainly not. It is only natural part
of being humans. More to the point, the public is able to gain a lot by learning about the lives and activities of celebrities.[16]

In Tanzania, celebrity has yet to be reduced to public attention where any
activity by any person is enough to generate a news story (Braudy 2000).
Still, celebrity is becoming a central concern for many youth who work
and live in the music economy. Particularly in urban areas where centralized community groups give way to a more expansive way of assessing
daily life, celebrities often provide a clear and public presentation of the
things that are considered moral and immoral, valued and devalued, successful and unsuccessful.

The strategies discussed in this section are new to the neoliberal period. Being well known has long been a part of the popular music scene
in Tanzania, whereas being famous has become a contemporary response
to growing media attention and public fascination with the individual.
Tanzania does not experience the same level of media focus on celebrity
as other parts of the world, but there is a growing interest in people's
lives. Since performers, along with models, radio broadcasters, and politicians, are prominent public figures, they tend to receive the most media
attention. In addition, an artist's life is always being performed in public,
which makes their mistakes or errors public events as well. Well-known
businessmen, academics, and judges do not encounter the same criticism
since they do not perform in public as frequently or conduct themselves in
ways that are easily recognizable in everyday life. Given the importance
of fame and popularity, artists must continually perform their roles as
well-known individuals whose daily activities can be, at any moment,
pulled in front of the public for everyone to see.

## WOMEN IN PERFORMANCE

In published literature on Tanzanian music, many researchers, including
myself, rely heavily on male voices to analyze local genres of music. This
approach would appear to make sense as men occupy most forms of em-

ployment in Tanzania's music economy. All the major music distributors, bar owners, music producers, and people who deal with copyright law are male. They work in a majority of positions in radio, television, and promotion. With the exception of singers and live music dancers, men dominate the music scene. To rely on male voices would therefore appear to provide a useful assessment of the music economy given the sexual divisions that statistically appear to exist in Tanzanian society.

My conception of gender, however, shifted after a series of interviews with young and well-educated women who dismissed many of my notions of male dominance in the music scene. These women offered an alternative conception of gender and music that helped me to see performance as a highly flexible medium of expression that carries few consistent traditions. Popular music is meant to be emergent, allowing new ideas to permeate into the composition and performance of songs. In this continually unfolding enterprise, many women find opportunities even when those opportunities did not exist in the past. According to several women, restrictions do not exist within the Tanzanian music economy; they only exist in the limitations one places on oneself. Luizer Mbutu, a well-known dansi singer, was one of the first people to make this point: "The women themselves often put themselves behind. They think that, 'Ah, I am a woman by myself, what can I do?' What has gotten into their minds is a lie that if there is a group of men gathered, they cannot participate. Something that is not true." For Mbutu and many other women, the only hindrance placed on women's ability to work and find success in the music economy is social apprehension of a male-dominated business. In other words, lack of confidence can be more all-consuming for female performers than any overt culturally defined social roles. From this point of view, male dominance is a manifestation of women's own inability to assert themselves in social situations.

Other individuals contest the idea that the limited opportunities available to women are in fact due to their own inhibitions. Stereotypes about women's inabilities to perform certain tasks or work in certain areas are often used as justifications for gender segregations (Clark 1994: 285). Social customs often inhibit women from taking on tasks deemed as male, such as handling band finances, and giving up roles deemed as female, such as helping feed the other performers during band practices. These socially created conceptions of gender create barriers for women that make it difficult for them to perform roles outside the socially defined categories of labor. It is rare for women to enter into occupations, roles, or activities defined as men's work and vice versa (Bujra 2000: 73).

In Tanzanian popular music, many areas are defined as being geared toward one sex or the other. These areas are permeable yet often reinforced categories for acceptable occupations and positions within the Tanzanian music economy. For instance, playing musical instruments is a position typically performed by men. With the exception of a handful of artists, such as Taji Mbaraka and Carola Kinasha, women do not play guitar, bass, drums, or keyboard. In traditional music, it is common for women to play instruments, as well as sing and dance. These women perform in a variety of contexts but tend to be pushed to the periphery of the Tanzanian music economy. For those few artists who do play instruments in popular music, people frequently comment that it is *ajabu* (strange) to see a female play an instrument such as an electric guitar or a drum kit. Interestingly, more acceptance for female instrumentalists may have existed in the past. During the 1960s, there was an all-female band called the TANU Youth League Women's Band, which formed in 1964, with women playing electric guitars, bass, and drums.[17] Currently, however, female artists who want to learn an instrument often struggle to convince anyone to teach them. By reinforcing the notion that women cannot learn to play an instrument, a barrier is erected that is reinforced with strong associations of male and female roles within popular music.

Aside from being a musician, stage performance in nightclubs, particularly with dansi, is often regarded as an activity for men. Several young female performers told me about parents who restricted their choices in finding jobs in music either due to the gendered nature of the work (all producers are male, ergo women cannot work as producers) or due to people's negative interpretations of women who go out at night to perform music. Generally, women who perform live music, with the exception of taarab and gospel singers, are considered to be more meretricious than other women who work at nightclubs, such as bartenders and waitresses. The association between a form of stage performance and overt sexuality certainly derives from the highly provocative dances that some women perform at live shows. It also emerges from the constant circulation of prostitutes who frequent some of the city's clubs. At California Dreamer, for instance, in downtown Dar es Salaam, female sex workers move freely through the club, and the club itself becomes a sort of stage for their performance and interaction with clients.

The association between the stage and sexuality is also reflected in the way audiences interact with performers. A man on stage often symbolizes power and prowess as he helps move the audience to a more cathartic state after a stressful work day. Many audience members do not consider women as possessing this ability—they do not purify people's emotions or educate audiences on the best ways to overcome the difficulties of living in the city. Instead, they create moments of intense sensuality. Their presence on stage establishes a sensation of sexuality and pleasure that is tied to associations with the female body rather than to the musicality of women as performers. There are significant exceptions to this phenomenon that I address below. Repeated analysis of audience interaction with performers at shows, however, as well as conversations with individuals who comment on gender and the stage, highlights a vivid contrast between the roles that men and women perform on stage and the perception of local audiences. Thus, due to the perception that women who dance and sing in front of audiences are more lascivious, female performers are frequently inhibited, by parents and peers, from performing on stage.

The view that stage performance renders women more lascivious than men also creates inappropriate forms of attention and action. Luizer Mbutu explains:

> There are problems because when people see you [women] performing many do not understand that you are working. They often think that you are a prostitute that just goes to any secret place to be awarded. This is something that is just not true. Even though I perform, I am not a prostitute. It is something that really disgusts me. Because, when we perform, I stand here and Ally Chocky stands here [motions that they stand side by side]. If someone comes up to tip Ally Chocky, he gives him money in his hand or in his shirt pocket. But, if he comes to tip me, he wants to put the tip down her [puts her hand inside her shirt]. Why? Or, someone else wants to put money here [taps her backside], but for men, tips are put in the hand. This is one of the biggest problems.

Mbutu receives a great deal of media attention, and her fame and talent as an artist has brought her respect among many of her peers and fans. Nonetheless, there is a noticeable difference between the roles that Chocky and Mbutu occupy as popular performers. Audiences are more

Luizer Mbutu (foreground), performing with Jesca Charles during an African Stars concert in May 2001. *Photo by author.*

deferential to Chocky, tipping him obeisantly, giving him space on stage, and treating him with esteem. Many audience members are discourteous to Mbutu in their actions, gestures, and proximity to her body. There is an expectation to treat Mbutu and other women as an object of desire rather than as a serious performer.

This treatment of female performers also impacts women once they join a band. Artists who enter the music business and attempt to get jobs with bands are increasingly exploited sexually. In 2007, a headline in the newspaper *Nipashe* read, "Tatizo la rushwa ya ngono katika muziki liangaliwe upya" (The problem of sex bribery in music should be re-examined afresh). The author, Abdul Mitumba, interviewed members of the music community to ask about sexual discrimination against women. All commented on the pervasiveness of sexual harassment, particularly among women who try to enter dansi bands. The interviewees explained situations where band leaders do not allow women into dansi bands because women are thought to have nothing to contribute; where women, even those with little skill as performers, must perform sexual favors to find their way on stage; and where many women are "demoralized" in bands that have multiple members who demand sexual favors for remaining in the group. As Gasper Tumaini, the secretary of TOT, commented to Mitumba, these problems are not limited to music, but are in evidence in many business and political sectors.

Another area defined as being for men is the ownership and control of musical groups. Most band decisions, such as finances, salaries, tour dates and schedules, practice routines, and band lineup, are made by men. Many groups have meetings after band practice with just the top men to talk about a band's business matters. Even solo artists often receive guidance from male managers, radio personalities, and producers. Carola Kinasha, a musician and former leader in local musicians' unions, explains this level of control that exists in popular music:

> Most forms of music in Tanzania see women musicians as cheap, sex objects who are only in music to attract people of the opposite sex. Taarab music is the one exception and women singers flourish here, but only as singers. . . . When I first started out as a musician I was told that being a musician was "not respectable work. You cannot make a living with music." Many women begin their careers by being asked to dance somewhere and then are later asked to add backing vocals. Until men decide that women can sing, they are left to dance.

There is certainly a dominant pressure for women to avoid music as a profession. Yet even once they decide to enter into music, many women argue that it is difficult to actually perform in ways that they would like. Many women are asked to perform more traditional roles as dancers, backup singers, or "showgirls." One exception to this phenomenon is African Stars, which I have emphasized in this section, partially because it is one of the only bands controlled by a woman, Asha Baraka. Perhaps due to Baraka's influence, African Stars has always had a strong group of female singers, such as Mbutu.

This position of women also moves off stage. In many band practices, women, including singers and dancers, are responsible for cooking and cleaning up all the food served to the band. Even if a singer does not cook the meal, she often has to wait for her male counterpart to eat before she can. Financial and general band decisions are typically left to the men in a group, and salaries reflect this division of labor and responsibility. After music responsibilities are finished, most male members are able to move through town conducting their other business. Women are left with little leisure time due to commitments toward home and family. Even dansi song lyrics encourage the maintenance of gendered social roles, and warn women "against questioning woman's present status in society" (Mekacha 1992: 113; see also Beck 1992).

Thus far, the discussion of divisions in musical performance has focused mainly on dansi music, the most popular form of live entertainment, and associated genres, such as soukous, mchiriku, and even rap groups. Taarab music offers an alternative vision of women on stage, though in recent years there has been a movement toward seeing taarab singers in a similar vein as those explained above. Most taarab bands feature female singers, and most of the attention, on stage and in the press, is paid to these singers. Khadija Kopa, for instance, is regularly featured in newspaper articles and her songs are widely played on the radio. Her wedding on August 27, 2008, became a national sensation appearing in almost every local paper and on the news. There are also many male taarab performers, but few receive the same notoriety as their female counterparts. Nevertheless, most females in taarab do little else than compose and sing in their groups. They typically do not play instruments, partake in a band's financial discussions, or advise a band on where to play. While singers do have power within a group and on the stage, many artists argue that power is often given to the singers by men who agree to allow them to perform.

In the opening to this section, I argued that many women challenge the notion of a patriarchal music business, and yet the examples presented thus far only confirm commonly held conceptions of male dominance in music. Despite the many obstacles encountered in the Tanzanian music economy, many women use popular music as a means to undermine and challenge gender conceptions that exist in society.

Mbutu's point that "what has gotten into [women's] minds is a lie" emphasizes that through innovative approaches to the arts, women can encourage cultural transformations of gender roles and interpersonal relationships. Mbutu and others draw attention to culture that is not bounded, static, or traditional but is flexible, dynamic, and continually subject to change. The obstacles discussed above prove challenging to many but are not absolute or permanent. They can be altered or undermined to provide opportunities where few existed before. The only hindrance, according to Mbutu and others, is in the restrictions that people place on themselves.

A great deal of the conflict over gender roles comes from interpretations of male and female identities in society. Khadija Kopa's appearance on a billboard advertising Foma laundry soap, for instance, can be thought of as a reification of gender roles in Tanzanian society since it emphasizes the role of women as homemakers. The caption to the billboard, which states that laundry soap is a woman's pleasure, only supports the notion of a bounded conception of women in society. The advertisement, however, also displays the commercial potential of Kopa's image and her power as an influential woman in society. It presents someone with business savvy and financial opportunities that garners respect among urban Tanzanians. Seeing the large image of Kopa plastered all over Dar es Salaam can be read as a demonstration of the economic and political potential of a woman asserting her rights to benefit from her popularity. The billboard can be both a means to maintain the bounded roles of women in society or a way to present a dynamic image of their commercial and political potential.

Some of the most interesting ethnographic examples of gender contestation have emerged from female performers in calypso music in Trinidad where several performers, such as Calypso Rose and Alison Hinds, use music as a means to counter sexual discrimination and segregation from the music scene through a combination of acceptance and manipulation of cultural practices (Dikobe 2003; Guilbault 2007; Niranjana 2006; Springer 2008). In Tanzania, a similar group of women also work within the parameters of the local music economy while attempting to alter perceptions of women. Stara Thomas, for instance, is a popular singer, a UNICEF advocate, and a widely respected figure in the local

An advertisement in downtown Dar es Salaam for Foma Gold detergent featuring the image of the taarab singer Khadija Kopa. The slogan for the detergent is "A Woman's Pleasure." *Photo by author.*

music scene. Her work with UNICEF has focused on maternal health, particularly on the importance of assisting pregnant women during birth, which she sings about in the song "Play Your Part." Her popularity has led to performances in front of political dignitaries, the use of her image in advertising campaigns, and a steady stream of positive press. In short, her campaign for woman's rights provides a means to communicate with audiences during performances and indirectly engage a broader public through identity marketing that positions her as a well-informed and established member of Tanzanian society.

In addition, through performing certain notions of being female, such as singing about maternal health, Thomas manages to maintain elements of female identity while subverting customary expectations of women within the music economy. She has gained fame and respect among a broad community of Tanzanians who see her as an individual who can create changes to social customs and public policies. If the essence of gender is something that is performed through a "sustained series of acts" (Butler 1990: xv), then the ability to slowly alter or subvert those acts becomes a central strategy toward changing perceptions. Thomas's ability to use direct and indirect engagement to push against the notion that female performers are merely sexual objects allows for a competing narrative to emerge about the place and role of women in popular music.

Another strategy used by women in the music business is to perform foreign genres of music. R&B, for instance, is a popular genre dominated by female performers, such as Lady Jay Dee (Judith Wambura), K-Lyinn (Jacqueline Kanyana Ntuyabaliwe), Ray C (Rehema Chalamila), and Renee (Irene Lwelamira). Tanzanian fashion magazines routinely feature these singers, and they appear on television and radio stations and at major events in Dar es Salaam. These performers imitate the dress, styles, dances, and persona of American r&b singers who appear to be powerful, well-dressed individuals who entertain large audiences and receive celebrity media attention. Through embodying this genre in a local setting, Tanzanian artists follow the popularity of foreign acts and redefine their place within the local music economy without appearing to subvert any dominant gender roles. Rather, these women highlight the flexibility of gender roles when alternative frameworks, such as new musical genres, exist (Oyegoke 1994). Even in sub-genres, such as the muziki wa injili (gospel music), women find more opportunities as composers and group leaders than in more established musical forms, such as kwaya (Sanga 2007). Tanzanian artists are able to draw on alternative notions of gender that circulate globally through adopting the characteristics of popular, foreign artists familiar to local audiences.

A third strategy used in the Tanzanian music economy is what Jeroen de Kloet (2001) refers to as a "denial of gender." Rather than focus on gender roles in performance, there is an increasing attempt to draw attention to musical aesthetics or alternative notions of meaning in music. This strategy is most effective in genres that can move the focus of music away from direct notions of physical sensuality. One of the clearest examples of this is muziki wa injili (gospel music). In videos and live performances, artists dress in conservative outfits and use more rigid, formal dance movements. Men and women often use the same choreography, negating obvious visual differences in movement. And many popular female gospel artists have male backup singers who wear more revealing outfits, such as shorts, than they do, thereby reversing some of the expected gender identities in popular music. Combined with the dominance of women as lead singers and the spirituality of the music, popular artists find numerous areas where they can subvert or deny common notions of gender.

One example of the denying of gender is the music of the gospel singer Rose Muhando. Muhando uses many genres, such as reggae and rumba, to create gospel songs. This allows her to explore different sounds that other women might not be able to employ, given restrictions within those genres. In concerts, she typically dresses conservatively and often in all-white or all-black outfits that give her an air of being exalted and powerful. She also changes outfits and hairstyles, adding another layer of sophistication to her image. The confidence she expresses in herself and her music also subverts many of the narratives of male dominance discussed in this section. Even when she appears in moments deemed as being for women, such as shopping for food, she does so in a way that promotes notions of sophistication. In the video "Yesu Nakupenda" (Jesus I Love You), for instance, she appears in a grocery store rather than a market, with a small basket where she purchases items for herself rather than for a family at home. The idea of self-empowerment is expressed here through the notion that, as a woman, she can focus on herself and her well-being rather than being the caretaker of a family or a spouse. It is a powerful alternative image of gender roles considering the dominant narrative that exists in Tanzania of women as providers for others rather than caretakers for themselves.

One reason that I chose Muhando to illustrate the denial of gender is also to emphasize the malleability of gender roles in certain genres of popular music. Whereas "Yesu Nakupenda," illustrates Muhando's ability to subvert dominant narratives, she employs gender in other songs to draw attention to her plight as a woman. Imani Sanga (2007) analyzes the song "Nipe Uvumilivu" (Give Me Endurance) in which Muhando describes the suffering she has encountered in life due to having borne children to unfaithful men. In real life and in the song, Muhando has children without being married to the father. Sanga illustrates that this is considered a Christian sin and a cultural transgression in Tanzania, and typically forces women to become outcasts. To circumvent this offense, Muhando sings about God being a father and husband and draws attention to the cultural roles of men as owners and providers. Toward the end of the song, she implores, "Unisitiri na adui zangu / Wewe umekuwa ngome wangu/ siku zote za maisha yangu" (Protect me from my enemies / You have been my Crusader / during all the days of my life). The notion of protection by a male figure, whether husband or father, articulates cultural traditions that become embodied in Muhando's song and rearticulate the roles of men and women in society. Even while she subverts notions of gender in other songs, "Nipe Uvumilivu" presents a conflicted individual searching for protection by male figures. The gender roles in Muhando's music are useful for interpreting the variances in meaning and identity in gendered spaces and the ability of artists to continually subvert or reinforce these spaces.

(4) A fourth strategy in Tanzania's music economy is a more direct approach of confronting sexual discrimination through songs. Many artists use their songs to attack social conventions or warn people about problems that exist in the relations between men and women. One of the best-known artists for this direct and confrontational approach is the Tanzanian rapper Zay B. Zay B uses her songs to confront stereotypical conceptions of gender in Tanzanian society. Most of her songs have an educational message aimed at young girls. Here Zay B explains her song "Monica":

You know, many female students here in Tanzania leave school and then fall into bad company. They start to follow the habits of their new peers. After a time, because those students are not used to it, they begin to ruin themselves more than the ones that they followed. "Monica" is about a girl and her friends. The girl is nice and everything, but later she encounters these friends who begin to change her. Her friend begins to direct her on issues of love [sex] with men in a way like a prostitute. Now, the one who was taught by her friend becomes pregnant. After she becomes pregnant, her friend teaches her how to get rid of it. She herself helps to terminate the pregnancy. After the abortion, she wants to die and her friend gives her some drugs/ medicine. She regrets what she's done. This is the song "Monica." Many young girls die from abortions here in Tanzania. Young girls, especially students, often die.

Zay B is clear that the reason for writing this song was to educate young girls about the dangers of unprotected sex and, more important, the issues that can arise from abortion. In the interview, she repeated the issue about people regretting having terminated a pregnancy, but she was also clear in warning young girls about the dangers that having sex can have on their overall quality of life: from an unhealthy lifestyle to death. Particularly for younger women in the Tanzanian music scene, neoliberalization has brought significant changes in the ways they conceptualize daily life, relationships, and sex. For Zay B and others, music needs to be a means to educate these young girls about the dangers that can arise in urban societies. Songs became a means to educate women as well as men about the consequences of their actions.

Barriers placed on women in society are commonplace within Tanzania's music economy, but so too are the strategies used to overcome those barriers. As more opportunities emerge, women are taking part in live performance and doing so in ways that empower other women and girls to become part of a live music scene. Although men continue to dominate in most areas of the music economy, the presence of women on stage, on the radio, on television, and in other areas of the economy create powerful new ways for other women to participate in the production and circulation of music. In addition, many male artists and members of the music community encourage these changes. While I intentionally focus on women performers in this section, numerous men also push against traditional gender roles in society even though others work to reinforce them. Considering that only a handful of women performed as singers in major bands in Tanzania during the 1980s, the several hundred that call themselves performers now is a measure of success in rearticulating the role of women as musicians in the contemporary music scene.

## ENCORE

Direct and indirect forms of engagement create an important framework for examining the role of performers in Tanzanian popular music. Both forms require artists to use strategies that can benefit their interactions with audiences inside and outside clubs and social halls. Failure to appreciate one or the other frequently results in an artist being unable to make it within the local music economy. This is common in popular music generally as there is often a high turnover in repertoire and as well as musicians who perform that music. The difference is that the safety nets that exist for artists elsewhere are absent in Tanzania. Few opportunities exist for musicians outside of stage performance. There are a limited number of teaching jobs or opportunities to tutor upcoming artists for financial gain. There are almost no music shops looking to hire knowledgeable and skilled professionals. The parallel economy that exists to support performers in several other parts of the world does not exist in Tanzania. If artists fail as performers, they routinely have to find other forms of employment. Furthermore, royalties are not lucrative even for highly prolific and popular composers.

The lack of support outside of state-sponsored groups can act as a deterrent for many people interested in music. Yet given the potential for financial and social success, people's interests in music have undergone significant transformations. Part of the change involves an imagined potential of performance as a career that can bring wealth, fame, and opportunities that tend not to exist elsewhere in the country. People become seduced by the "promise of compelling forms of identification and affiliation, which are facilitated by the presence of commodities and electronically disseminated images" (Weiss 2004: 8). Though not discussed in this ethnography, the presence of foreign and local music videos creates desires for wealth, power, and fame as visualized through images of performers. In videos, artists appear successful, content, and surrounded by consumer pleasure often unattainable to the average Tanzanian. This creates an immediate draw to the images on the screen, which become

reinforced in stage performance where popular artists perform to adoring fans.

The incorporation of a marketable identity and consumable forms
of celebrity are important in Tanzanian popular music. This works to reinforce the fantasy of success found in popular music even if that success
hides the failure of many others who came before. It is common for people
to become consumed by the idea that popular music can offer a means to
escape many of the circumstances that they encounter on a daily basis.
This pushes people to try careers as performers or find other areas of employment related to music. Before individuals consumed by the images
of success can become performers, however, they need to learn music, a
task that immediately complicates any ambitions that they may have.

# FOUR

# The Submerged Body

People think carefully,
Put more effort in your work.
Progress comes from your diligence,
Do not tire of learning,
Education has no end.

—DDC MLIMANI PARK ORCHESTRA "Historia ya kweli ya Mwanadamu"
(The True History of Human Beings)

The performance of music is only one part of being a musician. As Johannes Fabian discusses in his book *Power and Performance,* performance is just the visible tip; there is also the submerged body of rehearsal and repetition (1990: 12). To this I would add that musical learning, joining a group and remaining in it (repositioning), and high-risk promotion are other critical dimensions to being a performer. For Tanzanians, the road to arriving and remaining at the visible tip is not always clear or well lit. With only rudimentary formal music education in the country, most upcoming artists rely on the advice and teachings of other artists. Lacking instruments, they borrow from other musicians, make their own, or become singers. Dancers watch television and attend concerts to learn dance moves and routines, but often they do not receive one-on-one instruction until they join a group. Once these artists are established, they work to join successful groups and create a name for themselves within the local music community. The entire process, from musical learning to rehearsal to performance, is for many artists a test in self-learning. Arriving on stage as a performer signifies a person's long struggle in overcoming economic and social hurdles in musical development.

The submerged body of performance also includes numerous other individuals who help create the social life of performance. Many band owners in taarab and dansi music control the instruments, salaries, and resources for each musician. They can often determine when a band performs, how many days off the musicians receive each month, and sometimes decide the content of many compositions. In some circumstances, they are even given credit for composing the lyrics and music to songs in an approach akin to work-for-hire. Due to the relative power of band owners over musicians, they can create relationships that range from caustic to affectionate. In addition to band owners, promoters are vitally important for working with solo artists, organizing festivals and album releases, and putting on special events. While there were few promoters in the past, hundreds currently work in the local music scene, mainly due to the perceived value of music as a lucrative commodity.

Central to the submerged body of a performer are forms of musical learning: learning to become a musician, to practice music, to find lucrative music contracts, and to understand the interrelationships of people in the music economy. To acquire the indirect and direct forms of engagement needed to remain a performer requires imagination and ingenuity in acquiring musical knowledge. Elements of musical learning are sustained over generations as elders in the music economy share knowledge about events, participation, and music making (Jorgensen 1997: 1). Watching established musicians perform on stage, in practice, or in local communities fosters similar engagements with music and performance in the attainment of analogous levels of success. The admiration often found among junior members for more senior performers fosters some level of continuity between generations.

As in all popular music, a desire also exists to separate from the choices, rules, and aesthetics of previous generations. There is an interest by many up-and-coming artists to become musicians because it is enjoyable, interesting, and engaging, and it does not require them to narrow their behaviors to fit any particular method or approach (Amabile 1990: 86). It provides the possibility to express musical identities that connect with people of a similar age group and disassociate with certain principles extolled by others. For artists who want a career in music, commercial considerations create constant pressures to attain proficiency, knowledge, or skills that are related to the past but also connected to contemporary music. Musical learning is about navigating these various relationships and interconnections in order to generate and sustain a career in music. The submerged body forms the basis for arriving at the performative tip. The more established the body, the more capable the performer at remaining above water regardless of the difficulties that arise.

## MUSIC EDUCATION AND LEARNING MUSIC

Many scholars who write about music make a distinction between formal and informal learning. Formal education typically refers to more structured school-based training. Informal education commonly suggests learning though observation and imitation, often in people's homes, at band practices, or in communal spaces within a neighborhood. Jean Lave correctly points out that this distinction is problematic since training that could be labeled as informal, particularly in areas where apprenticeship occurs, is actually highly structured and formalized through lessons and pedagogical goals (Lave 1982: 182). Additionally, formal music education can include unstructured relationships between teachers and students that do not involve defined lessons or drills.

To avoid the inherent problems with this terminology, I continue to use the term formal education to examine school-based study, but I use self-learning to describe musical learning that ranges from short-term lessons with an artist to playing along with records at home (Finnegan 2007: 142). Self-learning embodies the notion that artists have certain desires in becoming musicians that they fulfill through casual study with other artists, members of their family, or through determined listening to sound recordings. Artists make decisions on what to learn based on potential opportunities rather than drawing on a school-based curriculum. Since all Tanzanian artists rely on their own abilities to gain musical knowledge, self-learning is far more ubiquitous than formal education. The limited options for school-based study, however, create associations of formal education with higher status and prestige, particularly given the economic success of those who are able to attain higher levels of education. Many artists argue that formal education provides skills to succeed regionally and internationally in ways that self-learning cannot.

In examining musical leaning, I begin by looking at formal musical education that includes instruction in the use of music notation, brass instruments, and foreign genres of music, such as choral music and ballroom dancing. While apprenticeship in traditional genres, where artists study an instrument or style of music with a teacher or group of teachers, should certainly be considered a form of formal learning, Tanzanian popular musicians rarely mention this form of study. Although some musicians did arrive in Dar es Salaam after working with traditional artists, they did not talk about these interactions as something that occurred over time under the tutelage and instruction of someone with advanced expertise and musical knowledge. Their interactions were more cursory, often unplanned, and done in contexts of performance or occasional gatherings. This was not just the case with music, but also with other forms of traditional knowledge where apprenticeship appears to have lost value as people seek other ways to acquire cultural knowledge (Herrick 1968: 174). I have therefore excluded traditional forms of apprenticeship from this discussion due to the lack of evidence in Tanzania's popular music scene.

## FORMAL LEARNING

One of the earliest and most significant forms of formal music education in Tanzania was based at Christian missionary stations. Christian missionaries entered East Africa in the mid-1800s, first landing on Zanzibar, moving into the coastal regions of the country and, on one well-known occasion, to Mount Kilimanjaro.[1] As the previously unknown interior of Africa was "discovered" by explorers and word returned to Europe about the continued slave practices in East Africa, other missionary organizations, such as the Universities Mission, the London Missionary Society, and White Fathers Mission, entered the territory. These missionaries brought significant changes to East Africa. Obviously, they converted people to Christianity—as many as 92,000 by the year 1900—but they also offered free education and medicine, both of which were important in drawing interest to their religion (Barrett, Kurian, and Johnson 2001: 729).

After the First World War, education became even more central to missionary work in East Africa. With the government offering financial assistance to mission schools, missionaries were encouraged to strengthen their role in education (Hastings 1967: 82). In August 1928, Monsignor Hinsley told a gathering of bishops in Dar es Salaam, "Where it is impossible for you to carry on both the immediate task of evangelization and your educational work, neglect your churches in order to perfect your schools" (quoted in Oliver 1952: 275). Putting education before evangelization created stronger schools and enticed parents to send their children for an education that was otherwise unattainable. For the next several decades, missionary schools educated many of Tanganyika's future political and social leaders. They also trained many popular musicians. Since the majority of the children who attended these schools were male, an overwhelming number of educated political and social leaders, as well as popular musicians, were male as well.

Roman Catholics, Lutherans, and Anglicans were the dominant missionary religions in Tanzania, and each established a strong choral tradition within its churches. Missionaries taught Tanzanians both how to sing and how to teach Western choral styles, thereby allowing choral music to spread quickly throughout the country, even where missionaries had not evangelized. This choral education was based on Western music ideals, as the following excerpt of a letter written by Gertrude Ward, an English Catholic who lived in Magila, Tanzania, working as both nurse and choir director, exemplifies:

> The one satisfactory achievement is that the boys have discovered they possess an upper register, and I believe they are almost as pleased at the discovery as I am. Last time I had all the new catechumens to the practice, and, after weeding out a few, had between thirty and forty left, and then set to work at scales downwards, and obtained at last an upper G and A that they had probably never heard before, certainly never produced. (Ward 1899: 81)

Teaching choral music was as much about religious evangelization as educating people about the "correct" ways to sing. It was a tradition that continued in many missionary and religious institutions over the next sixty years.

The skills, both practical and theoretical, learned from missionary or religious schools gave artists an advantage over others who may have had only rudimentary knowledge of music composition, practice, performance, and arrangement. In interviews, artists discussed this advantage in several ways, including improved chances of being hired for better jobs or of being able to create stronger original compositions. Knowledge of Western melodies, harmonies, and forms of musical proficiency were also particularly important in this regard. Attaining this knowledge, however, did not mean an abandonment of traditional notions of music making. Nor did it mean a privileging of foreign over local traditions. Rather, through religious musical training, many artists believed that they were able to expand their understanding and formulation of musical aesthetics. This was not bimusicality in the sense of learning two musical systems. It was a means to expand the vocabularies of playing an instrument, singing, composing, or performing.

Due to the rarity of attaining religious musical education, it became a source of prestige within the musical economy. Many formally trained artists became band leaders and composers in kwaya, dansi, and ngoma. John Komba, for instance, leader of Tanzania One Theatre (TOT)—the national party's musical unit that consists of kwaya, taarab, dansi, and ngoma groups and a drama troupe—studied at a mission station in Verimoti, Songea, which is a southern region of Tanzania. "My singing began in the church when I was seven," he recalled. "The white priests there saw that I had singing talent so they started to train me; how to sing, how to compose, how to write music, and how to play a few instruments, such as the church organ." After acquiring these skills at the mission station, Komba went on to lead choirs and singing groups throughout his primary and secondary schooling, in the military, and finally, in 1992, as head of TOT. His music, particularly the choral pieces he composed after the October 1999 death of Julius Nyerere, has become well known throughout the country. Most important, Komba credits his early education at the mission station for his success in music, particularly his abilities to teach and to compose for a choir.

Another Tanzanian musician, Kanku Kelly Kashamatubajike, who is the head of the band Kilimanjaro Connection—often referred to as one of the most efficiently run bands in the country—learned to play trumpet at a missionary school in the Congo: "We had a good brass band of youth from when I was 9 until 12 years old. Though we were young, we studied notation and everything. So, the trumpet, I learned in the Congo and it was there I got the inspiration to play music [for a living]." Because of the inspiration music gave him, Kanku Kelly ended up dropping out of school by form five to become a professional musician.[2] Once out of school, his practical music education continued as he went to play for groups in the Congo (Safari Encoy) and Tanzania (Maquis Original, Safari Sound, Kilimanjaro Connection). Though Kanku Kelly cut short his official education, the knowledge he gained in music from missionaries in the Congo gave him, in his opinion, enough expertise to lead his own group and become one of the top trumpeters in Tanzania.

Younger musicians, generally those born after 1970, have had less affiliation with missionary education, but many churches continue to provide formal instruction in music. Several churches hold weekly practices where members of the community gather to learn singing techniques, four-part harmony, and sight reading in order to sing with the choir. Some institutions also have rudimentary study of piano and keyboards. Given the decline in formal music education in the country, choir directors recognize that the level of education is rudimentary. In interviews in Arusha and Dar es Salaam, Tanzania, directors state that musical education never progresses far at local churches because members of choir groups are inconsistent with participation: they come for several weeks and then do not return for several more. Perhaps more interesting is that most choir directors are young and only learned music through concerted effort at other church choirs. For many directors, they regard this as self-learning since musical knowledge is attained through sitting with more experienced choir directors rather than lesson-based study.

A second area of formal education is from musical study in the military. Many popular musicians who play saxophone, tuba, or trumpet learned to do so in military bands. This tradition dates to the King's African Rifles (K.A.R.), which was a regiment of the British military that recruited members of local ethnic groups for military service. The British trained some of these recruits in the performance of brass band music, fife and drum, and bugle music, which was used at formal military ceremonies. Some of these recruits performed ballroom dance, including waltzes, foxtrots, and quicksteps, for expatriates in Dar es Salaam clubs. Led by an Indian bandmaster, the 6th Regiment K.A.R. Band performed their first public concert at a Bachelor's Dance in Dar es Salaam on July 24, 1920, and continued to perform regularly over the next several years (Moyse-Bartlett 1956; Martin 1980: 39).[3] African members of the military also composed some of their own music. In writing about the K.A.R. in Nyasaland (Malawi), Tim Lovering writes that songs emerged among African soldiers to boost morale or deal with military hierarchy. Even though songs become well-known standards for both British and African personnel, the songs could "often project soldiers' misgivings about the experience of war or the deprivations of military service" (2002: 79–80). In Tanganyika, many of the military songs were performed with traditional ngoma creating precursors to contemporary dansi music. In 1930, some of Nyasaland K.A.R. recorded military music for Columbia records in Dar es Salaam. Along with several ngoma songs, this was the first commercial recording made in the city.

After independence, the tradition of having a brass band, drum and fife, and bugle playing as part of both the military and the national service continued. The early post-independence military was modeled on the K.A.R. and was called the Tanganyika Rifles until 1964, when it became the *Jeshi la Wananchi wa Tanzania* (Tanzania Peoples' Defense Force). During the country's socialist period, every citizen was required to fulfill two years of national service, which included some members becoming involved in the brass band performance. Once out of these forms of service, some of the former military musicians played in local popular bands, such as dansi groups, and especially in *tarumbeta* (a form of brass band music used at weddings and other types of ceremonies). This formal training has mostly disappeared, although those who are able to gain some knowledge of brass band performance are more likely to join tarumbeta groups since popular bands have replaced horn sections with keyboards.

*schools* ③ A third area of formal music education can be found in the country's schools. After independence, the Tanzanian government established public schools and trained teachers throughout the country. Other than learning the Tanzanian national anthem and a few other nationalist songs, children rarely had opportunities to study music. Even in the late 1970s and 1980s, when the government attempted to educate teachers in music by offering them syllabi and training at area colleges, such as Butimba College of Education in Mwanza, primary and secondary schoolchildren never received a substantial education in music. John Mgandu, a professor at the University of Dar es Salaam, wrote that teachers trained in music would not teach the subject because "they realized how limited their knowledge of music was" (1987: 4).

Lack of music education courses at primary and secondary schools continues today, except for the few private institutions that offer elementary courses in playing instruments or singing. Core curriculum in Tanzania is centered on Swahili, English, social studies, civics, and mathematics, and these subjects receive far more attention than music or the arts in general. In public primary school, students are expected to have between one and two periods per week dedicated to music, while public secondary school students are expected to have three (Osaki 2000). Most schools, however, fill this time with other courses or only teach students to sing patriotic songs. A few private schools, particularly in Dar es Salaam, offer more advanced forms of musical education. These schools, such as Aga Khan Primary School and Upanga Primary School in Dar es Salaam—aimed at the local Asian population and upper-class African Tanzanians—offer rudimentary skills in musical performance and provide students a chance to play the piano, guitar, drums, and other such instruments. In general, however, private schools are owned by local communities and are run by contributions and fees from this community. If the community has more money, they have an easier time paying teachers and staff and buying equipment and musical instruments.

Aside from school-based education, there are also <u>institutions</u> scattered throughout Dar es Salaam that offer music education, such as the Chiriku Musiconsult and the Fine and Performing Arts Department at the University of Dar es Salaam. These institutions operate with limited budgets, but they provide instruction in traditional instruments, keyboard/piano, and choral singing. Other institutions also exist but do not operate with any regularity. The Music Conservatory of Tanzania, which is affiliated with the Royal Schools of Music in London, teaches the rudiments of theory, accompanied by exams established by the Royal Schools of Music. According to members of other music education organizations, the Conservatory had working facilities for a time, though no one could ever specify when it functioned or who may have studied there. By the mid-1990s, the Conservatory was essentially non-existent, even though a room in a building on the Dar es Salaam waterfront continues to mark its presence.

There are also many non-profit organizations that run music programs, particularly for disadvantaged youth or for those with disabilities. The Amana Vijana Centre (The Amana Youth Centre) offers classes in computers, language, and musical instruction. Owned by the Free Pentecostal Church of Tanzania, the facility provides youth the "knowledge to build self-reliance in their lives."[4] Students can take a three-month long class to learn both guitar and keyboard for $63 or learn one instrument

The outdoor chalkboard lists courses offered by the Amana Vijana Centre. On the right is a list of music classes including instruction in guitar, keyboard, or basic musical knowledge. Course fees were $45 for three months in 2005. By 2008, the price of the courses had risen to $64. *Photo by author.*

for one month for $21. Most students who attend the classes do not own instruments, so all musical learning must take place at the institution.

In addition to these institutions, occasional workshops organized by local organizations and embassies, such as the Alliance Français, the Korean Cultural Centre, and the Norwegian Embassy, offer some assistance for students who want to learn music. While these courses are frequently well attended, particularly when they are free, they are often limited in scope and resources. Education at several workshops only includes an introduction to ideas associated with composition or musical performance, and not consistent formal training. There is also Music Crossroads Tanzania, which is part of Music Crossroads International, a Belgium based non-profit that puts on festivals and competitions, and also offers short-term music instruction for young artists. In 2008, the organization gathered artists from around Tanzania for a ten-day workshop in lyric and melody writing, music arrangement, and studio technology. Finally, the Tanzania House of Talent (THT) offers dance, singing, and music instruction to disadvantaged youth.

Currently, only the Bagamoyo College of Arts (Chuo Cha Sanaa) offers long-term training in music performance. Located sixty kilometers north of Dar es Salaam, the Bagamoyo College of Arts is the sole institution devoted entirely to teaching art and performance. The dormitories and possibly a few of the classrooms for the school were originally built for a Nordic water project that started in 1974. After the project ended in 1980, the government decided to use the abandoned buildings to start an arts college. That same year, renovations were completed, and in 1981, the first courses started for sixty-four students studying music.[5]

Students have to audition for the three-year college and can enroll in a variety of courses, including acrobatics, dance choreography, performance, and drawing. Around twenty students are accepted in each class year. The facility has dorms and classrooms and had a small amphitheater with lighting, curtains, and props until it burned in an April 2001 fire.[6] Most music students of the college receive training in an amalgam of Tanzanian ngoma styles. They also learn to perform on several instruments and study dance. After college, most students return to rural areas to teach music, while a few attempt to make it as musicians in urban areas such as Dar es Salaam.

A great deal of the country's contemporary ngoma traditions have been filtered through the college, as students who pass through the school teach others the same dances and drumming they learned. The result has been a compression of many of the country's varied and disparate dance forms into a core, refined selection. The concern by many musicians is that through teaching the same styles of music and art year after year the institutions become more of an assembly line for artistic knowledge. Since the Bagamoyo College of Arts is the only institution specializing in formal music education, it has significant control over the artistic forms being learned and then reproduced throughout the country. There is anxiety among leaders in Tanzania's music communities that this restrictive approach to the arts does not account for change, musical development, or new skills needed to compete in the contemporary music economy.

This is a cartoon about the potential of Bagamoyo College of Arts to standardize and homogenize the country's musical traditions. The character asks, "What would it be like if all musicians followed in their steps?" The path leads to the Bagamoyo College of Arts. There is a reference at the top to Tanzania One Theatre, an established musical group whose members stated that they would train at the college to attain more musical skills. Originally published by Ibrahim Washokera in *Alhamisi*, May 23, 2002. *Photo courtesy of Ibrahim Washokera.*

Islamic schools also provide training for musicians and singers. Virginia Danielson writes in her study of the Egyptian singer Umm Kulthum that Qur'anic recitation was central to the foundation of Arabic song (1997: 141). Though the link between Qur'anic recitation and popular music is more tenuous in Tanzania, Islamic schools provide some level of musical instruction for artists. Starting at age seven, Mwinichumu Abubakar Mwinichumu learned to play the dufu (tambourine) in madrasa.[7] He is now the percussionist in Kilimanjaro Band. The rap artist Juma Nature (Juma Kassim Mohamed Kiroboto) also attended madrasa when he was 10 years old and learned to played dufu. He was also trained in qasida, a form of sung Arabic poetry. Many taarab artists, such as Shakila Saidi (JKT Taarab), Abbas Mzee (Egyptian Musical Club), and Bakari Abeid (Michenzani Social Club), also went to Qur'anic schools before joining popular taarab performance groups. Since most taarab lyrics are sung in Swahili instead of Arabic, particularly on mainland

Tanzania, Islamic schools aid singers in inflection and delivery of music rather than in pronunciation of words. Nonetheless, they still play a role in training singers in the ability to perform, sing, and compose poetic music.

Despite or perhaps because of the lack of music education in schools, many artists consider formal learning as a significant advantage in attaining social and economic power. Many artists argue that school-based learning provides more advantages than other forms of study. In the majority of interviews I conducted in Dar es Salaam, artists explained that formal education provides knowledge of composition and music theory; sight reading and musical notation; drills in practicing on instruments; and conceptualization of the relationships between people in a band. Formal learning can provide more focused instruction on musical aesthetics, melodies, and rhythms. Though other artists were more dismissive of formal education, providing examples of artists who succeeded in music without any official training, most perceived the lack of education as a sign of inferiority compared with other countries that had a more established educational system.[8]

To overcome the perception of musical inferiority, several established musicians have tried to acquire formal training by apprenticing with musicians who studied at formal institutions, or by taking short courses in music. Norbert Chenga explains how he attempted to train musicians in his group Muungano Cultural Troupe:

> Now, one thing that I was able to experience in this area of traditional music was to move or transfer local music into modern music and be able to play music that would be accepted even by foreigners. This was a real problem when we started because many traditional musicians did not have any education, even primary education. They did not know how to read or write. But they were very good in playing musical instruments. . . . The Ministry of Culture and Youth decided in this period [1975–1980] to give general music education for various cultural groups. Muungano Cultural Troupe was there. So, we went on like this and many [musicians] were able to understand basic music notation—not many, but some—which helped move the attitude in the group to learn and perform music as it was meant to be [performed].

Supplementing informal education with formal training has become more common, particularly as private institutions and non-governmental organizations offer clinics and free courses to local musicians. Some groups, such as Tanzanian One Theatre (TOT), will even pay their own way to study in order to try to get ahead. John Komba is quoted as saying, "I want to send my group to study in Bagamoyo and when we leave there, we will be so hot that we will go far."[9]

Perhaps more important, this discussion of formal music education points to the limits of creative practices. Where many artists desire more formal training in the arts, there is little long-term instruction available. Enticed by foreign forms of music education, artists struggle knowing that they are not provided the same opportunities in music as people in other countries. The playing field is not level. To many artists, as well as producers, managers, and radio announcers, neoliberal reforms have only increased their insecurities about musical knowledge and music qualifications. When asked whether he had musical training, the musician Banana Zorro comments, "Not at all, and this is not just my problem, it's the same with other artists. The biggest problem is, we don't have music schools in Tanzania, we have talent but it cannot be developed professionally in Tanzania. Going abroad [to study music] is very expensive for a local musician."[10] Several artists argued that traditional forms of music knowledge were sufficient to compete internationally, a fact they proved by naming many acts that had performed in Europe. Others argued that limited formal training was a disadvantage, particularly in competing against other groups that receive formal training and perform internationally.

Part of the desire to attain formal musical training can be found in the legacy of education in Tanzania's history. Julius Nyerere emphasized the need for education to liberate individual's ability to become self-reliant (Lema, Mbilinyi, and Rajani 2004: 185). For many years, Nyerere succeeded in bringing education to the masses, and Tanzania had one of the lowest illiteracy rates in Africa. Radio broadcast the importance of learning and included lessons in general education. The government produced short books on history, politics, and language, which were passed out to people throughout the country. The *Kitabu cha Elimu ya Watu Wazima* (Book of Adult Education), for instance, had lessons in African history, socialism, and the ills of capitalism.[11] The government distributed these books to many areas of the country in an effort to promote more knowledge and cultural awareness. The slogan for many of these efforts was "elimu haina mwisho" (education has no end) and symbolized the importance of continually learning over an entire life in order to become self-reliant. These efforts established an ethos that education was critical to triumph over any adversity.

During the economic crises of the 1980s, education suffered significant cutbacks, losing funding and abandoning the goal of eliminating illiteracy. Teachers left schools to find other work, and the salaries of those who stayed behind remained low. The ratio between student and teachers grew, reaching one teacher for every thirty-seven students. School supplies also ran short. In 1994, primary schools needed an estimated 1,658,064 school desks, but only 81,646 existed (Otieno 2000: 41–43; Komba et al. 2000). The education budget declined from 22 percent of the government's total expenditure in 1970 to 12 percent in 1990, in part due to the conditionalities of structural adjustment (Chachage 2009: 10). Given the low probability of attaining a quality education and the need for labor at home, dropout rates in schools were improbably high. In 2000, only 57 percent of school-age children attended primary school.[12] The plight of inadequate education left each subsequent generation further behind the previous one in terms of basic knowledge in math, science, and the arts. It also created tremendous frustration among children and teenagers who believed that they were being denied the same opportunities as those who had political and economic power.

Other issues taking place in the country's education system also impacted the local music economy. While gender parity was nearly equal in primary education, the ratio between boys and girls was two to one in secondary education (Osaki 2000: 229; Munishi 2000; UNDP 2007). That meant that half as many girls attended or completed secondary education as boys. This disparity increased through college and other forms of higher education, including journalism and broadcasting schools, which prepared many of the incoming group of broadcasters in Tanzania for work in radio and television. In addition, most students who wanted an education have to attend both regular classes and after-school tutoring in order to keep up to the standards of their grade. Paying for both school and tutoring was beyond the means of most students and forced many to drop out before they finished (Komba et al. 2000). Those who dropped out searched for work within the informal economy, through

A cartoon representing the increasing difficulty attaining access to education within Tanzania. The blackboard simply has the word "education" written at the top. Notice the last frame where the student is surprised and (in the originally published cartoon) angry, reflecting a popular sentiment of youth who believe that they do not have the same access to learning as in the past. Originally published by Adam Lutta in April 2001. Redrawn by Lutta for this publication. *Photo courtesy of Adam Lutta.*

selling goods on the street, working in public transportation, or other jobs where an education is unnecessary (see Tripp 1997: 128–33; Rizzo 2002).

Ironically, the growth of the music economy is partially attributable to the poor state of education in the country. Given the high dropout rates and limited potential for education, youth flocked to other possibilities in areas of the economy that were expanding or had the potential for growth. Economic possibilities in journalism, fashion, and music grew significantly between the mid-1990s and mid-2000s, which coincided with some of the weakest numbers in school attendance and graduation in the post-independence period. Newspapers emerged almost on a weekly basis in the early years of liberalization, as did opportunities in radio and television stations, recording studios, and live music. Aside from official journalists, education was less important in the emerging occupations in the city, which allowed people, educated or not, to pursue gainful employment.

In recent years, the Kikwete administration has encouraged education reforms that are more responsive to the needs of school-age children. In addition to making primary education compulsory and free for all children, he has also significantly raised the education budget. In the 2009/2010 budget cycle, the government increased support for education by 39 percent.[13] Given that 2010 was an election year, the increase and the high volume of publicity that it received may have been politically motivated. Even if all efforts become implemented, however, it is unlikely to affect formal music education. The push to increase attendance at primary schools stems, in part, from the World Bank's Millennium Development Goals (MDGs). The MDGs aims to have all boys and girls complete primary education with particular focus on language, math, and science. For many aspiring musicians, this education will not assist in attaining training in music and the arts. Their education in music will therefore need to come from non-school-based forms of learning.

### SELF-LEARNING *(informal)*

In Tanzania, the limited amount of formal instruction or direct commentary on one's artistic ability requires artists to be constantly aware of their place in a group and in the broader music scene. Especially for new artists, they need to keep up with contemporary sounds, techniques, and songs so that, whichever group they join, they can quickly keep pace with the other musicians in the group. It therefore becomes important for musicians, dancers, and singers to build a vocabulary of musical knowledge that can be tailored to different situations and performance routines. Building this musical vocabulary requires artists to creatively seek opportunities and experiences in self-learning that take place over time in numerous social contexts.

Self-learning, the informal processes by which musicians attempt to attain knowledge and proficiency in music, is a central creative practice in the Tanzanian music economy. It forces artists to rely on their own "eyes, ears, and memory" to acquire competency in local genres and styles of music (Nketia 1973: 88). It requires musical proficiency despite significant social and economic obstacles. Most important, self-learning involves establishing a network of individuals able to assist in the establishment of musical skills. The ability to form a network among fellow musicians, dancers, band leaders, bar owners, and others is part of creatively navigating through the Tanzanian music economy. Forming a network requires artists to be aware of the social context of musical knowledge and the forms of interaction that occur within music communities. It also entails locating areas where musical knowledge exists and mining that knowledge to create opportunities for learning about music. Self-learning is then about building musical knowledge through socially networked support. These networks form over time—among family members, friends, band members, and others—as prospective artists accrue musical skills and competency.

One of the most important forms of informal music education resides in the family. Regardless of the genre of music, acquiring musical knowledge from another family member is common practice for young artists. Charles Mhutu, who is the leader of the group Tatunane, explains:

> Everyone in my family played music, starting with my father. So, it was in my family that I learned music. . . . My major [experience] with music came while my brother had a band [the Comets] in 1976, 1977. There I tried to play instruments like drums, a little guitar, and I started to perform in the afternoon maybe one song. I continued like this in my brother's band until I mastered playing many songs. Then, after I finished school, I became a full time musician.

The parents of the ragga artists Steve 2K's were singers, and Steve 2K's father performed with the famed dansi musicians Mbaraka Mwinshehe. Referring to the fact that both his parents sang, he said:

> I think that since I was in my mother's belly I liked music. I remember singing since I was a little boy. I was told the story that when I was young I used to sing this old song called "Yeke Yeke." One day we went to see this band near Mt. Meru and the band asked if any child could sing. I went to the stage and asked the band to play "Yeke Yeke." They played it and I performed until every week I had to go there to sing "Yeke Yeke."

John Kitime, who performed with many popular bands, including Vijana Jazz and Kilimanjaro Band, had a similar experience: "My father and mother were teachers. My father played music on many instruments, and he used to sing with my mother. My father played trumpet, accordion, banjo, and guitar. Since I was around the house every day, I had music around me all the time while I was growing up."[14]

Family members, particularly older siblings and parents, create opportunities to learn and perform music that is often unavailable to young children. By having instruments around the house or performing at home, children and youth acquire skills in musicianship, performance techniques, and musical aesthetics. Learning songs from family also creates an appreciation of music that is often lacking in other urban environments. Problematically, instruments are in short supply in Tanzania. High importation taxes and the lack of music stores that sell instruments put them out of reach of most people. While traditional instruments are available, they too can be expensive and, more commonly, not popular among artists wanting to join contemporary music bands. The struggle over instruments makes musical learning and appreciation in the home less common despite the appreciable knowledge that can be gained.

Contrary to the support that some families provide for young people to learn music, many artists stop learning or studying music because it goes against the expectations of their families and communities. A strong stereotype exists of popular musicians as lower class and uneducated who face a life of struggle and hardship. Many musicians told me that their parents who played music discouraged and, in some cases, hindered them from going into music, fearing that their children would lead a similar lifestyle to the one they had lived. Due to recent income increases for many people in Tanzania's music economy, there is an equal movement emphasizing the potential prosperity and success that can be attained through the arts (see chapter 1). It is possible that many artists, who would have been discouraged in the past, will be encouraged due to the changing perceptions about careers in music.

A second means to learn music informally is through band rehearsals. In Tanzania, people are free to attend band practices, speak with musicians at their homes, and sit on the side of the stage during performances. Though some musicians are protective of their musical talents, others offer advice freely, lend upcoming artists their instruments, and give young musicians opportunities to play with bands. In many circumstances, young artists only need a desire to be a musician to gain support from a band. Shaaban Dede, leader of DDC Mlimani Park, states, "Yes, it is easy [to join a group], but it depends on how much time you have and how responsible you are." Self-reliance is highly valued in these circumstances, sometimes over musical proficiency, since bands frequently require the dedication, hard work, and promptness of younger artists.

One internationally known Tanzanian artist who became a musician through attending band practices was Cosmas Chidumule. When a bandleader brought instruments from Dar es Salaam to Songea (where Chidumule lived at the time) to form a band under the TANU Youth League, Chidumule had his first real chance to learn music.

> Already, as a child, I had an interest in talking with musicians and I wanted to know more. So, when I saw [the TANU Youth League band], I knew that this was my chance, and if I applied myself, I could join the group. But, I knew nothing about music. Yet, already inside of me was this desire to express myself. The band members agreed to let me join and asked what I could do. I told them that I could sing. So, I went to practice, which was hard for me because I really wanted to play guitar. Well, I stole a guitar one day and went to my room, shut the door, put on a hat like the other guitarists I had seen, and, in the mirror, tried to play guitar.

Though the TANU Youth League Band did not remain in Songea for long, Chidumule was able to use their instruments, since the person he worked for owned them and kept them at his house. From time to time, Chidumule would practice on the instruments and try to copy the music he heard from the radio, as well as what he learned from the band. Eventually, he was able to play with Butiama Jazz Band for three shows in Songea. Butiama Jazz Band's leader, Mustapha Mkwega, convinced Chidumule to join his group, which brought the young Chidumule into major cities around the country. Chidumule was also able to record with Butiama Jazz Band at Polygram in Nairobi and Radio Tanzania in Dar es Salaam. Since then, Chidumule has been associated with several of Tanzania's best groups, including DDC Mlimani Park Orchestra and Remmy Ongala and Orchestra Super Matimila.

Another musician, Professor Yahya Mkango, described his rise to become a professional musician through his association with a popular local band in Dar es Salaam. Initially, he spent his afternoons after

school playing music with friends, each teaching the other about makeshift instruments.

> One of the people who saw us practice said, "Why don't you form a band?"
> We said, "No, that is not possible. How can we play electric guitar when
> we still use these makeshift instruments?" He told us, "Tomorrow, there
> is a band coming here called Pole International from Vingunguti, Dar es
> Salaam." So we thought, okay, we will try to go, at least, to see if our music
> could work with electric instruments. By good fortune, the band brought
> the instruments there [to the club] early and we went and asked them if we
> could play. We told them, "We are musicians, but we do not have a band. We
> play at home for practice." After taking out their instruments and making
> the connections, they gave us the instruments and allowed us to play our
> music for a bit. It was then that we knew we had become musicians.

After playing with the instruments and learning a few tips from the band,
two of Mkango's friends joined Pole International. Though they were
second-string musicians for the band—meaning that during low points
in a concert, they would fill in for the main musicians—they were able
to perform with the group, to study and observe other musicians, and to
discover what it meant to be a professional Tanzanian musician. Mkango
eventually joined other groups himself and became a rhythm guitarist
and songwriter for one of Tanzania's most popular dansi groups, African
Stars Band.

   For many artists, such as Chidumule and Mkango, as well as Mhutu
and Kitime, learning music from experienced musicians or family is far
more attainable than studying at a school. It is usually free, relaxed, and
readily available. Perhaps most important, it gives prospective musicians
more experience and knowledge of the popular music scene than is available in any school. A musician can be brought into a band before learning
to play an instrument and, through practice, gain proficiency to work and
perform the music scene. Whereas these musicians may not have certain
skills often derived from formal education, such as reading and writing
music, they are well aware of the importance of creating dynamic performance routines, varying song structures, and finding ways to communicate with audiences through music. They attain a better sense of musical
engagement, a process illustrated in the previous chapter.

   One last source of music learning is from phonograms, radio, and
television. Although musicians in all genres use these media, rap, ragga,

and r&b artists use them predominantly. Phonograms, radio, and television act as instructional tapes that give prospective artists in these genres lessons on the delivery, flow, and style of these imported musics. The reliance on media has a lot to do with how Tanzanian youth were introduced to these genres. Inspekta Haroun, the founder of the rap group Gangwe Mobb, discussed his introduction to rap:

> I started to listen to rap when I was in primary school. I really liked to listen to music. During that time [1991–1992], I listened to Naughty by Nature, Wu-Tang Clan, and old school rap, like LL Cool J. I listened to a lot of rappers and they really inspired me, except that, at that time, I did not understand what they were saying. But, their flowing and how they spun their words on an instrumental really inspired me. Then this one musician sprang up who rapped in Swahili here in Tanzania, Saleh Aljabry. He really inspired me since he rapped in Swahili.

Almost all hip-hop artists and fans experienced rap, ragga, and r&b in a similar way. Starting in the mid-1980s, audio and videocassette tapes of American groups, such as Public Enemy, N.W.A., LL Cool J, and others were brought into the country, mainly by or for wealthy, urban youth (Perullo 2007). Due to the overwhelming focus on national music forms on Tanzania's airwaves, youth, curious about other foreign music, particularly African American music and ideas, avidly collected and passed these cassettes around. With increasing piracy in the country, tapes of American hip-hop artists circulated widely throughout Dar es Salaam, Mwanza, Arusha, and a few other towns.

Even if many young Tanzanians could not understand the lyrics, the powerful visual images of artists such as Tupac Shakur and Ice T, accompanied by their strong, confident, often angry voices inspired many young Tanzanian musicians. Professor Jay from the group the Hard Blasterz said, "In that time [1989], I liked to listen to rap like Public Enemy. They really attracted me to rapping because I saw the way black men liked the music and the way they searched for their own voice." For artists such as Jay, trying to imitate American rappers via cassettes, radio, and television was a means to symbolically overcome economic realities of local contexts. Imitation was a means to embody the persona of others imagined to be successful, powerful, and prosperous. Phonograms communicated ideas, knowledge, and meaning to Tanzanian artists, which they embraced in the creation of an indigenous hip-hop culture that responded to and then reconceptualized the importance of rap music in Tanzania.

Initially, many Tanzanians used cassette tapes to teach themselves to rap. They imitated lyrics and vocal timbres of American hip-hop artists, while also adding their original ideas to the music. Mr. II, whose real name is Joseph Mbilinyi and is also known by the name Sugu, explained that he would listen to rap cassettes repeatedly until he could mimic the English lyrics. Though he did not speak English at the time, he would sound out the words until he had a sense of the rhyming and "flow" of the song. After establishing the song's feel, Mr. II would create his own lyrics and rap over the music from an American rap tape. This reliance on the tapes played a strong part in the early years of Tanzanian hip-hop (1989–1995). Rappers tended to rely on the words, rhythms, and styles of their American counterparts. By the late 1990s, however, most rappers had developed Tanzanian sounding songs, mainly by composing lyrics in Swahili.

Regardless of the path that individuals take to becoming musicians, there is a great deal of self-learning involved. Individuals must seek opportunities wherever they can, from local institutions, band practices, family homes, and local media outlets. Often times, the artists that rise quickly through the local music scene are the ones who efficiently navigate the various spaces of musical learning. This requires forms of networking where the artists must establish contacts and reaffirm connections to members of local communities. It requires ingenuity in learning methods, techniques, processes, and vocabularies of musical phrases that can better prepare the artist to become a professional musician. Even finding an instrument to play takes skill in negotiating with people who do have instruments and in convincing bands to allow young artists to handle their equipment. Self-learning is, therefore, a rigorous process that demands a great deal of time and energy from artists. Though formal school-based education can be grueling and time consuming, self-learning is often more physically and emotionally taxing due to artists constantly searching for opportunities while encountering numerous impediments. In short, self-learning is central to many music cultures where institutions lack resources to educate local artists (Finnegan 2007; Ottenberg 1996: 56).

## MUSIC PRACTICE AS CREATIVE PRACTICE

The first time I attended an African Stars practice was on a Tuesday, the first day of the band's weekly routine. As I sat in the circle with members of the band, guitarist Bob Goddy began to teach the others a new song. Goddy vocalized the drum pattern to the drummer and the bass part to the bassist. For the guitarist and the keyboardists, he played their parts on his guitar, repeating the patterns for several minutes until they committed it to memory. As in most such practices, nothing was written down and the musicians relied on their listening ability to learn their parts quickly, as well as on the critical ears of other members who often pointed out if a note, chord, or rhythm was wrong. Even with everyone helping each other, Goddy had trouble teaching the song to the band. The drummer could not find the rhythm, which was in $\frac{5}{4}$ time, uncharacteristic of the typical $\frac{4}{4}$ time in which the band usually plays, and the keyboardist could not control the odd chords he was given. Unperturbed, Goddy continued to repeat all the parts until finally the band could play the first part of the song. The song Goddy had taught them was "Take Five" by the American jazz musician Dave Brubeck and would be the opening selection at one of the band's concerts.

When Ally Chocky, the lead singer of African Stars, walked into the room, the second-string (back-up) members left and the main players picked up the instruments. Within a few minutes, the band began work on a new song, which had been requested by a local beer company, Kibo Beer. Kibo Beer wrote the lyrics to a song meant to promote awareness for AIDS (as well as promote Kibo Beer) and asked African Stars to write accompanying music. African Stars would then sing the song at a promotional party for Kibo Beer at a club near the University of Dar es Salaam. The lyrics that Kibo wrote, as the band unanimously stated, were terrible, and though Chocky came up with a melody for the song, the group shook their heads at the material. Nonetheless, as Chocky's melody became clear, the band quickly filled in the gaps, with Professor Yahya strumming a rumba style rhythm on E and A chords, Abou Semhando drumming the standard African Stars beat, the backup singers Luizer Mbutu and Jesca Charles humming harmony parts, Jojo Jumanne adding the deep, percussive bass, and Victor Nkambi tying the various instruments together on keyboard. Within ten minutes, the group had built a song—modeled on other songs they had written—for the Kibo Beer promotion. Few spoke during the entire composing process; everyone listened to each other's music and came up with a sound that was characteristic of the group but without the need for appreciable verbal communication.

At 11:30 A.M., the band began its official practice, strengthening the arrangement and overall sound of their standard repertoire, discussing new song possibilities, and adding new instrumental bridges and breaks for the dancer's routine. Again, few words were spoken. And while Chocky appeared to be the bandleader, he did little more than sing, nod at the musicians, and sit against the back wall during the instrumental parts. Occasionally a member would stop the band while they were playing and explain a problem, but overall each instrumentalist strove to improve through practice and by listening to the music. Each person then took it upon him or herself to work, listen, and perfect their playing, especially since they all know that other comparable musicians are willing to replace anyone not meeting the standards of the group.

Dancers also need ample space and opportunities to practice, as their routines often move offstage close to the audience. In African Stars, the dancers try to incorporate new moves into their routines every week so audiences never complain of seeing the same material twice. In the practice session, Hassan Mussa "Super Manwela" Mohammed, the dance group leader and choreographer, taught four women and three men new moves to add to their repertoire. They added a slow, staggered fall to the floor after a long period of hip movement that was to be synchronized with Semhando's snare drum, though during practice the dancers clapped and sang the rhythm since the band was playing a different song. All the dancers continually spoke with one another, and Mohammed spent a great deal of time analyzing the dancers' moves. When someone did not bend low enough during a part where the dancer was supposed to sink to the floor, he made that person repeat the move until it was performed correctly. If a dancer's hips did not shake and swing in rhythm with the other dancers, he made everyone repeat the part.

The African Stars narrative is a fairly typical example of musical practice in popular Tanzanian music. First- and second-string musicians in a group, and even musical acolytes attempting to join a group, gather in a common space to work on old and new songs. New songs are taught through verbal recitation of the melody and rhythm, though each artist has ample room to modify suggestions to fit his style of playing. In more established bands, particularly among artists who have been in groups for a long time, learning a new song takes only a few minutes. Part of the reason that artists are so versatile and learn so quickly is that they rely on common vocabularies of chords, rhythms, and melodies that they can all refer to. Difficulties arise when artists stray from these vocabularies. In one dansi band practice session, for instance, a band leader taught the horn section a new melody where the emphasis of the descending line was on the second beat followed by a held note that began on an off beat. The rhythm was unusual though the melody was fairly standard. The horn players, all of whom had been playing for over a decade, easily recited the melody but struggled to get the rhythm since it did not correspond with their working vocabulary.

Musical practice in Tanzania also entails critical thinking and imagination, both necessary for keeping one's position in a group given the ready availability of other musicians looking for work. Music is experiential and contextual, moving beyond the mechanistic repetition of tasks that encompass other forms of musical learning (Jorgensen 1997: 10–11). Practice does not receive considerable attention among critics and scholars, aside from those in music education, perhaps because it appears ordinary and routine. In the interactions and responses of musicians within a group, practice is as engaging and important an event as actual performance. It removes the communication between the band and audience and focuses solely on the self and on dialogues between other artists. It also establishes critical means to experiment within a musical repertoire. For Tanzanian artists, musical practice is a proving ground for their skills and competence, and a dry run for performance that can potentially ensure greater social and financial rewards.

One of the main differences in practice routines among popular musicians is in the space they choose for practice. Many bands, such as FM Academia, Muungano Cultural Troupe, and Msondo Ngoma, practice in bars or clubs that are open to the public. Interested people can freely attend the practices and even dance with the music. Attending an FM Academia practice session is almost akin to seeing a show, though the attendees are all children and teenagers from the neighborhood. Other groups, such as African Stars and Tanzanian One Theatre (TOT), choose more secluded areas to learn new music. There are many

*but he mentions repetition @ the beginning*

reasons for choosing a secluded place: quieter location with fewer distractions; often more space to separate dancers and performers from one another; and higher status for having both a regular performance and practice space. For many bands, however, the main reason for selecting private locations far from performance spaces is to avoid anyone hearing new songs being composed. TOT, for instance, often leaves Dar es Salaam entirely to practice in a remote area where all the groups (taarab, dansi, ngoma, and theater) can work on new material. When they return to Dar es Salaam, all the bands are ready to perform their new songs at opening concerts.

Musicians in other musical genres, such as rap, r&b, and ragga, often practice more at home. Although practice competitions do occur in school courtyards, where artists can be heard trying out their technique in front of friends, hip-hop musicians first perfect their songs in the seclusion of their home or neighborhood. For most rap and r&b artists, practice is critical to perfecting their delivery, flow, and timing. Mr. Paul (Paul Mbenna), an r&b artist, explains: "I have to practice every day so that I make it a habit of mine. Many times, I like to study different singing techniques and how best to control my breathing while singing. And, when I do this, I discover many new things about singing that I did not know in the beginning [of practice]." Aside from improving one's skills, practice also ensures that an audience will better receive the messages of the songs, which is the core of most Tanzanian rap. Balozi Dola (Ahmed Dola) explains his approach to practicing: "I am the type of MC who is never satisfied with anything I do. I want to be one step ahead. Practice my voice; get it tighter. Get the message across to the people. I try to speak with clarity. I do not want any ambiguity. I always want people to understand the message that I am trying to send across." Locked in his bedroom, Dola spends his evenings after work developing his art and writing new songs either for a performance or to record. No one pushes Dola to practice, but he recognizes the stiff competition of the local hip-hop scene and the need to remain popular both for economic and social reasons. → relates to Consumerism

Religious groups, such as *kwaya kuu za usharika* (main choirs of a congregation) and *kwaya za uinjilisti* (evangelical choirs), use a slightly different model of practice but also have a different incentive in music. These groups gather several times a week, usually in a church or in a space

Dismas J. Mallya teaching basic music theory to choir members at
St. Joseph's Cathedral in downtown Dar es Salaam. *Photo by author.*

set aside for the church, and practice hymns for Sunday services, upcoming competitions, or recording dates. Most churches use new hymns every week, and choirs work for several hours each practice to learn new songs. Usually a choral instructor orally teaches each of the four sections (soprano, alto, tenor, bass) their parts, since the majority of singers do not read music. Each of the sections continues to work on its part as the instructor moves to teach other sections, until everyone has learned the complete song. Then, joining the parts together, occasionally with drums, guitars, piano, and/or other instruments, the choir attempts to sing through the song, stopping to improve on certain parts. As competitions with other churches, recordings, or television appearances near, the group will practice more frequently and for longer hours.

Kwaya members have a strong dedication to practice considering the obstacles they go through to attend. They are paid very little if at all and often leave work and head directly to choir practices without a meal. They stay for several hours and then head home late at night. In one group, St. Joseph's Cathedral Choir, most members live far from the church and do not arrive at home until after nine in the evening. Unlike artists in other genres who only practice this way knowing that their livelihood depends on it, kwaya members practice and dedicate themselves because of their devotion to the church, as well as for the hope of improving their own abilities as singers and religious knowledge holders. Even the most populist-oriented kwaya music can have low financial rewards for musicians, composers, and singers given the amount of time and effort spent practicing their craft.

Among popular musicians, practice is regarded as a critical obligation to performing well and remaining competitive in the local music scene. There is a Swahili proverb that reads *mcheza kwao hutunzwa* (he who dances at home is rewarded). The proverb refers to the need to practice before publicly demonstrating one's ability. In the proverb's example, dancing at home before going out to a musical event, such as an ngoma celebration, improves the dancer's public performance. Even though this proverb is no longer well known, it embodies a fundamental idea in Tanzanian popular music: the need to gain proficiency before attempting to perform in front of other people. Practicing music provides artists time to work with other artists and improve their musical capabilities, especially since instruments typically belong to band owners rather than musicians. It also gives bands time to refine their music, learn new songs, and discuss recent events in the music scene. It is an opportunity to gain more credibility as a performer and potentially move up in the band hierarchy. Further, musical practice provides an outlet to the stresses of competition in the music and performing in a live band, some of which perform five nights a week. Ally Chocky explains:

> Practice is important—without it, you cannot continue [in the music business]. So, our success depends on how much we practice. We do not practice for a long time since we play many shows. . . . Yet, a lot of energy is spent on the little time we have to practice. And, when there is an important show—such as an album release or a competition with another band—we can spend two or three weeks practicing until we put a strong program together.

Although music is not always played at practices, and time can be spent dealing with other issues, such as performance techniques, dance routines, or ideas for an album, rehearsals serve as a critical time for musicians to gather and work on their skills as performers. Practice is a compulsory form of being a performer and allows one to remain creative and open to new ideas. Due to the competitive market for musical proficiency, practice is central to both individual and group success. Musicians use practice to react to the popularity of other bands, adjust their music based on the comments of radio announcers and music critics, or respond to other pressures that shape the career of someone in music. In short, practice is a central space for musicians to conceptualize and adjust their musical skills in order to stay relevant in the music scene.

## REPOSITIONING IN JOINING A GROUP

Joining a group in Tanzania is one of the more complex social rituals in the popular music scene.[15] When I first went to Tanzania in 1998, I started a map diagramming which artists joined which band at which time. After only a few days of conversations with local musicians, my map looked like a little kid's drawing on an Etch-a-Sketch: lines went in every direction and it became impossible to truly envisage an artist's career. And it was not just that musicians changed groups in Dar es Salaam; they moved all over eastern and southern Africa and came from numerous places and ethnicities (Tsuruta 2001: 145). The careers of musicians were complex terrains, following the changes in economic and political circumstances of living in East Africa.

Artists, particularly those who are well known, tend to join a group, remain for a year or a few years, and then switch to another group that offers more pay or benefits. Even though the increased salary or benefits may not materialize, a compulsion still exists among many musicians to continually switch bands or even to leave music for a time to try to earn a more steady income. I refer to this constant switching between musical groups with the expectation of some better outcome as repositioning (Perullo 2008b). Borrowing from scholarship on positioning (Davies and Harré 1990; Leander 2004), repositioning highlights the common practice among artists in central Africa to constantly vie for power and negotiate new alignments within and between groups. By moving between groups, these artists reposition themselves—that is, they empower themselves both within their new group and toward the group they left—in order to escape bad contracts, take advantage of expectant opportunities, or improve economic and social status within the local music scene.

Repositioning has been a central part of the popular music scene in many eastern African countries since at least the 1960s. By the 1970s, parastatles of the Tanzanian government established national bands that promoted government initiatives and entertained local audiences. Members of these bands were often treated well and received housing, food, transportation, and other amenities. This helped create some stability within groups, although repositioning continued to occur particularly for well-known artists who were often enticed to join other local bands. Once these bands collapsed, the movement of artists between bands increased and it was—and still is—not uncommon for artists to switch between several bands each year.

To give a sense of repositioning since the 1970s, it is useful to look at the career of one artist. Shaaban Dede, currently leader of DDC Mlimani Park, explains his career both in joining bands and in working outside of music:

> In 1972, I officially joined the TANU Youth League Band. In September 1974, I moved to Bukoba and joined Police Jazz Band. Later I left, I went to Kigoma, in a band called Kashibabo, where I stayed in 1975 and 1976. I also studied music and began teaching myself to be a mechanic. I worked as a mechanic for a while, then in 1977 I moved to Tabora.
>
> In Tabora I played with the band Sonasona. I stayed there for a year and Tabora Jazz saw that I could sing. They sought me out and asked me to join their band. So, at the end of 1977, I joined Tabora Jazz until 1978 when I went to Dodoma. There I found a band that started called Dodoma International, where I played until September 1979.
>
> I came to Dar es Salaam and joined Msondo Ngoma [Juwata Jazz]. On April 2, 1982, I left Msondo Ngoma and came to Mlimani Park where I remained until 1983. I then went to Orchestra BIMA Lee. I was there until 1987 when the band started to threaten my job. There was an argument between myself and another singer. I returned to Juwata Jazz. I did not stay long, until around 1989. I stopped working, but then I asked for a job at the factory of Tanzania Foods, where I became a driver.
>
> In October or November 1989, I was sought out by the band Orchestra Safari Sound (OSS) for a week of performances. They ended up using me for a month, and then asked, "Why don't you become employed here?" I said,

"No problem," and we agreed. Then, I had a dispute in 1990 with the head
of the band. They [the other band members] dismissed me and Fresh Jumbe
[another musician] from the band. Fresh Jumbe went on to start the band
Bicco Stars Band. I went to work in a garage and also as a taxi driver.

Then, that same year, members of OSS came to me again and I joined
them for a month. I then returned to BIMA Insurance 1990, 1991, until 1994
when I was chosen to be leader of the band. I was leader until 1997 when my
mother died in Muscat. I got permission to leave [the band], but when I returned the band had already chosen another leader. I went to Mlimani Park
and became leader of the band in 2000.

Changing bands, on average, once every other year as Dede did is typical
of popular musicians.[16] It is also common for musicians to find other, non-
musical occupations, as mechanics, tailors, importers of luxury goods,
or farmers, all jobs held at one time or another by professional popular
musicians. Further, the ability to switch groups easily provides artists
with an economic and social freedom that is often difficult to find. Dede
explains:

If you want better benefits, you judge for yourself what to do. The government of your mind decides; the ministers of your brain give you advice....
Mlimani Park sought me out while I was at Msondo Ngoma. They persuaded
me. They came to me; we agreed. At that time, I was making a salary of Tsh
580—I started around Tsh 400. Mlimani Park wanted me and they offered
me a salary of Tsh 2200. So I left Msondo Ngoma.

The ability to "judge for yourself" gives artists control to use their musical
skills to enhance their economic and social positions. In other words, musicians have agency to take advantage of situations as they arise, which can
affect their salaries, benefits, and popularity. It is the freedom to switch
bands that gives musicians power, especially when they are employees
of bands owned by companies or wealthy businessmen.

Although money is often part of a musician's decision to leave a
group, internal conflicts also play an important role. As in other areas
of Tanzania's music economy, jealousy plays a large factor in a musician's
decision to leave a group. If one musician becomes better known and
builds a strong fan base, then another band member may envy him and
try to attain the same recognition. If the recognition does not come, the
musician will simply leave for a band that may bring more opportunities.
Once in a new band, however, the competition between the two artists

often continues. In one recent event, a singer, whom I refer to as Juma, became jealous of the popularity of the new lead singer of his old band (which he had left because of internal conflicts). In a concert attended by both Juma's new and old bands, he attempted to discredit the new singer. When introducing the singer on stage, Juma slightly changed the other singer's name to a word that translated as "homosexual." Due to the low social acceptability of homosexuality in Tanzania, the remark was considered offensive. The performance turned into a scandal, with extensive tabloid coverage and fistfights between band members and journalists. The scandal also caused a rift between the two bands and eventually produced further repositioning. It was also effectively used to market both bands in the media and in live concerts.

Even without artist conflict, frequent artist rotation causes a tremendous amount of competition between groups. Competition is central to Tanzania's music scene and affects every genre of music (Gunderson and Barz 2000). When an artist in one group is lured to a competing band, fans and former band members initially bear a great deal of animosity toward the artist.

> **Perullo:** When you leave, do members of the first band get upset?
> **Dede:** Yeah [gives a loud resounding yell]. They get upset, of course, but later they forgive you.
> **Perullo:** But if you went to Juwata Jazz from DDC Mlimani Park, it would not be like a war, would it?
> **Dede:** Ahh [shouts]. It was a war. When I left Juwata in 1982 to come to Mlimani, at the house where I lived, hooligans and fans fought each other. They wanted to burn the house down. They came with petrol. But there really was no violence. Later they just left. Then we went to play at the Equator Club, a fan of Msondo Ngoma [Juwata Jazz] came on Mlimani Park's bus with a knife. He tried to approach me, but we scared him off.

Fans take their favorite band seriously and are often offended when their best singer, guitarist, or percussionist leaves for a competing band. Nonetheless, the resulting feuds, competition, and gossip that stem from an artist "changing sides" creates excitement in Tanzania's music scene. It is a sort of musical soap opera, played out in repetitive cycles where no one is physically hurt, but where everyone is involved in a highly charged social event that makes music personal and exciting.

Of course, not all musicians pack their bags and head off to another group every time a more lucrative offer is made. Some bands, such as Kilimanjaro Band, Tatunane, and All-Star Taarab, have had a steady lineup of musicians for a decade or more. Other groups, such as Simba Theatre, Muungano Culture Troupe, and Kilimanjaro Connection, have had the same leaders (James Mbunju, Norbert Chenga, and Kanku Kelly Kashamatubajike, respectively) since the groups' inceptions. These instances of stability are fairly rare, however, and it is far more common for artists to give new opportunities a try rather than continue with one group.

A current trend in repositioning involves displays of financial wealth. Younger artists, in particular, constantly vie for new positions in bands based on visual cues of financial success and fame. Well-known artists often flaunt their wealth by wearing fancy clothes, driving cars, or wearing jewelry. Economic power becomes visual through the social meanings of brand name clothes and accoutrements. It fosters immediate reactions among those who compete with these performers, as well as other members of society who judge their own social value based on the artists that they respect. Reaction to the success of another artist, based on visual cues, creates frustration and jealousy that frequently pushes artists to reposition. Even in the same band, where a manager or owner controls finances, artists do not always know the salaries of other artists. At the beginning of the week, many bands are paid by the manager as they leave practice in sealed envelopes. Solo artists receive undisclosed amounts by promoters unless a collective contract has been signed. In these cases, the only knowledge of income appears in a person's visual displays.

Many artists come from similar economic backgrounds that prevent anyone from standing out before they join a group. Over time, a more popular performer in a band can earn a higher salary and begin to purchase commodities that set him or her apart from other band members. This financial wealth brings forms of power and prestige that frequently lead to jealousy and tensions within bands. Finances and salaries have often been at the center of disputes within musical groups, and are a frequent cause for repositioning. The attention to commodities in the new economy makes potential conflicts more visible and reflects shifts in perceiving the body as symbolic of a person's social status. Wealth and power are now more visually situated within the commodities that musicians purchase and wear, which has the potential to make conflict and repositioning more customary.

To help keep people from changing groups so often, band owners use contracts that artists sign when they join a group (not all bands use these contracts, but most do with well-known or established artists). The contracts require artists to stay with a band for a certain number of years or forfeit a percentage of their salary in fines. Band owners use these contracts to keep artists from changing bands or abandoning a group before big events, such as right before an album release where a tremendous amount of money has been invested in recording songs. If an artist repositions, then the artist could take many fans away from the old band owner, since they are sometimes loyal to certain performers rather than a particular group. For this reason, owners create strongly worded contracts that often frighten artists from considering shifting to another band.

Occasionally, scandalous examples of strongly worded contracts emerge that remind musicians to carefully read through these transactions. In one situation, a singer was discovered in a rural part of Tanzania by a band owner who promised the singer wealth and fame if she signed a contract with him. The singer did sign even though the contract made numerous stipulations about her rights, finances, and identity. The band owner refused to allow the singer to speak to the press, handle her own finances, or book any of her shows. All attempts to interview her were met with either stern refusals or accompaniment by the band owner. Although no one knows for sure, many journalists estimate that the singer actually made very little money from her shows as the band owner took most of the nightly earnings. The singer was even stranded after one show in Uganda when the owner, according to newspaper reports of the event, took the earnings of a sold-out concert and went back to Dar es Salaam without providing any means of transport for the singer. Although this narrative is mostly likely factually incorrect—the owner was unlikely to just leave his "investment" behind—it created an important rumor about the problems that can arise with contracts that force a musician to remain under the control of someone else. Given the potential lack of knowledge about contracts and lawsuits, it is often easy to entice naïve artists into signing confounding contracts.

Contracts can also stipulate many factors beneficial to the musicians, such as insuring that all health, housing, food, transportation, and salary costs will be met by the band owners, as long as the musician fulfills his or her responsibilities in the band. In situations where the owners agree to cover many daily expenses, just as occurred in the past with many parastatal bands, artists are more willing to sign the contracts since it provides a certain amount of protection. They are also more willing to work for the band, composing and performing better material. Band owners, therefore, often try to create lucrative contracts particularly for well-known artists who are, on occasion, provided homes, cars, and other luxuries to remain with a group. Though these enticements are still rare, they provide a counter narrative to the rumor discussed in the previous paragraph, and keep musicians signing contracts in the hopes of finding financial wealth.

Given that there are no legal cases to uphold the terms of these contracts, why do artists bother with them? Why not leave a group whenever one wants and ignore the fines? There are many reasons that artists pay attention to the terms of the contracts. First, forfeiting a contract and not paying a fine often means that another band owner will not sign an artist or take a risk on them. Second, band owners can use his (financial) power to persuade police and others to take his side and arrest the musicians on numerous charges (this has occurred on several occasions). Third, talented artists can join other bands and have the new band pay the fine to the old contract. This practice ensures that all terms are met with the contract and the artist can still reposition him or herself in the new group. Finally, along with contracts, most Tanzanian bands have constitutions that they are required to create in order to register with the National Arts Council, a government organization. The constitutions detail the members of the band, administrative officials, banks to be used for finances, and the group's finances (Askew 2002: 194). Artists realize that their relation with the National Arts Council, the band constitution, and other band members is important for their reputation. They therefore would rather not risk public embarrassment at being referred to as someone untrustworthy or disloyal to band mates, the band owner, and to the government. → System is self-governing

The conflict of repositioning and contracts presents an important dichotomy within the contemporary music economy. Artists use their musical talents to find ways to reposition between the growing numbers of bands in the city. The proliferation of groups reflects the growing financial gains that can be made in the local music economy, and artists attempt to seize those opportunities to find increasingly better opportunities. Of course, this creative movement between groups does not always benefit the musicians. Frequently artists find themselves in bands that are poorly managed or lacking in enough investment to make them competitive in the local market. This is particularly true in the abundance of new bands that emerge each year. This only encourages them to keep moving between groups as they search for a desired outcome or opportunity. Motivated by stories or rumors of other peoples' successes, artists constantly vie for the best situation, the ideal fit for their lifestyles.

Through contracts, band owners manage their investments in musicians and ensure some level of stability given the practice of repositioning. Though I do not want to suggest that all band owners have groups because of the financial rewards rather than their love of music, owning a group in Tanzania has become a means of self-promotion and financial gain combined with an interest in music. Many band owners are businessmen or politicians who want to benefit from music even as they enjoy listening to concerts performed by their band or artist. Other bands are funded by a promoter who expects to eventually be bought out by the musicians in the group. Often, the desire for profit, particularly in difficult economic times, encourages these owners to be unscrupulous in paying band members their salaries. The only cost that is expendable in performance is artist fees because most artists do not have the legal or economic means to force an owner to pay them. One of the main options available to artists is repositioning. The power play of repositioning and contracts creates one of the central struggles to joining a group or maintaining bands in Tanzania.

## HIGH RISK IN CONCERT PROMOTION

Even after learning music, finding a band, and practicing to gain proficiency in music, artists still have to find ways to perform in clubs, social halls, bars, and festivals. For larger bands, a band owner or manager makes arrangements for weekly performances. In most circumstances, the owner of a band purchases all instruments, hires people to dole out salaries, and employs a manager to negotiate performances with local clubs and social halls. Since so many large bands exist and continually emerge in Dar es

TABLE 4.1. Revenue for the Sunday, November 5, 2000,
performance by a popular dance band in Dar es Salaam, Tanzania

| Expenses | Amount (Tsh) | Amount (US$) |
|---|---|---|
| Entertainment tax | 40,000 | $44 |
| Transportation of people and instruments | 50,000 | $56 |
| Incentives | 22,500 | $25 |
| Other taxes[1] | 30,000 | $33 |
| Performance fee for top musicians | 50,000 | $56 |
| Performance fee for other musicians | 21,500 | $24 |
| Total | 214,000 | $238 |

Note: 1. Bands are required to pay additional taxes, including entertainment tax,
to district and regional cultural officers.

Salaam, the responsibility of these managers is to come up with creative
strategies for marketing the band. Often this means pushing a newly recorded song on the radio before the band performs any shows. If the song
is well received, then the manager has some leverage to use with bar and
club owners. Kickbacks are another common tactic by which a manager
agrees to pay either an additional percentage of the entrance fees to the
bar owner—in other words, 55 percent of the entrance fee rather than the
usual 40 percent—or agrees to pay a certain amount of money regardless
of the outcome of the show. If a band becomes successful, however, these
strategies tend to be used less since it is the bar and club owners who often
court popular bands with guaranteed performance fees.

Due to intense competition for performance spaces, most groups try
to establish a steady performance routine early on, by playing the same
clubs on the same nights, occasionally performing at festivals, or touring
the country to promote an album. Establishing a steady routine with a
consistent fan base leaves artists with more time to write songs, practice,
and record since it removes the added pressure of finding ways to draw in
new fans. Regular performances also bring in a steady income, which, for
bands that are not supported by an organization or business, is crucial to
their success. Even bands that have regular salaries from corporations or
publicly owned institutions rely on extra salaries. The average musician
in popular Tanzanian dance band, for instance, makes $150 per month
(salaries vary by band member status). At concerts, musicians can expect
to receive a performance fee, between $5 and $10 in addition to their

salaries (see table 4.1). The performance fee varies depending on the size of the audience and the day of the week of the show.[17] Musicians also receive "incentives," which often means free beer. Regular performances for dance band musicians can add up to $30 per week to their salaries.

For smaller bands, rappers, and groups that do not have the means to hire managers, they have to rely either on their own ability to make contacts with bar and club owners or they have to work with concert promoters. The number of concert promoters in Tanzania has increased 200 percent in the past ten years due to the imagined potential for profiting from the popularity of artists (see appendix D). These promoters work to put on shows throughout the country, establishing concerts for an album release, promotional or fund-raising events, festival, or "beach party," which I refer to collectively as one-time events since they usually do not occur more than once. Promoters of these events frequently coordinate renting the social hall and necessary equipment, such as speakers, mixers, and microphones. They hire designers to put up advertisements and pay for promotion on local radio stations and in newspapers. The high cost of entrance fees and the difficulty of finding late-night transportation often means that the larger shows are more likely to fail than succeed. To guarantee that they will at least break even, many promoters rely on bringing in foreign talent, such as Jay Z, Ja Rule, 50 Cent, Miriam Makeba, Koffi Olomide, and Awilo Longomba, who can fill large concert halls. Or, they use the sponsorship of large businesses, such as breweries and cell phone companies—to cover the high costs of renting equipment, social halls, buses, and other amenities.

Most promoters take on a significant amount of risk when they attempt to put on concerts. The potential for considerable profit, notoriety, and higher status provides impetus for many people to attempt to stage large concerts. In a well-read essay, Clifford Geertz refers to this high risk behavior as "deep play," where the more money one risks, the "more of a lot of other things, such as one's pride, one's poise, one's dispassion, one's masculinity, one also risks, again only momentarily but again very publicly as well" (Geertz 1973: 434). The high stakes involved in putting on shows has led to numerous failures and some success. More important, due to the strategies that promoters have used to get people to shows (including artists), many have earned the distinction of being manipulative and untrustworthy. Taji Liundi, who works at TBC FM and is a promoter

in Dar es Salaam, explains the combination of risk and strategy involved
in being a promoter:

> We have good promoters and fake promoters. I think everybody starts
> out with very good intentions. And you might do very well for the first two
> shows. Let me start with the money part. How much do we get? First of all, I
> don't think anyone ever pulls in a crowd of over six or seven hundred people.
> There seems to be a core audience all the time, you never miss those guys at a
> show. The entrance is usually Tsh 2,000 [$2]—it is very expensive. Tsh 1,500
> [$1.50] does not get you anybody because everyone feels that there are going
> to be too many people [and so they will not go to the show].
>
> Then, there is no real venue. You want to do something at the FM Club;
> it is way out in a rough area of town. And people do not expect to come out
> at 8:00 and stay until 12:00 at night. So, the people who go there know the
> area real well, ngangari.[18] The Bills complex [Billicanas] is difficult to work
> with because they want [a] 50/50 cut from the gate. Or else, to hire the hall
> for a day, that is not a disco night, it costs you almost half a million shillings
> [$500]. So you have to make sure you bring in at least another half million,
> or million to actually get your money back. Diamond Jubilee goes for half or
> one million shillings. That is a lot of money.
>
> Sponsors are not giving away money anymore, they are giving away pro-
> motional materials. And so, it becomes much more difficult to get money.
> The budget might be like this: The venue, a couple of hundred thousand
> shillings. You need posters in the streets—fortunately, there is no tax to
> put up that stuff—just put them at bus stops. You need maybe Tsh 150,000
> [$150]. The banners that you stick up, you have to pay a small fee for that,
> maybe Tsh 20,000 [$20]. As a city commission fee to even do a show, you
> could use another Tsh 60,000 [$60]. Then the big headache is the sound
> system and it seems that there is only one good one in town and they rent
> it out for Tsh 200,000 [$200]. You have to have a half a million [$500] to
> do a decent show, with no props, just a stage. And the stage is about Tsh
> 50,000 [$50].
>
> Sometime I do not get it back. When you do not [think that you are going
> to] get it back, you obviously do not start by signing a contract with anyone
> because you tell him, "Hey, let us look at what the weather is going to be like.
> If the sun is shining, I will be generous." When funding started drying up,
> it got a little bad. The good intention turned into animosity and wrangling
> over money. So you find the relationship between people who want to do
> concerts and artists is really sticky. It is really hard. They have got to be your
> friends.

Even with a good venue, a sunny day, and the support of local sponsors,
however, it can still cost a million shillings ($1,000) to put on a show in

advance of any financial benefit to the promoter. The high cost of these shows entails deep play given that many promoters have little financial capital of their own.

High risk involves intense strategies to get audiences and artists to shows. In a form of blackmail, many promoters write the names of artists on their posters and fliers, which they hang all over town, even though the artists have not been officially invited to perform. After seeing the signs, fans attend the show expecting the artist to perform. If the artist does not play, he or she risks being resented by fans, and losing their loyalty for future concerts. In other scenarios, promoters will collect money at the door during a show (advance tickets mainly exist for foreign acts in Tanzania), and then drive away while the band is playing. Promoters will also lie about the number of tickets sold and pocket money meant for the artists. And, in the ultimate blow, elite promoters occasionally blacklist artists—by not allowing other promoters to hire certain artists for shows—because they are seen as competition for musicians that they are trying to support. Blacklisted artists have a difficult time finding anyone to help them perform or organize a concert. Promoters also make numerous promises as they attempt to secure equipment and capital to put on a show: letters to attain sponsorship are written to local companies with grand claims of the performance lineup and potential audience size of a proposed concert; musicians are enticed to sign on to an event that they are guaranteed will receive television publicity, which rarely happens; and fans are frequently told that the culmination of some scandal will occur at a performance. This strategy is effective and often one of the few promises that promoters make that is routinely filled.

For performers, the problems with promoters always keep them alert and aware of what is happening in the local music scene. Occasionally, they will find the upper hand (e.g., by taking money from the door before the promoter is aware, not going on stage until the promoter pays them, or having a band's representative collect money at the door with the promoter). Many musicians secure parallel deals with a promoter, such as concurrent radio airplay of the artist's music, advertising time, or media support. There is also intense negotiation for position in the lineup of other bands and musicians performing during a show. The later in the show one performs, the more highly acclaimed they appear. Of course, the performance fee becomes a constant struggle in these promoted events. Band and musician fees range from Tsh 5,000 to Tsh 400,000 ($5 to $400). Most groups, particularly rap groups, are paid on the lower end of the scale. The more popular bands will make the higher rates. Nonetheless, the financial benefits of these shows are often extremely small. Again, Liundi explains:

> The big bands like FM Academia, they accept maybe Tsh 300,000, even 200,000 [$300, $200]. The smaller bands accept Tsh 100,000 [$100]. The smaller artists would get between Tsh 5,000 and Tsh 10,000 [$5 and $10]; Tsh 20,000 [$20] is very high for a show. Now if they have a group it is worse. The Hard Blasterz [a rap group with three rappers] would go for Tsh 100,000 [$100] and split it. It is better not to be too many in a group; it does not work too well money wise.

Due to the small salaries, many artists will not agree to do a show unless they are paid half of their fee upfront, except when they are friends with the promoter.

One of the results of this high-risk behavior in promotion is that, due to the high rate of failure, there has been a concentration of promotion into the hands of a few large companies that own sound equipment, magazines, radio stations, and have a network of radio hosts and artists popular enough to draw in large audiences across the country. The largest promotion company is PrimeTime Promotions, an affiliate of Clouds FM radio station, which can advertise for free on their radio station, have musicians guaranteed to show up (particularly if they want their music played on the radio station), and get sponsors who want their products promoted at the concert and on radio. In other words, Clouds Entertainment removes advertising expenses, equipment rental fees, and worries about finding sponsors, which essentially ensures a profit from their concerts. As a result, PrimeTime Promotions has put on large touring festivals, such as Fiesta Jirambe, sponsored by Kilimanjaro Premium Lager Beer, and Mkali Nani, sponsored by the cell phone company Tigo.

Despite the concentration of successful performance into the hands of a few promoters, the high risk involved in putting on one-time concerts helps to form a thriving music economy. Artists frequently gain wider exposure through one-time concerts and, therefore, sell more albums,

An advertisement for an all-day beach party at Mikadi Beach in Dar es Salaam. The show was for students who finished their Form Four exams. The event featured one of the winners of the television performance competition Bongo Star Search, Kala Jeramaya. The event took place on November 1, 2008. *Photo courtesy of Said Mdoe.*

attain more airplay, and gain credibility as performers in front of large audiences. In writing about financial traders in Chicago, Caitlin Zaloom writes, "Risk is a productive force.... Risk is the object around which traders organize their conduct and shape themselves. Traders stake capital on daily speculative competitions. Simultaneously, they wager definitions of the self" (2004: 383). Although, in 2008, the American economy saw the misuse of this practice, there is still a sense that risk is a means through which traders establish reputations and credibility and "sustain" the local market (Zaloom 2004: 366). Promoters in Tanzania do not have the same impact on the overall market that traders do, but hundreds of promoters who work to put on events in Tanzania dramatically impact the local music economy. Risk leads to creative strategies that push the boundaries and expectations of profit, success, and performance. It also expands the potential scope of the music economy by connecting local businesses, newspapers, social halls, performers, and traders in the local music economy.

## ABOVE WATER

Self-learning, repositioning, contracts, practice, and high-risk promotion are all strategies for handling the prospects of financial and social gain brought on by opportunities in music. These are creative practices that emerge from changes to extrinsic motivations with music, such as the prospect of more lucrative careers, salaries, and fame. Through an influx of new ideas about success, power, and wealth, neoliberal reforms brought alternative motivations in relation to the arts and new ways to achieve those motivations. Even though music remains a form of entertainment and carries notions of ceremony embedded in the participatory nature of performance routines, it is also shaped by people's interests in connecting sound to daily life. If music reflects "social and political organization, economic behavior, religious activity, and other structural divisions of society," then shifts to these "structures" become reflected both in the way people interact and use music (Merriam 1964: 248). Music, in other words, takes on new meanings as society undergoes economic and political transformations. These new meanings become reflected in the learning, practices, and promotion of popular music. Those who are better able to discover opportunities in training, repositioning, and practicing within cultural transitions occurring within music can more easily reach the visible tip. To play on the metaphor of the submerged body, they are able to rise above the surface of the water of performing, recording, and broadcasting music to find social and economic opportunities in the local music economy.

# Radio Revolution

Thanks to real news promoters, media moguls . . .
Clouds FM, Radio One, Magic and Kiss,
Radio Free East Africa thanks a lot, I am very thankful.
Radio Uhuru, Times FM, and Channel 5 . . .
I am thankful to those who like me and gave me a name
My respect is eternal.

—KING CRAZY GK "Tupo Pamoja" (We Are Together)

No single event changed the course of Tanzania's music economy more than the passage of the Broadcasting Services Act. Signed into law by President Ali Hassan Mwinyi on June 11, 1993, it allowed private businesses and individuals in the country to apply for broadcasting licenses and, with government approval, start private radio and television stations. Given that the government's radio stations, Radio Tanzania Dar es Salaam (RTD) and Radio Zanzibar, had controlled the country's airwaves since 1951, the new law ended the government's monopoly on media and signified the expansion of opportunities for listeners, musicians, and media employees.[1]

The introduction of television in and of itself created a major cultural transformation in the country. Though Television Zanzibar (TVZ) had existed since 1974 and was on the air for close to five hours a day during the 1990s, mainland viewers had few opportunities to watch.[2] There was a small number of videocassette players in Dar es Salaam at the time, which were often in high demand when videotapes began to circulate among the city's residents. As one of the more humorous *Daily News* articles pointed out, owners of these machines were considered "demi-gods" during soccer's World Cup.[3] A few residents even had satellites dishes to receive broadcasts from other parts of the world, particularly South Africa. Despite these few exceptions among wealthier members of Tanzanian society, television was still a rarity in the country, making Tanzania one of the last African countries to offer television to its citizens.

The reason for restricting the airwaves from television was simple. Former president Julius Nyerere viewed television as a capitalistic tool and thought that the country should not enter into such a costly enterprise until it had the ability to develop its own programming.[4] Nyerere feared that television stations would only pipe in news and shows from other parts of the world, particularly Europe and the United States, which would undermine the government's ability to maintain control over the media and the education of the country's citizens. Not surprisingly, after the Broadcasting Services Act passed and the first television stations appeared in 1994, television stations did exactly what Nyerere predicted. They aired programs from South Africa, the United States, and England, interspersed with local news briefings and occasional sports and arts coverage. By the year 2000, news programs, particularly from CNN and the BBC, American sitcoms such as *Diff'rent Strokes,The Steve Harvey Show,* and *Silver Spoons,* and American hip-hop music videos were broadcast on local television stations. It was not until 2006 that local movies, music videos, and documentaries started to overtake these foreign imports in the amount of local airtime and in popularity.[5]

The government restricted radio for slightly different reasons. During the socialist period, the government could have required independent stations to produce locally oriented programs, but it would have been unable to control the content of those programs the same way it could with a state-run station. By hindering competitors, the government ensured that it had full access to the country's population, or at least to those who had radios.[6] More important, government officials could be sure that all Tanzanians were receiving information filtered through institutions they controlled. Being the sole radio station for mainland Tanzania, Radio Tanzania Dar es Salaam effectively restricted the news, music, and ideas people received throughout the country.[7] It standardized ways of speaking, notions of education, sound, and the arts. By keeping radio and television as state enterprises, the government aimed to influence public presentation and perception of the government and its policies.

When the government introduced the Broadcasting Services Act, a gradual movement away from tight controls on radio broadcasting occurred. No longer could the government hope to manage popular opinion or educate the country's citizens as it had before. New broadcasting stations aired foreign music, news, and ideas. Deejays altered the way that they spoke and interacted with their listeners. And a gradual relaxation of censorship occurred. Given the importance of radio, however, the state did not allow complete independence to broadcasters. Judge Mark D. Bomani, former chairman of the Tanzania Broadcasting Commission (TBC), stated, "While remaining free in their work, the broadcasting stations are aware that they have to operate in the national interest" (Bomani 2000: 5). The "national interest" is an important phrase in Tanzanian political rhetoric; it signals the state's continued involvement in shaping popular opinion about political realities. This is certainly not unique to Tanzania since most governments attempt to create strategic versions of political realities through influencing the language, ideas, and expressions of radio and other media broadcasts.

Musicians, broadcasters, and media owners are also aware of the influence of broadcasting media and attempt to influence the content of radio programs. Radio stations in most African countries wield tremendous cultural power in determining tastes and interests of large listening audiences in ways that no other medium can achieve. In a survey published on December 17, 2009, in the Tanzanian newspaper the *Daily News*, 66 percent of the 25,000 respondents stated that they receive their news primarily from radio stations.[8] In another survey, 95 percent of people in certain areas of Tanzania, such as Dar es Salaam, reported that they listen to the radio on a daily basis.[9] Although television has certainly become more influential in the past few years, radio remains the most dominant enterprise in the production and presentation of music, language, news, and ideas.

The popularity of radio is attributable to several factors. Literacy is not a barrier to listening to the airwaves. Radio receivers are relatively inexpensive, and they constantly blare from restaurants, storefronts, public transportation, bars, street corners, office buildings, and homes. The popularity of radio creates a social circulation of ideas, phrases, music, and discourses that can be "recycled and reanimated in everyday usage, outside of the contexts of radio listening" (Spitulnik 1997: 162). This social circulation allows radios to influence a broad array of listeners. Richard Fardon and Graham Furniss write, "African public cultures are ... radio-driven cultures. This is why such vital interests come in the ownership, control, and design of what goes on the airwaves" (2000: 16–17).

The power to influence large audiences—to shape public cultures—creates an omnipotent quality to broadcasting. Unlike the strategies discussed so far regarding performance and musical education, the creative practices that emerge around radio broadcasts are unique in that they embody different notions of power and prestige. Radio announcers, who read the news and provide information on the air, and deejays, who play and talk about music, are influential because their decisions can be heard by thousands of people at any given time. A voice heard by many carries weight and authority. Listeners help to shape a broadcast through requesting songs or deciding which programs they enjoy. Radio personnel, however, are the ones who select, modify, and create broadcast content. This accords them power, influence, and cultural significance in shaping the sounds of popular culture. Even in the early days of radio in Tanzania, radio personnel wielded tremendous cultural influence and were treated as celebrities. Gaudens Makunja, a sound engineer at RTD, told me that, in the 1960s, "An announcer was not considered a normal person. If he walks into a bar and people knew who he was, he would get free beer. I will give you one example, Saidi Omari; a very, very good announcer famous all over East Africa. Wherever he went, girls chased him. He was popular." While the fame of radio announcers is not quite equal to the 1960s when Omari was on the air, they remain significant in shaping popular culture.

The next several sections look at independent broadcasting in Tanzania and focuses on key players, including the state, listeners, musicians, and radio staff, who influence the outcome of popular music on the radio. More than any other part of the music economy, radio has played a central role in the commodification of popular music through creating desires to hear, acquire, and be a part of the ideas being played over the airwaves. It simultaneously helps determine what is popular commercially and aesthetically. Given the economic and cultural importance of radio, the government maintains a vested interest in the country's broadcasting. The first section of this chapter examines the desire of the state in maintaining control of programming content and in establishing regulations meant to protect its interests even in a political economy that discourages government interferences in local markets. Subsequent sections move into interactions between radio broadcasters and listening audiences, and the effect that this relationship has on compositional strategies among local musicians. Finally, the last two sections move inside radio stations to analyze the role that radio presenters have as gatekeepers in the content of radio programs. There is a great deal at stake for musicians who want to air their music, deejays who want to attain strong listening audiences, and station owners who want to bring in more revenue than other local stations. Individuals such as deejays, announcers, and musicians approach radio as an important resource, one that provides them tremendous financial potential. It is in gaining access to and/or protecting this resource where creative practices emerge with great force and influence.

→ THink about how these forces
intersect with each other &
the for...! acculturation→

## COMMERCIAL BROADCASTING IN
## THE NATIONAL INTEREST

The importance of radio in African countries is not just that it reaches so many people on a daily basis. It is also that radio is the primary medium for influencing and affecting public cultures. The notion of public cultures refers to forms of consciousness created by producers and consumers of mass media, from radio to television and sports to cinema. Listening to a radio program can make audiences feel connected to other listeners as part of a social group. People tuning in to the same broadcast may share similar moral and ideological beliefs, aesthetic tastes, and worldviews. The shared meanings created in such public cultures not only provide a sense of belonging and community, but also establish trends from each radio broadcast. There is no single direction that public cultures may take. Nor is there anything homogenous about them. Instead, the notion of public culture signifies the creation of listening spaces for broadcasting that connect people together through providing them with ideas, stories, songs, and language that can then be refracted and moved to other areas of society. Public culture is a dialogue that emerges within people's interactions with mass media and shapes the direction of broader social and economic landscapes.

Due to the influence of radio on public cultures, many governments have a vested interest in controlling the content of broadcasts. The better

control the state has over public cultures, or so the logic goes, the more
power can remain vested in a country's political leaders and policies. Yet
even in Tanzania's socialist period, where the government fully controlled
broadcasting in the country, dissent emerged among employees and content providers: many musicians used metaphors and double entendres to
make criticisms of the state; radio script writers, particularly those who
wrote radio plays and educational programs, inserted suggestions of their
opposition to social and political issues; and announcers used humor
to make their discontent known. These practices, while subtle and not
often acknowledged as an organized movement, undermined the state's
ability to completely manage and control information coming over the
airwaves.        *Exactly what Krims said in order to debunk*
                  *→ Adorno's standardization (homogeneity) argument*

   What is interesting about the transition to private radio is that the
Tanzanian government remains in control of many aspects of broadcasting even as it allows for media freedoms. Legislation and regulations exist in Tanzania that provide policy makers and political leaders
latitude to censor or restrict the broadcasting practices of companies
or individuals. At the same time, journalists, musicians, and others are        *consent &*
able to criticize the state and its policies often without fear of retalia-      *→ control*
tion by government officials. This negotiation between censor and tol-           *GRAMSCI*
erance is critically important for the state, since creating opportunities       *hegemony*
for criticism is viewed inside and outside Tanzania as a means to achieve
a functioning democracy. Further, by allowing criticism, the state can
sometimes evade tactics used to undermine the government's efforts:
musicians no longer need disguise the meaning of their songs in metaphors and double entendres if they are able to speak openly about the
problems facing them. If the state is able to shape the content of public
criticisms and ensure that media content remains focused on key issues
as defined by government officials, then the media criticism will appear
more transparent and less severe than comments made secretively or
with fear of repercussions. The ability to allow for and control critical
commentary is a central strategy used in Tanzania's privatized media
landscape.    *→ Appearance of less gov't control, but*
              *in reality . . . .*
   Tanzania is not unique in using the tension between censor and toler-
ance as a means to promote state interests in the neoliberal period. Many
countries, including those in the West, employ strategies that grant the

state privileges in shaping media coverage, such as permitting certain information to be made public and others private; sending specific members
of the government to speak to journalists about key issues; and reminding
members of the government to remain united on specific topics. Savvy
politicians are often those who can most adroitly manage their public image by shaping the information that circulates about them within public
cultures. Given the unpredictability of political gaffes and scandals, it is
not always possible to manage public perceptions, but there are certainly
political leaders and even administrations that are far more astute in influencing media coverage and commentary. Many politicians can even
turn potential liabilities into opportunities depending on the way that
they manage themselves in public.

To illustrate political maneuvers and public image in Tanzania, it
is useful to examine correlation between corruption, broadcasting, and
popular culture. Corruption is a primary concern of many international
institutions, development organizations, and foreign governments that
imagine that nations without corruption would improve trade and economic sustainability in free market economies.[10] Discussions of reform-
ing corruption have therefore become a means to legitimize the nation-
state both to citizens and foreign interests (Foster 2002: 9). Central to this
legitimization effort is the ability to manage the image of the government
and its leaders. By fighting corruption, political leaders can appear strong
and committed to central social concerns, particularly since corruption
is considered by many Tanzanians as the most significant problem in
government.

Tanzania is generally regarded as a country that permits media independence and, as the watch group Media Institute of Southern Africa
(MISA) notes, political leaders are tolerant of journalists criticizing the
government.[11] The effectiveness of media criticism has led to increased
attention to corruption: newspapers regularly appear with several simultaneous stories about corruption printed in the same paper; television
soap operas and comedy sketches often focus on issues of bribery; radio
plays, news, and music frequently present people's views on this issue; and
musicians record songs that address political and social dishonesty. Irene
Sanga's "Salamu Zangu" (My Greetings) is one such song that received
steady radio airplay in 2009 and early 2010. In this song, the following
lines are spoken by Mrisho Mpoto:

| | |
|---|---|
| Rushwa, ni wimbo wa sumu, | Corruption, it is a song of poison, |
| Uliotapakaa kwenye ubongo wa kila | That has spread over everyone in this |
| mwana wa taifa hili, | nation. |
| Tubadililishie wimbo huu tafadhali, | Let us change this song, please, |
| Turudishie nyimbo zetu za ushujaa, | We must return to our songs of bravery, |
| yimbo za makuzi na jando la taifa. | Songs that will build a youthful and strong nation. |

The pressure by the media, musicians, and other citizens in condemning corruption has led to several media spectacles. In 2008, the government took unprecedented action in arresting prominent politicians, including the former ministers Basil Mramba and Daniel Yona and permanent secretary Gray Mgonja. Charged with enacting government notices that exempted taxes for a foreign firm auditing gold production, each of these individuals spent time in jail, and photographs of the men awaiting arraignment with their heads bowed were prominently displayed on the front page of local newspapers. Another corruption scandal led to the resignation of Prime Minister Edward Lowasa and several other politicians. While embarrassing for the administration, the public scandals won President Jakaya Kikwete praise for listening to public and media commentaries. Through embracing media criticism, he signaled his willingness to participate in a more open debate, thereby gaining favor with many people who consider media freedoms and public opinion fundamental to a functioning democracy. → *Demonstrates how mass culture can influence hegemonic forces, yet the*

Many questions emerged in the aftermath of these scandals. Other *hegemonic* prominent politicians, who were also involved in corruption, remained *still take the* in Kikwete's administration. Some called the sacking of a few politi- *control –* cal leaders either a means to scapegoat a minority group or a means to reshuffle the administration. The news of the corruption reported by the media ultimately came from the Prevention and Combating of Corruption Bureau (PCCB), which is a government organization under the control of the president.[12] The possibility exists that media coverage and results of the corruption scandal were a means for the administration to achieve simultaneous goals of ousting problematic members of government and attaining a media victory in the fight against corruption. These goals benefitted the administration's ability to remain politically strong among international donors and Tanzanian citizens. It was a means of shaping media content while appearing to be tolerant of public criticisms.

The purpose of discussing political maneuvers in Tanzania is twofold. First, it shows that the creative practices discussed in this ethnography are not unique to the local music economy. There is a broader movement of developing strategies to market image, to remain politically powerful, and to establish a reputation within public cultures. The state, in other words, helps to shape and is in turn influenced by the strategies employed in Tanzania to attain political and economic success. Second, examination of corruption emphasizes the way that public culture can be mediated by many individuals in Tanzanian society: politicians, broadcasters, journalists, and musicians. Even though the focus of this ethnography is on the music economy, it is difficult to separate spaces, such as radio broadcasting, from the other areas of society that are intimately connected to the formation of public cultures. Politicians pressure media outlets, which impacts announcers' commentaries and influences musicians' compositional strategies. Of course, the alternative, where musicians impact politicians through radio outlets, is also true. There is a recognition that radio can serve commercial purposes, in promoting a politician's or an artist's career, while also influencing broader cultural or national interests.

To better comprehend the simultaneous engagement with commercial and national interests, I now turn to examine the management of broadcasting in Tanzania, particularly the practices that most affect the local music economy. Three strategies are central to the formation of radio broadcasting: the use of legislation that provides legal power for the state to censor where needed; the enforcement of strict guidelines in broadcast licensing; and the limited breadth of independent broadcasting. The use of legislation to enforce political authority in the broadcast spectrum is done through a combination of regulations, legislative acts, and constitutional amendments. In Tanzania, there are twenty-seven legislations that affect media information and, according to MISA, seventeen of them "suppress access to information, press freedom and freedom of expression."[13] Many of the laws enacted in the socialist period are reformulations of British colonial law, including the Newspapers Act No.3 of 1976, which allows for provisions of the state in restricting certain press freedoms. More recent acts, such as the Prevention of Terrorism Act of 2002, modeled on the British terrorism laws, considers it an offense if anyone in the government knowingly makes public information held in possession of the state. Considering the colonial legacy on rule of law in African countries (Joireman 2001), it is not surprising that Tanzania depends so heavily on British legislation. Tanzania is, in many ways, building a broadcast system based on those in England, Canada, and the United States.

For radio stations, several pieces of legislation exist that create an environment of commercial broadcasting in the national interest. In addition to the Broadcasting Services Act of 1993, there is the Tanzania Communications Regulatory Authority Act of 2003 (TCRA Act), which merged the postal, broadcasting, and electronic communications industries. The TCRA Act has language that encourages profitability of broadcasters and other communication industries. The function of the TCRA includes "promoting effective competition and economic efficiency" and "protecting the interest of consumers."[14] The Broadcasting Services Act, however, pushes more nationalist ideals in its language. It stipulates that the commission in charge of broadcasting should "encourage the development of Tanzanian and African expression by providing a wide range of programming that reflects Tanzanian and African attitudes, opinions, ideas, values and artistic creativity." It should also "serve the needs and interests and reflect the circumstances and aspirations of Tanzania men, women and children in a democratic Tanzania society."[15]

To further strengthen national interests in broadcasting after the more commercially oriented TCRA Act passed, the Tanzanian government issued additional guidelines under the Broadcasting Services (Content) Regulations of 2005 (BSCR). Under Part III of the regulations, broadcasting programs in Tanzania need to uphold "national sovereignty, national unity, national interest, national security, and Tanzania's economic interests." They should also project "Tanzanian national values and national points of view," "uphold public morality," and protect "children from negative influences."[16] Other specific regulations are vague enough that any promotion of violence or sexuality could be considered an offense. Considering that the TCRA can fine broadcasters up to five millions Tanzanian shillings ($5,000) for a single offense, radio broadcasters have good reason to closely follow these regulations.

The language used in the Broadcasting Services Act and the BSCR are similar to the nationalization of radio in the years after independence. In 1963, Idris Wakil, Minister of Information and Tourism, stated: "We

want development now. . . . We cannot leave the studios in the hands
of a group of wealthy people who could use it as a shop for business only
[cries of 'Hear, Hear,' and applause], without minding the need of our
Republic [cries of 'Hear, Hear,' and applause]. The Government ought to
have the power in these studios [applause] and I and my Ministry will do
everything we can to see that our radio is working for the benefit of this
country [applause]."[17] With the exception of the TRCA Act, all legislation
aimed at broadcasting in the contemporary period maintains the "need"
or "national values" of the state. The contention over commercialization
of radio in both the post-independence and neoliberal periods reflects the
persistent concern with special interests, business, and capital influencing
the content of radio. While differences exist in earlier and contemporary
legislation, it is only by a matter of degrees rather than a complete reformulation of ideological principles.

Rev!

Musicians are inexorably linked to the combination of consumer
and national rhetoric of Tanzanian legislation. Artists nearly always release their songs on the radio before they distribute them on cassette and,
in many cases, before they perform them in public. A successful radio
hit is often enough to provide artists with distribution and performance
contracts, as well the potential for widespread popularity and financial
stability. Given the importance of radio, artists need to compose music
that captivates listeners, adheres to broadcast regulations, and creates an
enticing song for radio broadcasters. To achieve these three outcomes,
composers frequently tailor their music within the boundaries of social and political acceptability. Anticipatory self-censorship is prevalent
in the way artists compose music aimed for broadcast audiences. Yet
the boundaries of acceptability are far more fluid and permeable than
would be provided by strict forms of censor. Artists are capable of pushing against state regulations in broadcasting, but only if they do not go
too far.

Elsewhere I note that Tanzanian music is often politically and socially
engaged (2005). While this has changed substantially since 2005, most
songs still do not promote violence, disrespect, or otherwise undermine
the values of the nation. The few controversial songs that have aired on
private radio encountered tremendous criticism in newspapers and public
debates. The government took action against Dully Sykes's "Nyambizi,"

because it had overt sexual references (he re-released an edited version for the radio); Young Stars Modern Taarab had their song about AIDS banned on radio and television and in performance, mostly because it was misinterpreted; and "Cheers" by Mgunga Mwa-Mnyenyelwa was censored for its negative reference to privatization. These songs received tremendous media attention when they were first broadcast on the radio. Due to their confrontational topics, however, the government, through various culture and broadcasting regulatory agencies, took action by banning them from the airwaves. This form of censor only occurs on occasion, however, since broadcasters themselves opt not to air songs that may be too controversial or flaunt broadcasting regulations.

Other artists are able to cleverly push against the borders of state restrictions by writing songs that are widely accepted as being in the public interest but are also critical of the nation-state. One example of this type of song is "Nikipata Nauli" (If I Receive a Fare) by Mrisho Mpoto. In the song, Mpoto tells President Kikwete, whom he refers to as Mjomba (Uncle), that the government is not doing enough to help the people of Tanzania. In the chorus, Banana Zorro sings, "Bora kujenga daraja kuliko ukuta / Chemchem si temi / Ukitaka kunywa maji yake / Sharti uiname" (It's better to build a bridge than a wall / Spring water is not forceful/ But if you want to drink its water / You must bend down to it). The melody is sweet with a gentle flute playing in the background. The meaning, however, is rather forceful, stating that the government has built a wall rather than a bridge between the Kikwete administration and the people of Tanzania. The metaphor implies that, even if the government does not care for its citizens, the day will arrive when the state will need the country's people. Government leaders will then appeal to citizens (symbolized by bowing to the water), especially when votes are needed. The verses of the song are no less critical. At one point Mpoto even asks Kikwete, "Je unajua timu yako?" (Do you know what team you are playing for?), which refers to the perception that Kiwete is more interested in helping foreign governments than local citizens.

Given the strong message of the song, why does it remain a popular hit on the radio? When I asked artists and journalists why this song was not banned despite its criticism of Kikwete, they stated that the lyrics are ultimately respectful and use moderate forms of criticism to discuss the

separation of the government from its citizenry. Many verses are reverential, even one at the beginning that states that Kikwete has added the
"ubeti wa mwisho" (latest verse) of the country's political history since independence. By using the word "Mjombe," Mpoto portrays Kikwete as a
father figure who can make needed changes. Mpoto also uses metaphors,
some of which have multiple layers but which contain no direct attacks,
slander, or highly critical language. Not least of all, the music employs
traditional instruments and rhythms. Through combining notions of respect with traditional Tanzanian forms of music, poetry, symbolism, and
meaning, the song remains a popular radio (and television) hit despite its
strong message.

In addition to influencing the parameters of acceptability on the
radio, the state's ability to maintain its interests in public broadcasting
entails remaining closely connected to radio station owners, announcers,
and deejays. Due to close political ties between the government and many
broadcasting owners, as well as the control over licenses administered by
the government, there is a generally acknowledged support of the state in
the content of radio programming. Many shows present political leaders
in the same way that Mpoto did in his song: respectfully, with some level
of criticism. Further, radio presenters encourage up and coming artists
to strive for inspired and culturally engaged forms of songwriting if they
want to appear on the radio. These include songs that promote *maendeleo*
(progress) and the interests of the nation-state. Several radio shows play
works of lesser known artists in order to give them exposure but also to
critique their works. These public reviews allow presenters to shape the
content and quality of songs that they air. Frequently, the commentaries
and critiques heard on these shows align closely with dominant political
ideologies of the ruling party.

In order to maintain a strong playlist of music, radio deejays also visit
recording studios to find new songs and request from producers works
that are socially and politically beneficial. Prior to the 2010 presidential elections, for instance, a presenter from a prominent radio station in
Dar es Salaam visited Fish Crab Studio in Kariakoo, Dar es Salaam. The
presenter requested works that carried a strong and useful message. The
producer played Wagosi wa Kaya's new song "Miaka Kumi ya Maumivu"
(Ten Years of Pain):

| | |
|---|---|
| Wagosi tunaamini moyo wako hauko radhi na mtu uliyemchagua | Wagosi believe that you are not satisfied with the person you chose, |
| Ila umemchagua kwa sababu umekwisha nunuliwa, | Except that you voted because you were paid off, |
| Usikubali hata siku moja kuipoteza haki yako ya msingi, | Don't give up your primary rights even for one day. |
| Kura unampigia leo unaongozwa kwa miaka mingi, | The vote you make today will go on for many years. |
| Naona wakina mama na kina baba mmejitokeza kwa wingi, | I can see mothers and fathers coming out in force, |
| Ili mpige kura kwa wingi tayari mmeshahongwa shilingi. | For you all to come out and vote means you have already been bribed. |

The song was a strong attack on the use of money in voting for elected officials. The presenter planned to air the song on the radio as a support for people to consider the best ways to move forward in a democracy. Even though the song could have been taken as a critique of the ruling party, many regarded it as a welcome comment on the election process, thereby emphasizing the state's willingness to allow many divergent opinions to emerge publically.

Aside from the creation of legislation and the encouragement of broadcasters to air content supportive of government policies, a third approach used by the state to manage radio content is through issuing licenses, controlled by the TRCA. Most of the TRCA's requirements are typical of other broadcasting commissions, such as the establishment of a network plan, technical and equipment specifications, insurance of expertise and financial resources, and stipulation that the company is at least 51 percent owned by citizens of Tanzania. Other requirements mandate that stations maintain community initiatives in their broadcasts. There is also the possibility that the TRCA could attach conditions to licenses such that broadcasts are made in "the public interest" (United Republic of Tanzania 1993: 8–9). For many broadcasting applicants, comprehending these specifications is critical to their application for a license. Applicants need to convince the commission that their station can exist on its own—in other words, be commercially viable—and still serve the public interest, through news and educational programming. More important, stations need to clearly define the parameters of programming content to show that it will not counter the interests of the state. Ruge Mutahaba, who is general manager at Clouds FM, one of Dar es Salaam's most popular radio stations, discussed the process he and Joseph Kussaga, the head of Clouds FM, went through to receive a broadcasting license:

> **Mutahaba:** The worry was not how to run a station, but we did not expect the broadcasting commission to give us a license. We knew it was going to be a real difficult process. But we decided to try. We went and applied for a license. And we were so determined, going back again and again; I can imagine their feeling was like, "Oh, just give it to them."
>
> **Perullo:** What was the process like to get a license?
>
> **Mutahaba:** You have to go to the Tanzania Broadcasting Commission, get a form, fill it out. They take it back and they have a big meeting in the Prime Minister's office and they discuss all of the licenses that are put through. If yours is filtered to the next stage—each one is screened to the next stage—you go to an interview. So, Joseph and I went to Dodoma to have an interview in front of the whole commission. And they asked us questions about what we were going to do. See, our idea was to start a station, but it had to be an entertainment radio station. We argued a bit about that with them. . . . Our argument was that there are so many radio stations giving out information, we want to give out information in a different way. In a way, that the young people relate to us more. So, we defended our case. They said okay, we will give you a license. After we got the license, we were surprised. "Wow, we got the license, what do we do now?"

Mutahaba's summary makes the application process sound simple, but as he and others later told me, it is a long, costly process. Despite repeated visits to speak with the commission, follow up on the application, make necessary changes, and travel to interviews, an applicant is not guaranteed to receive a license. If an applicant is successful, then there is a list of fees that need to be paid. There are also costs to use radio booster stations, owned by the government. Even before purchasing equipment, renting office space, hiring staff, and buying music to air on the radio, an applicant has to invest a great deal.

On the whole, the financial obligations of a broadcasting license in Tanzania are equal to those in other countries. Similar to the United States, where commercial radio stations are often run by large businesses, media conglomerates own most of Tanzania's commercial radio stations. The remaining portion is owned by religious organizations, mostly

Christian, and are scattered throughout the country. Only a handful of stations, such as Clouds FM and Radio Free Africa, exist as independent radio stations, separated from other media companies and religious organizations. The owners of Clouds FM, however, do own several disco clubs, rent deejaying equipment, and enter into other music oriented projects, while Anthony M. Diallo, the owner of Radio Free Africa and its sister station Kiss FM, is a former businessman and a current member of Parliament. Even though radio is now independent in Tanzania, it is primarily owned and run by individuals and companies that are financially strong.

More important, many of the radio stations that do receive licenses are friendly with the ruling party CCM. This point is harder to prove with any explicit data though many informants in broadcasting often talk about the relationship between their station's owners and members of Parliament. Due to interest in CCM candidates, most broadcasters avoid making disparaging comments about those candidates even though they argue that they have the freedom to do so. This subtler form of censor is based on job insecurity where announcers, managers, and others are well aware that their employment and even the viability of companies depend on intelligent navigation of the political spectrum in the country. Musicians need to be aware of these subtler forms of regulation since any song that counters a dominant ideology of the station may not make it on the air. Further, during studio interviews, which is a prevalent part of radio broadcasting, musicians often need to refrain from being overtly political as they might be in daily life. In situations where topics become too controversial, radio presenters signal the guest to stop talking or change the subject in order not to offend station owners, media regulators, or even, when court cases are discussed, the public. This on-air editing is not heard over the airwaves, but is effective to controlling the content of live broadcasts.

In general, radio stations are required, upon receipt of a broadcast license, to comply with the conditions of the Broadcasting Services Act, set high standards (in other words, not use foul language or have inappropriate content), and have local and national news.[18] These "duties," as they are called in the law, attempt to "contribute through programming to shared national consciousness, identity, and continuity" (United Republic of Tanzania 1993: 10–11). The TRCA, with its limited resources, is unable to monitor all of the country's radio, cable, and television broadcasts throughout the day.[19] Nonetheless, several radio and television stations have had their licenses revoked for not complying with specific forms of legislation. The commission inspects license holders to determine if they are following the conditions and duties of the Broadcast Services Act. If they are not, they are warned or fined and may have their licenses revoked. On August 1, 1996, the TBC determined that twelve radio and television stations had failed to "implement their projects" set forth in their applications (Sturmer 1998: 191).

Finally, the last strategy used by the government to promote its interests within radio broadcasting is to maintain strict controls over the territorial reach of independent radio. On January 26, 1999, members of Parliament discussed expanding and upgrading national radio services to ensure that Radio Tanzania Dar es Salaam (RTD) could be heard throughout the country. Fatma Maghimbi, an opposition Member of Parliament, raised her concern about control over national airwaves:

> I just have one question to ask. There are other radio stations aside from Radio Tanzania that are heard in nearly the whole country, such as BBC, American radio [Voice of America], and German radio [Deutsche Welle Radio]. When will the Government stop restricting [independent broadcasters] such as ITV and Radio Free Africa from broadcasting to the entire country? Doesn't the Government see that it is hindering progress of Tanzanians and benefiting foreigners? When will the Government stop this practice?

Muhammed Seif Khatib, who was the Minister of State, replied that the Broadcasting Services Act only allows an independent radio station to be heard in 25 percent of the country.[20] He continued, "We cannot allow a person himself to reign over the entire country and control the news of the entire country; and this is not only Tanzania . . . even those with prominent democracies, such as the United States and England, do not allow this."[21] For Maghimbi, it was far better to have locally produced content heard throughout the country than foreign broadcasts. For Khatib, who had authority over broadcasting in the country, even the independent networks could not be trusted with the ability to broadcast to the entire country. This could undermine the ability of the state to maintain its interests in all regions of the country.

Of the strategies that the state uses to maintain control over broadcasting, this is the only one that has been significantly undermined. Savvy independent broadcasters with enough economic standing are now setting up broadcast relays in neighboring countries. Radio One, for instance, applied for a frequency from the Uganda National Frequency Registration Board that allowed a broadcast from Dar es Salaam to be carried to most areas of Tanzania, Uganda, and Kenya. Radio Free Africa has relays in sixteen areas of Tanzania, and can now be heard, according to their own analysis, in all of East Africa during the night (when radio signals travel better). These broadcasting expansions have made Radio Free Africa and Radio One far more powerful than even Tanzanian national radio. Other media enterprises are following suit, and there is a possibility for more regional interaction and competition to emerge in broadcasting over the next decade. The East African Economic Community (EAC), however, has signaled that it wants to regulate regional airwaves (Sorokobi 2001), which could either restrict the influence of individual nation's on broadcasting or, more likely, expand the potential to regulate independent media. At stake is the influence over national and regional public cultures that could provide tremendous lucrative power to whoever defines those regulations.

The combination of strategies used by the state to remain influential in broadcasting should not overshadow the many freedoms that artists have in Tanzania. Without the privatization of media, even the airing of rap, r&b, and ragga would not have occurred since these were viewed in the past as non-African musical forms. Currently, artists are able to compose music in any style and on most topics as long as they refrain from certain overt or direct forms of commentary. The boundaries that exist in radio are still being explored, and new songs regularly emerge that push the margins of radio broadcasting. The TRCA, as well as other government organizations, continue to react to music that pushes too hard on those borders. In addition, artists refrain from composing salacious songs out of a combination of respect, a lasting socialist idea that continues to permeate through artists' songs. Broadcasters also refrain from airing content that would be considered counter to national interests. At each level—from the composer to the broadcaster to the state—there are forms of self-regulation that keep music confined to certain topics, ideals, and values. These forms of regulation, however, are common to many media markets where broadcasters frequently avoid taking risks in the songs that they air. The commonalities in this approach to broadcasting signal Tanzania's emergence as a viable radio market equal to those in other parts of the world.

## PROGRAMMING, LISTENERS, AND POPULAR MUSIC

In 2001, I conducted a survey among one hundred radio listeners in Dar es Salaam to determine listening habits.[22] I was interested in understanding the ways private broadcasting altered people's interests and connections to radio. My questions focused on the amount of time people tuned in to local radio stations, as well as the use of other media, including television, the internet, and recorded music. I asked respondents to identify genres that they enjoyed the most, as well as the names of their favorite artists. On the survey form, I listed all the radio stations that could be heard in Dar es Salaam at that time (there were ten on the air), and had them select ones that they listened to with regularity. Finally, I asked the participants to explain the reasons that they listened to these stations.

The respondents ranged in age from 18 to 62. All listened to the radio for several hours each day, and only a few watched television or used the internet. Radio, for everyone who filled out the survey, was the most accessible and important media resource. They received a majority of their news, music, and enjoyment from tuning into local radio broadcasts.

In the survey answers, the reason for listening to radio stations was fairly consistent among respondents. One 30-year-old male stated that he tuned into local radio stations (he selected eight) because they "educate and entertain" him. The former dictum of socialist radio and recording studios remained a vested part of contemporary connections to broadcasting. A 22-year-old female wrote, "I enjoy these radio stations [she selected six radio stations] because they provide various programs that are very good. They have programs that teach our society about various concerns such as AIDS, youth employment, and still provide entertainment from various countries around the world, along with Tanzania." A 28-year-old male explained, "I like these stations [he selected six] since they have a good approach for providing entertainment and they play more songs from Tanzania." Others noted the importance of news and entertainment, or radio programs that encourage society to "move forward." The conceptualization of radio culture as first educational and then entertaining suggests a persistent legacy to the role of state radio in shaping people's reception of and interaction with broadcasting in Tanzania.

The survey results also showed that the content and meaning of radio broadcasts have undergone significant reformulations. In the 1990s, state radio programs often sounded like lectures or informative lessons about elements that the government believed to be important for all citizens. Radio plays started with interesting characters, dialogue, and well-developed plots only to break off into long lectures that rarely fit the content of the previous dialogue. Political speeches were regularly broadcast, as were long news segments that presented the merits of the state and the national party. Music, as discussed in chapter 2, was censored and did not address controversial issues or topics. Government-influenced education frequently became the focus of radio programming, which, according to both staff and listeners, made entertainment less entertaining.

When independent radio stations appeared in Dar es Salaam in 1994, broadcasting content changed significantly. The first radio station was Radio Tumaini followed by Radio One, a station owned by the business entrepreneur Reginald Mengi. In an article that announced Mengi's award as East Africa's second most respected CEO in 2000, James Mwakisyala writes, "Reginald Abraham Mengi is the man who brought television and independent radio stations to the country, changing Tanzanians' perspective and world outlook, wiping out the notion that broadcasting was the preserve of the government."[23] Radio One created programs around certain themes, such as a deejays' favorite songs (*DJ Choice*), popular hip-hop music (*DJ Show*), news and views from all over Africa (*Africa Panorama*), and slow, late-night music to help people wind down the day. The depth of programming gave listeners a wide variety of music and ideas unheard of in the past. There were catchy jingles, some made in Kenya, which gave the station a novel, commercial sound. Deejays, announcers, and program directors allowed on-air discussions and brought live debates to the airwaves. Radio One razed many of the stiff barriers fortified by public broadcasting and made radio vibrant and (eventually) more commercially lucrative.

Currently, over 2.9 million people own a radio in Dar es Salaam, compared with 565,000 in all of Tanzania in 1994. The increase in listenership is due to significant expansions in the types of content being offered.

Are radios being manufactured in Tanzania?

Even though many listeners want to have educational and entertaining programs, the meaning of those terms has undergone alterations in the neoliberal period. Rather than focus on socialist ideology, agriculture, and literacy, as was common in the programs of state radio, the most popular broadcasting time slots on independent radio tend to be filled with informational talk shows that discuss music, relationships, community activism, and public policy issues. There are programs about healthcare, employment, divorce, and land ownership. Music shows provide biographies and discographies of artists and their music. Even the government radio station has altered its programming. Their radio lineup on January 3, 2010, included call-in shows (*Simu ya Mkononi*), the best bongo flava songs of 2009 (*Bongo Flava Bora ya 2009*), and comedy programs (*Orijino Komedi*). None of these would have aired before the privatization of radio. In these cases, education and entertainment remains a fundamental part of Tanzanian broadcasting culture, but there are far more diverse interpretations of learning, enjoyment, and knowledge than occurred in the past.

In the 2001 survey, audiences also pointed out that they listened to several radio stations (an average of five) throughout the day. They would regularly switch to find a favorite song, announcer, or show. When competing popular programs were on at the same time, the respondents stated that they switched back and forth between the stations every few minutes to keep up with both. Scanning many radio stations throughout the day allows listeners to find content that connects with their interests, which they can then use to participate in discussions with others. Listeners construct a relation to public cultures through identifying programs, presenters, and content that articulates their concerns, hopes, and desires. It is a fragmented means of listening where radio establishes a creative space for individuals to develop their own attachments to and relations with local popular culture. Radio, in these situations, is interactive and dynamic, even though broadcasters and the state have a great deal of influence in shaping the content and information received by listeners. In short, the survey results emphasize actively engaged radio audiences rather than passive consumers of powerful media networks.

Knowing that listeners frequently switch stations, many program directors design radio schedules that capture as many different publics as possible during any given day. Thomas Chilala, a presenter at Radio

Tumaini, explains his station's variety of programming: "We are a mixed variety station; we do not discriminate. If you want a mix of music, you will get it. If you want religious programs or prayers, you will get it. If you want sports, you will get it on our radio station. If you want educational programs, you will get it." Although Chilala laments other stations that copy Radio Tumaini's programming style, he is careful to note that the station covers every area of radio listening in Tanzania and attracts a wide audience. He continues:

> Our listening audience is mixed. Adults and elders really love Radio Tumaini. For example, a few Ministers [gives their names] appreciate what we do, and they say that Radio Tumaini is listened to by people who have wisdom and respect. Youth also listen. During a program like *Salaam* [*Greetings*], many of them call in. Another program is *Vijana Leo na Kesho* [*Youth Today and Tomorrow*] where youth enter the studio to discuss life. . . . We also have programs for children.

The approach to present radio to a variety of listeners across social, economic, and educational lines is a result of the variability in audience interaction with radio broadcasts. It is also due to the lack of audience research, which often provides insights into how and why people tune in to radio shows. With more audience research, a radio station might shape a more cohesive daily schedule in order to maintain a steadier body of listeners.

For the local music economy, the most important result of the 2001 survey was the comments people made about the types of music that they regularly searched for on the radio: hip-hop, reggae, soul, jazz, r&b, rock 'n' roll, *ndombolo* (Congolese dance music), and *bolingo* (Congolese romantic music) were the most common genres mentioned. Several people also wrote the names of local forms of music, such as taarab and dansi, or identified local artists that they liked. Overwhelmingly, however, the focus of people's responses was toward foreign genres. Another question on the survey asked if respondents liked Tanzanian music. Almost everyone said that they did, and then proceeded to list groups such as African Stars, Mr. II, Lady Jay Dee, and Hamza Kalala and Bantu Group, bands and artists that most significantly incorporated foreign musical sounds into their compositions in the early 2000s. It was a strong commentary on the influence of foreign cultural forms, mediated by radio broadcasting, in shaping popular music in Tanzania.

## BANDS TUNE IN AND TAKE OUT

Along with other radio listeners, musicians rely on radio broadcasting to learn about trends and ideas emerging within popular culture. Few musicians use cassettes or compact discs to find out about new musical ideas and techniques. Instead, radio informs them about innovative studio aesthetics, vocal phrasings, instrumentation, and new vernacular words. It provides them with rhythmic and melodic ideas, as well as overall trends in tempo, timbre, and lyrical content. Artists become audiences who partake in a sense of social aesthetics where they "evaluate the style, coherence, and effectiveness of a particular performance" (Brenneis 1990: 173). Performance, in this case, is the broadcast of songs which, with repeated play, pushes artists to alter their compositions to attain airplay that connects commonalities in musical sound to a particular genre. A desire exists to be innovative while also being associated with popular radio hits. It is a balance that encourages creativity within the restrictions of commercial radio → *BALANCE is key here*

For Tanzanian musicians, independent radio broadcasting was initially detrimental to their careers. Between 1994 and 1996, independent radio stations rarely played local music, preferring the sounds of Michael Jackson, Toni Braxton, Boomerang, Bombastic, and other foreign pop sensations. The first one hundred CDs at Radio One were all pop music from Europe and the United States. Eventually, independent radio stations built libraries that included music from Africa, since this was a requirement for attaining broadcast licenses. Local music was added to the mix, but only intermittently since the quality of most Tanzanian recordings was poor compared to foreign compact discs. Deejays from the 1990s commented to me that they refused to play the "cheap" Tanzanian recordings next to high-quality foreign ones because the sound difference was just too drastic. Recordings in Tanzania sounded a bit like AM radio compared to the higher quality materials from other parts of the world.

The decline in radio airplay for local artists had a significant and enduring impact on the sounds of Tanzanian music. Refusing to play local artists, broadcasters searched for culturally appropriate African replacements since broadcasters were still required to have representation of African music in their radio shows. Congolese rumba became a quick and easy choice since it was better recorded and shared many musical and cultural connections with Tanzanian popular culture (Perullo 2008b). Radio popularity led to high cassette sales of Congolese music. Artists from Zaire/Democratic Republic of the Congo moved to Dar es Salaam and formed popular bands, such as FM Academia, Diamond Stars Band, and New Millennium Band (for classic Congolese artists and song, see PURL 5.1; for the group New Millennium, see PURL 5.2). The interest in all things Congolese led to a dramatic decline in Tanzania's indigenous dance bands. One journalist wrote, "In the 1990s, the mention of the Congolese—whose songs sold like hot cakes in Tanzania—sent shivers down the spines of many local musicians."[24] As a result of low radio airplay, many dansi groups lost their audiences and suddenly found themselves in the role of cover bands trying to play Congolese music to keep people attending shows. Even long-running bands, such as DDC Mlimani Park Orchestra, debated their future as audience size dwindled to as few as five people.

To regenerate interest in dansi, Tanzanian artists searched for ways of recapturing local audiences. One strategy was to draw on the popularity of classic Tanzanian dansi. Miguel Suleyman wrote in *The East African*, "Threatened by the immense success of Congolese music, musicians in Tanzania have in recent years embarked on a mission to restore the glory of East African dance music by revisiting the works and music styles of such artists as Mbaraka Mwinshehe, Marijani Rajabu, Hemedi Meneti, Fundi Kondi, and Daudi Kabaka."[25] A few local bands and musicians, such as Shikamoo Jazz, Ndala Kasheba, and King Kiki, found short-term success in performing the classic sounds of the 1960s, referred to as *zilipendwa* (literally, songs that were loved, sometimes referred to as "old is gold," PURL 5.3 and PURL 5.4). The audience for these shows, at least in the late 1990s and early 2000s, tended to be *wazee* (elders) who would attend one show a month and spend their money rather conservatively. Youth and young adults, despite their low incomes, were far more important in the urban music scene. They had the most disposable income to use and far outnumbered the city's elders. Recapturing their attendance at shows became a prime objective for many dansi groups.

The most successful dansi bands, such as African Stars, Chuchu Sound, TOT Band, and Hamza Kalala and Bantu Group, increased their fan base by releasing quality recordings on the radio that mixed local Tanzanian music with popular radio hits. Cognizant of the tremendous

*Demonstration of change in musical components / aesthetics*

success of Congolese rumba, many groups added rhythms, guitar lines, and especially vocal parts to their music that conjured the Congolese sound. For instance, on the song "Kitimoto" (Pork), Hamza Kalala and Bantu Group merge several elements of rumba, dansi, and traditional music to compete in the radio market. The opening line of "Kitimoto" is sung in Kinyamwezi and describes a conversation between two slaves in colonial times. One slave, Hussein, receives a pass to return to his family. The other slave, who continues to work, says goodbye to Hussein, telling him to greet everyone for him and tell them all is well. Kalala sings this opening section with the Sheggy brothers (Christian and Francis) in a slow two-part harmony that sounds like classic dansi music. Mixed with short guitar runs, the voices, guitar, and steady rhythm section produce a sound reminiscent of music from the 1970s (PURL 5.5 and PURL 5.6).

After singing the opening few lines of the song, the band moves to a faster-paced section. The vocal harmony is similar to previous Bantu group compositions, but the remainder mimics Congolese songs heard on the radio at that time. Drawing from the Congolese artist General Defao, Kalala uses a strong keyboard fill to present the melody and chords of the song. The lead guitarist harmonizes the melody line, and there are deep vocal shout-outs from Kalala. While praises are common in Tanzanian music, the style and timbre that Kalala uses are a direct reference to popular Congolese performers. Kalala also sings several praises in Lingala, the language often used in Congolese rumba. The drum pattern of "Kitimoto" and the punctuated staccato guitar breaks are derivative versions of ones that can be heard in "Gâté le Coin," a popular song by the Congolese singer Awilo Longomba. Even the overlapping, flowing guitar lines are reminiscent of the melodic phrasing characteristic in certain rumba styles, such as *soukous* and *ndombolo*.

Kalala's "Kitimoto" became a radio hit after its release. Lyrically and musically, the song tapped into the popular culture aesthetics dominant on the radio at that time, reviving the band's popularity in the local music scene. Though many gatekeepers of Tanzanian culture complained about the "copycat" tactics of Tanzanian bands, the commercial success that these groups found far outweighed any criticism they received.

Audience and broadcasting tastes also change over time, and by 2006 interest was moving back toward high quality, locally inspired dansi music. Band members of strictly Congolese music left their groups to join

*How did this transition occur?*

native Tanzanian groups. In one high-profile scenario, the local sponsor of the Congolese group FM Muzika dropped the band, citing weak profits at concerts. One journalist wrote in the early period of this movement, "Tanzanian musicians are elbowing out their rivals. . . . The Tanzanians boasted in separate interviews that they are no longer afraid of the Congolese in performing, recording, promoting, and selling their songs."[26] Many people acknowledged the shifts in interest from rumba to dansi as a result of radio support for local artists. In newspaper articles, musicians thanked radio stations for playing local Tanzanian music.[27] In my interviews with musicians, most acknowledged radio as the main reason their groups had become commercially successful. Even though radio initially encouraged dansi musicians to alter their sound and improve the quality of their recordings, most believed that radio benefited their music overall since it brought their songs to a wider audience. Independent radio was influential in reshaping the sound of a genre, but equally powerful in giving local artists a chance to achieve popularity and success through competing with foreign talent.

One of the results of relying on radio more than any other medium is that it fosters immediate and timely dialogue between groups. Recorded music can take time to circulate, and live performances tend to cultivate isolated communities rather than unified spaces of public dialogue. Radio broadcasts produce immediate impacts on audiences since so many people regularly tune in, call in, and react to the sounds they hear. The potential, therefore, exists for musical genres to attain more airtime if they provide similar interactive types of dialogue that generate strong audience reactions. The argument, according to one radio manager whom I spoke with, is that songs that encourage a reaction from listeners, whether amusement, frustration, anger, or shock, provide far better radio programs and should be broadcast on the airwaves.

Taarab music is a genre that generates dialogue and strong reactions in performance settings. For instance, during live shows, a person can request that a band play a song with a powerful social message. The messages in taarab songs can range from those that discuss extramarital affairs to dishonesty in social relationships. The person who requested the song then stands in a prominent place in a club and mouths the lyrics while looking at someone in the audience. The lyrics act as a means of condemning, criticizing, or challenging the recipient of the words.

These social commentaries can lead to further conflicts or help to resolve misunderstandings between two people. Inevitably, they generate
tremendous interest by audience members who watch the musical group
and the dialogue between the participants of the song.

Moving this confrontational style onto the radio meant that broadcasters could draw the controversies inherent in taarab songs into their
broadcasts. Even though taarab music was not commonly heard on radio
either in the socialist period or in the early years of independent broadcasting, several radio stations recognized the potential of the music
within the new radio culture. Problematically for broadcasters, taarab
audiences often have specialized knowledge of words, phrases, places,
and names that they use to understand the meaning of songs.

To move taarab to the radio, artists needed to shift their compositional approaches to the genre. Taarab musicians wanted to have their
music played on the air, and were frequently frustrated by the dominance
of other genres. In consultation with deejays, announcers, and other radio
personnel, taarab musicians made several changes to their compositions.
The most significant change, aimed at drawing on the types of songs commonly heard on the radio, was to make the meanings of confrontational
and inflammatory songs more direct, obvious, and enticing to the general
listener. This more direct form of confrontational style became known
as *mpasho.*

*Mpasho,* derived from the word *kupata,* "to get," is a form of communication through song lyrics that includes the ridicule of rival bands
or singers (Fargion 2000: 40). Rival bands enter into *mipasho* (the plural
of mpasho) to prove which group is better than another, and to critique
how another band acts, presents itself, and performs. While mpasho pre-
dates the influence of radio, broadcasting stations, ready to entice listeners onto the airwaves, picked up on the mpasho trend in 1998. Clouds
FM was the first independent, commercial radio station to offer taarab
as a regular part of mainland programming. Ruge Mutahaba, program
director at Clouds FM, explained that the airing of mipasho songs created
tremendous interest in a genre that had not been considered a part of the
independent radio movement. Through using controversy, the genre attracted critical acclaim by listeners who enjoyed attacks and rebuttals
between bands. Lyrics that were contentious, divisive, and, at times, cruel
came to be part of people's enjoyment with the broadcasting of this genre.

Tanzanian radio had always been a rather pristine place for songs sung in Swahili. The emergence of mpasho pushed the limits of acceptable broadcasting through airing insults, grievances, and discussions of private topics.

TOT Taarab and Muungano Cultural Troupe became the forerunners of the broadcast mpasho movement, and continually spilled out hits ridiculing one another. The rivalry between the groups started when TOT formed on August 18, 1992. According to the leader of Muungano Cultural Troupe, Norbert Chenga, TOT stole some of its band members to start their group. Chenga referred to his band's relationship with TOT Taarab: "We became neither friends nor enemies. We were in opposition. One day, they would come and steal one of my artists, and I would sit idle. After a month, I steal. I come and take one of their artists. So, when the fans of Muungano and the fans of TOT meet one another, they enjoy a lot." Chenga uses the word "enjoy" here, but as he continued to inform me, there is nothing friendly or humorous about mipasho.

> Someone can use the same song to attack another person. Someone rents a home and, maybe he/she has a falling out with the landlord or he/she has a falling out with the renter next door. He/she takes a [mpasho] tape, puts it in the radio, turns up the volume, and opens the door. Then the other person comes out of their house to do something. The message comes out [from the music] and reaches him or her. Perhaps that person is *sanamu la michelini* [very fat]. Now, that person gets the message. Sometimes [the conflict] goes until they take each other to court. Sometimes they fight, until they end up in the hospital. Because of the hatred [that exists between the people]. This is not humorous.[28]

Mipasho developed out of the fierce competition for both artists and fans between the two groups, which made both bands' concerts extremely successful. By the time Muungano released their hit single "Sanamu la Michelini"—literally, "Symbol of the Michelin [Man],"—aimed at the lead singer of TOT, who in size and weight is comparable to the Michelin Man—mipasho was one of the biggest draws in the Tanzanian music scene, heavily promoted on several local radio stations (PURL 5.7).

To reach broader radio audiences, particularly people less familiar with formal taarab compositions, musicians introduced several changes to the genre. Many of these changes began well before radio stations aired taarab music, yet the influence of radio helped to foster these transformations. Attacks needed to be punchier, more clear-cut, and more readily decipherable by listeners. Lyrics needed to be straightforward so as to appeal a wider audience not familiar with codes and metaphors of the genre. Referring to the taarab singer Aidha Haji Mohamedi Omar, John Ngahyoma writes, "Today's taarab poetry is not complex and deep like it was in the past. [Instead] today's poetry is light, making it easy to understand what the composer intended to say" (2001: 54). Some recent songs have even become so stark and stripped of deeper meaning that they have begun to resemble pop songs, unusual in a genre that relied so heavily on poetry and metaphor. Taarab songs also need to be shorter, five to six minutes long rather than the more typical 15 or 20 minutes (in cases where songs are not edited in the studio to the shorter length, they are cut during live broadcasts by deejays). Finally, the arrangements of many taarab songs merge elements of the cities' popular cultures with taarab aesthetics. These changes, both lyrically and musically, make taarab appealing for a broad array of listeners throughout Dar es Salaam and Tanzania.

Many older taarab musicians lament the destruction of taarab due to the current overuse of mpasho, which has often degenerated into foul language and other strategies deemed unacceptable (Askew 2002: 134–35). Yet, this sensational style of musical composition brings wide public interest to audiences across Tanzania, partially through its heavy promotion on the radio. When I conducted research in Dodoma, which is the capital of the country and removed from coastal traditions, all the cassette vendors said that the most popular form of music was mpasho due to its confrontational lyrics and frequent broadcast on radio. In 2010, taarab was the most popular music in Dar es Salaam in part due to the controversies stimulated by groups appearing on a variety of radio stations throughout the day.

Thus far, my argument has been that radio broadcasting impacts the compositional and recording choices of musicians due its influence in popular culture. In order to attain radio airplay, a coveted medium in Tanzania's music economy, musicians need to be responsive to the desires of broadcasters and their audiences. Creativity emerges in the techniques that musicians use to tailor popular music to the content of radio broadcasts. It is important to add, however, that not all radio stations are equal within the country's broadcasting spectrum. There are radio shows that are more dominant than others in influencing the sounds of popular music. These programs combine many elements, such as quality announcers, enticing topics, and frequently some measure of competition. In interviews and discussions with members of Tanzania's music community, as well as radio audiences, these radio shows are regularly mentioned for their prominence and popularity in the local music scene.

Radio One's *Nani Zaidi* (Who Is Better), for instance, has been on the air since 1994 and remains a critical program for popular music in Tanzania. The program airs every Sunday for two hours, and has two bands or groups with similar styles of music that compete against each other live on the air. In 1995, two early rap groups, Kwanza Unit and the Deplowmatz, competed on the program. When the Deplowmatz, the younger group, won, it created a significant rupture in the future of hip-hop in the country. The Deplowmatz would eventually sing in Swahili, while Kwanza Unit focused on keeping their style as close as possible to the American rap they heard on cassettes. The battle between the two bands took place at a moment just before these two ideological approaches separated, a significant transition in the popularity of rap in Tanzania. In addition to a live performance competition, called Yo! Rap Bonanza, *Nani Zaidi* set the tone for the future of the country's rap scene (Perullo 2007).

More recently, in January 2010, two classic dansi bands, Vijana Jazz Orchestra and Orchestra Safari Sound (O.S.S), competed against each other on the same show. Both bands were popular in the 1970s and 1980s, but had long lost their vitality as important groups on radio and in live performances. Since the mid-2000s, however, classic songs, zilipendwa, have become popular again due to their association with the country's post-independence period (the music has become popular even among young people, which is different that the initial resurgence of zilipendwa discussed above). Many music fans argue that life has become harder and more difficult during neoliberalism, while the past is imagined more idealistically as a time where the state "took care of you." Zilipendwa songs represent a nostalgia for an imagined past where there is comfort in the proto-nationalist music of a bygone society. In addition, zilipendwa songs are viewed in opposition to genres such as bongo flava that may feature angry and confrontational language, as well focus on money, wealth, and capitalism. Classic dansi songs tend to be about love, relationships, and problems living in the city and carry a more laid-back feel than other contemporary popular music songs.

The presence of two zilipendwa bands on the program *Nani Zaidi* symbolized the resurgence in classic dansi music. By appearing on a prominent competitive show, the bands were able to perform to listeners from various age groups, social classes, and regions of the country. It proved that classic dansi was still a viable musical form. Further, the stakes for the bands were high, since winning the on-air competition could potentially lead to more radio airplay, higher concert attendance, and greater cassette sales. In the end, Orchestra Vijana Jazz won the most votes among radio listeners and, at least over subsequent months, regenerated interest in their live shows.

*Nani Zaidi* is unique for its longevity and for the concept of airing a competition between bands. Yet other radio shows share similar broadcasting dominance in Tanzanian popular culture. These programs add a compelling mixture of interviews, interaction, and information that audiences find compelling. Although some of these shows remain popular simply due to audience attachment to them, the quality of the programming and subject matter make them stand out from the dozens of other shows being broadcast simultaneously. More important, audiences often comment that the quality of the announcers is the most compelling reason to tune in to a radio show. Popular announcers are frequently revered in Tanzania for their vocal clarity and ability to make topics engaging, entertaining, and educational.

## RADIO STAFF SIGN ON

On the afternoon of December 14, 2000, I sat in the on-air studio of Radio Uhuru waiting for the show's host, Sebastian Maganga, and his assistant, Oops (Asma Makau), to finish reading the top-ten song list. Maganga stood in front of the microphone, with one hand on the large mixer in front of him and the other on the dial of a CD player. Maganga's Fubu pants sagged several inches below his waist, while a long Sean John striped shirt fell low on his hips. Oops sat at the second microphone, injecting comments and information between Maganga's list of musicians and songs. The studio was filled with equipment: racks of minidisc, CD, and DAT players; turntables; speakers; and transmitter devices. A glass window separated the room we sat in from an adjoining interview, or live music, room. On the hot Dar es Salaam day, the room was kept icy cold, giving us all a most enjoyable set of goose bumps.

I had become a regular on the *Deiwaka* program, a show geared toward the avid rap, rhythm and blues, and ragga fans of the country, and I often entered into discussions with various musicians about hip-hop in Tanzania. As Maganga opened the second part of the show, he waved Oops off the second microphone and motioned me to take over. Without missing a beat, he began to move into a discussion about the top-ten list, all the while maintaining a steady stream of soft music in the background:

> Alright everyone today is moving forward, Thursday, December 14, the last month of the year 2000. A lot has certainly happened this year with music of the new generation ["kizazi kpiya"] and the *Deiwaka* show has been shoulder to shoulder in letting you know everything that has been happening. And, we would like to let you know of major changes happening in the *Deiwaka* show, specifically to make you aware that we will be playing music and bringing you inside music of the new generation from East Africa [rather than just Tanzania]. This change will take place soon. But, everyday you can be sure that there will be information about musicians and music from here in Tanzania. In addition, on Friday's we will evaluate the outcomes of r&b, rap, and ragga music and many more. Artists themselves, their music, their producers, and the music business, we will continue to look at all of these. To explain more, the expert Alex is here in the house to talk about music of the new generation. And, all of you listeners who want to join the conversation and call, you are free to do so without any worry.

Maganga then went on to ask me questions about popular rap songs. His knowledge was encyclopedic: he took apart lyrics, beats, and styles of performers to shed light on genealogies of songs, lyrical meanings, and conceptions of the music among listeners (important educational components in Tanzanian radio broadcasting). Our conversation moved through different songs in the top-ten list, and he provided a long introduction to each question before allowing me to provide my own analysis. Though he was kind to call me an expert, it was his knowledge that captivated listeners and created a formidable body of knowledge that greatly informed public cultures about the *muziki wa kizazi kipya* (music of the new generation).

Inside Radio Uhuru's studio with Sebastian Maganga (center), Oops (right), and Bernard. *Photo by author.*

In addition to his knowledge about rap music in eastern Africa, Maganga was a talented announcer and deejay. His speaking voice was smooth, steady, though extremely fast, and easily distinguishable from that of the other rap-style presenters who were broadcasting in the same time slots. In the numerous on-air discussions we had with each other, Maganga rarely fluttered or became lost in his words. Yet he never used written notes, unless reading a quote from an e-mail that the show had received. Maganga also held the reins as an excellent deejay. Gaps rarely appeared between songs; jingles he produced were mixed throughout the show; and commercials, which he often recorded when he was not on air, were played frequently. The only element that Maganga did not do in his two hours on air was read the news; another staff member did.

In Dar es Salaam, Maganga is not alone in being knowledgeable about music, deejaying, and announcing. Around the city, hundreds of excellent presenters hold the reins of various programs, making competition for listeners fierce. Even scanning through the radio stations during Maganga's show reveals the competency and distinctiveness of many deejays at the popular stations. On Clouds FM, the deep, Barry White-ish voice of ML Chris slides from the speakers as he introduces, in English, some of the best in international hip-hop. On Times FM, the youthful, fast-paced sounds of Soggy Doggy Anter bounce out of the radio as he interviews local rap groups. On Radio One, the singing voice of Sos B parades on the airwaves as he excitedly introduces a new American r&b sensation. Those who lack talent for broadcasting tend not to last on the airwaves in Dar es Salaam, particularly in coveted time slots when there is intense competition among the more charismatic and knowledgeable presenters.

The proliferation of new stations after the passage of the Broadcasting Act meant training an entire new sector of the music economy. Since radio stations employ a variety of people, including radio announcers, technicians, deejays, producers, program directors, journalists, librarians, administrators, and accountants, each station had the difficult task of combing the city and the country for talent. Some radio stations, such as Radio One, East Africa FM, and Radio Uhuru, relied on state radio expertise. These stations hired trained staff from RTD to help with programming, broadcasting technology, and announcing. By 1996, twenty RTD staff had left that station due to the frustration of working for a government institution and the exciting potential that independent stations offered (Kabalimu 1996: 58). Still, RTD was only one station, and even its approximately 500 employees, most of whom were technicians, drivers, and journalists, could not fill the more than 400 on-air jobs that would be needed at Dar es Salaam's radio stations by the year 2002. Taji Liundi describes the need for workers in the radio sector after the passage of the Broadcasting Act: "What I discovered is that everybody investing in this business does not have any prior experience or knowledge of this media and would not be able to operate eighty percent of the equipment that they buy. And so, that is where the major problem starts now. When you invest in something you do not really know anything about it. . . . Imagine."

Due to the need for employees with requisite broadcasting skills, club deejays and rappers suddenly found themselves in demand, as did bilingual (English and Swahili) speakers and those knowledgeable about music and politics. Engineers and computer experts, newspaper journalists, and recording studio engineers also found opportunities in the radio job market. Despite their inexperience at radio stations, they quickly filled in radio jobs and learned about broadcasting as they went. John Dilinga, known as DJ JD, a popular presenter on East Africa FM, explains the process he went through to work in radio:

> **Dilinga:** I had experience as a radio deejay because I had worked as a [club] deejay for a long time. For one reason or another, I listened to a lot of radio, especially when I traveled outside [of Tanzania]. If I traveled abroad, I would record many shows. I would listen carefully and follow presenters that I admired. I kept on training myself without actually going on the radio. So that is the reason, when I went to interview at a radio station, I was given the job straight away. I remember on the day of the interview, there were more than sixty people that went to the interview. By good fortune, out of the sixty, I was the only one to get the job.
>
> **Perullo:** Can you explain the interview?
>
> **Dilinga:** They checked my CV . . . they did an interview and recorded my voice. They asked me questions that if I were to become a radio deejay what would I do? And other things like this. It was most important to record my voice and see how I could present like a radio deejay. And from their experience, even though I made small mistakes, they were able to know that I had the ability to do the job even though I had never been on radio. A short time after receiving the chance to broadcast, almost all of Dar es Salaam knew that there is this person, DJ JD. A bit later, I was able to do shows on Radio One Stereo, as almost all of Tanzania recognized that there is a new person in town who has brought a lot of changes on the radio.

For Dilinga, training to become a radio deejay started from listening to other presenters and studying their speaking and presentation techniques. Dilinga's self-discipline to train his voice gave him an advantage over the other candidates for the radio position. Even though Dilinga never went to a journalism school and had never entered a radio studio before his interview, his clear, deep voice—honed through practice at home—allowed him to beat out other competitors.

In interviews, radio station managers and owners perceive the overall lack of training differently depending on previous experience in broadcasting and expectations of commercial revenue. When Monaliza Bongera, program director of Classic FM, first began looking for radio hosts, she became exceedingly frustrated by the lack of professionalism, experience, and knowledge of job candidates. Bongera, who came from India to work at Classic FM, had specific expectations of the role that radio personalities needed to have at the station, and she ultimately found herself training all the staff she hired in all aspects of radio. Training the staff, however, took considerable time away from her ability to promote the station and attract commercial sponsors. Ultimately, stations that expected to turn a profit from the liberalization of the airwaves—through advertising from national and international business—were the most frustrated by the lack of knowledge about radio, while stations that existed as publicity for political and business leaders were less concerned about the mix in talent coming to the stations.

Although the majority of individuals entering into radio broadcasting in the 1990s and early 2000s had no radio trainings, a few schools, most notably the Tanzania School of Journalism and the Morogoro School of Journalism, offered courses in radio broadcasting. Often the courses at these programs focused on approaches to announcing, deejaying, programming, and on-air etiquette, but did not provide any on-air experience or training. Thomas Chilala, a presenter at Radio Tumaini, described his schooling in radio:

> I was a troublemaker when it came to listening to the radio. Even when I was in Form 5 and Form 6, I was really drawn to the program *Majira* on RTD. I was also really attracted to the announcer Charles Hilary, who did sports. It came to the point where I went to my Padre [at the seminary school] and said, "I really like announcing." He said, "Really. Okay, let us look for a way for you to enter radio." I said, "Okay." Now, the next day I read in the paper that a college in Morogoro, which is now called the Morogoro School of Journalism, offered training. I said, "If I try, I will be able to join." I went to my mother and said, "Mom, there is this college in Morogoro that I would like to join." This was in December 1995.
>
> In January, I had to go to Morogoro for one year of courses in journalism: there were courses on printing and announcing. We learned everything. After a year and a half, I finished school. By good fortune, when I was in Morogoro, I was given the opportunity to do an internship at Radio

Tumaini. My professors knew that I had gone through seminary and thought I was perfect for Radio Tumaini. So, they told me to go. I interned at Radio Tumaini for two months and then returned to College to take my exams.

One of the questions that I was asked on the exams was how to prepare a radio program. By good fortune, at Radio Tumaini I had already prepared programs. So, I answered that question well. Another question was, what is a microphone? How do you use a microphone? I finished my exams and did very well.

After leaving school—it was either April or May 1997—Padre Francisco at Radio Tumaini told me that he wanted to take me in as a full-time employee because I had done well as an intern. I was very thankful. So, in 1997, I started work at Radio Tumaini as a radio announcer.

Actually working at the radio station Radio Tumaini proved invaluable to Chilala as it offered experience and knowledge for school exams. While there is a radio station currently affiliated with Morogoro School of Journalism, many students argued that it did little to prepare them for the skills needed to compete in Tanzania's major radio stations, particularly those in Dar es Salaam.

When not training at a radio station or a vocational school, potential radio hosts develop numerous strategies for attaining jobs at local radio stations. One of the primary skills that radio announcers must acquire is a proper speaking voice. Due to the historic influence of state radio on public cultures, many radio announcers began their self-training through listening to the voices of RTD radio hosts. Male announcers have deep baritone voices that draw out the vowel sounds of Swahili speech to make the words rhythmic and dynamic. Most sentences end with a dramatic drop-off of the last vowel, as if the speaker's voice is taking a nice slow walk off a cliff. This aesthetic is deeply admired and encourages many would-be radio hosts to listen to RTD announcers and mimic their vocal inflections, speech patterns, and word choices. Even with attempts to move away from the national models of radio, the lasting influence of the station's fifty-year dominance can be heard in the broadcast of the spoken word throughout the country.

Nevertheless, many radio hosts realize that the quality and characteristics of their speaking voice holds value as a commodified product that can attract listeners to tune in or tune out. This commercial potential encourages radio hosts to adopt new techniques that cater more to a postsocialist broadcasting culture. The stereotypical RTD voice is slow and meant to be heard over inexpensive radios in rural parts of the country. This approach does not represent the sounds of cities. Many announcers, therefore, choose to take elements of the RTD voice and speed it up, incorporate local vernacular speech, and add elements of originality that separate their voices from other popular radio announcers. Part of developing a speaking voice comes from experimentation at home, with friends, or on stage in clubs as bongo flava artists. Even this form of self-training has limitations, particularly in an environment where distinctiveness of voice can often make the difference in attaining a radio job. To acquire unique characteristics, other than those born to the individual, many announcers acquire cassette tapes from radio stations they most want to emulate, including those in the United States, Europe, and India (the New York station HOT 97, for instance, was a model for early Clouds FM announcers). Some radio hosts have even turned to languages other than Swahili and English, oral traditions, and religious speech for ideas on how best to incorporate a unique sound to their voice. Each announcer has to develop a way of speaking to make his or her voices memorable and clearly audible on the radio. Some have referred to this as the "trademarking" of the voice to make it distinctive, hip, audible, and, ultimately, commercially successful.

In addition to trademarking, radio hosts also develop practical forms of consciousness. Practical consciousness is a form of knowledge where professional skills become a part of "embodied performance" (Downing and Husband 2005: 175–76). The ability to select a hit song out of a hundred possible choices, describe an engrossing event that listeners want to hear, or use a vernacular term that becomes a popular saying are all ways of employing this knowledge. Practical consciousness is not taught or, in many cases, described since it relies on direct engagement with culturally appropriate aesthetics.

Practical consciousness establishes a form of creativity that moves beyond basic techniques of running a radio station to more specialized ways of acquiring a unique approach to drawing in listeners. The Radio Uhuru stalwart Masoud Masoud is a highly regarded deejay primarily because of his encyclopedic knowledge of dansi music. Abubakari Sadiki and Abdallah Mwaipaya, both of Radio One, provide specialized insight into the music of local artists based on their close association with artists in multiple genres. The Magic FM radio hosts Dj Majizo and Dizzo One often receive praise from both listeners and local journalists for their ability to weave insightful stories about artists with local cultural information. The brother and sister Dativus and Fina Mango, at Magic FM and Clouds FM, respectively, have warm on-air personalities that listeners enjoy. Each of these radio hosts moves beyond the basic knowledge needed to conduct a radio show and creates a broadcast identity that conveys an experience and association with a specific demographic. This practical consciousness becomes central in broadcasting a unique voice that does not mimic the sound of other stations and can attract both advertisers and large audiences. The skills needed to create an original sound are not taught in any direct way, but are formed through the hosts' interaction with other staff, radio stations, and ultimately his or her interest in the public presentation of the self. It is, therefore, the obligation of the radio hosts to create distinctive dialogue with audiences that represents the intentions of radio station owners, the interests of listeners, and the public personality of the presenters.

The most important presentation of practical consciousness occurs in the shows that radio hosts create. While these shows have to be approved by the administration of stations, it is up to the hosts to establish a distinctive approach to radio with promotional segments, guests, and ideas that do not mimic other radio shows internally or externally. The specific pieces of the program, including when to do call-in segments, creating suspense before unveiling a new song, and designing top-ten lists, are up to the discretion of the hosts. These pieces help to create an overall sound for the radio show that formulate in the minds of listeners the overall quality of the hosts and stations. Those unable to create original programs may be placed into undesirable time slots, such as midnight to four in the morning. Or, as has happened in many cases, the radio hosts are let go to make way for more innovative deejays.

Playlists are a particularly important part of creative practice within radio programming. A radio host is just as expressive with his or her song choices as with the words used to speak to an audience. Even though fans make requests to radio station staff, it is up to the presenters to select songs that appear on shows. The selection of songs, however, can be rather daunting. At Times FM, for instance, the station receives hundreds of songs each month from local artists. The hosts sort through

Dj Venture of Clouds FM spinning records on the air. Although less common these days, deejays would often mix records on the air just as they would in clubs. *Photo by author.*

these materials to find potential hits before other radio stations. This is not unique to Tanzanian radio. Nevertheless, the lack of any mediation between radio host and musicians is rather unusual. The musicians sit outside the studios waiting for the deejays and announcers to appear. Waiting rooms of radio stations are often full of young artists holding CDs or cassette tapes of their music—particularly from genres associated with bongo flava—which they hope to give to the station's most popular hosts. In these exchanges, the host holds tremendous power in deciding the fate of artists, particularly those who are just starting out in the music business. An artist often pays a tremendous amount from personal finances to record a single song, and a radio host controls the success or failure of the artist. This power is not lost on radio hosts, who use it to maintain their credibility as central figures in the local music scene. Still, the host needs to work through all the songs that they receive in order to find the material that will become popular on air. In essence, radio hosts are both broadcasting personalities and talent scouts who must search through both local and foreign music to attract a listening audience.

Finally, radio hosts need to develop acute ways of understanding the broader role of broadcasting in the country. They need political skills to understand social issues that impact radio listeners and clarity about the rules and regulations of radio broadcasting in Tanzania. Many hosts develop slogans, promotional advertisements, and even commercials for leading advertisers in order to keep their show and the station economically viable. They must be clear about ownership of their station to understand where an owner stands on political issues. During election times, for instance, it is not uncommon to hear a radio host quickly cut off a segment where call-in audiences criticize members of Parliament or the president who may be friendly with the station owner. Despite the idea that censorship does not exist in contemporary radio, this form of self-censoring, prominent at most commercial radio stations, is a fundamental tactic that radio hosts use to remain on good terms with advertisers, radio station owners, and members of the political elite.

There is a similarity between the forms of learning and practice that occurs among radio hosts and musicians. Both demographics need to form a bundle of skills necessary to out-compete the many other individuals vying for the same opportunities in gaining employment. These skills include specific expertise associated with each profession; the ability to network within the space of employment; attaining technological proficiency in equipment emerging within each profession; realizing the political and cultural context of one's position in society; and finding strategies to best profit from one's craft. Most radio hosts and musicians lack guidance offered by managers, educators, and record companies. While notions of community certainly exist in Tanzania, there is also a survival of the fittest, a bongo mentality, which frames the way that deejays and artists need to learn their profession. The bundle of skills needs to develop from an individual's ability to make the proper connections, learn the structures of music production and broadcasting, and create opportunities to exploit the potential of knowledge gained. The bundle of skills, in other words, emerges forcefully in response to the pressure of making a living on a daily basis. Competition for resources, as well as the general lack of a formalized industry of music, creates an intense struggle that requires individuals to use their ingenuity and resourcefulness to find the best ways to make a living from their craft.

## PAY TO PLAY

Despite the social, political, and technological bundle of skills needed to attain employment at Tanzanian radio stations, salaries for hosts are often (though not always) improbably low. These low salaries have forced a few radio hosts to leave Tanzania for higher-paying radio jobs and others to seek alternative forms of employment outside of radio broadcasting. Far more commonly, however, the combination of the social power and low salaries creates an ideal situation for radio hosts to use their resourcefulness to find alternative ways to profit from their craft. Creative practice may be central to becoming a radio personality in the first place, but it is just as important to making a living as one.

It bears reiteration that within Tanzania, radio hosts are extraordinarily powerful. This is perhaps best articulated in an issue of *Baub Kubwa,* a glossy music magazine that focuses on music, film, and youth cultures. In the June/July 2008 issue, the editor opened the magazine with the following statement for young musicians (I provide the original Swahili version here due to the unusual forcefulness of the language):

| **Wachawi Kwenye Radio** | **Witches on the Radio** |
|---|---|
| Ili msanii utoke ni lazima upate air-play ya kutosha redioni, siku hizi FM radioz ziko za kumwaga japokuwa kuna zile muhimu ambazo ni lazima ngoma zako zichezwe humo na ziki-sema no, umeumia. | For an artist to be known/popular it's important to get airplay on the radio, these days there are plenty of FM radios, although there are those good ones where your song must be played by them and if they say no you're a loser. |
| Mwisho wa mchezo kuna watu wanaitwa PRESENTERS, hawa ni very very important kwenye redio stesh-eni yoyote ile, kama wewe ni artist then don't f**ck with them if you don't kuwa kama wale wanaolala-mika kila siku "nimebaniwa." | At the end of the game are people called PRESENTERS, they are very very important on all radio station, if you are an artist then don't f**ck [sic] with them if you [do] then you'll be like those people who complain every day "I'm being squeezed [out of the music business]." |

My guess is that the author is a current or former radio presenter since the next line states that most Tanzanian presenters could leave Tanzania and work in Europe or the United States like Ryan Seacrest. The author then continues that money is not a factor in the decisions by radio presenters; their sole desire is to be on the radio. Most important, the author points to the social power of radio presenters who can determine the careers of upcoming artists. Even the title of the article, "Witches on the Radio," is suggestive of a more occult and clairvoyant purpose to this profession: there is some level of mystical power attributed to voices coming over airwaves and influencing local populations.

The tremendous cultural and perhaps mystical influence provides a means for presenters to control radio airwaves for their economic benefit. The strategies that radio hosts use are rather diverse and dependent on the type of music that they play. Some radio station personnel who work in bongo flava ask artists to sign contracts with them in much the same way that an American artist would sign a contract with a record company. The Tanzanian radio station then becomes the exclusive representative of that artist. Radio station managers help the artists record an album, find a local distributor, and set up sponsors for a tour. The radio station, specifically the radio personality who helped find the artist and get him or her to sign a contract, serves to benefit financially from legal and ille-gal kickbacks from sponsors and album sales. A few radio stations profit tremendously by promoting an artist on their broadcasts and then using

Cover of the music and culture magazine Baab Kubwa with the radio hosts
Didi wa Mchops (left), Adam Mchomvu, and Salama Jabir. The cover reads,
"These are the Witches of the Radio." *Used with permission.*

the artist's popularity to sell albums, fill concert halls, and draw on local sponsors where the station receives a percentage of the overall earnings of an artist.

This same approach exists in the United States and Europe and is referred to as a 360 deal. In these deals, an artist agrees to share the revenue from album sales, merchandising, advertising, concerts, and other incomes streams in exchange for comprehensive promotion to all forms of media. The *New York Times* even referred to this as "The New Deal: Band as Brand."[29] The Tanzanian radio station strategy emerged earlier than 360 deals—some of the first examples came out in 2000 when Clouds FM signed several artists to their station and the spinoff division, PrimeTime Promotions—but both showcase a desire to commodify music and the artist. Branding here is central to the success of both the radio station and the artist. Clothing lines, commercials, billboard advertising, and music singles all emerge from an ability to turn an artist and his or her music into a brand that people want to buy into.

One of the first artists to receive this type of branding was Lady Jay Dee (PURL 5.8). In the early part of her career, she was a mediocre singer who recorded a few hit songs as part of her deal with Clouds FM. Over time, the radio station helped her to record and promote several albums, film one of the first commercially successful music videos with a high-end production company, and emerge as one of the first symbols of the neoliberal female. She won numerous awards during some of the earliest music awards ceremonies in Tanzania, though many journalists have argued that the shows were staged to promote her music and that of other "selected" artists. Most of her career was managed by Ruge Mutahaba, who was for many years the program manager at Clouds FM. Mutahaba composed many of the lyrics for Lady Jay Dee and arranged for her to appear in numerous local rap songs.

As a result of the support from Clouds FM, Lady Jay Dee has become one of the most successful members of the local music scene, winning more awards nationally and internationally than any other artist in the country, performing in front of dignitaries, and being the only Tanzanian artist to be nominated four times at the Kora Awards (the South African music awards). In September 2008, a local phone company, Zain, named Lady Jay Dee as "Zain's ambassadors for its world's first borderless mobile network services."[30] Her wedding to the radio presenter Gardner Habash became a major media event and was featured on the July/August 2005 cover of the glossy lifestyle magazine *bang!*

The success of Lady Jay Dee can be seen as a further commodification of the musician. By employing both privatized technologies, such as radio, recording studios, and print advertising, and flexible forms of artistic specialization, such as shaping songs to fit the interests of businesses, advertisers, and international award competitions, an artist can become part of a dynamic campaign to attain financial profit. Put another way, the strategies involved in using private technologies and artistic specialization are central to the transformation of artists into brands within Tanzania's music scene. To become a commercial brand signifies an artist's ability to move beyond using only songs as a source of income, but also image, dress, name, and identity (discussed in more detail in chapter 3).

Although many people are involved in transforming an artist into a brand, radio personalities have been the forerunners of this practice; in this regard they most resemble record companies in the United States and Europe. The way record companies in the United States, for instance, and radio personalities in Tanzania search for talent, write contracts, promote careers, connect to local businesses, and then profit from that relationship is similar in both industries. There is a possible conflict of interest between radio hosts as public figures and radio hosts as private investors in local talent, yet Lady Jay Dee's manager (and husband), radio host Gardner Habash, defends his dual duties: "Artists like presenters to be their managers because they have a lot of potential to help them sell [their music]."[31] Of course, presenters also enjoy the relationship with musicians since the economic benefits add significantly to their salaries. Since no regulations exist that restrict the radio personality/artist relationship, it is likely to continue unabated in the years to come.

In addition to working closely with artists, radio personnel also have other means of profiting from music. The most significant is payola, meaning that radio employees are paid to guarantee a certain amount of on-air radio time for an artist's songs. The payment can come from artists or from other radio stations that represent artists. Some radio hosts have payment schemes that take into account the time of day, a program's popularity, and the amount of airplay: the more airplay, the higher the cost. Other deejays will play an artist's recordings in return for gifts: deejays can find extra money on their phone card with a message identifying the benefactor (in Tanzania, phone cards are needed to add minutes to cell phones); they might receive free meals at fancy restaurants; and, though less common, there have been sexual favors. All these gifts are meant to sway the radio host toward airing an artist's music.

Tanzanian radio personnel have two strategies to make use of payola. The first is to pay deejays at other radio stations to play and even not play certain artist's music. For instance, if a radio station staff represents Artist A, they will pay other radio stations to play Artist A's music. They will also pay those same stations to not play Artist B, who competes with Artist A for album sales and commercial appeal. The initial radio station has to be careful, however, to not undercut the business of "friendly" stations who allow payola to occur. If the station that represents Artist A pays a station to not play Artist B even though that station represents Artist B, then conflicts can occur. Given the secrecy involved in these interactions, artists, radio hosts, and radio managers must be savvy enough to comprehend the connections between the principals.

By far, the most dominant strategy in payola is for artists to pay radio deejays directly. Referred to as *promo* as in *nataka promo* (I want some promotion), musicians in all genres of music have become increasingly pressured to pay deejays money in order to obtain air time. To extrapolate fees for this service, two coalitions of deejays have come together under the names Kwafujo Deejays and Nyuki Deejays. Kwafujo is the better known of the two, possibly because it covers deejays at two radio stations, including Abubakari Sadick Muhina (from Radio One), Dj Majizo (Magic FM), and Dizzo One (Magic Fm). Kwafujo Deejays also runs a clothing store in Sinza, Dar es Salaam, called Kwafujo Classic, and manages numerous local artists. Nyuki Deejays is a coalition of deejays from Clouds FM, including Dj Venture, Steve B, Dj Nelly, Molli B, and Dj Fatty. Both of these groups require artists to pay them money to ensure that the artist's song will be aired on all the deejays' radio shows. According to several deejays, some of these fees are extraordinarily high, upward of Tsh 100,000 (US$100) for moderate airplay over a one-month period on one radio show.

Artists lament these high costs since, according to many, it removes their ability to attain airplay simply for the quality of the music. During socialism, the government-controlled radio station censored songs and restricted the types of music that it played, particularly those that did not fit within state ideologies. Several independent radio stations also restrict airplay, but for pecuniary rather than ideological reasons. The transition from socialist educational content to neoliberal reforms of capital investments is one of the more dramatic shifts in Tanzania's music economy. Many artists deplore this transition, since it removes the social significance of music. Afande Sele, a Tanzanian rapper, sings about this transition in "Watu na Pesa" (People and Money).

| | |
|---|---|
| Tatizo mapromota na maredio presenta, | The problem with promoters and radio presenters [is that], |
| Wachache sasa wanafuata, | Few people follow [the music scene], |
| Fani wanaiboronga, | They are ruining the hip hop scene, |
| Top teni za kupanga, | They fix the top ten lists, |
| Yaani hawajali ubora | That is, they do not care about quality |
| Watakazo ndio wanaopiga, | They play what they want, |
| Nyimbo za ujingajinga | Songs of ignorance |
| Kila muda wanatwanga | They play repeatedly |
| Bila ya kujali ujumbe, | Without caring about the message, |
| Ilimuradi umekata panga | So long as you pay a bribe [you can be on the air] |
| Kama huna kitu, | If you cannot bribe them, |
| Basi utakoma kuringa, | Well, you will no longer be able to boast, |
| Mimi nalipinga, | I am against this, |
| Japo kwangu afadhali, | and I am not in the worst position, |
| Vipi wasanii wachanga? | What are the chances for young [upcoming] artists? |

The last line of the song is particularly important for many artists who considered the neoliberal music economy to mean that anyone can make it as long as they had musical skills and talents. For many artists, including several highly regarded figures in bongo flava who left Tanzania all together after being denied radio airplay, payola has removed the neutrality of radio stations in deciding music on the basis of an artist's image, sound, or lyrics. For them, radio is as restrictive now as during the socialist period even though the reasons for censorship are ideologically different.

Not all radio stations take part in payola, however, and many deejays deride the practice. John Dilinga, a radio deejay with East Africa FM, discussed his role in promoting local hip-hop artists:

> Other deejays play music by artists or promote artists who they know or who gives him money. What I believe is that if you make a good song—I love the song and the song is good for the listeners—I promote you. Whether I know

you or not. If I know you and the music is bad, it does not make any sense to
society, I do not play it. If I think that it is leading society astray, I do not play
it. If I think that it is educating society, I play it, promote it.

For Dilinga and other popular youth-oriented presenters, their job requires them to find music suitable for their audience. More important, the
music, as Dilinga states, needs to make sense to society. Similar to RTD's
approach to music, some presenters from independent radio stations pick
and choose songs that they consider worthwhile for their listeners to hear.
A tension therefore exists on the airwaves between those stations that
have adapted payola and those that consider the educational qualities
of music a priority. Artists, who depend on radio to promote their music,
have a difficult task deciding which strategies and which radio stations
they will use to have their singles broadcast on the air.

There are some artists that are popular enough that they can avoid
payola. Every time these top artists release new material, radio listeners
search the radio stations to hear them. According to several radio station
program directors, a popular song can be played on a single radio station
upward of eight or more times per day, particularly on broadcasting stations that organize programming into block periods (two- to three-hour
time slots). A hit song will appear in each of these blocks, since radio
listeners enjoy hearing a new hit on a regular basis. If a radio station does
not air a popular song throughout the day, radio listeners switch to other
stations. Wagosi wa Kaya and Professor Jay, who do not use payola, continue to attain radio airplay due to their popularity and visibility in the
local music economy. A station that does not play their music can lose
credibility among radio listeners.

The development of payola in Tanzania has a number of qualities
of the post-socialist music economy. It points out the commercial potential of artists and their music and the resultant strategies used to take
advantage of that potential. Similar strategies exist in the United States,
where independent promoters, called "indies," pay radio stations to play
artists music.[32] Radio, in these scenarios, becomes implicated in the commodification of sounds due to the influence of broadcasts in affecting
listeners' tastes. Payola, 360 deals, bribing journalists, and other strategies
emerge in response to the commercial potential of music in a pattern that
exists where public interest "can be distorted by unregulated privatized

expropriation" (Nash 2007: 622). In the past, the communal potential of broadcasting was emphasized in the educational focus of radio and the government-run radio station that promoted nationalist ideologies. The privatization of this medium ushered in diverse sounds, ideas, and aesthetics and, through the increased commodification of music, new business strategies for benefiting from the power of radio to determine the success or failure of an artist's career.

## SIGNING OFF

One afternoon I sat on a bench in downtown Dar es Salaam reading the local paper. An older man sat down next to me and began to stare at my notepad. On it, I had written several radio stations and the contact people at each. Glancing from the notepad to me, and seeing that I was reading a Swahili newspaper, he began to talk to me about local businesses. "Do you know what the major problem with local business is?" Without waiting for my reply, he answered, "Lack of creativity. Once one person starts a successful business, everyone follows and does the exact same thing. When one business begins to make money, fifty others copy it. For this reason, all make no money because there is not enough business." To make his point clearer, he gestured to a young man sitting at a makeshift table across the street. The young man sat with his elbow on the table, eyes half closed in a midday dream. On the front of his table, a sign read "Mihuri" (stamps). The young man's business was making rubber stamps that were used mostly by other local businesses to stamp receipts or items in stores. The older man turned to me and said, "Do you know, when the first one of these little businesses opened, it was very successful. Now, there is one on every corner and none make any money."

Throughout my time in Tanzania, many more people gave me the same analysis—once one successful business appears, many more arrive and destroy anyone's chances at creating a successful enterprise. From the direction of the older man's conversation, I inferred that he considered radio to be the same way. Seventeen years after the Tanzanian Broadcasting Bill passed, over fifty stations were in operation in Tanzania, most competing for the same listeners and advertising dollars. Using the man's philosophy of Tanzanian business, if stations continued to start and compete for funding, the local economy would eventually not support them.

Even the government newspaper the *Daily News* expressed concern about the future of Tanzanian radio when a reporter wrote, "Industry watchers say the market [for radio and television] may soon be saturated."[33] Tanzania's radio culture had moved from a monopoly of one government station to an oversaturation of broadcasting networks, which, according to many local analysts, would eventually use up all the commercial funding options available to them.

While stamp vendors always produce similar products that can easily be mimicked, local radio stations are different: programming and song selection allow radio stations to develop diverse strategies for attaining and maintaining listenership. After abiding by government regulations, there is relative freedom to creatively position broadcasts within the interests of public cultures. Deejays and announcers become critical voices in speaking to audiences and selecting music that impacts local interests in music. Perhaps, more important, there is a strong desire among radio listeners to hear a diversity of content that reflects their interests. In chapter 2 I argued that music, even within the same genre, has multiple meanings and interpretations depending on the perspectives and contexts of those who are listening. Similarly, radio stations produce varied meanings depending on interests of broadcasters and listeners. This allows radio stations to avoid direct repetition of competitors since there are so many interpretations of and interests in broadcasts heard in Tanzanian urban society. Until other mediums, such as television or the internet, become more dominant, radio stations will continue to attract a broad array of listeners interested in finding a diversity of educational and entertaining programs.

# SIX

# Analog, Digital . . . Knobs, Buttons

If music is hooliganism, why do you buy cassettes?
If music is hooliganism, why do you request songs on the radio?
If music is hooliganism, why do you buy records?
If music is hooliganism, why do you dance to music?

—REMMY ONGALA, "Muziki Asili Yake Wapi"
(Where Did Music Originate From?)

In March 2001, rappers from Holland and South Africa flew to Tanzania to hold a series of workshops. Sponsored by the Netherlands Institute for Southern Africa (NiZA) under the Tanzanian PREACH Education Project, the workshops aimed to create dialogue between rappers from disparate backgrounds and give them an opportunity to exchange ideas, experiences, and rapping techniques.[1] Along with the workshops, all the rappers were scheduled to participate in a recording session, where they would collaborate on a series of hip-hop songs and then perform a concert in Dar es Salaam.

The first workshop, held in the dilapidated, government-owned Kilimanjaro Hotel, was meant to open dialogue between the rappers.[2] The conversation started slowly with Skate the Great and Too Tall from Holland discussing the Dutch hip-hop scene, the maintenance of the four pillars of hip-hop (rapping, deejaying, break dancing, and graffiti), and meaning in their rap lyrics. Devious and EJ (Elimiza Jones) from South Africa spoke about hip-hop in their country, their relationship to music, and the importance of local groups, such as Prophets of Da City. The Tanzanian rappers, a bit timidly, discussed the formation of an indigenous hip-hop scene in the 1990s and the importance of socially conscious lyrics that stimulate youth action. For several hours, the informal dialogue continued, with rappers, along with some journalists and organizers, teaching each other about their respective hip-hop cultures. Aside from a few tense moments when the Dutch rappers questioned the lack of graffiti art in Tanzania—to which one of the Tanzanians replied, with some hostility, "This is a formerly socialist government: you paint a building, and you spend a long time in jail. Besides, who can afford paint?"—comradeship developed from the workshop, with all the rappers seemingly looking forward to the next week of projects.

A few weeks later, the Dutch and South African rappers gathered in another room of the Kilimanjaro Hotel along with fifty Tanzanian musicians, deejays, and reporters. Almost all the Tanzanian musicians who were at the first meeting did not attend the second, and the crowd was mostly novices or upcoming rappers. The Dutch and South African rappers looked tired, and they sat impatiently at a long wooden table waiting for everyone to arrive. About half an hour after the scheduled time, the meeting began with questions being thrown at the visiting rappers only to be quickly tossed back to the audience. The room was tense and the comradeship of the first meeting appeared to be significantly weakened. Tanzanians asked why they had come to their country, and one of the South African rappers asked if local artists had any sense of goals or future outlooks. Another Tanzanian asked why he was not invited to perform with the other musicians, and one of the Dutch rappers expressed anger at the disarray of the local music economy. The interaction between the various youth appeared to be a colossal failure, one that left all those involved with a sense of bitterness and distrust of the other.

After some time, everyone began to relax. The airing of frustrations had apparently led them to realize that they were achieving little from their verbal condemnations. The audience, therefore, turned to respectful questions about Dutch and South African music industries, marketing music, and opinions of local rappers. The Dutch and South African rappers responded politely and expressed their admiration for those in Tanzania, encouraging them to continue working on their craft and promoting their music. Yet, a sense of tension remained. It was not until someone asked about the recent recording project between local rappers and the guests that the source of much of the frustration became evident. As politely as they could, each guest rapper vented his anger. Skate the Great began:

It was hard, man. It was hard. I have to be honest with you. I am not trying to diss [disrespect] anyone here, but I have a problem with the mentality over here. It's not just a mentality of the people who do hip-hop; I think it is a Tanzanian thing, you know? We have an appointment at 11:00 o'clock in front of the studio, [and we were] waiting for two or three hours. We are on a hectic schedule over here. But for some reason, people don't cling on to that. Everything is going so slow, what's up with that? You all want to make moves. It's about discipline. In my opinion, people lack a certain discipline.

Too Tall continued:

[In the studio] it went from one thing to the next, from no key to no extension cord. I can't get angry because I understand that it is different over here. [But] if you have an appointment with someone at eleven, you should be there. If this happened in Amsterdam, we would be saying, all right, I'll see you in two hours, and we'd just go [to another studio]. It took us almost two complete days to have the music together and that was because somebody turned off the sampler, the problems with the ADAT and the computer. If a producer in Holland doesn't deliver . . . it's like bye-bye, you get someone else to deliver.[3]

Each of the four rappers discussed their disbelief at the "lack of professionalism" exhibited at the recording sessions. The producers (known as sound engineers in other countries) never arrived on time, were unable to keep their equipment running, and often had to leave to search for cables, extension cords, and other studio parts.[4] The first time I arrived at a recording session, Skate the Great and Too Tall were in the studio by themselves composing some beats for a new song, while a few of the Tanzanian rappers mingled outside, waiting for one of the producers to arrive. The second time I went, one of the Tanzanian rappers was asleep on a bench outside the studio, while a few others sat and talked, again waiting for a producer to arrive and open the studio. What was planned to be a multiple song recording opportunity produced only two tracks. The visiting artists were pleased with the songs, but their frustration with the producers, as well as some other members of Tanzania's music community, was unmistakable.

Despite the comments made by Skate the Great and Too Tall, it would have been possible for the artists to try other local studios just as they argue is possible in the Netherlands. With numerous qualified producers in Dar es Salaam, the entire project could have shifted to another studio.

The chosen producers were considered the best in the country, and there was a strong desire by the organizers to have the names of those producers on the recordings. So what created the problems within the studios and between the artists and the producers? The source of everyone's frustration was due to a perceived injustice made against one of the producers who felt that his career and success was being threatened by the project. His studio was being used but he was not chosen as the main producer. Instead, his strongest competitor was selected to create the beats and orchestrate the overall recording of the songs. Rather than cooperate, he decided to inhibit the success of the project, which led to mysteriously malfunctioning equipment, sabotaged samples, and missing cords and wires. The perceived ineptitude of Tanzanian recording was largely due to the foot-dragging of one individual.

At the end of the trip, the perception among several of the foreign rappers who had traveled to Tanzania was that local recording studios and, perhaps, the entire music economy lacked professionalism. Though up to date in technology, producers were not modern in practice. The most prominent illustration of this lack of professionalism, from the point of view of the guest rappers, was in various forms of resistance that took place and the apparent disdain for the presence of the foreigners. Was this one event emblematic of the entire music economy? Did sound engineers and music producers typically sabotage the success of recording project? And, more important, does this reflect the way independent recording studios operate on a daily basis?

The production of recorded music is a critical means to inform popular aesthetics in music economies. Whereas radio establishes trends through song selection and the formation of public cultures, record producers shape, develop, and document the sounds of popular music. The growing body of literature examining the production of popular music provides evidence of scholarly interest in understanding creative processes involved in recording studios (Greene and Porcello 2005; Katz 2004; Théberge 1997; Meinjtes 2005; Porcello 1998, 2004; Wallach 2008). This chapter works from these previous studies to consider strategies that producers use to respond to pressures of increasingly competitive markets. Creativity in Tanzania's music economy includes learning a variety of technological and acoustic skills in order to record quality tracks that can become popular in the local music economy. It involves dealing with the intense competition in the market among the hundreds of producers attempting to find commercial success. And, as the opening narrative illustrates, it entails comprehending sabotage, foot-dragging, and the use of the occult in dealing with the anxieties of competition. Located as a nexus between artists, radio stations, distributors, and music fans, producers are responsible for transforming songs into commercially viable and aesthetically appealing creations that can win accolades, media attention, and financial stability. It is a task that has made studio production the most competitive and, at times, volatile space in Tanzania's music economy.

## STUDIOS ON THE RISE

In the United States, Europe, and many other parts of the world, the term record or music producer often signifies the person who schedules and organizes recording sessions, guides musicians on material to record, and works with the sound engineer to create the best sound for artists. The producer, in other words, orchestrates the recording session, handling budgets, personnel, and many aesthetic choices during recording. The sound engineer, also referred to as the recording engineer, works in the control room and operates the mixing boards, recording devices, and other technologies. He or she has knowledge of acoustics, music theory, engineering, and even arranging in order to make suggestions to the artists in the studio on how best to present their music. The work of producers and sound engineers thus requires a great deal of knowledge and skill in order to handle the many obstacles that can arise during a recording session. In most professional recording situations, it is difficult to complete any project without the presence and input of both.

In Tanzania, the term producer signifies an individual who is both a recording engineer and a producer, as well as a studio musician, composer, and arranger in some genres of music. This conflation of duties to a single individual makes becoming a producer extraordinarily challenging. A Tanzanian producer must be able to operate recording equipment, mixers, sound effects machines, and other technologies; help artists decide on the music that they want to record; orchestrate the recording sessions and bring in any needed studio musicians; arrange the microphones and instruments that best fit the acoustics of a room; fix any equipment problems as they arise; handle the scheduling of the sessions; and com-

TABLE 6.1. Dar es Salaam's Commercial Recording Studios, 1991–2009

| Studio Name | Engineers/Producers | Year Started[1] |
|---|---|---|
| 41 Records | Ambrose Dunga and Lufunyo Mvungi. | 2008 |
| 69 Records | T.C (Timothy Chelula) | 2008 |
| Aegis Records | Peter Rutta (Nice P) and Arthur | 2003 |
| Akili Records | Castro Fusi and Mr. Akili | 2003 |
| Amani Studio | Joseph Anania and Jerry Gumbo | 1999 |
| ASET Productions | Bakunde Mbilima | 2004 |
| B on 2 Records | Steve White | 2008 |
| Backyard Productions | John Sagati, Mr. Yusuph, Abdiel Mengi, Huko Msasani | 2002 |
| Baucha Records | Ally Baucha, Mbwana Mponda | 2003 |
| Bigapple Studio | Man V. | 2005 |
| Bigboy Studios | Profesa Ludigo | |
| Bigtimes Studios | Said Comorien | 2003 |
| Bongo Records | P Funk | 1993 |
| CBM Studio | Moses | 2006 |
| CMK Studio | Jack P | 2006 |
| Dhahabu Records | Dully Sykes | 2007 |
| Don Bosco | Athanas Shelukindo | 1991 |
| Down Town Records | Damian (DMan) | 2000 |
| Empty Souls Production | Queen Tiny and Solomon Lamba | 2002 |
| Fabrice Studio | Shomari Abdalaah | 2004 |
| Fish Crab Records | Lamar | 2008 |
| FM Production | John Merry | 1999 |
| G Records | Gullu | 2002 |
| G2 Records | Roy Aaron Bukuku and Jacob Mahuwi | 2000 |
| Highland Studio | Richard Mloka and Edwin | 2003 |
| Jug's Records | Garder G | 2004–2007 |
| Kama Kawa Records | Yudi and Rajabu Marijani | 2006 |
| Kawa Kawa Records | Gerald Mwanjoka (G-Solo) | 2009 |
| Kubwa Records | Siga | 2006 |
| Magic Star Studio | Adax | 2004 |
| Mahewa Studio | Matrix (Martin Arico) | 2007 |
| Malone Linje Studio | Malone Linje | 2006 |
| Mambo Jambo Records | Benjamin | 2002[2] |
| Marimba Studio | Keppy Kiombile and Samuel Ngosha | 1999 |
| Mawingu Studio | Bonnie Luv | 1993–1996 |
| Mawingu Tafsiri Records | Bonnie Luv and Juma Rajabu (Jay) | 2001 |
| Metro Studio | Allan Mapigo and Anicety Apolinal | 2003 |
| MF Studios | Abdul Salvador and Richard Mloka | 2003 |
| MJ Productions | Joachim Kimario (Master Jay) and Mako Challi | 1997 (1991) |

TABLE 6.1. (*cont.*) Dar es Salaam's Commercial Recording Studios, 1991–2009

| Studio Name | Engineers/Producers | Year Started[1] |
|---|---|---|
| Mo Records Rock City | Q (Nicholaus Owiti), owned by Monica Manyaga | |
| Nash Records | Shadrock Masaga | 2004 |
| O.M. Records | Omary Mkali | 2007 |
| Poa Records | Amit Bhajaj (Mental) | 2002[3] |
| Praise Production Studio | Amonoso Synth (Chyna). | 2008 |
| Raja Records | Ras Raja | 2005 |
| Royal Productions | Ephaim Kameta | 2002 |
| Sei Records | Sei | 2006 |
| Sofia Records | Ababuu Mwanazanzibari, Musa Kisoki | 2003 |
| Soundcrafters | Enrico and Bizman Ntavyo | 1993–2002[4] 2005 |
| Studio Makuti | Rosa and Michel Tyabji | 1998–2002 |
| Tazara Hotel | | Defunct |
| Up-town Records | Man Walter | 2006 |

*Notes:* 1. Year started refers to the year that the recording studios commenced recording with the intent of creating commercially available music.
2. Mambo Jambo Records temporarily halted studio production in early 2003.
3. Poa Records merged with Backyard Productions in 2003.
4. In 2002, Soundcrafters moved to Mwanza, Tanzania.

plete the numerous other tasks involved in recording music. In addition, these same individuals must keep up to date in recording techniques, equipment, and musical effects.[5] They therefore must be active listeners of local, regional, and international music so that an artist who arrives at a studio with an interest in recording a specific sound can ask the producer to create that sound. In short, a Tanzanian producer must be knowledgeable in several subjects, such as business, music, technology, and acoustics, all areas in which it is difficult to gain competence in Tanzania.

Despite the numerous challenges and responsibilities of Tanzanian studio producers—challenges that should have limited the number of people involved in studio production—the number of studios and producers in the country have risen significantly since the mid-1990s. Between 2001 and 2004 and again between 2004 and 2008, the number of studios in Dar es Salaam doubled. By 2008, there were fifty-one commercial studios in Dar es Salaam (see table 6.1). It should be noted that these figures only include commercially active recording studios that have a steady base of clients and regular output of recordings. Smaller, less viable studios also populate Dar es Salaam's neighborhoods, particularly in people's homes and in small businesses looking to expand or diversify their production. While it is impossible to accurately estimate the number of these smaller studios, several producers believe that there are two to three times the total number of commercial studios in the city. This burgeoning sub-commercial economy creates a constant circulation of informally produced music that provides producers and artists with the ability to develop their skills, record demonstration (demo) tracks, and potentially gain the notice of more established members of the music community.

The dramatic rise of independent recording studios occurred for several reasons. In the broader context of Tanzania's economy, the transition of the ruling party from socialism to more laissez-faire economic reforms in the 1980s led to increased incentives for people to create their own businesses. As discussed elsewhere in this book, Tanzania's second president, Ali Hassan Mwinyi, ran an administration that granted autonomy for people to start businesses or generate incomes by any means they could. Without the need for permits to set up recording studios and the ability to illegally import equipment (thereby avoiding taxes), many aspiring producers found little hindrance to their efforts in starting studios. All that producers needed was startup capital to buy equipment and space to set up a studio. From there, they could generate an income that, in the hands of a talented technician, could be extremely profitable. The incentives of high profits with few restrictions made recording studios a popular option, particularly for youth interested in building a career in music.

The second reason that the number of studios increased so significantly was due to the influence of foreign music. Liberalization increased the importation of foreign genres of music, particularly rap, r&b, and ragga. Many youth emulated the sounds they heard, using the instrumental tracks on foreign records and cassettes as backing tracks for their rapping. Over time, the desire to imitate transitioned into a desire to create original backing tracks. The formation of studios was partially in response to people's craving to produce foreign genres locally. Despite limited technical knowledge, deejays and rappers started studios in an effort to produce beats in the early period of bongo flava. Many studios formed in the 1990s with the sole purpose to record rap music and, even today, most studios in the country produce and record bongo flava music.

(3)    The third reason for the dramatic increase in studios was the significant decrease in the price of studio equipment, such as computers, software, and recording devices. In 1997, an average studio in Dar es Salaam could cost as much as $6,000 to purchase and over $10,000 to import legally into Tanzania. By 2007, that price had dropped to a total cost of $2,000 to $4,000. This price included a mixing board, microphones, a computer, speakers, and a keyboard, which was often used to compose beats for rap music. The price of equipment was also low due to the extensive use of pirated software that freely passed among producers. Some of the software being used could cost several thousand dollars and include recording software, effects plug-ins, and sound libraries. Given the low cost of equipment and software, the potential to make profits was even more likely considering that many studios would eventually charge high fees for each song recorded.

The first independent studio to open in Tanzania was at the Don Bosco Youth Center in Upanga, Dar es Salaam. The Salesians of Don Bosco are one of the largest Catholic religious orders in the world. Founded by Saint John Bosco in 1859, Salesians focus on missionary work to improve the lives of poor people through education. In 1980, the Salesians entered Tanzania, first in Dodoma and Iringa, where they opened trade schools, and two years later in Dar es Salaam, where they started a secondary school and a youth center. At the Dar es Salaam center, youth were provided facilities to play sports, learn arts and crafts, and attend educational seminars. Between 1990 and 1991, a Salesian missionary constructed a recording studio with a Tascam portastudio tape recorder, effects processors, compressor, microphones, and instruments to give youth a chance to develop their talents through music. As Samuel "Ngosha" Luhende, engineer at Don Bosco from 1998 until early 2002, explained:

> Father Peter Paulo, who during this time was the head of Don Bosco, saw that he should not leave music behind. He saw that it was better to start a band and part of his vision was to start a studio. So that was his dream and he made it true. So, he opened a studio for youth and the objective was to make them grow their talent. But, along with youth, any musician could record because it was a center for recording—they would not restrict someone from recording because he was an elder. Yet, the main use of the studio was for youth, especially those who had a talent for music.

The Salesian missionary, Father Peter Paulo, who started the studio, was also a musician and formed a group with local youth who frequented the Center. The Center became an important resource for musicians interested in recording and learning music without relying on government institutions.

Many of the earliest groups that worked at the Don Bosco Center were choirs or performers from religious backgrounds, though secular bands and rap artists also made use of the studio. The first local sound engineer was Justin Kalikawe, who became a well-known reggae star in Tanzania, followed by Marlone Linje, who is now considered one of the preeminent producers for dance band music. These producers recorded some of the first rap tapes by Mr. II, Mac Mooger, and others, as well as albums that would have been passed over or not permitted to be recorded by the government radio station Radio Tanzania Dar es Salaam (RTD). Slowly, through word of mouth, people learned about the potential for recording at the center. One popular singer, Spider, received his start in music there:

> After I finished primary school in 1987, my parents did not have much money. I worked on a *daladala* on the Morogoro/Dar es Salaam route until 1990. I then studied Form I at JKT Mgulani. I officially started music with the help of Marlone at Don Bosco. In the studio, I did not know how to sing, I just knew that I wanted to be involved in floor or rap music. By good fortune, when I was there singing, they [the staff at the studio] saw that I could sing and decided to train me. So, I officially started music by being taught by Marlone at Don Bosco.

Similar to other formative studios in other parts of the world, such as Sun Records and Stax in the United States, the early producers and artists who worked at Don Bosco Youth Center in the early 1990s created a dynamic and thriving music community that became widely recognized for their distinctive and popular sound.

While the recordings made at Don Bosco were comparable to cheap home recordings in other countries, for many Tanzanians they represented the first time artists had control over their music. At Radio Tanzania Dar es Salaam, recorded music was controlled—as far as lyrical content and overall sound—by studio managers or radio staff. The final product (the actual master tape) became the property of RTD, not the artists who composed and performed the songs. The practices at Don Bosco and other early independent studios in Tanzania altered the relationship between the studio and artist by granting more creative freedom. In recording sessions, musicians could experiment with instruments, including their voice, to achieve desired outcomes. They could receive instruction from other artists and producers who lingered around the studio. Artists tended not to be rushed, and there was a collegial relationship in experimenting with sound, timbres, and aesthetics. Many youth-oriented forms of music benefitted from the availability of recording technology that, in the early years, did not involve economic or political considerations. The acquisition of recording knowledge blossomed in this period since that was the main reason for being in the studio.

In 1993, Mawingu Studio opened in Dar es Salaam. Like Don Bosco, Mawingu gave artists an opportunity, after paying a fee, to record music and keep their master tape. Unlike Don Bosco, however, Tanzanian youth founded Mawingu as an outlet for other youth; no religious or foreign donor helped fund the studio. Started by the same people who opened Clouds Disco, which developed into Clouds FM, Mawingu Studio began as a grassroots project where former club deejays learned to engineer and produce music, while artists continued their self-discovery as hip-hop musicians. Mawingu Studio also opened with somewhat better equipment than Don Bosco, with a Korg drum machine, 8-track Tascam recorder, Fostex mixer, and effects processors, as well as a keyboard and bass.

Bonnie Luv was the main engineer and producer at Mawingu Studio. Growing up in Upanga, Dar es Salaam, listening to records and deejaying shows around the city in the early 1980s, Luv joined Clouds Disco in 1987. Through two people, Joseph Kussaga, the head of Clouds Disco, and an English expatriate, Luv learned about deejaying techniques, mixing music, and genres of music (a concept he said was previously unknown to him). He became a well known and respected deejay for concerts throughout Dar es Salaam, especially at his main venues, Hotel Agip, New Africa Hotel, and Bahari Beach Hotel, due to his in-depth knowledge of music. Deejaying gave Luv experience with the production styles of national and international recording engineers. Using this musical knowledge in Mawingu Studio, Luv became adept at editing and mixing instrumental tracks for upcoming rappers, such as GWM, Raiders Posse, the Villains, Kwanza Unit, KBC, and Tribe X, early popular rappers in Tanzania. He also worked on the first successful singles of rap sung in English, by groups such as Kwanza Unit, the Hard Blasterz, and Die Young Mob. Through his experience as a deejay and willingness to experiment in the studio, Luv created some of the earliest and most influential Tanzanian rap songs.

Through Mawingu Studio and Don Bosco, as well as two other local studios that began in the mid-1990s, Soundcrafters and P Funk's Studio (now Bongo Records), foreign-influenced music prospered, especially rap and rhythm and blues. Nonetheless, artists of other musical genres, such as taarab, dansi, and kwaya, also viewed new studios positively. Bands and artists who had been restricted in their recordings at RTD and TFC were given more freedom in areas of production, including arranging times for recording sessions, choosing studio engineers, and selecting music without worry of censor. Recording sessions could even be spread over several months, a practice unheard of in the past. Other artists used to traveling to Kenya, Zimbabwe, or abroad found solace in working in their own country, using local musicians and being able to communicate ideas in their own language. Many artists explained that independent studios allowed them to creatively explore certain musical ideas, sounds, and effects. Even though several bands and artists continued to record at RTD, the diversity of production possibilities allowed for more dynamic and creative fixation of sounds to emerge.

As demand for studio time increased, many of the largest studios hired additional producers. One producer, Master J, who owns his own studio, hired Marlone Linje from Don Bosco to record rumba and taarab while he continued to work with r&b and rap artists. FM Studio had Miikka Kari Mwamba from Finland recording rap and r&b, while John Merry, a Congolese producer, recorded choirs. Perhaps due to the division of labor by genre, MJ Production and FM Studio, established in 1997 and 1999, respectively, became two of the most popular studios, prized for their ability to create high-quality recordings in any genre. Other studios continued to focus on one genre, such as Amani Studio (kwaya) and Bongo Records (rap), while Don Bosco, Soundcrafters, and Studio Marimba used as many as four different producers to record anyone who came into the studio and did not limit a producer to a particular genre. All studios competed with one another for local talent and always kept

an ear out to hear which producer bought which new piece of equipment
and what technique each producer was using.

With each producer always watching the other, however, it only took
a few years for independent studios to lose their novelty and for producers to turn recording into a highly competitive business. Producers, once
content to spend days working on tracks without pay, began to charge by
the hour or per song for their services. The several days of experimentation and testing it once took to record a song shrank to a single day to
record an entire album. Producers suddenly found themselves constantly
busy, recording, mixing, and meeting with new clients, unable to play
around in the studio and meet with other producers to talk about recording techniques. Antagonism among the various studios became intense,
particularly among producers who realized that their economic survival
depended on their ability to entice the best of the country's musical talent. Several producers explained having anxiety or depression, fearing
that they might not create a hit song as they had in the past. These fears
pushed some producers to bad-mouth their peers and carried the once
open and prosperous recording studios into a hazardous state of secrecy.
Several interviews with producers even turned quiet when I asked them
about studio techniques, technology, and clientele (though other producers allowed me to sit and watch during entire recording sessions). Too
much depended on specific recording and compositional techniques for
trade secrets to be made public.

Despite the influx of numerous studios and the intense competition
for studio talent, established producers still command large fees for their
productions. In 2000, many of these producers charged around $60 per
song, but increased their fees to $115 in 2001. By 2005, the rate jumped to
$300 and, in 2008, the price moved to $500. Under these rates, studios can
make close to $5,000 on a single album. (Don Bosco, which records in
analog, still charges $20 per song.) In 2000, during the first surge in costs,
Master J discussed the evolution and future direction of studio fees:

> You have to understand, when I started doing this it was free; three years ago
> an album was Tsh 150,000 [$US150]; now an album is one million [$1000].
> Next year an album will be two [million]. This is the long-term plan that
> I am telling you. Just think of it within those three years. We move from a
> 150,000 to a million and the market is paying well. If you tell distributors
> that they have to pay me one million for studio time, no problem.

Creating a hit or a series of hit songs ensures that producers are able to continually raise their prices. Artists pay for both the studio name, which can symbolize some level of esteem and aesthetic quality, and time to actually record in the studio. Paying higher studio fees can also provide artists access to the producers' networks of contacts within radio stations and among distributors. Paying high costs to record songs is, therefore, often viewed as a means to gain access to the potential of the local music economy.

Producers also search for new talent that they want to record. In the American music industry, talented artists are often sought after by record companies, A&R (artists and repertoire) personnel, as well as agents, managers, and others whose jobs are dependent on a musician's career. In Tanzania, the main scouts for new talent are producers. Even though radio announcers do work in clubs listening to young artists and promoters are always searching for new talent, producers' studios are frequently flooded with young, aspiring artists attempting to gain the ear of the producer. Producers listen to these artists and, occasionally, allow them to record with the studio for free until the artist begins to earn money from the sale of their songs. The producer P Funk, also known as Manjani, heard the music of Juma Nature around the year 2000 and brought him into the studio to record.[6] Through a series of singles recorded and promoted by P Funk, Nature became one of the more influential rap artists in the country, and his group, Wanaume, holds a significant place in the history of Tanzanian music.

The relationship between artist and producer is one that uses resourcefulness and innovation to establish or maintain credibility within the music scene. The producer has to be conscious of his role as a talent scout, as well as a composer, arranger, technician, and marketing specialist. He has to use each artist as a platform for creating future sustainability since few are secure enough financially to continually experiment with their songs and sustain a string of potential failures. The longer a producer goes without a hit song, the greater his risk of losing his clients and his source of income. Of course, this relationship exists in other parts of the world as well, where a producer's job depends on quality of recorded music. Tanzanian producers have the added burden of filling many additional positions in the relation between artists and the final sound recording. They need to be self-reliant, depending on the combina-

The producer Complex in Aegis Studio, June 2005, Dar es Salaam. Complex, whose real name was Simon Sayi, died in a car accident two months after this photograph was taken. *Photo by author.*

tion of musical and technological knowledge to foster relationships with many different people in the music economy. They also need to be aware of popular musical aesthetics that will resonate among consumers. It is an environment that creates a great deal of tension and avarice in the ways that producers approach each recording session.

## BECOMING A PRODUCER

On the early years of recording in the United States, Susan Schmidt Horning writes, "Grasping 'subtleties,' possessing 'mechanical finesse,' and working without written instructions figured prominently in the early recordist's job description, and not everyone fits the bill" (Horning

2004: 705). Similarly, in Tanzania, the specific requirements of being a producer entail certain intrinsic forms of interacting with technology and music, such as mechanical finesse and musical appreciation, which target the personalities and sensibilities of particular people. Although any profession attracts specific individuals, being a producer tends to draw an even more focused population. All producers who work in independent studios are male (including Queen Tiny, listed in table 6.1), and most started working in a studio sometime between the ages of 18 and 30. The majority of producers tend to be from middle-class backgrounds, and as such they grew up with access to technology such as radios, televisions, computers, and sound equipment. Perhaps most important, all the producers I met during my research enjoy sitting for long hours, often alone, in front of mixers, computers, and other devices manipulating and recording sound. This self-imposed isolation can deter many individuals from working in a studio despite their curiosity with sound.

From interviews with Tanzanian producers, most explained that their interest in recording music came from either a strong connection to performance or extensive interaction with technology as a deejay, sound engineer during live events, or in other areas connected to music. Bizman Ntavyo, for instance, who emerged as an important producer for composing Tanzanian sounding beats within bongo flava, first became interested in sound engineering as a performer in Inafrika Band. During shows, Bizman assisted with mixing the sound as well as arranging the instruments for performance. From these initial musical and technical forays, Bizman became interested in working with music he composed but in ways that were only possible in a recording studio. In 2001, he began working with P Funk while continuing to perform with Inafrika Band. Many other artists, such as Keppy Kiombile, Bakunde Mbilima, and Said Comorien, also became interested in recording through their work as performers. Family connections to music are also a significant motivating factor for many artists. Current producers, such as Rajab Marijani, Dully Sykes, and Master J, all had fathers who performed music.

For these and other individuals interested in becoming a producer, the best means to learn about music production is through some form of apprenticeship. Though two producers studied music production overseas, the majority of producers do not have access to schools or institutions that teach recording engineering. Apprenticeship is therefore the best and more reliable means to gain the diversity of skills needed to work within the local music economy. Apprenticing with a producer often involves sitting in a studio and watching a producer, then moving toward assisting with some aspect of recording (setting up microphones, mixing levels, and so on), until finally taking control of a recording session. Most producers rely on inductive transmission of knowledge whereby the more senior producer does the work and the apprentice observes before attempting to replicate similar movements and aesthetics. Apprenticeship is always done in the recording studio.

In the early 1990s, before studios became a highly competitive and secretive enterprise, it was easy for individuals to sit in with a producer and watch him work. Samuel "Ngosha" Luhende discusses how he learned to be a recording engineer:

> [In 1995] I went to Nairobi, Kenya. In Kenya, I started to venture into the
> studio, as a studio musician for gospel music. For a short time in 1995, I
> worked in the studio and then I returned [to Dar es Salaam] to be a studio
> musician at Don Bosco. There I learned how to record. I would just use my
> eyes—I looked at the engineers and studied what they did. I was given very
> little instruction. I started to work as a producer in 1998. And, I also got
> new tools, such as books to study about studio recording. There are some
> instructions that you need to be given like programming, mixing, sound
> recording. Sometimes I learned by observing how engineers were doing
> their work which made me not have many problems when I was hired here
> as sound engineer. The first album I recorded came out very well. It was
> of Tanzania One Theatre.

Being a studio musician, Ngosha had no trouble watching producers in both Kenya and Tanzania, picking up ideas, and teaching himself to be an engineer. Recording is a very tactile and auditory experience. Through watching and listening, Ngosha was able to educate himself in the art of recording and then simply sit down in front of a mixer and record his first album of one of Tanzania's most popular bands, Tanzania One Theatre.

Master J, who was one of the first independent producers to focus exclusively on recording rap music, did work with some producers to learn the basics of recording, but he spent considerable time learning the craft on his own:

Master J (center) has several studios in the same facility.
This is one of the secondary studios. *Photo by author.*

> Since I never studied sound engineering, I learn the most from reading
> books and listening to a lot of foreign music. At home, I put on headphones
> and just listen for a half hour or hour a day. I want to listen to how they [the
> foreign producers] use the stereo spectrum; what do they do to the chorus,
> the vocals; what effect do they use and how do they use it; you know, these
> are things that I listen to a lot. Because, I don't know, I didn't study recording
> engineering. So, I learn a lot of things through listening to foreign music and
> reading books.

Dozens of other producers follow a path similar to Ngosha and Master J.
These individuals then train other prospective producers to create a lin-
eage of production practices and techniques. In 2003, for instance, Master
J hired two producers, Professor Ludigo and Said Comorie, to record r&b
and rap at his studio. He continually monitored their work and encouraged them to develop their own sound. Both producers now work at other
studios where they are the head producers training a new group of sound
engineers.

Ally Baucha in his recording studio called Baucha Records. Baucha's recording studio was decorated with rap and pop records from the 1980s and 1990s that represent his early career as a competitive dancer in local clubs. *Photo by author.*

In the past few years, several producers have also been able to take computer courses at area technical colleges. Omari Mkali, who was a musician in the band Chuchu Sound, decided that he wanted to become a producer. In 2004, he enrolled in general computer courses at the Chuo cha Computer cha Forodhani (the Forodhani Computer College) and was eventually able to learn about recording software. These courses offer general knowledge about programs, but do not provide the technical and mechanical knowledge actually needed to run a studio. Mkali was fortunate in that he already had experience with mixers, microphones, and other sound equipment before he starting taking computer courses. Mkali has since set out to learn various instruments, such as trumpet and keyboards, as well as to continue to sing with various groups, such as Tango Stars and Chuchu Sound. For Mkali, his education and skill as a producer is in his musical abilities to appreciate and understand sound. Given the amount that a producer needs to compose or work on an arrangement for bands, musical skill is seen as a vital asset to creating high quality songs.

In addition to the resourcefulness needed to become a studio engineer, producers also need to find and maintain up-to-date recording equipment. Funding for many studios comes from local businesses, wealthy parents, or occasionally from the producer working other jobs. All recording equipment in Tanzania is imported from outside Africa, and a majority of it enters the country illegally. In Tanzania, recording equipment, as well as musical instruments, is heavily taxed. In visits to the Tanzania Revenue Authority, for instance, I sat with a tax specialist to determine the cost of bringing in equipment from overseas. Although the tax rates vary, generally the government applies three taxes on recording equipment and musical instruments. There is a 30 percent customs duty tax; a 30 percent excise tax; and a 20 percent VAT (value added tax). This means that a $100 piece of equipment costs $80 in taxes to import into Tanzania. In conversations and in published documents, the excise tax specifically targets "goods whose consumption is seen by the society as immoral." Generally, immoral goods refer to beer, cigarettes, and petroleum products, but luxury products fall under this purview. This is partially because luxury products are seen through the socialist lens, as being unnecessary for social development. Studio musicians, however, see the issues of imports differently. Master J, exasperated by the issue of taxes on equipment, stated:

> The problem is taxes. If taxes were smaller we would be bringing in equipment like rain. You know, even the equipment we do bring in allows for progress in Tanzanian music. I don't understand why they charge such [high] taxes. [He pauses and draws in air with exasperation.] That is, you can buy a $600 piece of equipment and they will charge you $600 dollars in taxes. What is this? On the side of technology, we fail to bring in a lot of equipment because of the large taxes. For equipment, if I go to a country like England, I can bring the whole container of equipment because the second-hand equipment there costs almost nothing. I mean cheap, cheap. But musical instruments are classified as luxury goods so they can even charge 100% in taxes. No joke. Ask them. P Funk paid it for his equipment. What is this? I am thinking that this is ridiculous. That is another battle we fight

every day, but we'll never win. Maybe if someone with a lot of [political] weight is able to help us. But we ourselves cannot. Because of such a thing, we have had to be creative. Of course we are creative; we are not going to do it straight. And you know what: I do not feel guilty because it helps the standard of Tanzanian music. For *Tanzania*. For *Tan-za-ni-a*.

J's argument is that high taxes only limit the potential growth of the Tanzanian music economy and society more broadly. He draws on nationalist sentiment to proclaim that the importation of more equipment and, therefore, the creation of better quality songs would only help to promote Tanzanian music regionally and internationally. Popular culture could become a means to promote the country as a whole if there were fewer taxes.

Due to the excessive costs of importing luxury goods, finding ways around paying taxes makes it far easier for small-scale producers to purchase high-quality equipment. Producers, therefore, use various creative practices to import equipment, such as bribing custom officials, smuggling goods across borders, or creating false receipts for the cost of the equipment, thereby getting lower taxes. Many producers also use legal means in being creative, such as relying on second-hand equipment and purchasing large quantities at once, which can often receive discounts at the time of importation. Of course, since most producers use computer-based recording technology, the piracy of computer software is common, which also saves producers financial investment. Without these illicit activities—bribery and piracy—the music business would be far less successful. It is therefore ironic that Tanzania's music economy can be called a success of neoliberalism even though the way that success is often achieved is through undermining legitimate forms of trade and exchange. → key!

## CREATING VALUE IN SONGS

In studies on value creation in capitalist-oriented markets, particularly in the academic discipline of business, many scholars debate the way in which people come to associate value with commodities. Value creation often refers to business interest in establishing connections between consumers and a brand; the greater the social and economic importance of a brand, the better a business has done at conveying the worth of their products. Debates emerge about the ways businesses invest in a brand or the ways customers relate to products that they purchase. In management studies, some scholars base their thinking on assembly line work and establish a linear model that emphasizes associations between businesses that generate interdependence between established firms. The central argument here is that value is created through relationships, commitments, and dependence of businesses on one another (Holm et al. 1999). Recognizing the limitations of this approach, other scholars posit a notion of value co-production in which people's interests in commodities is more synchronic and interactive. These studies emphasize the importance of customers and society in forming value through constant negotiation over the social significance and meaning of the goods that they purchase. Rafael Ramirez argues that this approach recognizes a "multiplicity of values" in relations to "multiple actors" (1999: 55). Rather than view value as something created solely by a company or a group of companies, the recognition here is that it is something constantly negotiated between various people and businesses in society. This notion has been referred to as an economy of qualities whereby commodities become defined by the "characteristics attributed to them in successive qualifications and requalifications, including those enacted by consumers" (Foster 2007: 713).

To become a successful producer means to have an awareness of value creation within the Tanzanian music economy. Producers need to comprehend the movement of their works through various areas of society. People listen to songs at home and at work. They are played in public transportation throughout the city and are regularly heard in shops, stalls, supermarkets, and other places of business. Bars and restaurants play recorded music on a daily basis. Youth who gather in certain areas of town regularly listen to the radio. Pushcart vendors blare music as they push their carts filled with cassettes throughout the city. Even at night, security guards sit with small portable radios to listen to music. Few spaces in Tanzanian urban society go untouched by the music recorded in local studios. This presents a powerful means for producers to interpret the value of their profession within the local music economy. Since producers are also listening to music—on buses, in homes, and in shops—they interpret aesthetics, sounds, and cultural meanings in the movement of music throughout the city and country. Using this knowledge, they work in recording studios to build on the public circulation of popular music: they want to tap into the circulation while also being original.

Creating value in Tanzania music studios means understanding the many ways that Tanzanians interact with recordings. From incidental consumers (those who listen to the radio) to intermediate consumers (those who attend live shows) to end consumers (those who purchase an album), studio producers focus greatly on the implications of their works on a broader public. In interviews with producers, many discuss their interest in interpreting the desires of listening audiences through following top-ten lists, popular radio shows, and comments they receive from music fans and artists. Through following commercially valued music, they attempt to creatively work from that knowledge to produce music that will attain recognition locally, nationally, and regionally in eastern Africa. The greater the public interest in a producer's works, the more attention the producer receives. The more attention a producer receives, the more clients come into the studio to record. Value is created in the composition of musical works but is sustained in the response of the producers to the desires and demands of artists and public cultures. ─ key!

Most attention in the music economy is paid to the work of producers who compose for bongo flava. These producers take an artist's vocal part and compose all the music for a song. They do not maintain ownership in their works since their composition becomes a work-for-hire where the artist hires the producer to compose a song, after which the artist becomes the owner of that material. Despite losing ownership in their compositions, they do create the sound that people identify with the genre. Considering that some of the same producers, such as Master J and P Funk, have been composing popular hits in Tanzania since the mid-1990s, they play a significant role in shaping the cultural and economic importance of popular music. In many respects, the longevity of their careers suggests that producers are the architects of bongo flava.

This is not to deny the importance of artists who compose the lyrics and perform the music in concerts. Yet considering that most rap artists use a producer's songs as the backing tracks to live concerts, the producer's work is, in effect, always with the artist. It becomes associated with that artist's sound, career, and artistic abilities. A talented producer can take even mediocre lyrics and performance skills and create compositions that allow an artist to stand out on the radio, in performance spaces, and in album sales. Or course, the opposite also occurs. The relationship between the producer and artist is best thought of as value co-creation. Value co-creation is the ability of a producer and artist to combine their efforts to compose songs that will be appealing to a broad listening public or a selected demographic. It is a central facet in the cultural dynamics of the recording studio.

There are many issues that interest studio producers in their attempts to create value in their recordings. Their relationship and opinion of an artist, for instance, matters significantly in their willingness to produce quality tracks. If the producer does not believe that the track will be a hit, then they will not put much effort into producing a quality work. If a local radio station funds a studio project, producers put more exertion into their recordings. The hope in these relationships is that the more successful the producer, the more business the radio station will send his way. Competition with other producers also informs the producer's work within the studio. If a producer has had a string of hits, then another producer may mimic those recordings. Finally, critics, radio deejays, and government officials play a large role in informing producers about their work. Being called "out of touch" or "irrelevant," as several producers have, is seen as a significant offense since it can lessen the draw of the studio to new talent and listeners.

Part of the reason producers or recording engineers garner so much attention is their ability to shape and transform songs through their knowledge of acoustics, music, technology, and sound. Even the selection of microphones for different voices or instruments shapes the final outcome. The amount of reverb, chorus, or other effects inspires different reactions in listeners. Allowing bands to warm up before performing and encouraging them to try something new are strategies used to produce different outcomes. A comparison might be made to language: anyone who studies a language learns a vocabulary of words and phrases. The way that a person puts those words together distinguishes him from other people. In a recording studio, the engineer is not creating the words or phrases; that is the job of the musicians. Instead, he edits them and moves them around. He turns weak sounds into powerful and effective sonic experiences. Talented producers, similar to skilled editors, make a work stand out and become exceptional. The producer would be unable to do this without the work produced by the artists. The artists, on the other hand, depend on the studio technician to refine their work. This is the process of value co-production.

A producer's work also has implications for the choices that artists make in their performances. Mark Katz suggests that recordings influenced the use of vibrato in concert violinists in the 1910s (2004: 93). Vibrato may have hidden imperfection in intonation and produced a greater sound on record. When some of the more talented violinists recorded with vibrato, it inspired others to incorporate the technique into their music. Tanzanian studios produce similar outcomes with their aesthetic choices. The use of auto-tune, for instance, is popular in many bongo flava songs. In Western recording studios, auto-tune is commonly used as a process for pitch correcting a singer's voice. If a singer is flat or sharp in singing a note, the computer software corrects the error. Overuse of this process produces an interesting digital melisma where the voice sounds as if it is moving on digital steps. The technique is mainly done in the studio and has become a popular aesthetic effect in many Tanzanian songs.

Due to the emergence of numerous studios in Dar es Salaam, producers have to distinguish their style or technical abilities from other recording studios. They need to create value in the sounds that emerge from their studios in order to make it familiar and desirable. There are two ways they can do this. The first approach is to create a style that is recognizable by both consumers and other producers. In the same way that many musical groups create a sound distinct from bands in the same genre, many Tanzanian producers attempt to find a particular aesthetic that listeners, artists, and other producers can easily identify among other songs being produced in the same genre. Ideally, the signature sound should emerge early in the song so that people can recognize the producer before the singing or rapping appears. The style should also be replicable and interesting across a variety of recordings. → *But what to do when this changes?*

P Funk (Paul Matthysse), also known as Manjani, began producing bongo flava music in 1995. His productions are unique in that he frequently inserts a thick layering of aggressive effects that often sound simultaneously cautious and confrontational. On the song "CNN" by Mangwair, the opening begins with a synthesized violin sound mixed with a punctuated rhythm reminiscent of timpani. Similar to his other recordings, P Funk leaves space around the main instrumental sounds and connects them with a sustained chord played on a synthesizer. A voice also repeats a single word in a rhythmic whisper that adds to the somewhat eerie quality of the recording. Before Mangwair begins to rap, the song is already distinguishable as a P Funk creation.

On other songs, particularly older recordings, P Funk uses a similar open and aggressive production technique, but also adds atypical sounds that add texture and interest. His recordings have included cowboy themes, presidential speeches, and samples from popular records. On Juma Nature's song "Njaa Mbaya" (Severe Hunger), P Funk adds a wavering, sustained note reminiscent of the sound used to represent satellites on old television cartoons from the United States. Other variously pitched notes enter the recording, which adds depth and texture to the song. No one else in Tanzania produces a similar sound or attempts to incorporate a similar array of textures.

Finally, P Funk uses the musicality found in the rhythms of the music to compose his backing tracks. The rhythm of the song, according to P Funk, should be melodic and follow the direction of the artist's words. P Funk listens to an artist perform without any music before figuring the best production style to match that voice. There is responsiveness to each rhythm that builds on and encourages the listener to invest energy in the lyrics to a song. On Professor Jay's song "Zali la Mentali" (The Luck of the Crazy One), P Funk uses the keyboards and rhythms to follow and move along with Professor Jay's voice. When Jay sings, "'Dada habari samahani naomba niulize swali" (Excuse me sister, permit me to ask a question), P Funk places pauses in the music and shifts the rhythm, which makes it sound as if Jay is stuttering, nervous while talking to an attractive woman. For the woman's response, the music returns to the song's main rhythm. After the two finish talking and the woman pushes Jay aside, P Funk adds a single, lonely sustained note under the music, which shows the longing interest that Jay has in the woman. Jay's voice does not change much during his performance. Instead, the music provides the sentiment of the lyrics through creatively manipulating notes and rhythms.

Given his distinct production style, many listeners can easily recognize P Funk's songs. This allows him to attract artists interested in creating similar projects. He can also create a consumer base of people who want to purchase his recordings. Due to the popularity of his work, P Funk is often recognized within the music economy as one of the top producers in the country. In 2003 and again in 2005, he won awards at the

ORIGINALITY:
① Signature sound
② Diverse production techniques

Kili Music Awards in Tanzania. At other awards shows, he won in the best producer category for album of the year, song of the year, and hip-hop album of the year. These accolades symbolize P Funk's ability to capture the interests of listeners while establishing an innovative style that is associated only with his compositions and efforts in the studio.

②    A second approach used to create value in sound recordings is more responsive to the interests of artists. Rather than create an identifiable style of production, producers in this second category create a variety of technical and aural approaches to recording songs, which can be tailored to the sound of a particular artist or band. Originality comes from establishing diverse production techniques to accommodate a number of approaches and interests in music. Many bongo flava producers, for instance, need to be able to compose a broad spectrum of backing tracks, from those that imitate American hip-hop to those that rely on traditional genres of music. Bizman explains this recording practice as a combination of artists and producers attempting to bring bongo flava to multiple music markets. He explains the way he works with different musicians:

> For example, in bongo flava, you encounter ragga beats and artists come [into the studio] and say that they like the beats that foreign artists use in their music, especially from America. So, if you want to make beats for ragga, you have to listen to an archive of ragga material to get ideas. I don't take foreign artists' beats, but I use their music as an example. The bongo flava artists, from what I can see, are just keeping up with what is happening in the world. If we compose really good beats it can be heard throughout the world. The beats are a means for capturing the interest of many people.

The notion that beats capture the "interests of many people" is a key cultural component for understanding the way that Tanzanian artists imagine their place in a global community of musicians. Engaging with this community means establishing a repertoire of sounds that fits within the body of musical repertoires inside and outside the country. The producer's responsibility is to ensure that the work he creates usefully and effectively builds on preexisting songs without mimicking them. He must create new productions by approximating the feel and sound of the original source.

Both approaches to distinguishing a producer's style require originality, a form of creative practice central to any music economy. The term originality is often equated with newness, freshness, and innovation. To be original is to think of something that has never been thought of before.

Mkoloni (Frederick Mariki) recording for the 2006 release of an album by his group Wagosi wa Kaya. *Photo by author.*

Many social theorists acknowledge, however, that there is rarely anything actually new and, instead, originality needs to refer to creative and inventive ways of engaging with people, ideas, and society. The British scholar T. Sharper Knowlson writes, "Originality is the expression of the individual self in relation to its environment; its significance does not lie in newness so much as in sincerity" (1918: 4). The idea encompasses the notion of being distinctive from others in a cultural context. Imitation can also be considered a form of originality, depending on the way it is used and the degree to which something is imitated. Returning to Knowlson, he states, "In social life, in economic matters, and in the intellectual sphere, also, imitation is a method of progress" (1918: 10). The notion that originality can come from imitation of someone else's ideas is particularly relevant to Tanzania's music economy and to the way value is created in many production projects.

Given the multifaceted ways that people interact and react to songs, originality is a matter of opinion, circumstance, and social position. In Tanzania's music economy, originality within specific genres of music is often equated with popularity; the more popular a song is, the more original it must be since listeners enjoy hearing new ideas and sounds. The ultimate goal of most producers is to have several songs in the top-ten lists of local radio stations, which often, though certainly not always, signifies the ability of artistic works to stand out from the hundreds of others being concurrently released. The use of innovation in the establishment of originality is a central part of value creation within Tanzanian recording studios. Whichever techniques the producers uses, the goal for most is to attain recognition for musical works that reflect the desires and interest of listening audiences. The production of culture evidenced in recording studios is a means to establish value in a song as both a musical work that people enjoy and as a commodity that people want to purchase in recorded form.

## IN THE STUDIO

A central part of originality is the materialization of new recording technologies. The transition from analog to digital recording, which mirrored the move, to some extent, from state-controlled to independent studios, brought many shifts in the way that sound was being manipulated in the studio. Recordings no longer needed to be thought of in a linear fashion since any segment of recording could be rearranged, edited, overdubbed, replaced, or transformed during the recording process. A song became something that could be segmented, measured, and edited in ways that were not possible when reel-to-reel tape machines were used. James Williams writes, "A song may begin in one form, with performances recorded according to a template established early in the project, and yet be so re-arranged and re-configured via non-linear editing that the resulting recording is essentially a new composition" (Williams 2006: 423). The malleability and flexibility of digital recording technology offers infinitely more forms of innovation than previously existed.

To illustrate originality within digital technology, particularly in non-bongo flava genres, it is useful to look at a single producer's efforts to differentiate two bands that perform in the same genre of music. Marlone Linje is considered by many dansi bands to be the best producer in Tanzania. He is known for taking mediocre songs and transforming them into high-quality radio hits. Listening to the recordings made by Linje, one can hear the variety of methods he uses to keep each song sounding fresh, even with bands that sound similar. One of the central issues that Linje has to confront in recording dansi songs is that his work needs to have a sense of liveness, as if they are emitting from the speakers at a concert. Regarding South African studios, Louise Meinjtes writes, "Liveness is an illusion of sounding live that is constructed through technological intervention in the studio and mediated symbolically through discourses about the natural and the artistic" (2003: 112). For Tanzanian producers, a great deal of energy is spent considering the best ways to not only capture a sense of liveness, but also enhance that experience. Most producers are well aware that studio technology in Tanzania surpasses the equipment used in concerts. For this reason, producers believe that they can create a better sense of liveness—a simulacra of performance—than one can actually achieve at a show. Studio recordings are clearer and achieve more spatial separation between instruments than the muddied sounds of live shows.

In 2004 and 2005, respectively, Linje recorded albums for DDC Mlimani Park Orchestra and Msondo Ngoma (formerly OTTU Jazz Band). Both bands have been in competition with one another since the late

1970s and battle each other for audience attendance, radio airplay, and even musicians. Linje had a particular responsibility to highlight each of the band's strengths without allowing one to claim that he failed to record a quality recording.

Linje's recording of "Kaza Moyo" (Courageous) by Msondo Ngoma is distinctive for the clarity and space that surrounds each of the instruments. Each instrumental voice—trumpet, saxophone, drums, bass, guitar, and vocals—is audible even as the instruments layer on top of one another. The use of digital technology where the producer can create clear, multi-track recordings of each of the voices certainly helps in this song. For instance, in recording the background vocals, Linje uses different microphones for each singer, and pans the voices to different channels (right, center, and left). When TX Moshi William, Muhiddin Maalim Gurumo, Maina Joseph, and Athuman Momba sing the chorus, the effect is that the singers are standing in different places in the room, similar to a live performance, even though one hears each of the voices in each channel. In addition, the way Linje layers the voices in his mixing of the song and adds reverb also makes the voices distinguishable when they sing in unison instead of muddied together as they often are in live concerts. Further, because of his use of quality microphones and digital effects, the voices sound warm and are mixed to appear closer to you than the other instruments: the ideal similitude for liveness since the sensation is that the band is singing directly to you in an intimate club setting.

DDC Mlimani Park's song "Maneno Maneno" (Rumor) also has very clear separation between instruments. Linje, however, creates a different vocal aesthetic through the use of heavy delay on the vocals, which better suits the singing of the group. When the lead singer, Hassani Bitchuka, sings, "Maneno maneno sikuzoea, Maneno maneno mimi sipendelei [I am not used to rumor, I don't like rumor]," there is a slight echo at the end of each of his phrases. The effect is meant to create the illusion of a live hall where the sound emanates from the speakers toward the audience and then bounces off the walls back to the audience, thereby reaching the listener's ears twice. When the background singers enter, the vocals have a thick, heavy quality to them meant to sound like a large group of singers. Only two singers, however, were recorded for the background vocals. Linje then took each vocal track, panned one to the left and one to the right, and then copied each vocal track several times to create a thick layering of sound. The overall vocal quality is distinctive and differs from vocal sound in Linje's work with Msondo Ngoma. Where one is warm and each voice separable, the other is thick and punchier, helping to drive the song. Both aesthetics are well liked in Tanzania since they provide the illusory sense of sitting in a club and listening to a band that is performing on excellent sound equipment.

The separate strategies in recording two similar sounding bands emphasize the acoustic and musical considerations that must be made. First, it demonstrates Linje's knowledge of the dansi genre. He put consideration into all the other instruments on the recordings but focused particular attention on the singing. They are placed more to the front of the recording and only the rhythm guitar is as audible during the singing. At the end of phrases, other instruments, including lead guitar and saxophone, fill in the spaces. This fits customary aesthetics of classic dansi music. Second, Linje draws out the strengths of the vocalists. Msondo Ngoma's singers each have unique vocal timbres that should be drawn out to present the distinctiveness of the band. In the opening phrase, "Nitakaza moyo / dunia hii / walimwengu wanavyotaka tukaze moyo" (I have to be courageous / In this world / people want us to be bold), the vocalists sing in harmony with a balance between the timbres of each singer: from more nasally tenor to a throatier baritone. The recording uses the timbres as strength to support the overall sound. On the Mlimani Park recording, he draws the most attention to Bitchuka's voice. He sings alone for most of the verse and, to allow his voice to stand out, Linje pushes the other instruments and voices aside. On the recording, one almost has the sense that Bitchuka is standing in the middle of the room surrounded, at a distance, by the instrumentalists.

The culmination of these recording strategies is a pair of songs that draw from the strengths of the bands, maintain the aesthetics of the dansi genre, and create two popular hits considered innovative by consumers, radio staff, and music critics. Studio producers must attain these types of results on a regular basis. The tight deadlines, competition, and desires for steady incomes provide impetus to manipulate sounds to attain something that fosters excitement within the music economy. Value co-creation and originality become creative practices necessary to remain competitive among an array of producers simultaneously releasing songs into the local market. Even with artists and songs that sound similar, there is innovation in the manipulation of digital sounds that hits listeners' ears as novel, unique, or innovative, thereby creating marketability for the music.

## BRANDING

In addition to originality and digital technology, the creation of value in studio production also encompasses the entirety of works that a producer creates. The songs that a studio producer engineers over a period of time become identified as that producer's sound and contribution to the local music scene. While this identity or musical brand shifts over time, artists and fans learn the subtle techniques and styles of local music producers. Producers attempt to build a brand for themselves that will continue to attract fans and artists to the studio. Branding is no small task since it establishes a producer's reputation and identity within the local music economy. The investment in studios names and public image is similar to that of brands in that the name often carries connotations of the quality and meaning of the studio, as well as the biography of the producer. There is also a cumulative effect of associating a producer with a particular sound that has appeared on previous recordings. Though these associations and conceptions of the producer and his studio continually unfold over time, it also has a certain level of rigidity given that most producers have similar formulas and approaches to all their recordings.

Branding is not unique to recording studios. Some of the influence of creating a particular style of recording may have come from mtindo used in dansi music. Dansi bands typically identify the rhythm and style of their music through a particular name, referred to as the mtindo. DDC Mlimani Park's mtindo is called sikinde. The term sikinde comes from an ngoma of the Zaramo people who live in and around Dar es Salaam. Even though Mlimani Park does not rely on only this one ngoma in all its music, it is the dominant rhythm for the group and one that appears on all its album covers, press releases, and advertisements. When Msondo Ngoma became an independent band in the early 2000s, the musicians decided to use their mtindo (msondo ngoma) to replace its old name (OTTU Jazz) since most people were familiar with the mtindo. The band, in other words, believed that it was important to keep the mtindo so that

Mchizi Mox, a Tanzanian rapper, wearing a T-shirt with his own moniker. The "established in" date on the shirt was the year he was born. The shirts are sold in Dar es Salaam and help advertise or brand the artists to a broader public. *Photo by author.*

people's image, association, and understanding of the group would not disappear with a name change. The msondo ngoma refers to a rhythm and dance from the Wadengereko peoples in Dar es Salaam.

In more recent years, many younger artists have also attempted to brand their style of playing. Bongo flava artists create names that define their specific style of music. Mr. Nice calls his style takeu, an acronym that stands for Tanzania, Kenya, and Uganda. Zozo refers to his style, heavily influenced by ngoma music, as bongo culture. Some artists have even made T-shirts with their names on them and then the words "established on" followed by the year of their birth. In essence, the artist's moniker becomes the brand, which started on his or her date of birth. Similarly, some producers create styles that identify their music. Said Comorien, who runs Metro Studio, produces beats that he calls African American or Africa-U.S.A., a reference to the mixture of African and American sounds in his productions. Other producers never label their style but create consistent hits in a sound that becomes identified with their studio name. Think about branding in terms of Taylor-

Branding creates a value for the studio and its producer, just as it has for bands and artists in the past. The creation and maintenance of brand value come from a variety of places. It originates in the techniques that producers use in the studio, emerges through the songs that producers record and mix, and becomes public on cassettes, on the radio, and in performances. Consumer interaction with and interpretation of those songs inform a broader public of the role that the studio plays within the local music economy. In writing about the use of branded goods, Adam Arvidsson writes, "Consumers use goods . . . to produce a common framework in which goods can have a use-value" (2005: 242). Consumers thus creatively use brands to establish a shared meaning for that brand even though brand products undergo continual transformations in the way people interpret and use them. The use of goods becomes a "communicative process," to use Robert Foster's term, where brands "function for their owners as stable platforms for the perpetual destabilization or requalification of products" (2007: 719). In other words, the brand may continue to have a shared meaning among consumers even as the products manufactured by the brand continually undergo transformations in uses and meanings. For producers, the name of the studio represents a brand while songs are the commodities. The use of studio techniques thus reflects the way in which producers attempt to articulate the branding of their studio.

The purpose of originality and branding is to create a studio production that distinguishes a producer both technologically and competitively. While early producers were less concerned about the financial ramifications of their images and even, to some extent, the overall quality of their recordings, the successful manipulation of sound into hit songs and the successful marketing of one's studios have become central strategies for remaining competitive in the music scene. Samuel Ngosha describes Tanzania's modern studios as follows:

> Now, we have business competition. In this business competition, we are able to support Tanzanian music, which is different from the past when there were few studios. Even attention to recording was not there in the past because you were in the studio by yourself and you had a lot of customers. If you compare older products and recent ones [you will notice a difference]. Now, there are a lot of studios, which is good because if you record badly, you will lose customers. If you do well, you will get customers. Now, studios and studio engineers are more attentive in their job recording music. This is very good for promoting Tanzanian music.

Aware of the many other talented producers in Dar es Salaam competing for the fees of local artists, producers continually search for ways to make their recordings and their studio name appear distinctive. Generating value in the production of songs is a central creative practice for the contemporary producer in Tanzania.

## UNDOING SUCCESS

Thus far, I have described the ways individuals discover the means both to become producers and to use their resources to establish a specific style that becomes identified with their recordings. Many of the creative practices discussed, such as branding and originality, present a rather business or market-oriented approach to becoming a producer. Yet being a producer entails other forms of engagement with music and society. This chapter's opening narrative, for instance, emphasizes the foot-dragging and sabotage that occurred in the recording session with guests from South Africa and Holland. These forms of creative practice play a significant role in the music economy but are perhaps most prevalent in the competitive and secretive area of studio recording.

Unlike other areas of the local music economy, recording studios tend to be owned and run by one or two individuals. The actions of one person can, therefore, have a profound impact on any project connected to his studio. In this chapter's opening narrative, the one producer who owned a successful studio resisted the cooptation of his equipment by a competing producer. James Scott describes similar actions as "everyday forms of resistance," which are informal, often covert, and concerned with immediate gains (1985: 32–33). The producer who sabotaged his own equipment and frequently showed up late to unlock his studio wanted to ensure that the other producer would not find success from the project. If the producer who owned the studio outright withdrew from the project and refused to share his equipment, he would have simply shown his unwillingness to cooperate and may have been passed over in future recording situations. His main goal was to undermine the success of the other producer without tarnishing his name. He chose to sabotage his own studio to ensure the overall failure of the endeavor.

Many members of Tanzania's music economy encounter or employ similar forms of resistance in their daily lives. Among producers and artists working in recording studios, disruption of other studio projects is common and is often discussed as a reaction to increased competition between local studios, particularly as perceived notions of wealth, power, and fame become intertwined with the fate of one song or one album. In the past decade, numerous instances of sabotage and evasion have taken place within the local music scene: producers paying individuals to disrupt another producer's recording sessions; artists being paid to sit in on a recording session but performing badly, thus ruining the quality of the overall song; or providing misinformation about the way to use a new technology, which can delay the release of a song or album. In addition to these more benign forms of creative practices, there are numerous instances of sabotage that destroyed the work and labor of up-and-coming producers and artists: several studios have mysteriously burned down or been robbed; albums in the process of being recorded or mixed in the studio disappear; and at least one artist has been held at gun point and robbed for importing equipment to begin a studio and promotion company. In each of these cases, no one has ever been arrested or caught for the crime (though numerous people have been implicated in rumor). Instead, the act of sabotage successfully disrupted the potential success of a studio, producer, or artist.

Derived from Arabic, the Swahili verb "kuhujumu" or the noun "hujuma" refers to this purposeful act of destroying or damaging something in order to hinder it from being successful. The word is commonly used to refer to any act of sabotage by anyone or anything. Disease, for instance, can be said to "hujuma afya na uchumi" (destroy health and the economy);[8] youth can "kufanya hujumu" (commit sabotage) when they burn down their school;[9] and terrorists can "kuhujumu utawala wa mwenzie" (sabotage an opponent's establishment).[10] Kuhujumu can also refer to less violent or lethal forms of undoing success, such as removing the only available cord used to run an important machine in a studio. Central to the idea of hujuma is the undoing of something, either through some form of destruction, foot-dragging, or sabotage, in order that the success of someone or something is avoided. Thus, hujuma is to undo success whether it is the success of a healthy body, a school, a government, or a recording studio.

As has become important in this and other chapters, competition and financial insecurity has brought increased anxiety of someone else's success. In his book *Kupilikula,* Harry West writes about neoliberal reform and dangerous displays of ambition among Muedans, a population that lives on the Mueda plateau in northern Mozambique. Among Muedans, West explains, conflicts emerge between neoliberal development goals intended to create opportunities for local peoples and attempts by those people to undermine displays of ambition. This tension between development and undoing that development makes individual enhancement perilous: "In this environment of actual mutual suspicion, anything that might be accomplished by anyone was undone (kupilikula) even in the moment of its doing, making impossible not only advancement on the part of the 'ambitious' but also maintenance of the dwindling commonwealth upon which Muedans of all ambitions depended" (West 2005: 244). Part of the reason for this continual state of "transcendent maneuvers" among Muedans is alternate conceptions of living daily life: a constructive act for one may appear ruinous to another (West 2007: x). Thus, Muedans use various tactics to invert, reverse, or overturn previous actions considered overly ambitious.

There are similarities in the transcendent maneuvers of the Muedans and the strategies used by Tanzanian producers. Driven by intense
competition for talented artists, popularity, and wealth, there is an increasing push to undo the success—imagined or real—of anyone who
appears overly ambitious. There are many direct ways that people find to
disrupt or undo the work of another producer: the theft of money given
to producers traveling abroad to buy equipment for other producers; machines malfunctioning and parts disappearing at studios; the deletion
of songs and albums from computer hard drives; and so on. Of course,
not all producers participate in the cutthroat studio environment, but
many are brought into the competitive market simply by establishing a
studio. Studio Makuti, organized under the Urithi Arts Program, was
one of the new local studios whose owners quickly found their studio
being threatened by other local producers. Rosa and Michel Tyabji, who
formerly lived in New York, moved to Tanzania in 1998 with the idea
of creating high-quality recordings of traditional music. Because the organization was designed more as a non-profit than as a business venture,
it received assistance from the National Arts Council (BASATA) and the
Ministry of Education and Culture, which provided tax exemption on the
importation of goods and assistance with finding groups to record. After
setting up their studio at the BASATA offices in the Ilala district of Dar es
Salaam, the Tyabji's began to look for local artists to record. After only a
few weeks, several local producers visited the Tyabji's studio. Rosa Tyabji
explains a visit by one local producer:

> He [the local producer] casually says to us, "You know, there has been a lot
> of tension and some studios get burned down." Just casually letting us know
> the scene. Michel and I were like, we do not want that. All we knew was that
> this really sharp looking guy, in a cream suit with snake skin boots, big gold
> rings, and 1970s sunglasses shows up and says, "studios get burned down."
> He did not need to spell it out for us. I thought it was a sincere statement,
> and Michel and I acted accordingly.

Not wanting to enter into the hazardous fray of the commercial studio
business, the Tyabjis decided to record only traditional music or popular
artists that had limited local market value but could be sold internationally. This allowed them to work in Dar es Salaam without being perceived
as competition by other producers within the popular music scene.

Many other individuals told me similar stories of violence or threats of violence against their studio. Although no one was ever hurt in these interactions, new production facilities present a risk that can be potentially ruinous to others. In my own research in Tanzania, I was unaware of the ways that other producers were inspecting my presence in the country. Although all appeared to believe that I was conducting research on the local music economy, a few also decided to ensure that I was not recording any local artists for commercial use. One producer even came to my apartment, looked around, and then left after asking many questions about my research equipment. At the time, I thought that the producer was just visiting my home as a goodwill gesture. On reflection (and the fact that he never returned again), I now realize that he was looking in my home for signs of recording equipment and ensuring that I did not present any competition to him within the local economy.

In addition to the more direct approaches toward undoing success of others, there is also an increasing movement toward using the invisible realm to negatively impact other producers. In writing about the Ihanzu in Tanzania, the anthropologist Todd Sanders focuses on issues of witchcraft and modern wealth. He writes that witches "intensely dislike development, modernity, or progress, all terms glossed as *maendeleo*" (2003a: 164). They destroy any attempts at showing individual prosperity and wealth, and numerous cases emerged in Sanders's fieldwork where witches allegedly destroyed modern goods, fostering the notion that witches and modernity cannot coexist. Sanders also shows, however, that certain forms of witchcraft are employed to creatively engage and envisage forms of tradition and, by extension, modernity: "Notions of African witchcraft have proved surprisingly flexible and thus survive—indeed thrive—in novel postcolonial contexts. This conceptual flexibility implies that while the African witch *may* be about modernity, it may also be about other things, too" (2003b: 338, his emphasis). In other words, the flexible use of witchcraft is a means for some to establish "a modernity on their own terms" (2003b: 347).

The presence of anti-modern individuals working within the invisible realm is not unique to eastern Africa but has been recorded in numerous contexts over the past half century (Ardener 1970; Geschiere 1998; Gluckman 1956; Friedson 1996; Sanders 2003b). In Tanzania, there is a great deal of emphasis and concern about the practice of witchcraft, both in the health of the nation and in the image that non-Tanzanians hear about that country. The Tanzanian press has emphasized the presence of witchcraft in the contemporary world and frequently carries stories of curses made by one person against another. There are also numerous reports of suspected witches being killed.[11] In January 2003, *Harper's* magazine reported that five hundred people were killed in Tanzania because of witchcraft in 2002. Compare this figure to the estimated 3,692 "witches" who were killed in Tanzania between 1970 and 1984 (Mesaki 1994), an average of 260 per year. The current rate at which "witches" are killed is almost double what it was during the period of socialism, though these numbers are obviously questionable both due to the way crimes about suspected witches are reported and in the way the statistics are compiled. Nonetheless, a general trend exists in both fear and use of action in the invisible realm.

It is not surprising, then, that for many people working in the Tanzanian music economy, the invisible realm is an important means to deal with the difficulties and insecurities brought on by neoliberalization (PURL 6.1). Todd Sanders argues well that "structural adjustment and the changes it has unleashed are themselves responsible for the recent rise of occult idioms and practices across Tanzania" (2001: 177). As people find innovative ways of make a living within the new economy, they disrupt, in a sense, perceptions of daily life that once existed in a community, among neighbors, or between friends. Jennifer Widner explains that witchcraft helps "'level' inequalities in status and wealth, bringing down the successful innovators as well as those whose gains were ill-gotten" (2001: 382). The use of witchcraft, as well as other forms of sabotage, also illustrates the bitterness that comes from recent emphasis on success, wealth, and material goods in the neoliberal period even as most people's lives remain one of hardship (Meyer 1998). Undoing the success of others can therefore be seen as a response to cultural shifts taking place in daily life due to neoliberal reforms.

Among producers, who continually struggle to keep up or stay ahead of their colleagues, accusations of witchcraft are a common response to explain why something is going wrong in one studio or going well in another. Some producers visit *wachawi* (those who use secret knowledge to harm others) or *waganga* (healers that use their powers for good) to counteract curses they believe are put on them by other producers. They also place curses on others, thereby creating a strong sense of balance within the occult world. Others use the healers to attain better skills, talents, or success. In a 2009 e-mail, one Tanzanian producer explained to me:

> There are some producers who believe in going to healers to help them attract artists to their studio and to become more popular inside and outside Tanzania. A producer can go to see a *mganga* and be tricked into believing that the medicine he is given helps him compose a song that becomes popular when it is actually his talent all along. Those who believe in this do not believe in themselves and are only confused. I am not sure why they think it is important to go to see healers; I think it is a desire to build a name quickly at any cost and earn money quickly.

Witchcraft has become a psychological and invisible means to deal with the competition that exists between studios and the anxiety of trying to remain on top within the recording business. In many cases, producers seek help from an occult practitioner simply to provide assistance for their success.

Although interest in the invisible realm is common among many Tanzanian producers, it is difficult to provide statistics on its prevalence. Producers as well as artists often spoke to me about the occult but they did so in the abstract. They explained situations in which the occult was used to hinder the popularity of their studio recordings, cause a particularly important piece of recording equipment to malfunction, or drive away prospective clients. Most, however, never stated that they sought the assistance of a mchawi or mganga. When I pressed about the potential number of producers who went to see a mchawi or mganga, the numbers given were often high, ranging from 50 to 80 percent of all producers. One journalist assured me that these numbers were far too low.

One final note: even though intense competition creates conflict between studios and producers, some musicians use it to their advantage. Balozi Dola, who recorded his album *Balozi Wenu* at two studios in 1999, commented on his tactic of getting two competing producers to work to make his songs sound the best they could in the shortest amount of time:

I booked at Master J's studio and P Funk's studio. I really wanted them to work fast. I pressured one, "Hey, how come you're not working man, I've already recorded two songs with this guy, I haven't even recorded one with you." I take one to listen to another's track and he goes, "Damn, I must make a better beat." That actually got them working hard and brought out the best in me.

In eleven days, Balozi Dola recorded his album, mainly because he perfected his parts before entering the studio and then pushed the producers to compose accompanying tracks. Since an album can take months to complete and producers are tied up in so many projects, Dola's ability to record and mix his album in eleven days was stunning. As a result, the release of *Balozi Wenu* became a critical album in the hip-hop scene and a model for other artists attempting to record in studios. Other rappers wanting to record albums followed Dola's lead, recording at multiple studios to ensure that their albums had diverse beats and were well produced. More important, Dola found a way to manipulate the way competition is experienced within studios by pushing two dominant producers to work on creating a single album.

## FADE OUT

Success is experienced, lived, and undermined in many different ways in Tanzania's music economy. Certainly, the dramatic expansion of studios and producers represents an overall growth in studio production and points to the desire to record, document, and sell recorded music. The undermining of that success also shows the tension that arises from intense studio competition. These fluctuations of engagement with success present one of the everyday realties of working within Tanzania's music economy. For producers, learning their craft, experimenting within the studio, establishing a particular style and brand, competing for talented artists, and encountering the success of other producers all present a constant need to employ creative practices, such as attaining an apprenticeship; finding innovative ways to import equipment; networking with other producers and artists; attaining knowledge of music and studio techniques; establishing a reputation for a particular, unique studio style; working within the visible and invisible realm to discourage the success of others; and finding ways to create value within one's own work. These creative practices are central to the way music production is lived in Dar es Salaam and other areas of Tanzania. Since any recording situation has multiple outcomes, with which the producer engages in order to interpret his place within the music scene, there is a strong impetus for producers to find ingenious ways to make the most of any recording situation and best the competition.

# SEVEN

# Legend of the Pirates

There came a call for us,
To create self-employment.
At first, as usual, we agreed.
We should create self employment.
But things they are not calm on the streets, sometimes there is violence.
Street traders they are fighting with the state.
Employment now is a problem and cannot be resolved.
And if it cannot be resolved then a lot of other problems cannot be resolved.

—JUSTIN KALIKAWE "Ajira" (Employment)

Once music is recorded in a fixed and tangible medium, artists have several options. They can take copies of their songs to radio presenters in hopes of receiving airplay. They can work with managers and promoters to try to market the music in local clubs and potentially generate performance opportunities. Or, artists can attempt to make deals with record distributors to sell the recordings throughout Tanzania, eastern Africa, or, in the most lucrative arrangements, internationally. Attaining a contract with local distributors, however, is rather difficult since musicians need to have already convinced radio presenters, listeners, and others that their music is popular and worth selling. A distributor rarely offers contracts to artists who do not already have media exposure and a fan base. To overcome these obstacles, talented artists sign contracts with music producers or managers who have relationships with radio presenters who, in turn, are friendly with distributors. There is vast network of connections between the most influential people in the music business. Contracts are common at each node of these connections, though there is little or no legal representation at any point in the creation or signing of deals. This is often to the disadvantage of artists who find their music part of an outsized commodity chain that leaves them with a significantly reduced income.

Whether working alone or with someone else, attaining a lucrative distribution deal is a significant rite of passage in the career of artists and bands. Distributors, referred to as wasambazaji, purchase the rights to sell an album for a certain length of time in specific locations, such as Tanzania, eastern Africa, or southern Africa. The distributor then takes on the responsibility of creating the covers for sound recordings and then making copies of a designated number of albums. Artists can earn royalties on each album sold or, more commonly, are paid a lump sum based on an estimated amount that the artist is expected to sell. The potential for large payments and mass distribution represents an essential objective for artists who aspire to improve their economic and social status within the local music economy.

The most successful distributors in Dar es Salaam have a unique relationship to other members of the music economy. They are almost all Asian Tanzanians. They hold a monopoly on the distribution of music in the country. And they are often considered extraordinarily wealthy though stingy in their contracts. Many African Tanzanians resent the economic power of Asians, and several musicians believe that these businesses should be owned by Africans, which harkens to the nationalization efforts of the 1970s. The resentment toward Asian distributors is particularly vehement when discussions turn to music piracy. It is widely believed that many distributors sell albums illegally, even those that are under contract. These duplicitous actions have been described as a form of imperialism where music pirates pilfer the rights and labor of Africans for their own prosperity.

The stories of Asian piracy, however, are partially legend. Like any legend, they begin with some basic narrative drawn from historical fact. Many Asian businesses did (and do) illegally sell music and many profited tremendously from this practice. They were not, however, the first group to not pay royalties to musicians, nor did initial forms of piracy harm musicians' careers in the way that is often argued. It was common before the 1990s for music sold in Tanzania to serve as a form of publicity rather than as an object of profit, and royalties were only paid by a few companies. Recordings were often considered a form of advertising to draw audiences to performances.

In addition, the legend of music piracy promotes the idea that the early sale of music throughout Tanzania damaged the local economy of music. Without piracy, however, Tanzanian music would not be as prosperous and successful as it is now. Between 1979 and 1989, the distribution of music cassettes throughout Tanzania moved albums into people's homes at unprecedented rates. Since they were inexpensive to manufacture, people could buy many cassettes of their favorite artists and even keep collections of music in the home. This was an uncommon practice during socialism, particularly due to the collapse of industries capable of supporting a viable record industry. Cassettes, however, provided more opportunities for any enterprising person to create a market of consumer interest where none had existed before. By keeping the cost low, piracy provided an impetus for people to become consumers of popular music. It established social practices and classifications that formed a demand for people to conceptualize music as a commodity (Appadurai 1986: 29). It was an illicit creative practice that benefited the early commodification of music.

Once consumer interests emerged, artists realized the commercial value in sound recordings and the potential to profit from their works. They led several movements to hinder piracy, including leading protests at the state house, and helped to create stronger laws and means to enforce intellectual property rights. In a 1999 interview with the Chief Executive Registrar of Companies, Business Names, Patents, and Trade and Service Marks, E. E. Mahingila commented that these movements created the impetus to pass a new law in the first place:

> We received a lot of complaints from stakeholders: musicians, artists, authors of literary works. . . . Everyone came and complained that we are not receiving protection here in Tanzania. Then, the importation laws in this country are not very strong. There is a lot of piracy and trade in counterfeit goods. Our neighboring countries were complaining that Tanzania has major problems and that you need to do something to make the situation better. Therefore, we decided to make changes and create a new law.

The 1999 Copyright Act emerged from the pressure of musicians, as well as international organizations. Initially, copyright law restricted the number of illegal cassettes and compact discs appearing in the market. It provided royalties to musicians, brought official action against the illegal duplication of cassettes, and educated the public about author's rights. Then digital technology emerged. Many argue that, since around 2007, piracy has actually become more problematic despite efforts to en-

force copyright legislation. Even royalty payments by the Copyright Society of Tanzania (COSOTA) are minimal compared to losses incurred
through contemporary forms of piracy. Unlike the early period where
piracy expanded the commodification of music, the current movement
is doing far more to undermine the ability of artists to earn a living from
music.

This chapter is a genealogy of music distribution that traces the relationship between distribution and the commercialization of music over
time and among different populations. I begin by looking at two parallel historical narratives that give shape to the distribution of music. The
first is state efforts to form legitimate recording and distribution facilities, and the second is the control by Asian Tanzanians in the sale and
distribution of music. The two narratives show that piracy did not just
appear, but slowly emerged from the concomitant collapse of a functioning state music industry and the long history of Asians in the distribution
of popular music. Understanding this history supports discussion in later
sections that emphasize the influence of cassette technology, controlled
by Asian Tanzanians, on capturing a new populace of people interested
in purchasing music. Cassettes rebuilt people's interests in consuming
popular music and created demand in people's associations with music
as a consumable commodity.

The second half of the chapter turns toward changes to music distribution due to the introduction of the 1999 Copyright Act. Given the
lack of lawyers, judges, customs officials, and law enforcement agencies
familiar with copyright law, many people expected that the law would
do little to hinder piracy. Legislation, however, has a particular power
in and of itself to affect social action among populations. Anticipation
over the possibilities brought on by the introduction of a new law, as well
as numerous meetings for musicians to talk about piracy, ownership,
and rights, invigorated interests in reconceptualizing the distribution
of music in Tanzania. This altered interactions between musicians and
distributors and expanded notions of ownership in songs. As presented
in the final section of this chapter, however, the benefits of copyright law
in hindering piracy and expanding the potential for ownership in sound
recordings may be already drawing to a close.

Ultimately, the following sections investigate the strategies used to
encourage people to own music both as a physical item and as intellectual

property. It takes apart the most prevalent creative practice (piracy) and the counterresponse to limit the impact of the illegal sale of music (copyright law). Of all the creative practices discussed in this ethnography, none is of greater concern to global music economies than piracy. Music executives worldwide blame illegal downloading for the significant decline in the sale of recorded music. Even though piracy helped to encourage the early growth of sound recordings in Tanzania, similar to trends occurring globally, it may be the most significant element undermining the continued prosperity of the music business in the country.

## CORRUPTED RECORDINGS

On March 22, 1968, the Tanzanian government established the Tanzania Film Company Limited (TFC) to develop the country's film and music industry. Initially, the company focused on importing, producing, and distributing cinematographic pictures and acted as a commission agent, receiving revenue from the distribution of foreign films throughout the country. In August 1969, all shares of the company were transferred from the National Development Corporation (NDC) to the Tanzania Tourist Corporation (TTC), though the purpose of the company remained to "control on behalf of the state, national cultural sovereignty in the business of production and distribution of cinematic, music and other similar leisure time services" (TFC 1995: 3).[1] Distribution of American, British, and Indian films, and by the 1980s Chinese, Russian, and other Asian movies, accounted for 95 percent of the company's total income.[2] By 1991, distributing to thirty-five theaters throughout the country, the company grossed $180,200 (TFC 1995: 10).

While the TFC's film distribution accounted for most of the company's gross income, film production often resulted in financial losses, since some investors and clients failed to pay the company for producing films. Nonetheless, the TFC managed to produce fifty-two films, most of which were short commercials for government departments, which aired prior to the showing of foreign films in cinemas. State companies would go to the TFC with a script and the TFC would locate local actors, take care of any logistics, such as permits and technical support, and shoot and edit the commercial before distributing it to various cinemas. Through the cooperation of the Danish International Development Agency (DANIDA),

TFC also produced several feature films, such as *The Land of Kilimanjaro*, and, in 1973, *Fimbo ya Mnyonge* (Poor Man's Salvation). In the 1980s and 1990s, the company worked with the American filmmaker Ron Mulvill on two films, *Harusi ya Mariamu* (The Marriage of Mariamu) and *Maangamizi* (Catastrophe), the latter of which the Tanzanian government submitted to the Academy of Motion Picture Arts and Sciences for the 2002 Academy Awards in the category of Best Foreign Film.

The establishment of an "indigenous music industry" was also a major objective of the TFC and the Tanzanian government. Like the film industry, a music industry needed to reflect the history, culture, values, and politics of Tanzanians. It was considered crucial to bringing social and economic "development" to the country (TFC 1995: 5). In particular, there was concern by members of the TFC, as well as the Ministry of National Education, that consumption of music produced by foreign companies would corrupt nationalization efforts, thus spurring the TFC to reinforce a strong unified national culture. In addition, the TFC wanted to establish an indigenous economy that was self-sustaining and did not rely on neighboring or international countries for support or commercial products.

The TFC began to create a music industry in 1971 when the company formed a department responsible for film music and picture postcard production. Despite the odd pairing, film music became the company's first venture into composing and recording. Two years later, the company released its first records under the Uhuru Stars label. This was followed by other labels, including Sindimba (1974), TFC (1976), Azimio, and its most recognizable label, Kwetu (1976). With limited recording opportunities, the creation of so many labels was certainly excessive, especially since each label may have only released a handful of records. The label names and cover depictions, however, were symbolic of the company's goals and proposed achievements. Azimio means "declaration," referring to the socialist Arusha Declaration. Sindimba, a traditional ngoma associated with the Makonde people's initiation rites, was popular in schools during the 1960s and 1970s (PURL 7.1).[3] Uhuru means "freedom" and referred to the post-independent period. Kwetu, the most prolific of the labels, means "ours." It was an important national reference that emphasized belonging and cultural unity within the production of popular music. The songs were the property of Tanzanian citizens.

A 45 rpm disc released by the Tanzanian Film Company in 1976. The label
Kwetu means "ours," as in "our music" and, by the image, "our country."

The excess of labels that the TFC produced was certainly meant to
show the company's establishment of a credible music industry that could
promote the country's artists. For the most part, the effort failed. Recording for the other government-owned recording studio, Radio Tanzania
Dar es Salaam (RTD), could produce consistent airplay and publicity. The
engineers at RTD were skilled at their profession and constantly scouted
for musical talent. The TFC also had skilled engineers who made recordings by some of the best bands of the 1970s, including Ndala Kasheba
and Orchestra Safari Sound, Black Star Taarab, and Western Jazz. The
company, however, had a weak distribution network and received limited
airplay on RTD. In Dar es Salaam, only a few stores carried TFC recordings in the 1970s.

Due to the limited commercial distribution of recordings by the TFC, many private bands opted to travel to Kenya to sell their recordings or record anew at Kenyan recording studios. Contracts from the Kenyan studios could be rather lucrative and provide an additional source of income, particularly for private bands that did not have the support of the Tanzanian government. Orchestra Super Talakaka with Remmy Ongala signed a contract with Polygram Records Limited in 1982 that allowed the group to maintain the copyright in all their musical works and earn royalties from each of their recordings. The contract ensured that Super Talakaka would only record for Polygram, that they would remain with the company for three years, and that the company could use the artists and their likeness in any publicity. The royalties were generous and even allowed the band to "have the Royalty statements checked by an independent pubic certified accountant." There were clauses in the contract for use of songs on television, the possibility of video recording concerts, and the creation of compilation records. Even compared to contracts in the United States and Europe, the Polygram contract gave artists generous rights and leniency in their recordings.[4]

Most contracts were not as lucrative as Orchestra Super Talakaka's. For those that received lump-sum payments, they frequently lost the rights to their music. In 1966, the famed Kenyan musician Fadhili William stated, "A musician takes, let's say, three months to compose a song. Then he goes into the studio and after singing, he is paid Ksh 300 and loses his rights in the song that he recorded—copyright. I know of many companies especially those owned by Indians where you are only paid Ksh 60. The Indian takes advantage of the musicians before the musician realizes it."[5] Despite the loss in copyright, Tanzanian artists who did sign deals stated that they either regularly received royalty statements or lump-sum payments that were financially useful. The low rates that William mentions appeared not to impact Tanzanian artists, partially because recorded music was still viewed as a form of publicity rather than a commodity. Any money received was an added benefit to the continued professionalization and commercialization of music.

Artists who attempted to benefit from record distributors in Kenya could sell their music simultaneously to multiple companies. Similar to blues musicians in the United States during the 1920s and 1930s, Tanzanian musicians recorded the same songs at different studios; they licensed/sold the rights to the same songs to multiple distributors; or they changed the band name to avoid any contract disputes. DDC Mlimani Park Orchestra, for instance, had a five-year contract with Polygram, but members of the band illicitly recorded under the name the Black Warriors for CBS's Ken-Tanza label. One of the songs they recorded, "Nawashukuru Wazazi Wangu" (I'm Grateful to my Parents), was recorded both by the Black Warriors and DDC Mlimani Park Orchestra, which proved problematic for the song's distribution by both Polygram and CBS. Another album included a picture of a woman wearing a bikini while being held by a gorilla, which apparently angered socialist sensibilities in Tanzania (Wallis and Malm 1984: 95). Other popular bands composed and recorded an abundance of songs in a short period of time in order to sell as many records as possible. Between 1967 and 1976, for instance, Western Jazz Band licensed over fifty songs to Kenyan record labels, including Africa and Moto Moto, both subsidiaries of A.I.T. Records, Philips, and TFC (see table 7.1). Artists had to be creative about ways to sell their music to multiple labels, convince distributors to give them a chance, and, at a more basic level, produce songs that people wanted to hear.

Tanzanian music circulated widely in the early 1970s, and there were plenty of Kenyan record labels willing to take on enthusiastic bands forming in Dar es Salaam and in other parts of the country. Bands such as Orchestra Vijana Jazz, Jamhuri Jazz Band, Urafiki Jazz, and Morogoro Jazz Band became popular performers in several countries. They appeared in local magazines, such *Nyota Afrika,* which further pushed people's interest in the commodification of music. According to musicians and music fans in this period, records were widely consumed in cities and towns across eastern and central Africa. Waziri Ally stated:

> In the 1960s and 1970s, Tanzania was a musical leader in East Africa except that music was not a business like it was in Kenya and Uganda. Here there were many bands, more than the other countries. Kenya did have recording studios and companies to press records from Europe and America. All Tanzanian musicians either recorded for Radio Tanzania and tapes [reel-to-reels] were sent to Kenya (many times secretly) and pressed into records or bands went to Kenya to record.

TABLE 7.1. Western Jazz Band Songs Released by Kenyan Distributors, 1967–1976

| | | | |
|---|---|---|---|
| Afroshirazi Na Tanu (A-Side) | | Philips | HL 7-84 |
| Amina Maliza Masomo (A-Side) | 1974 | Africa | AFR 7-900 |
| Anna Anton (B-Side) | 1974 | Moto Moto | MOTO 7-117 |
| Asante (A-Side) | 1974 | Africa | AFR 7-903 |
| Aza (B-Side) | 1974 | Africa | AFR 7-901 |
| Baba Nitakuja (A-Side) | 1973 | Moto Moto | MOTO 7-99 |
| Baibui Mkononi (A-Side) | 1974 | Africa | AFR 7-904 |
| Balaa Limeni Andama (B-Side) | 1974 | Africa | AFR 7-900 |
| Bibi Mwamini (A-Side) | 1972 | Moto Moto | MOTO 49 |
| Eliza Mpenzi (A-Side) | 1974 | Africa | AFR 7-906 |
| Ellina (A-Side) | 1974 | Moto Moto | MOTO 7-117 |
| F.C. Young Africans (A-Side) | c. 1971 | Moto Moto | MOTO 7-4 |
| Helena No. 1 (A-Side) | 1973 | Moto Moto | MOTO 7-62 |
| Heri Mapenzi (B-Side) | 1972 | Moto Moto | MOTO 49 |
| Karolina (A-Side) | 1976 | TFC | TFC2006A |
| Kazi ni Kazi (B-Side) | 1976 | TFC | TFC 2006B |
| Kubadili Dini (A-Side) | 1973 | Africa | AFR 7-33 |
| Magdelena (B-Side) | 1974 | Moto Moto | MOTO 7-118 |
| Majumba ya Kupanga (B-Side) | | Moto Moto | MOTO 7-98 |
| Mama Mariana (B-Side) | 1972 | Moto Moto | MOTO 7-42 |
| Mimi Naogopa (B-Side) | 1973 | Moto Moto | MOTO 7-63 |
| Mke Mlevi (A-Side) | 1974 | Africa | AFR 7-901 |
| Mke Wangu (B-Side) | c. 1971 | Moto Moto | MOTO 7-4 |
| Mpenzi Rukia (B-Side) | 1974 | Africa | AFR 7-905 |
| Muedina Wangu (A-Side) | c. 1971 | Moto Moto | MOTO 7-13 |
| Mwajabu (B-Side) | 1973 | Africa | AFR 7-5 |
| Mwali (B-Side) | 1974 | Africa | AFR 7-904 |
| Mwanahawa (A-Side) | 1972 | Moto Moto | MOTO 48 |
| Mwanahawa (A-Side) | 1972 | Moto Moto | MOTO 7-44 |
| Mwanangu Rudi (B-Side) | 1973 | Moto Moto | MOTO 7-62 |
| Nami Naridhika (A-Side) | 1973 | Africa | AFR 7-5 |
| Nashindwa Kusema (B-Side) | 1973 | Moto Moto | MOTO 7-61 |
| Nashindwa Na Tabia Yako (A-Side) | 1974 | Africa | AFR 7-907 |
| Nitafurahi Ukitumwa Tena (A Side) | 1967 | Philips | PK 7-9007 |
| Pesa Nyingi Nimepoteza (B-Side) | | Philips | HL 7-84 |
| Pokea Salaam (B-Side) | 1974 | Africa | AFR 7-903 |
| Pokea Salaam(B-Side) | 1974 | Africa | AFR 7-903 |
| Rosa (B-Side) | 1973 | Afirca | AFR 7-32 |
| Saboso Moto-Moto (B-Side) | 1973 | Moto Moto | MOTO 7-99 |
| Sasa Tucheza Cha Cha (B Side) | 1967 | Philips | PK 7-7019 |
| Shani (A-Side) | 1974 | Moto Moto | MOTO 7-118 |

TABLE 7.1. Western Jazz Band Songs Released by Kenyan Distributors, 1967–1976

| | | | |
|---|---|---|---|
| Shemeji (A-Side) | 1974 | Africa | AFR 7-905 |
| Si Kulaumu (B-Side) | 1972 | Moto Moto | MOTO 7-44 |
| Simuachi Mpenzi Wangu (B-Side) | 1974 | Africa | AFR 7-907 |
| Simuachi Mpenzi Wangu (B-Side) | 1974 | Africa | AFR 7-907 |
| Soko la Mapenzi (A-Side) | 1973 | Moto Moto | MOTO 7-63 |
| Tangu Umeondoka (B Side) | 1967 | Philips | PK 7-9007 |
| Tanzania (A-Side) | | Moto Moto | MOTO 7-98 |
| Tu Shauriana Wanainchi (B-Side) | c. 1971 | Moto Moto | MOTO 7-13 |
| Tuliya Mama (A Side) | 1967 | Philips | PK 7-9019 |
| Ulivyo Amua (B-Side) | 1972 | Moto Moto | MOTO 48 |
| Usiamini Binadamu (B-Side) | 1974 | Africa | AFR 7-906 |
| Vigelegele (B-Side) | 1973 | Africa | AFR 7-33 |
| Wanaifanya Saboso (A-Side) | 1972 | Moto Moto | MOTO 7-42 |
| Wenzangu Nawauliza (A-Side) | 1973 | Africa | AFR 7-32 |
| Wivu Wako (A-Side) | 1973 | Moto Moto | MOTO 7-61 |

The popularity of Tanzanian bands throughout East Africa created a market for their music. People wanted to purchase singles that celebrated independence, regional popular cultures, and other pan-African issues. Records were a sign of prestige, and people included them in their self-portraits to show that they were fashionable and trendy. Retailers opened small stores in many towns throughout eastern Africa, thereby helping to make music more readily available. Further, there were strong networks of musicians who moved between Zaire, Uganda, Kenya, Rwanda, Zambia, and Tanzania, performing rumba beats that were popular throughout the region (Perullo 2008b). People could use any of the national currencies (Kenyan, Ugandan, or Tanzanian) throughout East Africa, which further encouraged significant interaction between populations. The rise in record distribution, retailers, performance outlets, and regional cooperation fostered consumer demand for popular, post-independent styles of music that supported Africanization efforts and people's desires for entertaining dance music. By any accounts, this should have been the formative years for a regional East African economy of music.

By 1975, however, the burgeoning regional music economy started to fragment and collapse. On December 27, 1975, the government banned foreign music on Radio Tanzania Dar es Salaam's Idhaa ya Kiswahili (Swahili Service) in order to promote local artists.[6] Even though regional records were still played, there was a strong push to play only national and socialist-oriented music. In 1977, the border between Kenya and Tanzania closed, preventing musicians from freely traveling to Kenya to record and perform music. Further, socialist restrictions on the importation of luxury goods, such as record players and records, made these items disappear from store shelves. During the 1960s, many stores in Dar es Salaam sold record players, including the Victor Company of Japan's portable record players.[7] By the late 1970s, these companies sold far fewer record players and focused mostly on radio receivers. Records remained popular among many middle- and upper-class residents who did own and purchase record players. Nonetheless, the costs of sound recordings eventually put them out of reach of most people and made the consumption of music a relatively elite or specialized practice. This produced a reversal or at least a dramatic slowdown in the commodification of music since recorded albums became less consumed and less socially relevant for audiences that gravitated increasingly toward radio and live performance spaces.

For TFC, the decline in imported records, the closing of the border with Kenya, and the move toward stronger Swahili radio programming provided strong incentives to develop the production and distribution of music. In 1978 the TFC formed a new studio at the Sine Club in Msasani, Dar es Salaam, to record bands and choirs. Amari Bakari, who was, before the company's liquidation, the accountant, internal auditor, and acting general manager for TFC, told me that the company charged by the song during the late 1970s. On the weekends, the studio recorded four to six songs a day, and one song on the weekdays between four and eight P.M. The studio itself, according to Bakari, was soundproof and included air conditioning and state-of-the-art recording equipment. Once a recording was made, the master was sent to Teal Records in Zambia to be pressed into records and then sent back to TFC for distribution (Teal was partially owned by the South African Broadcasting Cooperation).

Musicians who paid to have their songs recorded at TFC could take the master tape and use it as they wished. Since the TFC did not have a significant local market for the sale of music and, according to some musicians, did not pay well for albums that were licensed to them, most artists took the master tapes elsewhere. Often these companies were in Kenya, and there was a small stream of Tanzanian music being released by Kenyan companies throughout the 1970s and 1980s, even despite the closing of the border between the countries.[8] Other artists, however, opted for more lucrative contracts. The Revolution Band, for instance, recorded their album at TFC and then brought it to a distributor in England. The album was one of the few sold outside eastern African during the 1970s, and gives some sense to the isolation of Tanzanian music during this period. Even into the 1980s, only a handful of bands were able to launch popular recordings outside of eastern Africa. Several who tried, however, relied on the TFC since, after paying the recording fees, bands could walk away with their recorded material, which they could not do at the only other recording studio in the country, RTD.

For wealthier residents of Dar es Salaam, the scarcity of foreign music on the radio and in recordings created a craving to find new pop music. There was an urge to hear that which was being restricted and forbidden. Popular discotheques, such as the Silversands Hotel, Msasani Beach Club, The New Black and White Discotheque, and Mbowe Hotel, attracted middle- and upper-class youth who wanted to hear and dance to foreign popular music, mainly from the United States and Europe. Genres such as r&b, soul, and funk, as well as rock bands, such as the Rolling Stones and the Beatles, were popular in Dar es Salaam discotheques. (This is also the reasons that the government wanted either to shut the discotheques down or force them to play local music.) For youths who could afford the taxi fares for these clubs, the entrance fees, and cost of beer, these clubs encouraged their fascination with recorded music. Deejays who knew someone traveling abroad would ask them to bring back as many recordings as possible. When they did, the deejays would become stars due to the rarity and popularity of the songs that they possessed.

Realizing the interest in foreign music, the TFC company began to distribute international recordings to local audiences. There was an obvious attempt to find ways to get people to purchase music. Since only foreign music was selling in Dar es Salaam, the push was to focus on these recordings. In a December 12, 1984, advertisement for the company, the TFC sold albums by local star Ndala Kasheba, the Ubongo Lutheran Church Choir, and foreign artists, such as Bob Marley, Michael Jackson, The Jackson 5, Osibisa, the Pointer Sisters, the Rolling Stones, Chaka Khan, Tabu Ley Rochereau, Randy Crawford, Evelyn King, Donna Summer, and Dolly Parton.[9] This effort would have helped to move the TFC

toward profitability, except that by the early 1980s people had almost completely stopped using record players in favor of cassettes. Perhaps, more
ironically, the release of foreign music undermined the mission of the
TFC in promoting a cultural industry based on African music.

Socialist states are not particularly adept at creating or keeping up
with technologies involved in the production of culture. In Tanzania's
case, state organizations continued to invest in record technology even
as cassettes were emerging regionally and internationally as an easier and
cheaper alternative. In 1979, despite advice to invest in cassette technology, the TFC designed a facility to house a record-pressing plant and purchased machinery and materials from abroad for pressing both long-play-
ing (LPs) and seven-inch records (45 rpm) (Malm and Wallis 1992: 110).
The following year, the company invested Tsh 27 million (US$90,000)
to build a plant in Kijitonyama, Dar es Salaam, but stopped in December 1981 after equipment imported by the TFC from the Federal Republic of Germany "disappeared" at the Dar es Salaam port. Undeterred,
the TFC collected insurance from the National Insurance Corporation
(NIC) to import new equipment. In 1985, when cassettes were already
dominating the region, the company was slated to begin operation and
produce one million 45s and 500,000 LPs in its first year (8,000 45s and
4,000 LPs per day).[10]

With the building 95 percent complete and set to open in August,
Tanzania appeared ready to finally establish an indigenous music industry. But something went wrong. According to the TFC staff, just as the
company was set to start production, someone stole the generators meant
to operate the entire plant. With a lack of generators, the plant would have
to rely on electricity from the national electric company, TANESCO,
whose capabilities in the 1980s were erratic at best. Since the TFC did not
receive insurance for the stolen generators, the company decided to sell all
the equipment and the plant, which is now the Tanzania School of Journalism. Why the company opted to sell all it acquired instead of searching
for alternatives is unclear. Perhaps the economy was so unstable in 1985
that the company realized it would lose even more money if it continued
to invest in a record-pressing plant. Or, perhaps the stolen generators were
only a piece of the corruption that existed within the company. More
likely, however, the loan that the company took in 1979–80 was increasingly becoming a factor in the company's ability to operate. In 1989, the

loan reached Tsh 55 million (US$430,000), at which point the government finally stopped charging interest and fixed the amount (TFC 1995: 2).

Regardless of the reasons for the company's failure, its first attempt to record, produce, and distribute music highlighted the economic and political difficulty that Tanzania faced in forming an indigenous music industry. The few records that the TFC produced and distributed through pressing at Teal Records were important for preserving Tanzanian music, but, with limited circulation, they never made the company an asset to the local music scene. In fact, the TFC's actions showed the government's inability to comprehend the production of music and provided evidence of the corruption that existed in the country as people sought ways to make a living under increasingly pressing conditions. Further, the company's reliance on earnings from film distribution became its downfall, as the liberalization of the country's economy led to the importation of videocassettes, essentially removing the need for public theaters. Videocassette recorders became the standard form of nightly entertainment in place of theaters, and pirated tapes, imported from Oman and India, became the standard media (Malm and Wallis 1992: 109). Unable to compete with videotapes, the company's income slowly declined, and, despite efforts to privatize, the TFC eventually went bankrupt and was liquidated in 2001.[11]

The failure of the TFC in the 1980s left Tanzania without a viable recording studio, aside from the one that existed at RTD, and gave artists no options to release their music commercially in Tanzania. Kenya's music industry had started to collapse in the early to mid-1980s due to government corruption, piracy, and a weakening infrastructure for live music. Tanzanian artists became uncomfortably aware of the limited options for recording. Carola Kinasha, who along with her husband had a group called Shada, expressed her dismay at the studio options of the late 1980s: "The songs that we wrote we decided to record, but, during that time [1987], there were no recording studios at all. There was Radio Tanzania that had two tracks and there was the TFC studio, which also had two tracks, but they were not helpful to us. During that time, we had already heard foreign music and we were aware of the level one needed to enter [a studio] in order to do well." Kinasha and other musicians knew that they needed to do more to compete regionally and internationally than rely on local studios. Many groups traveled to other countries, such as

Zimbabwe, Japan, England, Sweden, and Germany to record and perform music. These efforts kept many groups solvent, but the 1980s would prove to be a constant struggle to record and release sound recordings.

## ASIAN TANZANIAN OWNERSHIP

It is important here to present a parallel historical narrative to the one just discussed. Whereas state control attempted to create a nationalist music industry, the distribution of music was long associated with Asian Tanzanian communities. Lured by the prospects of employment or encouraged to migrate by religious leaders, people from India began arriving in Tanganyika in the 1800s. Despite arriving poor, many became important shopkeepers both on the coast and inland where, in the words of John Iliffe, they were "crucial intermediaries of Tanganyika's colonial economy" (1979: 138). After the First World War, when Britain took over the Tanganyika territory under the British Mandate of 1922, the British recruited more Indians to become clerks and artisans. Encouraged by the prospects of life in Tanganyika, Indian migration grew significantly, expanding from 8,698 people in 1912 to 25,144 in 1932. By the 1930s, Indians controlled many of the central business and residential sections of Dar es Salaam, leaving the outlying areas to Africans.

As records and gramophones became a popular pastime after the Second World War, Asians opened several stores in Dar es Salaam that carried musical items (see chapter 2). The oldest music store that continues to operate in Tanzania opened in the 1940s as Assanand and Sons. Assanand and Sons was a Kenyan company that produced and sold records in Mombasa, Nairobi, and Kampala. They opened a branch in Dar es Salaam to expand the sale of their music. In 1959, Dalichand Kothari, born in Tanzania of South Asian decent, decided to buy the shop, which was located next to his father-in-law's store. The Dar es Salaam store was dependent on expatriates, who sought classical, ballroom, and popular music, and a strong clientele of local Tanzanians.

One of Kothari's sons, Ramesh, who now runs the shop, called Dar es Salaam Music and Sport, fondly remembered the 1960s as a period of growth and prosperity for phonograms. Kothari explained: "We were the sole selling agents for Polygram at that time. We sold Zairian records from France. Zairian music was more popular than Kenyan. We used to get instruments from UK, Italy, India, and Germany. Records from UK, Holland, Germany, USA, and Nairobi were our main source of records. People would buy Otis Redding, James Brown, and country music." Remembering the Peace Corps workers, professors, diplomats, and average Tanzanians who used to frequent his store, he continued, "At that time, we were on top in East Africa—we were known among all the record companies. . . . Those days will never come back."

His store, still located on Samora Avenue and called Dar es Salaam Music and Sport, is now mostly empty of music, with shelves sitting idle, holding a few records and tapes (the primary business now is sporting equipment). Waving his hand across the room, Kothari told me, "This whole section was filled with guitars, records, three to four thousand LPs and 45s all in stock. Nobody else really knew records." When records were still big business, 45s came in boxes of twenty-five and, looking at Kothari's store, one can see shelves made to fit these boxes.[12] With eight-foot-high shelves surrounding the room, all made for records, the store must have been impressive when fully stocked and with customers crowding the aisles.

The difficulties encountered at Kothari's store, like other local Asian businesses in the 1960s and 1970s, was a result of the political changes sweeping the country. Under socialism, the Tanzanian government attempted to balance the country's wealth and resources, which meant removing individual ownership of the country's major industries and putting them under the control of the government. Beginning with the nationalization of banks, flour mills, import and export companies, tobacco and alcohol companies, sisal plantations, and numerous other institutions from February 6 to 11, 1967, and the nationalization of buildings after the Acquisition of Buildings Act of 1971, the Asian population lost their shares in or ownership of many local businesses. Many Asians left Tanzania for other countries, especially Canada, India, and England, figuring that they could make a better living elsewhere. The population of 93,300 Asians in Tanzania dwindled dramatically and today, even after the return of families since the country's liberalization, there are only 58,720 on both the mainland and Zanzibar (Lobo 2000: 20–21).

For those who were able to continue their trade, including Dar es Salaam Music and Sport, the nationalization of buildings and businesses led to several significant changes. The cost of renting office space increased each year after nationalization making it difficult for people to pay bills, particularly since they were no longer allowed to freely import goods. Records and record players, now considered luxury goods, had to be ordered through the TFC or through the Domestic Appliances and Bicycle Company (DABCO). The TFC and DABCO were both government agencies that controlled import licenses on any musical item coming into the country, from instruments to guitar strings and records to styluses for recorded players. If a local business went directly to the Ministry of Trade for a license to import goods, they would be denied. The TFC and DABCO, however, rarely supplied the quantities of goods that local stores wanted, which meant that many local businesses in downtown Dar es Salaam struggled to keep items in stores. Several businessmen also had to deal with growing corruption that existed among government officials who controlled import licenses. Bribery became a commonplace means of doing business given the control of all legal imports by a few government agencies.

Due to the exodus of many Asian business owners and the worsening economic relations between Tanzania and neighboring countries in the late 1970s, the importation of records waned and only continued to worsen throughout the 1970s. John Kitime writes: "The closure of the border [with Kenya in 1977] left Tanzanians with no source of recorded music. Smugglers began bringing in records from Zambia. But, at the time, the radio was the only source of music. Around this period, the audio compact cassette began getting popular. Enterprising businessmen began copying hit songs and selling them to the music starved market" (Kitime n.d.: 2). Kitime's notion of a starved market is an apt description of the state of Tanzanian popular culture in the late 1970s and early 1980s. Even though cassettes and records of foreign music were available, it was never enough to satisfy the local market. People wanted to be a part of the music communities outside the country. State radio, while extremely popular, could not satisfy the cosmopolitan desires of urban communities.

By 1984, several stores opened in major towns and cities all over eastern Africa, providing consumers the opportunity to record a variety of songs from records or cassettes. The Dar es Salaam–based Kizenga Music Recording, for instance, offered customers cassette recordings of the latest hits. In the photograph of the studio, several popular records are propped up against three towers of cassette decks, amplifiers, mixers, and turntables. The advertising slogan for the store was, "NO tape-to-tape recording.... its STRAIGHT from the RECORD."[13] Since most cassettes were of poor quality, especially copies that were several generations removed from the original, better quality recording practices drew enthusiastic music fans interested in sound recordings. Numerous other small businesses started in this period, including those in Dar es Salaam that were mostly owned by Asian Tanzanians quick to capitalize on the growing demand for recorded music. These small businesses drew interest back toward the commercialization of recordings. The recession of the 1980s left so many people struggling for basic necessities that foreign popular music connected people's imagination and desires with life outside the country. For those that could afford them, mixed cassettes of popular music became important for attaining enjoyment and pleasure, aural escapes from daily life.

The state's struggles to produce a legitimate music industry allowed independent Tanzanian distributors to fill a void in the commodification of recorded songs. For Tanzania's music economy, the importance of this period is that the people who took control of the distribution of cassettes remain the most prominent and profitable individuals in the sale of recorded sound. Almost all distributors in Dar es Salaam are Asian Tanzanian, and continue a long history of controlling the distribution of music throughout Tanzania. To remain profitable and viable within the changing economic conditions of Tanzanian societies, Asian distributors have shown the same innovations and flexibility prominent in other areas of the music economy. This has allowed them to maintain a monopoly on music distribution by using piracy to turn liberalization against itself.

## TURNING TOWARD CASSETTES

Cassette duplicating stores significantly expanded the economic potential of music and put the control of recordings into the hands of customers. The more interest consumers had in specific genres of music, the more stores searched for records in that genre. Networking became the most important part of the growing trade in cassette duplication since locating popular hit records before anyone else ensured that enterprising music sellers could draw in customers. Often records arrived in Tanzania with relatives or friends who were flying back from foreign countries. They could also be brought in from neighboring countries that could more easily import foreign music. These networks became rather sophisticated and hit records could arrive in local stores while they were still popular overseas. One friend who lived in Dar es Salaam during the late 1970s and early 1980s remembers that when Michael Jackson's *Off the Wall* came into Dar es Salaam, it became a sensation among youth who were able to hear and copy it. The album circulated among a variety of youth and ended up in all the major discotheques in Dar es Salaam within a few days. Genres that were once hard to find in Dar es Salaam, such as rap, rhythm and blues, ragga, country, and pop music, became familiar. Cassettes made the commercialization of recorded songs possible by allowing the commodification of music to be simple, popular, and flexible.

Cassettes remain the most widely used sound technology throughout Tanzania, as well as Africa more generally, and appear only now to be losing ground to other formats, such as compact discs and digital files. Considering that almost all the music in Tanzania is recorded digitally, why are consumers drawn to what is frequently considered an outdated analog technology? Compared to other technologies, cassettes are easy to transport, do not require expensive technology to produce, and are difficult to damage. They can record as well as play music, which decentralizes ownership and control of recordings. This allows anyone to make an album of music without much skill or know-how (Manuel 1993: 2–3). Even compact discs do not offer the amenities of cassettes. Similar to records, CDs can be easily scratched or damaged under common living conditions in Tanzania. They are more expensive to produce and machines for playing compact discs are far more expensive than cassette players. Further, unlike consumer CDs, cassettes can be reused by anyone with a cassette recorder and easily manipulated. For all these reasons, cassettes have remained a dominant commercial medium in Tanzania, as well as other areas of Africa, since the early 1980s.

The same democratic qualities that allow cassettes to be easily manipulated and used by consumers make them attractive to music distributors as well. Even though digital duplication can be easier and faster to complete, it is often more expensive and involves greater technological knowledge of computers, software, and hardware. Cassettes involve machines, lots of them, and wires that can be visually manipulated in a straightforward manner to produce a desired result. There is also little possibility of encountering corrupted media, as is common with compact discs or computer files. And even though cassette tape can get caught in a machine, that problem can be fixed with a screwdriver, pencil, or well-articulated finger. The utilitarian nature of cassettes allows anyone with limited resources to copy and distribute music. It is also what makes cassettes such a practical technology for music piracy.

Piracy of recordings is often divided into three parts: pirate recording, counterfeit piracy, and bootlegging. Pirate recording is the unauthorized reproduction of someone's phonogram (record, cassette, compact disc, or digital file), where the copy does not look like the original but sounds the same. Counterfeit piracy is the illegal duplication of someone's phonogram, where the original and the copy look identical. Bootlegging is the illegal recording of concert performances. Of these three forms, only the first two occur consistently in Tanzania. Initially, pirated cassettes in Tanzania were poor duplications, with hand-drawn covers and, usually, poor sound quality. Counterfeit piracy came mainly from Dubai and India, and the cassettes were imported and sold by local distributors. It took time for Tanzanians to develop sophisticated counterfeit piracy, but once color photocopiers and high-speed cassette copying machines arrived, it was virtually impossible to tell the difference between original and pirated cassettes.

Through the late 1970s and 1980s, music piracy appeared in Indonesia, India, the Gulf States, and, by the 1980s, Africa. The movement of piracy followed government crackdowns on the illegal trade, pushing the market to move to wherever there was weak copyright enforcement. David Attard of the International Federation of the Phonographic Industry writes: "Throughout the 1970s, the piracy of music recording flourished, unchallenged and uncontrolled. The greatest threat came from the Far East. . . . Research has shown that, in one year alone, Singapore exported some 60 million unauthorized music cassettes to the Gulf market" (1993: 5). Piracy moved into Africa through trade with the Gulf States, particularly Oman, during the early 1980s and destroyed legitimate industries that could not compete with cheaper cassettes. The result of piracy's presence in many countries was an extreme disruption in legitimate record production. In Ghana, for instance, multinational companies during the 1990s were forced to compete with the rise of 2,700 dubbing shops, which turned out two million cassettes a year. The major record companies, HMV and

Decca, were unable to compete with the high influx of cheap cassettes. Without a workable copyright law, both companies left Ghana (Wallis and Malm 1984: 84; Manuel 1993: 30–31).

While Tanzania's piracy grew and became more sophisticated, major companies, such as Polygram and A.I.T., tried to restrict the practice in Kenya by limiting the availability of cassettes and promoting records to consumers. As early as 1981, Polygram and possibly A.I.T. took individuals to court for illegally duplicating sound recordings.[14] Though the record companies obstructed piracy to a degree, piracy still became a major business strategy within the Kenyan music economy. In 1985, Alex Seago wrote, "Home taping in Kenya has reached epidemic proportions and has reduced what little income bands were receiving from record sales to a trickle." While major labels in Kenya used to sell as many as 100,000 singles in 1976, less than a decade later they could sell fewer than 10,000, even though music had remained popular (Seago 1987: 176). These companies tried to revive their business by lowering prices. Yet when they raised prices again, customers became irate and questioned company motives. By the early 1990s, all the major record companies established in Kenya had left the country.

Ironically, while they were still in business during the 1980s, the major record companies ignored the developing piracy in Tanzania. In 1986, the Tanzanian musician Patrick Balisidya recorded an album, *Bahati,* for A.I.T. Records in Nairobi, which was subsequently copied illegally and sold in Dar es Salaam. Balisidya filed a lawsuit and, with the assistance of Professor Jwani Mwaikusa at the University of Dar es Salaam, brought the case to court in Tanzania. The case was dismissed, however, since A.I.T. opted not to become involved, even though they owned the rights to the album. Left untouched, Dar es Salaam distributors continued to sell *Bahati* and perhaps realized their unique state of economic freedom. Neither the Tanzanian government nor the record companies in Kenya were interested in Tanzania's growing piracy business. Distributors were therefore able to build their trade without competition or restrictions.

Eventually, the Kenyan recording industry collapsed under the weight or problems brought on by piracy and the country's increasingly autocratic political policies. The fall of legitimate record companies opened many opportunities for Tanzania's growing network of cassette distributors, as well as those from other parts of Africa. With connections in Canada, England, France, Oman, India, and regionally in Africa, Tanzanian distributors expanded their operations significantly. Albums could be sent to Dar es Salaam as soon as they were released in other parts of the world, quickly copied, and sold throughout eastern and southern Africa. A new release from Malawi, for instance, could be bought, sent to Tanzania, and returned to Malawi in bulk quickly enough to draw profits away from the company or individual who released the original album. The network that Dar es Salaam distributors created became massive and, as Serman Chavula, who now runs the Copyright Society of Malawi (COSOMA), found, daunting: "At the SADC [Southern African Development Community] seminar on copyright held at Mangochi, Malawi in 1994, it was reported that in Tanzania, the Government licenses about 65 companies to reproduce and distribute sound recordings. These eventually end up in Botswana, Malawi, Mozambique, and Zambia, where it can be safely said that over 90% of the audio and videocassettes being sold are pirated" (Chavula 1998: 9).

Other studies, such as in the *New African*, found similar statistics that estimated the percentage of pirated cassettes in Tanzania to be close to a hundred percent in 1988. Ten years later, John Kitime reported that 98 percent of foreign and local music sold was pirated. Herald Tagama wrote, "Sales of pirated sound tapes in Tanzania net a whopping Tsh 3.5 billion a year ($4.2 million)," while Bob Karashani of the *East African* stated that the Tanzanian government was losing at least Tsh 15 billion ($22 million) from pirated video and audio tapes.[15] Kenya and Uganda also practiced piracy, as did other nearby African countries, but Tanzania dominated the eastern and southern African communities from the late 1980s onward, establishing distribution points and networks throughout the region. What began as a simple business practice—provide cheap cassettes to consumers—turned into one of the biggest music networks in Africa.

What is even more impressive, however, is that this highly organized and sophisticated distribution of music was orchestrated by a small group of people. These few Tanzanian distributors were extremely skilled in saturating markets with cheap cassettes of popular Congolese, non-African, as well as the country's own music that were nearly identical to more expensive originals. The less attention the Tanzanian government paid to these illicit practices, the better businesses grew. The weaker piracy was in other countries—either because other countries had stronger copyright laws, powerful record companies, or less crafty businessmen—the more Tanzanian distributors profited. The creativity of a few in the illegal use of music led to their dominance in the East African music scene and set the stage for making Tanzania the most successful music economy in the region. Piracy, in other words, brought unparalleled success to the commercialization of Tanzanian music, making consumption of sound recordings popular and profitable.

## PIRATES, AHOY?

The term "music pirate" is rather problematic. It conjures images of unsavory individuals more concerned with pillaging property than their own (or anyone else's) health. Dictionary definitions include people who reproduce copyrighted works without authorization. But it is misleading to suggest that piracy on the high seas and the illegal duplication of music are the same. All the Dar es Salaam distributors are middle-class businessmen who started to sell music when there were few commercially available services for sound recordings. There was little conception of copyright law or theft in musical works within the production and consumption of the arts. The socialist government considered property, whether tangible or intangible, collectively owned. Nyerere once stated, "I do not believe in land ownership as you Europeans do; land cannot be 'owned' in the same sense as you own a T-shirt, or as I own my sandals. You can only have the right to use it."[16] Intellectual property rights found in music, including sound recordings, often fell into a similar purview even though some musicians and distributors had become aware of copyright law in their dealings with foreign record companies. Nationally, however, cassette duplication fed people's interest in foreign music. By the time people became more concerned with the practice, profits were soaring, which led to more duplicitous actions on the part of the music distributors to continue their businesses.

Though the term music pirate technically applies to the distribution of cassettes in Tanzania, it fails to capture the creative practices taking place in the distribution of sound recordings. A more useful means to explain the activities of music distribution is clever deception. Clever deception is creatively and intentionally misrepresenting one's actions for personal gain. It requires deliberately misleading others into believing that a fake product is real, that something false is true. Margaret Wilson found that, "in certain parts of Brazilian society, clever deception is applauded and given positive reinforcement. . . . The ability to use a person or situation to one's advantage [is] considered vital for the sophisticated Brazilian" (2001: 26). Clever deception is certainly not applauded when used by music distributors in Tanzania. Deception, however, is given positive reinforcement through the economic gains from illegally selling music. The combination of weak enforcement and high profits provides a caustic mix that encourages distributors to search for possibilities to remain viable. The more people learn about music and copyright, the more deception needs to occur.

To sell music illegally is to convince someone that the product is good, cheaper than the original, and not harming anyone else's interests. During the 1990s and early 2000s, distributors made exact duplicates of albums that appeared just like the original (even though they were pirated copies); they produced contracts to show that they were legally allowed to sell a foreign artist's music (even though the contracts were fabricated); they sat on copyright committees to show their desire to find solutions to piracy (sitting on copyright committees simply allowed them to figure out how to stay a step ahead of law enforcement); they showed account books to many musicians to prove that they were only selling a certain number of albums (again, most likely fabricated); and they bribed police and custom officials in several countries to ignore their business practices (though this is less trickery than just plain corruption). The combination of these strategies allowed music distributors to maintain tight control on the distribution of most music being sold in Tanzania. These practices, however, took time to develop and were not a part of the early years of cassette duplication. Initially, most distributors started out small and sold music as they would any other tradable goods.

As musicians and others became more interested in protecting their copyrights, the distributors developed more creative strategies to maintain their business interests. Musicians explained numerous instances where they tried to confront distributors over the illegal sale of their music. The most common narrative centered on walking through a market somewhere in Tanzania and finding pirated cassettes being sold. In most narratives, the musician finds pirated copies of his or her music being sold by a street seller. The seller tells the musician that the cassettes were purchased from a distributor in Dar es Salaam. The musician then goes to the distributor's store, shows the pirated copies, and asks to be reimbursed for losses. From here, the narrative splits into many versions. Occasionally, the distributor pays the musician to avoid trouble. In other cases, the distributor denies the charges, at which point the musician realizes that there is nothing that can be done to stop the illegal sale of the cassettes. Or, the distributor agrees to new terms for selling the artist's music in the local economy. In all these versions, the narratives come back together for the conclusion: the next day, week, or month, pirated copies of the artist's music are back in the market.

The earliest examples of this narrative date to 1987 with the illegal duplication of kwaya music (Perullo 2003). Given that there was not an effective copyright law or enforcement, early efforts to hinder piracy proved fruitless. Over the next decade, artists became increasingly interested in hindering the illegal duplication of their music. Attempts were made to create a collective voice for the music community: music committees formed; workshops and meetings were held; draft legislation was created; and numerous other actions were taken by the artists and government officials to establish more robust copyright legislation. Musicians also encouraged raids on music vendors all over Tanzania. Journalists even published photographs of the backrooms of local businesses showing stacks of VCRs and cassette recorders capable of duplicating hundreds of recordings per hour. Despite these efforts, piracy continued to flourish, due in part to the duplicitous actions of distributors capable of hiding, covering, and manipulating the dealings of their operations.

In April 1994, after increased pressure from external lenders, the Tanzanian government appeared to be making progress toward establishing a new copyright law. The Ministry of Industries and Trade agreed to deliver a new draft to Parliament. In a bewildering series of events, the draft documents disappeared. Tales of high-level corruption abounded. Many people, including journalists and artists, accused politicians and music leaders of accepting bribes from local distributors to hinder the passage of the draft document. Based on conversations with an undisclosed source, Muhidini Issa Michuzi reported that "the amendments, which could turn a new chapter in the welfare of local artists, have been lying idle in the Ministry [of Trade and Industries] since January. . . . Findings by this paper have it that some of the businessmen engaged in the video and audio cassette business are conspiring with the authorities in order to continue with the exercise [piracy]."[17] Officially, the government claimed that it needed $500 to print copies of the draft legislation and distribute them to members of Parliament. Musicians offered to hold a concert to raise the needed money. But the offer was refused.

During my research, I encountered numerous other narratives where corruption, collusion, or other deceitful tactics were used to hinder copyright legislation. The evidence from these narratives was that the practice of paying people to ignore illicit activities was a significant part of the music distribution business. One prominent distributor even made attempts to bribe me during an interview. It was ironic to ask questions about distribution and copyright law and then be enthusiastically offered an assortment of pirated products. Among many distributors, bribery had become a customary defense mechanism and a means to escape legal obstacles. It was an effort to retain legitimacy given the influence that even small amounts of money could have when used effectively as a bribe. Bribery is frequently effective in removing obstacles, providing a means to sell music without significant encounters with the police or the country's legal system.

In my research, I spent a great deal of time with music distributors attempting to learn their perspective on the music business. One distributor who spoke with me at length was Chandra Doshi, the owner of distributions company Galaxy.[18] Galaxy started in 1992 as Galaxy Recording Studio. Doshi initially owned a clothing store on Uhuru Street in Kariakoo but became more interested in earning a living from selling cassettes. He decided to buy a store behind the central market in Kariakoo in order to be closer to the other local distributors. In the early years, Doshi bought, copied, and sold cassettes out of his small store, creating a large clientele of both street vendors, to whom he sold tapes at a discount, and regular customers. Like most people in Dar es Salaam in the early 1990s, Doshi took advantage of the growing economy to expand his financial potential. Selling cassettes was as good a prospect as any, and Doshi invested time and effort to make sure his business thrived. And thrive it did.

Up until the early 1990s, most music distributors, such as Doshi, worked independently of one another. Although almost all of them carried out their business in the same neighborhood, Kariakoo (a section of Dar es Salaam), each tried to establish a niche market. One distributor, for instance, would focus on importing Zairian music and redistributing it throughout southern Africa, while another would market American hip-hop and popular music in Tanzania. Some distributors focused their business just on Dar es Salaam and did not bother investing in selling cassettes elsewhere in Africa. And while it is difficult to believe that companies did not compete with one another, duplicating the same cassettes and selling them in the same regions, there was so much opportunity for pirated music from the late 1980s that distributors had few reasons to interfere with each other's markets. At least that was true with the piracy of foreign music.

Music recorded by local artists was often treated differently than foreign music. In the 1990s, artists who recorded at one of the local recording studios would take their cassettes and try to sell them to a local distributor. The distributor, depending on his opinion of the artist, would offer to buy the rights to the master tape. Referred to as lump-sum payments, artists would often accept the money, usually between $20 and $100, to quickly recoup part of their investment in recording the album. Artists also thought that they had no other options to sell their music and would therefore sign distributor's contracts. In signing, the artists typically lost the rights to their recordings in perpetuity.

Most distributors profited from attaining the rights to albums by local musicians, but were limited to selling cassettes of only the artists they signed. Cassettes sold by one distributor could not be sold by another. Several distributors, however, made it a habit of copying and selling albums of local music owned by someone else without first gaining permission. This underhanded tactic caused a great deal of anger among other distributors who believed that they could not safely make an investment in buying the rights to an artist's album without having another distributor try and "illegally" copy those tapes. The fact that these businesses were also pirating music from foreign companies seemed unimportant. It mattered more that their investments in local music could not be protected.

Due to the problems caused by each signing with different artists, five companies, Mamu Stores, S.F.B., Down Town, Galaxy, and Congo Corridor, decided to merge in 1994. Identified collectively as the Big Five, each company retained its own name, but artists would sign a contract with all five companies. The tapes would then be marketed and sold by each of the businesses throughout Tanzania and eastern Africa. Since each distributor controlled different markets, the merger gave each business interest the opportunity to exploit the music within eastern Africa, while still keeping down the cost of buying the rights to recordings. Of course, it also helped that the owners of each of the companies were cousins and, to a degree, could trust one another.

The contracts of the Big Five were simple one-page documents that were also extraordinarily manipulative though potentially not legally binding. In the contracts, the musicians (assignor) and the company (assignees) agreed to only three conditions. What follows is almost the entirety of the body of the contract:

1. The assignor hereby assigns all their rights . . . to the assignees
2. The assignees are the only people who have the rights to produce and distribute the cassettes in Tanzania.
3. No other person shall have such rights.

The brief contract essentially argued that the Big Five was the only company that could sell a specific recording in Tanzania and that all the rights in the recordings were given to the company. Even compared to the contracts signed with Kenyan companies in the early 1980s, the contract lacked significant detail for the sale of music. The contracts should have specified the frequency and number of albums to be manufactured; any payment of royalties and the amount that would be paid to the musician in advance; deductions to be made on the sale of each album for making album covers, purchasing cassette stock, and marketing the albums; the names of key people involved in the contract aside from the musician; and any auditing rights and limitations, such as existed in the Kenya contracts explained above.

The reason for pointing out the weaknesses of the Big Five contract is to emphasize the murky rules governing the sale of sound recordings. Conventions in the music business emerged over time as new issues and ideas arose. There were no set rules or legal guidelines for creating agreements, nor was there any enforcement of the terms in contracts. According to interviews and analysis of court records, the court system was never used to debate the legality of these business transactions. There was an implied notion of understanding involved in these business dealings, which established certain codes of conduct between artists and distributors. Still, there was nothing to hinder distributors from underpaying

How did this happen?

musicians for the commercial value of their recordings. No one tracked
the number of albums sold, and it was not possible to trust the accounts
provided by the distributors.

More
*fruchic*
*acult vct*

In 1996, the Big Five merged with three other companies.[19] For some
reason, this new conglomeration was called the Big Seven even though it
was made up of eight separate businesses. The Big Seven was the largest
organization of music distribution in eastern Africa. Through the merger
and increased success regionally, the conglomerate expanded their distribution networks to reach into Zimbabwe and Zambia, and continued
to distribute to Malawi, Uganda, Kenya, Rwanda, and Burundi. Other
companies, such as Tajdin and FM Music, continued to grow as well but
not as extensively as the Big Seven. The regional control of popular music
up and down the coast of eastern Africa provided significant economic
and political clout to the Asian distributors.

In 1999, a scandal broke out within the Big Seven. One explanation
for the scandal was that one of the partners bought the rights to sell an
album of mchiriku and sold the tape independently of the other businesses. Several months later, he gave the tapes to the other stores and
asked them to pay their share of the royalties and cassette copying fees,
even though he had already profited from the tapes' sale. Angered by
the scam, the other companies in the Big Seven decided to separate.
Another underlying explanation for the demise of the Big Seven is that
other tensions had started to mount within the organization. Musicians
were continuing to pressure distributors for larger payments on the sale
of their master tapes and brought in police and local organizations to
fight the distributors on pirated materials. The Big Seven was an easy target and may have found the mounting allegations and pressure difficult
to handle. Further, due to the diverse business tactics used by members
of the Big Seven, the pressure to change their relationship with artists
may have caused controversy within the group. Regardless of the exact
reason(s), however, the organization collapsed and splintered into two
units similar to their arrangement before the formation of the Big Seven.
F.K. Mitha, Kings Brothers, and Wananchi Stores joined together (under
the acronym FKW). Galaxy's owner decided to no longer work with local
artists and instead only distribute cassettes that he could purchase at discount from the other companies. Space Recordings moved to distribute
mainly Indian, Arabic, and Zaïrian music. The remaining three compa-

A music kiosk in City Centre, Dar es Salaam. *Photo by James Nindi.*

nies, Global Sounds Ltd., Mamu Stores, and Congo Corridor, joined to become GMC, currently the most profitable company for local music in the country.

### TROUBLE IN THE STREETS

Although the storeowners described above import, duplicate, and distribute music, most Tanzanians buy their music from local street vendors. In Dar es Salaam, there are two types of street vendors: those that use pushcarts to walk throughout a designated area selling their goods and those that have a stall in a permanent location. Generally, the pushcarts are small box-like carriages with a glass top displaying albums, a music system in the base, and a storage area that holds between two and four hundred cassettes. The stalls are small, wooden structures that have shelves

A pushcart vendor selling cassettes in Kariakoo, Dar es Salaam.
*Photo by James Nindi.*

inside that hold over a thousand cassettes and a larger, more powerful
sound system. At least one hundred street vendors sell cassettes in Dar es
Salaam, most of whom are concentrated in the downtown areas.

Collectively referred to as *machinga,* street sellers are the public face
of the informal economy in Dar es Salaam. They move throughout commercial neighborhoods, public streets, and market areas hawking their
wares to anyone they see. They walk up close to people eating in restaurants to sell bootlegged movies, music, and, more recently, pornography.
At stoplights of major roads, vendors walk between cars, selling everything from newspapers to machetes, while holding their goods in front
of car windows and yelling, "Good price." Their presence is ubiquitous in
urban Africa, where anything and everything becomes a marketable item.

Used clothes, tires, and electronic parts, mostly from the United States and Europe, as well as books, magazines, posters, and furniture, can all be acquired along Dar es Salaam's thoroughfares. There are also many misappropriated goods that appear in the wares of machinga. When a truck carrying cereal crashed just outside Dar es Salaam in 2002, boxes of Frosted Flakes appeared throughout the city. Robberies of inexpensive items, such as costume jewelry or clothes, also often make it into the hands of street sellers. The informal economy functions in part due to the presence of machinga throughout the city, whether in the sale of legal or illegal products.

In Tanzania, street vendors have long had problems with the state government, police, and *askari,* locally recruited soldiers, guards, militia, or police used to enforce city regulations. At issue is the association of machinga with vagrancy and laziness. Dating back to the colonial period, Africans in Dar es Salaam who did not have a pass, were unemployed, and/or were in the wrong sections of town could be repatriated to their rural homes. Andrew Burton (2005) explains that up to 2,000 people were forcibly repatriated each year during the 1950s. The post-independence government held similar views to the unemployed or underemployed and referred to them as *kupe* (parasites), *wazururaji* (loiterers), *wavivu* (idlers), and *maadui wa siasa ya ujamaa na kujitegemea* (enemies of the policy of socialism and self-reliance). In 1972, the government launched *Operation Kupe* (Operation Parasite) to send jobless youth in Dar es Salaam to rural areas of the country. Four years later, the government initiated *Operation Kila Mtu Afanye Kazi* (Everyone Must Work). But in 1983, the Tanzanian government took its strongest attack on the urban joblessness, including among youths. Through the Human Resources Deployment Act (popularly known as *Nguvu Kazi*), 15,000 people were arrested in a three-month period. The unemployed were sent back to their home areas or, alternatively, required to work on sisal estates (Burton 2005).

Even in recent years, the Tanzanian government continues to crack down on the urban poor, the unemployed, and machinga. During raids, street sellers and the unemployed are arrested, beaten, and removed from the downtown areas of the city (Moyer 2003). Kiosks and stales are destroyed. Bribery is common as street sellers attempt to avoid being arrested. In response to these attacks, street sellers have become more organized, forming organizations such as Chama cha Wauza Mitumba (Association

of Used Clothing Sellers) and banks (Tanzania Bank of Machinga Ltd.).[20]
There have also been mass protests against the militia in charge of removing machinga from areas of Dar es Salaam.[21] Despite these efforts at collective organization, police brutality and extortion remain prevalent.

Music sellers frequently become the recipients of these forms of harassment. Even with a *kitambulisho* (licenses/identification cards) to
sell their wares in certain areas of the city, street sellers complain about
being attacked by the police or forced to pay bribes. In a survey I conducted with sixty street vendors in Dar es Salaam, police brutality was
a major concern:

> Do police officers or askari give you any problems in operating your business?
> *Vendor #35:* Yes, I received problems form the police: (1) I am arrested by
> a city Askari for not having a license; (2) arrested by police when you
> leave a store [and have money]; and (3) I receive problems from the
> ownership of this business.
> *Vendor #22:* The police chase us away from various areas. They claim that
> we should keep moving, that we should not sit in one spot. This is a
> nuisance to us because it is difficult to continually push a cassette cart.
> *Vendor #6:* The police arrest us by claiming that we do not have a business
> license. They tell us that we need to get a license from them. We listen
> to them and we get a license. Later they [return and] say that they do
> not recognize what is on the license and they go and tell the police.
> The police do not recognize the license and I do not know what it is for.
> And, if they nationalize the business they must give you an opening
> of a month.
> *Vendor #28:* The police claim that I am doing business in the streets. They
> do not leave me alone until I bribe them.
> *Vendor #30:* One day I was selling cassettes in an area that I was not permitted
> to. A city Askari arrested me and sent me to city court and destroyed my
> entire business.

Machinga are easy targets because they have no political or social representation beyond their organizations. Members of city government frequently deride the practices of machinga, which provides opportunities
for the police to abuse this population without fear of political recourse.

Interestingly, most police brutality is concentrated in downtown areas, suggesting that street sellers in other areas of the city encounter fewer
instances of extortion from police. The downtown has many wealthy
citizens of mixed races. The noise and presence caused by street vendors

may be at issue, causing residents of downtown to pay the police to take action.

> Vendor #41: It is my opinion, we who sell cassettes are bothered by Indians because they say it is illegal to make so much noise. The Indians pay the police to arrest me and they move me to another location. Is there such a law [about noise] in Tanzania?

In response to the long history of conflict between residents and machinga, two buildings have been built in Ilala, Dar es Salaam, to confine the efforts of the sellers. Referred to as the Machinga Complex, it is unclear whether music sellers will also be encouraged to move into these buildings at some point in the future.

Perhaps the biggest concern among many vendors, particularly in the downtown areas, is that they would be caught selling pirated cassettes.

> How has the 1999 Copyright Act affected your business?
> *Vendor #3:* When I started selling I sold original cassettes by artists that I liked. To my surprise, some of those tapes were stolen from a church so that the people of the church looked for them and found one in my cart. They got the police and arrested me, but the problem eventually went away.
> *Vendor #25:* One problem is that I can buy cassettes from an Indian store-owner and maybe he has not paid for the copyright on the original. If I sell these tapes without knowing [that they are pirated] and a police officer comes, he can arrest me and nationalize my business straight away.

The fear of having one's business "nationalized" or taken over by the government stems from police crackdown on illegal businesses, particularly in election periods. Some vendors had their radios taken from their pushcarts and others had their entire shops confiscated, which was the reason the pushcart owner stated that his shop could become nationalized. Although no one was sure why the police were increasing their threats to local vendors, the rumor was that the government was telling police to raid local businesses to regain the money spent on election campaigns. These rumors helped to place blame for the abuses on those in political power.

Another threat to street vendors comes from musicians. Although most musicians realize that street vendors purchase their merchandise from distributors, some still became angry at seeing pirated copies of their music sold on the street. In one highly publicized instance in 2001, a musician found pirated copies of his music in a pushcart and proceeded to smash the cart, tapes and all. By smashing the pushcart, the musician was showing that piracy would no longer be tolerated and changes needed to be made. To vendors, the attention local musicians gave to their business constituted another threat. The musician who destroyed the vendor's shop was never charged for the crime and, most likely, the pushcart vendor was never reimbursed for his losses. The message the musician sent to street vendors was clear: be prepared to accept responsibility for the music you sell. But with dishonest distributors and a fuzzy idea of the difference between pirated and original cassettes, street vendors are easy targets for frustrated local musicians.[22]

Due to the difficult environment of selling cassettes, most street vendors do not stay in the business long. All the cassette sellers are male African Tanzanians, mostly under 25 years old with an interest in music. Two-thirds own their pushcarts or stalls, while others work for a family, friend, or an employer. Most vendors earn anywhere from $1 to $15 per day, for twelve hours of work, usually six days a week. Others earn as much as $40 per day. Considering that there is a yearly tax of $50 in addition to the costs of purchasing merchandise and a pushcart ($300) or stall ($380), most vendors can expect to earn a decent income by the end of their first year. Yet all the vendors surveyed, with the exception of two, had only been in business for five or fewer years (and most under a year), which shows the transient nature of cassette selling. The long days and harassment from local police, askari, and musicians push many to move on to other opportunities.

Street vendors are also the most visible sign of piracy for foreign artists who visit Tanzania. In one incident, the Congolese artist General Defao traveled to Tanzania in June 1999 to perform several concerts. The accompanying comic strip highlights central moments in Defao's visit. In the first frame, he is welcomed by scores of admiring fans. In the second, he meets a young sheikh who curses Defao and sends him to the hospital. In the final frame, Defao has found illegal cassette copies of his new album on the Dar es Salaam streets. He exclaims, "My God. There are also copyright thieves here." To which the music vendor replies, "Don't be surprised. Even the Lost Boyz had rings stolen off their fingers here in Tanzania." (The Lost Boyz was an American rap band that toured Tanzania in May 1998.) After finding that his music had been pirated, Defao

Comic strip of the Congolese musician General Defao in Dar es Salaam, Tanzania. The first frame shows how famous Defao is in Tanzania. General Defao is being driven from the Dar es Salaam airport with the heading, "When he came to Tanzania at the end of June [1999], numerous people received him with smiling faces." Then, in the same frame, Defao says, "Thank you. Here it is as if I am in paradise." The next two frames explain how Defao became sick in Tanzania because of a curse by a young sheikh. When he recovers, he finds that all his music is being pirated on the streets. *Photo courtesy of King Kinya.*

was shown on the evening news weeping, uncontrollably at times, while the press interviewed him about the Tanzanian pirates.[23]

Given their encounters with local and foreign musicians, street vendors can best be described as the frontline of the cassette and compact disc market. They are the ones that push new albums, interact with the public, and try to discern legitimate and illegitimate cassettes from the albums they buy from distributors. Still, street vendors have to be considered on the periphery of the music economy: they do not influence the recording, production, and distribution of recordings. They do not hinder pirated music, since that is the domain of the distributors. And while they do impact the popularity of an album by increasing sales, radio is far more influential than individual vendors. They do, however, have a critical importance in *proving* the popularity of an album through actual sales. This creates demand for more recorded music. In essence, street vendors provide an indispensable service to Tanzania's music economy by keeping cassettes visible to the public and working every day to sell artists' albums.

Similar to other areas of the Tanzanian music economy, street vendors have to be self-reliant and ingenious in order to survive in the local market. Vendors need to raise money to buy a cart or a stall and an initial supply of cassettes. They need to register their business and pay taxes. If they are unable to read or write, they have to find someone trustworthy to assist them. Once a shop has been purchased and the business registered, the vendors have to learn to integrate into the heavily populated cassette market. Without experience in business or a business education, they have to set out to develop ways—targeting specific clients, locating an open area of land that no other vendor is using, or selling only one genre of music (such as *kwaya*)—to make their business successful. Problems with copyright law, the police, and comprehending the general music market add to the difficulties of making a living from selling music. Overall, the risks, responsibilities, and rewards of the street vendor business make it a lifestyle where only those with a bongo mentality can succeed.

## CONTROL, COLLAPSE, CONTRACTS, AND COPYRIGHT LAW

I was fortunate to live in Tanzania when the 1999 Copyright Act was signed into law. Given the uproar that artists made to have their music protected, I expected to see celebrations and excitement once the act became official. I thought that many artists would start to make use of the new law as quickly as possible, since they were so desperate for changes in the way their albums were being sold. In the following months, however, very little occurred: there were no major events marking its passage or increased threats to sue distributors who illegally sold recorded albums. Musicians discussed ideas about protecting and enforcing their rights, yet without an effective organization to take charge, most believed that there was nothing worth celebrating. Some musicians were optimistic that more changes would come. Salim Mohammed Zahoro, former leader of Shikamoo Jazz, explained his hope for the law the same month it was signed by President Mkapa: "The Honorable President signed the law. He agreed that now this law will start to work. I believe that now there is really a lot of support for the law. It will work . . . it will be good for Tanzanian musicians."[24]

Khalid Ponera, a popular announcer at RTD from the 1960s until 2000, was also optimistic that the new law would become effective:

> After the copyright law starts, the situation will improve. I think that our musicians receive a lot of problems, which is the reason so many enter into abject poverty. They compose many songs but do not receive anything for them. [Many older musicians] do not have anything. They are unable to play music anymore. So, they are left with nothing. Many die like this, without anything. They are worried in the city. You do not know that they were musicians because they have no salary of any kind, they do not have the ability to play music, and they are unable to do any other work. They are left without a thing. Now that copyright has started, I believe that their situation will improve.

Ponera, who passed away in 2000, watched many musicians he worked with at Radio Tanzania Dar es Salaam become poor and destitute. They were too weak to perform music and often too ill or old to have any other occupation. He hoped and believed that copyright would improve the way artists benefited from their music and possibly give them resources to live secure lives.

The year after the 1999 Copyright Act was signed into law, I returned to Tanzania. On the day I arrived, Hamza Kalala, a dansi musician, picked me up in his car with several of our friends. After catching up on the few months that passed since we last saw each other, I asked him about the effectiveness of the Copyright Act. Had it started to work and benefit musicians? Silent for a moment, he then turned to me and said with a slight smile, "*Ipo kama haipo*" (It is there but it is like it is not there). The simple Swahili phrase made everyone in the car laugh, including Kalala, and was a poignant reflection of the situation. Here was a law that was expected to protect artists' rights but remained, according to Kalala, ineffective: piracy continued, local organizations battled for authority over enforcing the law, and artists still found themselves losing money to music distributors. A minute later, Kalala repeated the phrase again to show that it was exactly what he wanted to say and, again, everyone laughed.

Despite the sense that the law did little to hinder piracy or expand the economic potential of musical works, many changes did occur in the years after the passage of the Copyright Act. The law provided support to artists through legitimizing their complaints against distributors. Threats of lawsuits had more weight, particularly as the governing body in charge of copyright, the Copyright Society of Tanzania (COSOTA), educated custom officials, law enforcement, lawyers, and judges throughout the country. Whereas in 1999, more people associated the word copyright with cover songs played by bands, a decade later most people affiliated with the music economy regarded sound recordings and musical compositions as forms of property that could be owned and profited from. Even traditional artists that I interviewed in other areas of Tanzania had started to register the music that they performed.

To understand the social and cultural shifts that occurred subsequent to the passage of the Copyright Act, I examine five changes in the relationship between artists, distributors, and musical works. The first is alterations to power relations between artists and distributors. Distributors became increasingly concerned with their public image the more people focused on copyright and piracy. Well-publicized raids of music stores occurred throughout Tanzania and were met with fanfare in the media. Politicians spoke about the importance of intellectual property law at various national and international meetings and conferences. International groups, such as the World Intellectual Property Organization, held meetings with visual and performance-based artists to discuss rights in original works. And musicians continued to pressure distributors for improved contracts. These efforts represented shifts in public knowledge and concern about intellectual property rights. It also created focused resentment on the practices of distributors, particularly those based in Dar es Salaam.

Realizing that their reputations, social standing, and ability to conduct better business depended on improving their relationship with artists, distributors started to more actively foster equitable connections within their *public* business dealings. The rap artist Mr. II, also known as Sugu, explains one instance:

The relationship with distributors changed a bit since the issue of copyright started to be debated. Really, the situation has changed because, even now, when you make an appointment with an Indian, you sit and talk serious business. That is, the Indian respects the artist. In the past, the artist chased after the Indian. Today, the Indian calls the artist, "Hey Bwana, how is the album coming?" "I have not started yet." He replies, "Bwana, I want to talk to you about your next album. Can we meet at the New Africa Hotel?" So, you go there and you meet with the Indian. Not everyone receives this attention. But not everyone who performs is given a Cadillac to sign a contract.

The Copyright Act shifted the influence of both parties involved in contract negotiations. The new legislation provided moral and legislative support to artists, which gave them confidence and knowledge in discussing the value of their recordings. It also made music sellers more wary of trying to distribute material without firm agreements and connections with the creators of recorded material. The more popular an artist, the more power they had in these business relationships. For Mr. II, this meant that the Asian storeowner courted him and took him to a fancy hotel to talk business.

The increased influence of artists in contract negotiations did not completely alter their relationship with producers. Distributors still controlled the finances and, after contracts were signed, the rights to the music. Norbert Chenga, head of Muungano Cultural Troupe, explains:

There are these Indian distributors that look for the work of artists. If they see that you are good, they give you encouragement: "Do you want to make another album?" "Yes." So they give you money to rehearse and then you enter the studio. They then ask you, "How much do you want for the album?" Then, they pay you $800 to $900 and continue to produce tapes. You do not receive any more money. They paid you to rehearse, to enter the studio, they bought the tapes, they paid for everything. What rights do you have in the tape? You have rights in the words that remain in your head, which do not have much value, at least as I see it.

Chenga's comments provide insight into the state of rights in Tanzania. Copyright law can cover intellectual property in both sound recordings and in musical compositions. If an artist gives an exclusive license to a distributor to sell his sound recording, than the artist is unable to sell or license that work to any other person. This is Chenga's point about not having any rights in his sound recordings. If the same artist is also the composer of the songs in the sound recording, than he also has rights to benefit from the lyrics and music. In other music economies, these rights allow artists to earn royalties from publishing their music. In Tanzania, music publishing is still relatively new, which means that most artists do not earn an income directly from their compositions. This is Chenga's point about the compositions not having much value.

For the distributor/artist relationship, Chenga's comments emphasize the continued authority of distributors over sound recordings. Artists are paid for their works, but once they enter into the commodity flows of the Tanzanian economy, it becomes the property of distributors for the duration of a contract. Even though artists have more power in courting music sellers, copyright law emphasizes the potential for distributors to continue to own and control musical recordings. Of course, this is fairly typical of many music economies where contracts grant record companies the right to publicly reproduce and distribute sound recordings. This is often referred to as acquiring exclusive rights. The difference between the handling of these rights is that there is no monitoring or auditing of the sale of sound recordings in Tanzania. Distributors retain the exclusive right to sell an artist's music and have no responsibility to prove that royalty payments reflect the actual number of albums sold. In cases where piracy is suspected, the distributor can point to a contract that stipulates exclusive rights to sell without also needing to prove that the number of tapes in the market equals the accounts for the royalty payments being made. While power in initial encounters has shifted to the benefit of artists, in some ways copyright law has only strengthened and legitimized the economic power of distributors in the sale of sound recordings.

Recognizing the initial interactions of distributors as the first shift, a second area that has undergone transformation since the 1999 Copyright Act is contracts. In late January 2001, I accompanied John Mjema, a local rapper, to negotiate a contract for the release of his album *Mimi Sio Mwizi* (I Am Not a Thief). Mjema had used his own money to pay recording studio fees at Don Bosco Studio and, with the popularity of his first song, "Mimi Sio Mwizi," had established enough of a reputation to sign a potentially lucrative contract (PURL 7.2). But Mjema still had to be cautious considering he had never made a distribution deal before.

He decided to first try FKW, whose owner was willing to offer Mjema a royalty of 25 cents on every cassette sold. Considering that a single cassette cost $1 at that time, FKW guaranteed Mjema a 25 percent royalty for every album sold. Tanzanian royalties, at that point, tended to be between 10 to 15 cents, which meant that the owner of FKW was offering Mjema the highest reported royalty in Tanzanian history.[25] For a new artist, the deal was obviously suspicious. Perhaps the distributor knew that Mjema could never tour the country to monitor the sale of his album, allowing the distributor to pay Mjema for just those albums sold in Dar es Salaam.

Realizing the risks of signing with FKW, Mjema decided to try GMC. When Mjema sat down in the back room of Mamu Stores in Kariakoo, where GMC's main office is located, he was handed a contract in English. Since Mjema was more comfortable with Swahili, there was an immediate tension in negotiating the terms of the contract. The contract itself was far more robust than those previously associated with local distributors. GMC, for instance, would have the right to sell Mjema's album throughout East Africa. The company would also be able to sell the albums at whatever price they saw fit. In addition, the following terms were specified:

1. Mjema would receive a Tsh 150 (15 cents) royalty for every cassette, with a cash advance for the first 10,000 copies.
2. Mjema and the other members of his group, Mambo Poa, would remain the copyright owners of the album.
3. Mjema could distribute compact discs on his own.
4. Mjema would need to have a unique rubber stamp made, which he would use to place a mark on every cassette sold. This would allow Mjema to stamp every cassette himself and then, in monitoring his cassettes in stores, be able to immediately identify a pirated copy.
5. GMC would also place their stamp on every cassette sold.
6. GMC would be responsible to track pirated tapes and share any collected fines with Mjema.
7. The contract would be registered by a court official, thereby adding legitimacy to the terms.

On the surface, the contract was a testament to shifts in the distributor/artist relationship after the introduction of the Copyright Act. GMC was not only willing to pay Mjema one and a half million Tanzanian shillings up front, but they would continue to give Mjema royalties on every tape sold after the first ten thousand. By stamping every album, Mjema was also given assurance that his album could not be easily pirated (although copying a rubber stamp is not beyond enterprising entrepreneurs). And, in case of piracy by another company, GMC would take responsibility for pressing charges.[26]

Other points in the contract present significant uncertainties. What does it mean that Mjema would remain the copyright owner of the album? This suggests something akin to a non-exclusive license, which means that Mjema could theoretically take his recordings to another distributor and enter into a second contract. Distributors do not typically allow this type of language because it means that any investment they put into the sale of recorded music can be undermined by competitors. Another issue with the contract is the registration with court officials. Who exactly are they? In 2001, there was no official body able to register the works of authors. It would take several more years before COSOTA was able to conduct this service, but this organization has no connection to the courts. In taking apart these elements of the contract, there is an obvious use of clever deception. The language appeased artists' concerns over their rights, as well as piracy and copyright law, but it was mostly false pretense aimed at gaining artists' trust.

Despite the deceit of this and other contracts, the post–Copyright Act negotiations symbolize a profound transition in the formalization of the artist/distributor relationship. By allowing artists to stamp cassettes, earn higher royalties, and sell compact discs on their own, there is an acknowledgment of the importance of sound recordings in the livelihood of artists. Distributors are more willing to support the careers of artists since the prospective benefits are significant. Investing in a talented band, for instance, has the potential to encourage additional recordings from that band that can then be sold by the distributors. These business relations promote a system of exchange that recognizes the potential value of supporting music as both a work and a commodity.

In 2009, contracts continue to present similar terms as those offered to Mjema. Popular artists are able to negotiate higher initial lump-sum payments based on the premise that their music is going to sell well. Several musicians reportedly sign deals for an initial payment between

$4,000 to $6,000, while a few are able to go as high as $10,000. They can also continue to earn royalties if their album sells beyond the number included in this initial payment. Particularly for younger artists who do not have other financial obligations, these payouts are enormous and have allowed an entire group of musicians to earn a comfortable living. Many bongo flava artists purchase cars, nice clothes, and other items simply from these payouts. For these artists, the rights in the actual recordings is less important since, after a year, most lose popularity and rarely generate additional sales. The commodification of sound recordings remains an active process with a significant turnover in repertoire.

A third shift occurring in the artist/distributor relationship is in the potential efforts by distributors to hinder piracy. Publicly, many of the major distributors attempt to obstruct the illegal sale of the albums that they sell. The difficulty is gauging whether these are genuine efforts or mere trickery. It is not uncommon for businesses to legitimately sell the same goods that they sell illegally. International headlines are replete with stories about the two-faced natures of many contemporary business deals: an arms dealer using a legal weapons business as a front for more profitable illegal sales; an investment banker investing legitimate funds but also running a Ponzi scheme; or a construction company that extorts money from clients, business, and the government. These two-directional business practices, where the legal covers the illegal, are a familiar aspect of business generally, but are arguably more inevitable during deregulation efforts. Left on their own, individuals search for profitable alternatives that draw in more financial benefits even if these alternatives are illegal or immoral. In Tanzania, where there are few copyright enforcement agencies outside Dar es Salaam, the ability to monitor the sale of cassettes is limited. The territory is large, frequently remote, and traverses many topographic regions, from lakes to mountains and savannah to cities. There is no real means to survey these areas, especially if one is looking for fraudulent cassette tapes. Even with an occasional raid or breakup in the supply of pirated tapes, distributors could easily continue to sell music illegally throughout the country with few financial drawbacks. In this scenario, Dar es Salaam becomes the front for the more illicit activities occurring throughout the country.

These album covers feature two popular Tanzanian artists, Ally Chocky and Bahati Bukuku. On the cover of Bukuku's albums there is a holographic sticker used exclusively by the distribution company GMC. FKW, which released Chocky's album, does not use such stickers. *Used with permission.*

There is some evidence, however, that distributors take seriously their claims at operating legitimate business practices. One technique that several producers are using to track and prove legitimacy of cassettes is placing holographic stickers on their albums. The stickers typically have the name of the distributor on them and reflect light when tilted back and forth. For customers, the stickers are meant to provide a level of assurance about the originality of the recordings: if a sticker is broken or missing, then the album must be a fake, a pirated copy; if the stickers are untouched, then the customer can feel confident that the album is

legitimate and that the artist is being paid royalties. Of course, a sticker is unlikely to dissuade enterprising individuals from duplicating an album and selling the copies. The sticker does not even hinder someone from opening the cassette box: they can unclip the hinges on the outer box and then remove the cassette. This leaves the sticker intact but provides access to the music and liner notes. Still, a consumer culture has emerged in Dar es Salaam that searches for legitimate cassettes given their better sound quality and authenticity. This is attributable to the passage of the Copyright Act and the educational efforts of artists, copyright societies, and even distributors.

Even if locally recorded music released on cassette is being pirated less than in the past, most foreign albums sold in Tanzania continue to be illegally copied. The reason for the lack of legitimate foreign music sales is twofold. First, local artists continually monitor their album sales, with band members, fans, and friends checking stores after a new album is released to ensure that only legitimate albums are sold. Foreign artists, on the other hand, rarely tour Tanzania and are therefore unable to keep checking sales of their albums. The second reason foreign albums are continually pirated is that many people are unaware of the difference between original and pirated albums in foreign music. The quality of pirated foreign albums, with fancy covers and plastic wrap, gives the impression that the products are original. On almost all original albums made in India, Europe, and the United States, however, a record company's address or the album's ISBN number appears on the back cover or in the liner notes. On pirated copies, the address and ISBN number are removed or altered in some way, so a customer cannot contact the original company reporting the illegal tape. Further, there are no holographic stickers on legitimate or pirated copies of foreign music, making it difficult to verify an album's authenticity.

A fourth shift in the relationship between artists and distributors is in increased efforts to market popular music. Recorded albums have attained recognition as commodities that need to be supported and pushed into the local market. One major distributor has partnered with a local radio station that manages artists. Where the radio stations manages and promotes the artists on the radio and in performance, the distributor pushes the albums in markets throughout eastern Africa. In addition, distributors, radio stations, and managers assist with promoting an artist's album or hire an outside promoter who pushes the album into the local market. Glossy advertisements appear regularly in local music magazines featuring information about upcoming album releases. There are also sponsorships from local food and alcohol companies who try to draw on the popularity of artists to sell their products. The continual addition of more people needed to sell an album points to the specialization developing in Tanzania's music economy as music becomes more financially lucrative. It also emphasizes the increasing ways that creativity needs to exist through print advertisements, radio airplay, clothing lines, music production, and partnerships with advertisers. Artists, radio personnel, and distributors continue to establish broader networks of people willing to find new ways to develop consumer interest in all aspects of recorded music.

Advertisement for the artist MB Dog. Toward the top it reads, "An album release bigger than any other in bongo." Notice also the text-message style writing at the top, common in music magazines. *Used with permission.*

⑤ Finally, a fifth shift does not involve music distributors, only artists and their compositions. The 1999 Copyright Act expanded potential forms of ownership within musical works. Prior to the act, artists could conceptualize ownership in several ways. ①One was in terms of socialist policies in which their musical works served to benefit society. The signing of contracts with Radio Tanzania Dar es Salaam (RTD) was an example where musicians permitted the broadcasting of their music on the station indefinitely. RTD also sold artists sound recordings beginning in the late 1980s or early 1990s. Artists did not fight the sale of their songs since there was still a conception of state ownership over recordings made at the radio station.②A second form of ownership prior to the act was a community's relation with traditional musical forms. In my interviews with traditional artists in Arusha, Bagamoyo, and Dodoma, there was much discussion of musical works having cultural significance for the maintenance of group identity. Certain traditions were seen as belonging exclusively to a specific community or cultural group. Other

② Does this mean the $ went to the communities

forms of ownership also existed, such as band owners' control of songs over composers, and works-for-hire, in which institutions paid artists for the rights to their compositions.

The Copyright Act provides for additional forms of ownership through allowing individual rights in sound recordings and compositions. Central to any copyright law is determining the author of a musical work. If an individual composes a song, then he can claim to be the author of that song. It is his property. If two people write music together, then there is the potential for joint ownership. The more people who contribute to a composition, the harder it is to determine authorship in a song.

Since many music bands compose songs in groups, the notion of establishing identifiable authors has created a number of shifts in people's relations to musical works. Traditional artists are increasingly claiming copyright in their music in order to protect their rights in songs, even if they are based on community-based music. Artists from socialist bands state that they are the sole composers of well-known compositions even though there is often little ability to verify these claims. In interviews, musicians frequently list songs they compose, which establishes a claim to authorship in a journalist's or researcher's publications. There is recognition of individual property rights in music even though other forms of ownership (socialist, traditional, etc.) continue to exist.

For artists, the difficulty is getting media organizations, band owners, and copyright officials to accept claims of ownership considering the impracticality of verifying authorship. Many conflicts have resulted from artists who state that they are the sole composer of songs. Whenever money is involved, such as in the resale of classic Tanzanian songs in the local market, several members of bands claim to be composers (composers can earn more from a re-release of their music as an author rather than just a performer). There are regular attempts to protect one's intellectual property even though there is no means to verify the authors of songs written in the past. Several artists have even claimed to be the author of songs that appear to have been written by another artist who passed away. Family members are less likely to fight for the rights of a relative who composed a well-known song in the past, particularly since the ownership of music is still a relatively new concept and not well defined outside the local music economy. Given the murkiness of ownership in music, songs appear up for grabs, where the most persistent and well-informed individual can stake a claim in compositions before anyone else does.

Bands in Tanzania have become more aware of rights in compositions and thus have established legal guidelines for artists to determine authorship in songs. Ally Chocky explains his compositional process:

> What I do when I have a new song is, first, I get the rhythm. I get the rhythm on guitar. Once I have established the rhythm [melody and the lyrics], the band can sit together and add solo guitar and bass. Then keyboard. Then drums. So, during a practice, everyone will get together and give their ideas. "Let's do this or let's do this." A new song is, therefore, a mixture of everyone's idea: From the first person who came up with the idea until the song sounds good. For example, I tell my singers, "Okay, every singer searches for a word to put here so we can 'please' the other words." So, they look for a word and they put it there. This is one example of the mixture of ideas of the musicians. A song does not happen by yourself. It does not matter which song, you cannot compose it by yourself.

> Perullo: Does this cause a problem with copyright?
> Chocky: Our company [that owns the band] is good. They pay the *mtunzi* [composer] and they pay those who assisted with the song. You see? Those people who assisted me are the *washiriki* [associates]. The song is mine, but there are the *washiriki*. For the *mtunzi*, they pay a rate that is different than the *mshiriki* [associate]. *Mshiriki* receives a standard rate.

The establishment of *mtunzi* and *mshiriki* suited many bands because it recognizes the primacy of the initial idea and the importance of collective compositional processes. There is no legal precedence to the terms created by Chocky's band. Rather, there is an emergent quality to create terms that best suit the band members and their compositions.

The many different claims to music in the local economy have created a varied landscape of intellectual property rights in Tanzanian society. Recombinant property is a concept put forth by the sociologist David Stark to address the plurality of mixed property forms—"hybrid mixtures of public ownership and private initiative" (1989: 167–68)—that exists within and between public and private sectors of Eastern Europe's post-socialist period. For Stark, recombinant property is a form of "organizational hedging" in which actors living in formerly socialist countries respond to market uncertainty by "diversifying their assets, redefining and recombining resources" (1997: 38). Tanzanian artists, attempting to earn a living from their musical works, also redefine and recombine resources to improve their ability to profit from their profession. For most musicians, this means using copyright law and previous notions of ownership to create multiple conceptions of rights that can be applied to many different scenarios. The terms created in Chocky's band may not be the same as those used in another group or among traditional artists, the state, or private institutions. Without legal precedent, ownership remains flexible, adapting to people's interest in recorded sound. This process, which I refer to as recombinant ownership, allows artists to easily maneuver within different situations to negotiate for the best results. In essence, recombinant ownership is a way of manipulating multiple situations based on desires of immediately profiting from the commodification of musical works.

The passage of the 1999 Copyright Act in Tanzania was an effort to establish standards in the way that people conceive of owning artistic and scientific creations. Sally Falk Moore describes these legal changes as "processes of regularization" where "conscious efforts are made to build and/or reproduce durable social and symbolic orders" (1978: 6). Most African countries receive intense pressure from international organizations to establish legislation that meets requirements for establishing free trade. These requirements encourage countries to pass or update their legislation, educate the public and the body of professionals responsible for upholding them, and create a common body of case law that establishes the parameters of newly passed legislation. Even though laws tend to be thought of as durable and permanent—rules that remain fixed regardless of time or context—they are more accurately seen as active processes where shifts and adjustments are made based on competition, communication, the exercise of power, and the continual modification of legislation. The way people interpret, use, and ignore laws work to undermine any notion of stasis that exists around the regularization process. This does not mean that legislation should be viewed as an element of constant or continual change. Moore writes, "If the categories of analysis treat *change* as in some sense the opposite of *regularity*, there is not sufficient place given to indeterminacy, to elements in situations which are neither regular nor changing, but are rather matters of open or multiple option" (1978: 47, her emphasis). Attempts at regularization, through the passage of new laws, create opportunities for multiple interpretations and uses of the social and symbolic orders contained within legislation.

The multiple interpretations of copyright law have made the transitions taking place in the country more responsive to the needs of the music economy. Controlling property rights is an important aspect of Western cultural industries, and means that large record companies or media conglomerates manage information, communication, and the commodification of popular culture (Bettig 1996). In Tanzania, the law remains less all-encompassing due to the lack of regularization or enforcement in the law. This has potential benefits for the music economy since it leaves ownership, rights, and property in the hands of locally based companies and individuals.

## PIRACY À LA MODE

The increased focus on composers and ownership has brought some additional financial benefits to musicians. The Copyright Society of Tanzania (COSOTA) collects fees from any business that broadcasts music, including hotels, buses, broadcast media, or supermarkets. It also registers the works of copyright holders in the country. By 2010, nine hundred people had registered with COSOTA and over $250,000 in royalties have been distributed over the previous eight years. The royalty payments have led to some contention between bands and artists over who actually composes songs, as well as questions over the collection and distribution of royalties by COSOTA. Generally, however, many argue that the royalties have not significantly altered people's relations to music because the payments remain rather limited. If the royalties are split between nine hundred people over eight years, each person only receives $35 per year. Since there are hierarchies of royalty payments based on the frequency of radio airplay or the number of songs that artists register, these royalty payments fluctuate considerably. Remmy Ongala's payment of $121 on August 25, 2006, represents a high royalty payment. Still, the final amount pales in comparison to the payouts by distributors of locally recorded music.

COSOTA has made attempts to introduce reforms in the distribution of cassettes. In a 2005 draft bill, for instance, the organization introduced legislation to have all cassettes sold or imported into Tanzania affixed with an official *hakigram* seal. A hakigram is typically a holographic sticker, difficult to reproduce, that would need to be affixed to any audio-visual recording sold in the country. Under the legislation, a cassette lacking a *hakigram* would be grounds for any audio-visual material to be seized and destroyed. Though the draft bill was discussed in Tanzanian Parliament in 2006, it has not materialized in any effective way within Tanzania's music economy.[27]

The most significant obstacle for the enforcement of copyright law, particularly in the distribution of music, is in the country's legal system. If an artist wants to take a case to court, he or she faces expensive legal fees and a failing court system. Magistrates are underpaid and sometimes even run out of paper on which to write out their verdicts. There are no stenographers, and the judges have to take all the notes of a case by themselves. Many magistrates, lawyers, and clerks take bribes and kickbacks. Clerks, for instance, are sometimes paid to lose or temporarily misplace files. Police falsely arrest people and receive a kickback from magistrates once the accused pays to win his or her release (Widner 2001: 276). Corruption in Tanzanian courts has been a problem since the 1970s, and efforts have been made—particularly the adoption of the American Bar Association's Canons of Judicial Ethics, and the dismissal of judicial personnel—to hinder its development (Widner 2001: 282). Yet it remains a problem, particularly for financially strapped artists who often do not have the resources to push/bribe their way into the courts.

Even more problematic is that only a handful of significant intellectual property rights cases have ever made it into Tanzanian courts. On July 3, 1995, the Tanzanian High Court case deliberated a trademark case between Tanzania Distillers Limited and Vitamin Foods Ltd. The case examined infringement in the names that the companies used to market liquor gin, Konyagi and Ginyagi, respectively. The confusing verdict ruled that the similarity of Ginyagi to the Konyagi was not a trademark violation. In civil case no. 295 of 1999, Cable Television Network (CTV) Limited brought a case against Star Cable TV Network Limited for infringing CTV's exclusive right to broadcast television programs from Sony Entertainment Television. A handful of other intellectual property cases were heard in the High Court of Tanzania, but they did not establish any precedence for judges and lawyers to interpret copyright law and music in Tanzania.

More recently, several lawsuits have been filed against businesses illegally dubbing cassettes, using artwork in a calendar without the artists' permission, or photocopying books. Many of these cases are settled out of court or not settled at all, which limits the legal discussion over copyright and musical rights. Nonetheless, the regularity with which court cases are emerging, at least in Dar es Salaam, suggests that there is increased awareness to intellectual property rights. The most important of these may be a 2004 lawsuit that revealed the future of music distribution in Tanzania and a significant fallibility in the timing of copyright legislation. The case was against a secretarial store that sold office supplies and provided photocopying services. The charge was that the store allowed customers to purchase compact discs of pirated music: anyone could enter the store, select songs from a handwritten list, and leave with a compilation compact disc of current hit songs.[28] The lawsuit claimed that the store infringed the rights of hundreds of artists whose music was found on the store's computer.

The lawsuit against the secretarial store brought attention to a new form of piracy that is occurring with greater frequency than in those discussed in previous sections of this chapter. Whereas a group of distributors controlled the sale of cassette tapes in the past, the contemporary practice can be done by anyone with a computer. Businesses and individuals throughout Dar es Salaam can participate in this informal economy with little investment or knowledge. The technology allows for flexibility and innovative, central characteristics of creative practices. It fits people's desires to purchase and own recorded music, particularly songs that appear on the radio but have yet to be released in a sound recording. Compact discs mixed at stores are also less expensive than original compact discs sold in the market. Since more people are interested in purchasing better quality sound recordings but cannot afford the high costs of originals, the new form of piracy fits people's desires for high quality, affordable audio products.

Here is the way the current situation works: an artist records a song at a recording studio. The artist leaves while the song is being mixed down. The producer or someone else who has access to the recording studio takes the finished recording and places it on a compact disc or other media format. The song is then given to a worker at local internet cafes or secretarial stores. Through word of mouth, people hear about the stores that are able to get the best new songs, often before they appear on the radio. A customer can purchase a compact disc of a variety of music for $2, which is a fifth of the price for an original compact disc. The purchased disc then often goes to other stores throughout Dar es Salaam and other areas of the country.

Radio staff are also implicated in the movement of songs in the local music economy. Since they frequently have access to a wealth of the latest songs in the market, they easily sell a variety of music to local distributors. There has even been an emergence of young people with laptop computers that start businesses selling pirated songs to friends, family, and classmates. A friend of mine even told me about an office supply company that provides free mixed CDs of pirated music to customers who enter the store.

Even though some stores and businesses have been fined for these forms of digital piracy, the business is so profitable that it is unlikely to wane anytime soon. COSOTA filed five lawsuits in 2010 against people illegally selling music, but there appears to be little if any effect on the sale of pirated digital files. So many people sell digital files that there is recognition that no amount of law enforcement could stop all of them. Since it takes little effort to acquire a database of Tanzanian music, the benefits of earning a steady income outweighs fear of any risks involved. There are even several websites that provide bundled downloads of hundreds of Tanzanian songs for free. These websites allow Tanzanians with computers to keep their data stored offsite, which can then be downloaded and saved for customers by request. At this time, no law enforcement agency would be capable of prosecuting such practices in Tanzanian courts.

Unlike in the past, when piracy helped to create a consumer interest in recorded music and expanded the economic potential of popular music, the current effort by so many individuals (deejays, announcers, producers, students, business people) has the potential to create an entirely different outcome. The creative practices of so many individuals may push for the return of recorded music as a vehicle of publicity. Even in Western music economies, there is recognition that album sales will remain less profitable than in the past despite legislation, lawsuits, and software aimed to prevent illegal downloading in music. While legitimate digital music sales increased significantly since the mid-2000s, many American and European record companies and artists have focused on making profits through touring, merchandising, music publishing, and licensing music for movies, commercials, and video games. A similar trend could emerge in Tanzania if digital piracy remains endemic and other avenues of financial profit emerge in the commodification of popular music.

### SOLD OUT

In this ethnography, I have argued that creative practices emerge due to people taking advantage of the increased commodification of social and economic resources. Of the creative practices discussed here, including performance strategies, marketing identities, repositioning, self-learning, payola, and branding, piracy may be the most responsive to the economic conditions of Tanzania. The cost of technology continues to decline to the point where many enterprising individuals can afford inexpensive software and hardware to duplicate music. They can then network to attain music singles and sell those singles on compact discs throughout Dar es Salaam, Tanzania, or eastern Africa. Little knowledge or expertise is needed other than to learn to operate the software on a computer that can burn files to a disc. Law enforcement is still unaware of many parameters in copyright law, and there is little investment in measures to hinder the practice. Among those who practice piracy, there are no taxes, job training skills, or other impediments to social advancement. The potential for profits is, quite frankly, stunning considering investments of time and energy. Piracy is the simplest and most effective creative practice currently taking place in the music economy.

Even though piracy initially expanded the commercialization of music in Tanzania, its continuation may undermine the future efficacy of the economy. The lucrative contracts that some artists sign with distributors could disappear as music sellers lose their ability to control the sale of sound recordings. Concerts may return as the most prevalent form of musical income for artists in the music scene. And recorded music could become a form of publicity for getting people to buy other merchandise (shirts, posters, and so on) and attend concerts. It is ironic that the business of distributors could be undermined by a practice that initially brought them financial and economic success.

Several efforts are underway to halt digital piracy. In a speech in January 2010 at an event promoting the use of mosquito nets, President Jakaya

Kikwete talked about forming a task force between the police, the Ministry of Industries and Trade, the Tanzania Revenue Authority (TRA), and COSOTA to halt or hinder piracy in the country. The Department for International Development (DFID), a part of the United Kingdom government, has also given aid to local arts organizations that attempt to improve musicians' rights and hinder piracy. In partnership with Denmark, the Netherlands, and Sweden, they have established the Business Environment Strengthening for Tanzania Programme (BEST), which has, as of 2008, provided $19 million to support better business practices. The arts organization RULU Arts Promotion has received several grants from DFID to find strategies to limit piracy. Several discussions have also emerged about creating online stores where people could download songs for a fee.

Whereas other areas of the music economy have settled into some general relationships and patterns in the commodification of popular music, music distribution remains volatile and likely to impact all other areas of the economy in the future. Considering that several African music economies suffered from the illegal sale of music by Tanzanian distributors, which helped the growth of Tanzania's music scene, the less demarcated borders of contemporary piracy may have the effect of limiting the growth of music in African contexts that remain unable to control content distributed by foreign internet sites. However, given the adaptive and creative strategies used to find economic wealth in the music scene, it is likely that the growth in digital piracy will push performers, composers, radio stations, promoters, producers, and others to search for alternative means to benefit from music as both a commodity and a work of art.

# EIGHT

# Everything Is Life

The world is harsh.
My father said,
"I see that now and I agree.
Others prefer to be happy,
When they hear someone has died.
People's death is planned by God."
I ask the Almighty to give me life.

—NDALA KASHEBA "Dunia Msongamano"
(The World Is Harsh, PURL 8.1)

Scholars often divide African history into succinct periods, such as pre-colonial, colonial, post-colonial, and post-socialist, based on the influence of outside forces on internal peoples. The bulk of this externally based periodization revolves around the concept of colonial, and many authors draw our attention to the domination and power of Western states in African contexts. In contemporary writing on Africa, a similar method is used, but rather than focus attention on Western governments, globalization scholarship is concerned with processes and flows that transform African cultures (the "local") to the point where they become riddled with the ideas, symbols, practices, and language of powerful, unstoppable capitalist forces. Globalization, similar to colonialism, is often examined as processes of dramatic change, loss of traditional cultural practices, and the hegemony of capitalist paradigms that alter the local to the point where it is completely transformed. In discussing discourses of globalization, Stuart Hall states that there is an idea that "*everything* is transformed; *everything* is an outcast in the same way by the global processes. There isn't any local that isn't written, re-written through and through by the global. That just doesn't seem to me to be true. It doesn't ring true; I think it's a myth" (Hall 1999, his emphasis).

Few scholars would deny that the processes involved in colonialism and globalization impacted African peoples. These processes were distortions of power and identities where daily lives, interests, and desires took on new meanings (Ranger 1996). Thus, dividing time into periods based on external effectual patterns can be useful in identifying these larger distortions. Nevertheless, externally based periodization does run the risk, even if unintentional, of (1) seeing the past solely as a series of dramatic ruptures from one period to the next (i.e., from colonialism to independence and socialism to neoliberalization); (2) privileging the concepts of change and transformation over continuity and stasis; and (3) ignoring the cultural particulars of time from the perspective of local peoples who are imagined to be significantly impacted by dramatic ruptures. There are always cultural referents that connect the present with the past into a continuous expanse of subtle and dramatic changes. Even in periods of significant transformations, many routines, habits, beliefs, and cultural forms progress subtly and unevenly. Changes and stasis often coexist, which marks time as far more fluid and continuous than the notion of ruptures would suggest.

In articulating the importance of transitions, rather than dramatic ruptures, I want to emphasize that the processes of commodification evidenced in this ethnography are not new or unique to Tanzania's music economy. There is a long history to the role that demand, consumption, and economic systems have on individual choices and social relations within Africa. Even the notion that globalization fosters dramatically new forms of interaction misses the long history of trans-regional and global integration that has taken place in East Africa (Prestholdt 2008). Illustrated in this ethnography are many relationships that Tanzanians have had with foreign and regional musical forms, such as military music, ballroom dance, rumba, soul, r&b, soukous, and rap. Consumption of music in recorded form dates to the 1920s when gramophones first started appearing in the region with regularity. Even the trading of musical instruments in eastern Africa, a process that no doubt has a long history even among pre-colonial populations, illustrates transitions in people's relationships with musical production and consumption. This long history of global engagement brings regular and consistent attention to alternative sounds, ideas, and experiences that become intertwined within everyday practices of people's lives. It also presents a longer expanse of time to the emergence of Tanzania's contemporary music economy.

This is not to deny that there is something unique about global interactions in the contemporary period. Other scholars point out the dramatic acceleration of global interactions, as the internet, cell phones, and global satellite broadcasts compress time and distance, making communication and consumption more expansive (Inda and Rosaldo 2002). This combination of compression and expansion reshapes people's interactions. Even in this ethnographic research, the distance between me and my Tanzanian colleagues has shifted over the twelve years of my research. In 1998, when I first conducted interviews in Dar es Salaam, my only means to contact people was through going to peoples homes or setting up meetings through an intermediary contact. Only a handful of people had telephones in their homes. In March 2010, however, I am able to e-mail and phone the majority of people who appear in this study. This fosters new bonds and relationships. It makes asking questions and clarifying details far easier. Yet it does not establish altogether new experiences or logics of social interaction. While I have become closer to many people in my research due to our ability to maintain contact with one another, I remain a researcher asking questions. My colleagues remain the experts. There is continuity even in the significant technological changes taking place.

The current transitions occurring around music provide a means to interpret people's relationship to past and present conceptualizations of cultural forms. The production and consumption of music is inexorably imitative, rooted in the practices, habits, and cultural beliefs of predecessors, yet they are also innovative in the reimagining of songs as commodities. To look for transitions is to interpret shifts in people's desires, demands, and relationships to cultural forms. Transitions may be more useful for interpreting alterations and innovations to people's daily lives than for examining rupture or more dramatic events that represent transformations in everyday forms of interaction.

In the remainder of this chapter, I examine five transitions that evidence broader movements in the commodification of arts that is taking place in many parts of Africa. These transitions look toward future outcomes in the commodification of music in urban societies and suggest issues that will most significantly impact the production and consumption of artistic forms. In arguing for the notion of transitions, evidence of future outcomes should already be visible in the subtle shifts taking place now. Future outcomes are decipherable in contemporary practices through examining the patterns, concerns, and struggles within contemporary societies.

The first transition is the increasing formality of interactions between individuals in the commodification of arts. Economies establish relationships between many individuals seeking to benefit from artistic forms. Due to the increasing profitability of the arts, there is a concomitant effort to make casual relationships more formal. Transactions need to include contracts or other formal agreements; conceptions of property, ownership, and individual rights become a focus of attention; and regimes of accumulation greatly inform the extent of formality being considered. The competitive pursuit of profit pushes people to create new forms of interaction that define relationships in terms of what should be instead of what could be. By this I mean to suggest that formality brings more expectations to people's relationships than casual agreements that are relational, active, and ongoing.

Turning to the Tanzanian music economy, several chapters of this ethnography illustrate increased formality: the rise of managers creating formal relationships with musicians; payola; distribution contracts; and contracts signed within bands. Associations that could have been formed in verbal agreements or casual conversations in the past are now replete with formally negotiated contracts. This encourages additional regulation in preserving the interests of each person's contractual agreements. Further, there is evidence that these official associations lead to disagreements, threats of court cases, and potential lawsuits. In the opening to this ethnography, I mention that lawyers are mostly absent from the Tanzanian music economy. In the escalating directives of negotiations and contracts, their presence may grow and add an additional layer of regulations in the commercialization of music.

To illustrate the increasing formality of associations in the music economy, particularly in the way that many areas of the music economy become intertwined, I use part of an interview with a radio station director about his attempts to work with a local musician in putting on a show:

I was asked to put on a show by [a large international institution] and they
wanted a young Tanzanian rapper to do a hip-hop song. So I contacted
Msela X [a pseudonym] and I told him what it was. He said, "Talk to my
manager." So I said, "I know you, Msela X, I'm talking to you." He says,
"No, no, talk to my manager." I said, "Your manager negotiates the fee?"
He says, "Yes." "You don't want to know how much?" "No." Okay, fine,
management. I call the guy, he negotiates five minutes [for the length of the
composition] half a million shillings [$500] for a single song. I tell him it
is too much, and for three or four days we barter. Eventually, I have to put
on somebody and Msela X is the best ; he has the best song out in the past
year. So, I agree with the manager. I call Msela X, he asks how much, and he
agrees. Though I ask him, as a friend, "Do you think that you could help me
reduce the amount a little because I have other commitments with the budget that I was given." He says, "No." He explains to me that the money goes
to him, his manager, his original musical group, and his producer. That's
four people he has to split $500. I don't know the percentages, but Msela X
is seriously losing out.

Five years earlier, the director's relationship and interaction with Msela
X would have only involved Msela X. A contract may have been used
between the radio station director and the international institution, but
there would not have been negotiations with other people involved. The
radio station program director was frustrated by the many layers of contracts, since they were impersonal and limited the capabilities of those
who put on shows. Most important, the director was quick to point out
the financial losses of Msela X, who composes and performs his own work
yet receives only a share of the income.

Many artists have become increasingly frustrated by these complicated transactions (PURL 8.2 and PURL 8.3). Currently, the music economy, as well as other areas of society, frequently benefits those who are
most astute in negotiating their relationships and connections with others. Those who want only to compose and perform music find themselves
discouraged by the increasing commercialization and competition found
in music. Artists have held press conferences to discuss the problems
and even retired from music in frustration. Others have changed their
names to get out of manipulative contracts. In another self-destructive
act, artists have recorded several consecutive albums within a short period of time in order to get out of the terms of their contracts. The impact
of these changes may be the loss of talented performers who cannot man-

TABLE 8.1. IPP Media Holdings

| Television | Newspapers and Publishing | New Media |
|---|---|---|
| ITV | The Guardian | ippmedia.com |
| CS East Africa TV | This Day | darhotwire.com |
| Pulse Africa TV | Financial Times | elimuimara.com |
| Channel M (Uganda) | Sunday Observer | |
| | Evening News | **Other** |
| **Radio** | Nipashe | Press Services Tanzania |
| Radio One | Nipashe Jumapili | Starfish Mobile East Africa |
| Sky FM | Alasiri | (Mobile Marketing) |
| Capitol One FM | Lete Rahe | U&I Entertainment |
| East Africa FM | Kasheshe | |
| | Komesha | |

age to both compose music and negotiate legal agreements with so many people. In these situations, power may fall to managers, radio station staff, and others who can formalize relationships with all interested parties and find economic benefits in musical commodities.

Coinciding with the formation of more formal business relationships is the transition toward media and entertainment conglomerates. Already discussed in the previous chapters is the decline of state control in media, recording studios, and other areas that has led to the proliferation of privately owned companies. The businesses that were able to capitalize on privatization early on formed strong empires that steadily expanded. IPP Media Holdings, started by Reginald Mengi in the 1990s, is the largest conglomeration of media formats in Tanzania. Featuring eight television and radio stations, as well fourteen newspapers and other media, IPP Media controls a significant stake in the local music economy (see table 8.1). In Dar es Salaam alone, IPP Media shapes a considerable amount of the information and ideas heard and seen in a given day. It has a much more public presence than most other media businesses in the city and nation as a whole.

Other companies also have a significant stake in local media. Classic FM Radio, Magic FM, Channel Ten Television, Dar Es Salaam Television (DTV), C2C Television, and Coastal Television Network (CTN) are controlled by the same seven stakeholders.[1] Clouds FM Entertainment operates a popular radio station, PrimeTime Promotions, *Kitangoma* magazine, and Mawingu Studio, as well as other media enterprises.

The dominance of these institutions allows them to shape and direct significant policies that impact the local music economy. For instance, the ability of promoters to put on successful shows depends on the support of one or more of these media conglomerates. Without advertising on the radio and television, audiences are unlikely to hear about an upcoming show. Numerous independent promoters who refuse to work with media conglomerates have ended up with poor attendance at their events. Even a hip-hop concert by an international superstar failed to draw a large audience due to the promoter's inability to attain the support of media conglomerates.

The privatization of media brought a plurality of voices and content to broadcasting in Tanzania and other African countries. It also exacerbated unequal power relations between producers and users of the media. The analysis of payola and radio station managers found in chapter 4 illustrates this point. The contradiction within neoliberalism is that there is an allowance for the formation of media monopolies that have significant authority in local markets, while a simultaneous effort is made to support increased competition and a celebration of individual freedoms (Freedman 2008). Individual agency depends on relations with people in positions of power, which does not provide a means to attain the level playing field imagined in neoliberal economic reforms. Whereas during socialism, state control required adaptation to a political vision of development, the privatization of media encourages financial investment, social networks, and political savvy to participate. In both contexts, the prominence of media significantly influences the content of popular culture and the interaction between musicians and the airwaves. It also creates opportunities for radio staff to undermine the ability of musicians, listeners, and others to freely participate in the broadcasting of music.

A third transition occurring around music is perhaps the most significant: the conceptualization of songs as property that can benefit society creatively and economically. One of the key ideas repeated within institutional publications is that better protection of intellectual property rights produces more creativity and, thus, more economic wealth. The argument generally states that by providing people the potential to benefit from their creations, they will be able to continue their creative endeavors. If economic benefits are restricted, then authors, musicians, and artists need to look for other sources of income, thereby limiting their productivity. Greenfield Chilongo, executive director of the Zimbabwean Reproduction Rights Organization, writes, "The works worthy of copyright protection have been produced. All that remains is for the rightsholders to be committed and steadfast in their effort to encourage Governments to create a conducive legal framework for the effective protection of copyright and mobilize users for economic support. With that the drive to develop a sustainable creativity culture in Africa will be guaranteed" (2003: 1). Many institutions and governments that promote intellectual property legislation follow a similar argument in connecting control of intellectual property with creative and economic benefits. Between 1999 and 2007, for instance, this connection was made in over one thousand World Intellectual Property Organization (WIPO) documents.

What are the real benefits of copyright law to creativity? Is there truly a connection between copyright law, economic benefits, and increased creativity? In the United States, which has conducted extensive legislative deliberation of copyright law, the answer is rather unclear. Considering that many musicians no longer rely on the sales of their music to support their careers but rather use touring and merchandising, it is difficult to convincingly argue that copyright law supports enough economic incentives to spur on creativity. The ethnomusicologist Anthony Seeger puts it more succinctly by stating that the litigation over musical ideas actually stifles the musical creative process (1991, 1992, and 2006). In Ghana, John Collins writes about families paying a tax to play traditional music that has passed down through the generations, which limits the amount that performers can do creatively (1993). Similar hindrances are placed on directors, writers, and musicians in many other contexts throughout the world (Arledge 2009; Guy 2003; Jaszi 1992; McCann 2002). This raises the question as to whether copyright laws benefit, alter, or restrict the way artists are able to create new works. Does copyright law promote or stifle creativity? And could copyright law undermine the ability of artists to continue to strengthen the music economy?

The introduction of Trade-Related Aspects of Intellectual Property Rights (TRIPS), a World Trade Organization (WTO) agreement, further complicates the notion of property. Under the TRIPS agreement, the WTO requires countries to update their intellectual property laws (trademark, patent, and copyright law) in order to be recognized as a potential trading partner. A country that fails to meet the requirements of TRIPS "can find itself taken to a dispute settlement panel and, ultimately, subject to the possibility of trade sanctions if it fails to put matters right" (Koroye-Crooks 1999: 2; see also Kongolo 1999). Given the desire by many African countries to open trade routes with other parts of the world, most opt to pass new legislation that meets the requirements of the WTO. Yet many argue that the reason African countries are being encouraged to pass new legislation is to protect Western forms of property. Susan Sell (2003), for instance, writes that TRIPS emerged through the lobbying of powerful multinational corporations that sought to protect their interests. Other scholars call for strong copyright legislation in international laws to protect copyright owners across national boundaries (Goldstein 2003: 210). A significant debate has therefore emerged between those that view these laws as a new form of imperialism and those that see them as an opportunity to promote and safeguard the interests of all copyright holders.

In disputes emerging over ownership, it is clear that musicians are altering their conception and valuation of music to accommodate copyright law. There is a strong desire to earn money from song compositions, which is leading to more direct forms of possession over those songs. Frowin Nyoni, lecturer in the Department of Fine and Performing Arts at the University of Dar es Salaam, states:

> The transformation from centralized economy to free market economy has tremendous impact on artists and artistic practices in Tanzania. The free market economy is a significant move from the earlier communal-based artistic production and performance processes when the arts were communal property and no one could claim copyright. Today the arts are individual properties and have become economical assets and tools that help one to survive in the existing free market economy. No other time has copyright been so crucial to the development of the arts and artists as now.[2]

The ideas that music has moved from communal to individual ownership is a prominent argument in conceptualizations of African music. Elsewhere, I argue that the notion of communalism misses the diverse relationships to music that existed before copyright law (Perullo 2008c). The notion of communalism is an imagined ideal that seeks to remove local-level interests and claims in the rights of song compositions. Nonetheless, Nyoni's point illustrates the broader significance of the introduction of copyright laws: these laws encourage artists to reconsider their position in relation to song compositions. This alters the way songs are composed (as a group or individually); the role of imitation in popular music; the use of sampling in song compositions, and the interests of artists in ensuring that they are compensated for the use of their songs. While economic benefits do encourage artists to protect their music more, creativity often appears to be undermined. Quoting other artists musically or lyrically in a song composition can be creative, but it is also illegal in the contemporary music scene. Given that most Tanzanian music, like all forms of popular song, emerges through imitation, notions of ownership can restrict the ability of artists to create new songs.

What is at stake in the promotion of copyright law in Tanzania is a potential conflict between compositional strategies of the past and present. Copyright law does not promote creativity but provides additional support of musical careers. This is important for many musicians and artists who are looking to depend increasingly on their song compositions and music recordings for financial wealth. Yet if delineations defined by copyright legislation in the United States and Europe were produced in Tanzania, then many popular songs in Tanzania would be considered as infringing upon other people's works. Tanzanian artists argue that a separation needs to emerge that would allow them to benefit from songs they compose and record, but also grant them the freedom to imitate, sample, and borrow, which would help to create a more diverse and interesting body of compositions. Creativity and economic viability should not, in other words, be mixed together. They are separate considerations that need to be based on context and cultural significance in order to allow ownership and authorship to become more responsive to formations of popular music forms.

A fourth transition in the contemporary music economy relates to musicianship. There has been a movement in popular music from performance on instruments, such as guitars, drum sets, and wind instruments, to electronic-based music, generated by keyboards, computers, and drum machines. The dansi singer Kasongo Mpinda Clayton explains that, in the past, people knew more about performing and playing music, but musicians now really do not know music or instruments. Music now is about business and not as much about learning a craft. Kasongo's point is often made by the older generation of Tanzanian artists concerned about the future of popular music in the country. What happens when people want something other than digitized sounds? What if few musicians are able to play any instruments well? Will the music economy simply collapse? Or will the digital composition of music with computers, synthesizers, and sampling become the status quo for popular music?

The central critique of many of these narratives is toward youth music, particularly bongo flava. The incorporation of rap, ragga, and r&b into Tanzanian music has created two divergent outcomes. The first is that youth attention to bongo flava is part of the reason that a prosperous music economy emerged in Tanzania. Most recording studios and several radio stations formed around the genre bongo flava. Thousands of young people gravitated toward the music because it required no financial investment. Only an ability to compose quality lyrics and keep time with the music (beats) mattered. There was no need to buy an instrument, study with an instructor, or spend several years as the backup musician to other band members. Artists could write a few rhymes at home or school and perform them at local shows regardless of age, class, religion, or race (gender did matter in the early years of bongo flava). It also connected Tanzanian youth to notions of power, wealth, and fame that they heard and saw in foreign songs and videos. Bongo flava gave many young people the ability to openly speak about their problems and attain a broad audience of people who shared similar interests.

A second outcome of the interest in bongo flava is a movement away from performance and musical practices associated with post-independence Tanzanian society. Several musicians and radio deejays argue that a generational gap has emerged between those who grew up watching and learning music from their families and the current generation that conceptualizes music differently. Bongo flava artists frequently hone their verbal and singing skills in isolation without participating with anyone else. The overwhelming focus is on the voice as an instrument at the cost of other forms of instrumental and social communication. Bongo flava musicians, as well as many muziki wa injili (gospel) artists, perform live shows over pre-recorded music. The stage is bare except for a few singers and dancers. There are no drummers, guitarists, or other musicians to provide live musical interaction. For many members of the music community, this is a concern as they believe it to be a weakening of the relationship between artists and music. Without physical instruments that performers use to communicate with one another and the audience, the engagement with music is far weaker and less emotional. Digital sound cannot replicate the direct forms of interaction of live instruments.

Those who deal with cultural policy in Tanzania share similar sentiments about the state of music in the country. In the 2001 Cultural Development Master Plan for Tanzania (see chapter 1), the authors levy their strongest critiques at bongo flava music. They write that bongo flava artists have a misconception that by aping foreign music, they will gain contracts with foreign companies and keep up with the times. The authors continue: "In this self-delusion they regard Tanzanian indigenous traditional stage performance art as a closed chapter—a thing of the past, something to be ashamed of. They vie to beat the Americans in 'rap' and 'hip-hop' music and export Tanzanian versions 'Rhythms and Blues' music to Europe! The Master Plan seeks to rectify this degrading situation by placing control measures which will restore the humane characteristic of Tanzanian stage performance art."[3] While the state has always attempted to foster more interest in traditional music, the exasperated gasp of this paragraph points to a more significant rift between policy makers and bongo flava youth culture. Even though there is little that the state can do to rectify the situation, there is a strong sense of frustration in the Master Plan that suggests both the failure of previous state policies meant to promote traditional over foreign cultural forms and the continued conception that all things foreign are problematic.

Many young people present a different interpretation of the interest in bongo flava. There is an argument that bongo flava resembles many traditional forms of music with rhythms underneath and singing on top. Rap music, in other words, is modern ngoma. Artists mention in interviews that the first time they heard rap music they were reminded of ngoma songs. Even government employees, though obviously not the authors of the Master Plan, told me that many rap songs resemble ngoma in terms of rhythm and the interaction of the lyrics with the music. The song "Are U Down" by the Deplowmatz plays on this idea: "Deplowmatz, We bring serious fever / Like modern ngoma / For the current generation."

In addition, the interest in bongo flava is not so much imitation of the West as being included in the international dialogues among youth. Rap and r&b are not just popular in the United States and Tanzania, but exist in most parts of the world. To not be a part of that conversation would be to undermine critical forms of interaction that take place among youth globally. By performing and writing music, the current generation is more usefully able to situate Tanzanian music in a much larger cultural sphere. If they did not participate, Tanzanians might be left out of this dialogue and consider themselves alienated in global forms of musical interaction.

Returning to Kasongo's point about declines in musical knowledge, however, many youths agree: younger artists know less about music than those of previous generations. They also add several key points. The movement toward digital technology is a response to the lack of instruments, instruction, and state policies aimed at supporting other creative endeavors. Any time workshops occur in Dar es Salaam to teach people about how to play an instrument, hundreds of youths sign up. The desire exists among youth to learn more about music. They want to play instruments; they want to have a chance to study with other artists. Youths argue that the framework and opportunities for musical study are nonexistent in the contemporary music economy.

Problematically, in many parts of Africa, there have been fundamental declines in musical knowledge due to a lack of educational policies that could replace traditional forms of apprenticeship and musical instruction. In some places, traditional forms of learning are being replaced by more business interactions (Reed 2003: 40), while in others they are not being replaced at all. The Tanzanian musician Waziri Ally draws attention to the cultural issues facing Tanzania's future music economy:

> The number of musicians with musical expertise—either a lot or a little— keeps declining in Tanzania. There are only a few artists that have the urge to put effort into studying music. This means that musicians in the current generation, who will be the ones handling music [in the music economy], do not genuinely know music well. I do not agree with people who say that the contemporary music is bad. This is not true for all music must change. It is, however, essential that musical expertise and knowledge continues so that as the music changes it continues to get better. What makes me the most disappointed is the removal of music classes in primary and secondary schools. It is important that the government looks into this so that musical studies return to school syllabi. It is ironic that there is a College of Arts (Bagamoyo College of Arts) in Tanzania that teaches about all of the arts including music, but these same studies have been obliterated from the pre-college education system. It is critically important for the government to return music education to primary and secondary school so that young musicians can better learn about music.

The band Mambo Poa and the security guard Francis Mlomwezi in a staged shot for an album cover. *Photo by author.*

In many other parts of the world, music education is also in decline. The difference is that for-profit and a non-profit arts sector has emerged in these areas to provide more substantive forms of musical learning. With the exception of arts organizations on Zanzibar, mainland Tanzania has very little to offer young people. The Tanzanian Cultural Trust does provide funding for several arts initiatives, including musical training for disadvantage youth. These would need to be dramatically expanded to compensate for the waning forms of musical knowledge that people argue is occurring in the country.

The last transition expands on music to address broader issues of living in Tanzanian society. My purpose here is to explore one of the constant concerns among many people living in Tanzania: the rise of insecurities associated with daily life. In numerous interviews and conversations, people talk about increasing anxieties due to competition for resources and access to opportunities. While recognizing that living in Dar es

} Fetishization

Salaam or other African cities has always been difficult, many argue that the significant attention toward consumption is leading to an erosion or alteration of interpersonal relationships. It is more difficult to rely on family and friends than it was in the past. Competition has led to animosity, jealousy, and, as evidenced on several occasions, violence. Perhaps most significant, many people believe that living—avoiding death—is becoming increasingly complicated by the competition for resources, the decline in healthcare, the increase in life-threatening illnesses and crime, and other trends in contemporary urban society. My interest is not to determine that life is harder now than in the past, but to illustrate the increasing anxieties emerging in African societies.

I staged the accompanying photograph that features the bongo flava group Mambo Poa being questioned by the security guard Francis Mlomwezi to help promote the band's album *Mimi sio Mwizi* (I Am Not a Thief), which featured a hit song of the same title in the early 2000s. The photograph used to make me laugh every time I looked at it. All the people in the image were friends of mine, and the process of staging it on a Sunday morning was filled with many antics as we wandered the streets of downtown Dar es Salaam imagining ideas for an album cover. The morning became more comical as we kept getting caught in massive downpours. Luckily, each of the band members brought several outfits to change into, which allowed them to appear dry in each photo session.

I worked closely with Mambo Poa for a number of years; each of the band members provided different vantage points of the music scene. Steve 2K, from Arusha, was one of the few people in the 1990s performing in the Jamaican ragga style, which is now popular in eastern Africa. Spider was an r&b style singer who got his start in Dar es Salaam recording studios. And John Mjema was a pop-oriented rap artist who also worked at the state house. I was with the group early in their careers and was able to watch them move from relative unknowns to popular artists. I documented their preparation for shows, their interactions with fans, and their movements in the music economy (PURL 8.4). Tracking everything from their formation to their eventual breakup years later, I received tremendous insight into the workings of a young group of artists attempting to make a career in music.

Looking at the image of Mambo Poa now, I am left with only great sadness. Steve 2K, recognized as one of the kindest musicians in Dar es

Salaam, was stabbed to death in 2004. A drunk individual was harassing a young woman when Steve 2K stepped in to protect her. As a consequence, he was stabbed with the drunkard's knife and died of his wounds. In a memorial in the November-December 2004 issue of the music magazine *Kitangoma,* an advertisement appeared featuring Steve 2K dressed a kurta and a turban, which is traditional Punjabi dress for men. The advertisement read: "We loved you, we continue to treasure you, God rest your spirit in heaven Steve." Although Steve 2K was not Indian, his memorialization in Punjabi dress acknowledged his work with the Asian artist Akili and in particular their song "Regina." In the song, Steve 2K dresses and dances in Punjabi style. He is considered the first bongo flava musician to cross over between Asians and Africans in Dar es Salaam. The effect was powerful and the song was expected to have a lasting impact on the two communities, particularly as Akili and Steve 2K planned to perform and record additional songs together.

Four years later, in another great tragedy, John Mjema died in uncertain circumstances. The newspapers reported that he took his own life by cutting his throat with a knife because he was frustrated that he was not famous enough. His was the first instance of reported suicide that I had heard in Tanzania. Most people told me that though uncommon, the pressures of the music economy and desires of fame can be extreme. In response to Mjema's suicide, Afande Sele said, "I understand that he died from seeing that the state of his life was not going according to the work he was doing in society. This is the reason that he came to the decision to take his own life."[4] Sele drew attention to the desire that people have to achieve success and the belief that hard work can bring significant rewards. Often imagining those rewards can also bring great disappointment. Mjema was thirty when he died.

During my research in Tanzania, over forty people I worked with passed away, many involving tragic circumstances. The elders Ndala Kasheba, Patrick Balisidya, Khalid Ponera, Gaudens Makunja, Michael Enoch, DJ Kim, and Nasma Khamis Kidogo all passed away soon after I worked with them; car accidents took the life of Simon Sayi (Complex), Issa Matona, and James Dandu (Mtoto wa Dandu); disease carried away far too many for me to list.[5] Once I sat in the dansi musician Shem Karenga's house as he showed me a photograph of his band MK Band. Most of the people in the image were smiling after just finishing a successful performance. I asked Karenga to tell me the names of everyone in the band. As he did, he also mentioned who had died and how they had died. When he finished, I went over the list and realized that, out of fourteen members of the group, only three were still alive. The photograph was not that old. I looked at Karenga and asked how this was possible. He stared at the photograph for a moment and said nothing.

Death may be the ultimate struggle in life. The struggle is to avoid its approach, its quickness, its appetite. Creative practices are not just a means to get by in any basic sense. They are also a means to prolong the inevitable that appears all too often in Tanzania. The Tanzanian expression "Everything is life" is meant to suggest that even death is part of the way people live. It is part of life. Ndala Kasheba's sings, "Hata nikifa,sitamaliza vifo, wala sijazi ardhi / Nitakwenda kwenye kaburi langu mwenyewe / Usiwe na wasiwasi na wewe la kwako lipo / Sababu na wewe pia ni marehemu mtarajiwa, linakusubiri" (Even if I die, I will not cease living or being a part of this land / I will only go into my grave / Do not worry, your grave is also there / Since you are also expected, it waits for you").

Despite the prominence of death and anxiety over living, there remains an undercurrent of hopefulness. Though Tanzanian friends cautioned me not to confuse hope with happiness, creative practices suggest more than just strategies used to get by, but also the potential for believing that alternatives exist. People's hopes motivate them to trust that options, an escape, or a better future are available to them. Even for those who do not have economic and social security, hope remains an important means for ensuring future health and security. It is a form of desire that depends on the agency of something else: God, fate, chance, and so on (Crapanzano 2003: 6). It counters the many inconsistencies, strains, and unknowns that make up urban life in Dar es Salaam and elsewhere in the world.

Even though people talk about having hope or being hopeful, it is difficult to accurately capture what that means. Hope is contextually based and dependent on too many factors to derive an accurate consensus on why or how it appears. There is some research that suggests that people in Tanzania do not lose hope as often as people in other parts of the world, but these studies are far from conclusive and may be misleading.[6] When I spoke with people about being hopeful, they suggested that the continued connections between family, home, and community provides a means to counter the problems occurring in Tanzanian society. Eileen Moyer's work among street children in Dar es Salaam emphasizes the way that people who are highly transient and without permanent residence continually search for places to call home. There is a desire to fashion places of belonging, develop social networks, and find security in relationships with other people (Moyer 2003: chap. 7). Without those networks, there is a lack of security and interpersonal relationships that create happiness. Hope may be inspired by close networks with others, particularly family members, but it disappears quickly when those networks break down.

Over the past ten years, hopefulness has also been under attack through movements that undercut its legitimacy. It is difficult to ignore the way that many members of the Tanzanian music economy internalize notions of success, power, and prestige associated with the West. Desires for money, consumer goods, and fame push many to alter their worldview and their relations to others. Drawing on the work of Karl Marx, Henri Lefebvre writes, "Under capitalist regimes, 'to exist' and 'to have' are identical. 'The man who has nothing is nothing.' The man who has nothing finds himself 'separated from existence in general' and a fortiori from human existence; he is separated from that 'world of objects,' i.e. the real world, without which no human existence is possible" (2008: 155). Consumerism may be eroding the foundation that has kept Tanzanians hopeful through creating desires for things that are separate from the everyday interactions, bonds, and relationships that ultimately give meaning to people's existences. The decrease in social bonds leads to increased anxieties about daily life, aspirations, and livelihood.

People in Tanzanian society react to this movement away from personal to consumer relationships with frustration. While few articulate what should be done to counter increased anxieties, there are many who expose declines of interpersonal networks and social responsibility. In response to John Mjema's death, one person writes:

> All of the artists are hypocrites; they claim to be sad about the death
> of Mjema but the obvious truth is that they are hypocrites at best. While one
> of your own was having problem you failed to help him and you abandoned
> him without any shame. He needed comfort from you. But you love each

other only when money is involved. Once your fellow friend is not stable you abandoned him. You are supposed to have unity [umoja] and love in bad and good times. Mjema decided to take his life after realizing that his life had no value after you artists abandoned him.[7]

People's interests in money over relationships reflect the broader transition of citizens becoming consumers. The concomitant anxiety emerging from this movement is becoming deeply felt in the dissatisfaction people have within urban areas of society.

Music also frequently illustrates the conflicting shape of life in Tanzania. The Mvita Dancing Troupe's song "Haiwezekani" (It is not possible) illustrates anxieties of life in the tension over hopefulness and hopelessness (PURL 8.5).

| | |
|---|---|
| Haiwezekani (jaamani) | It's not possible (people) |
| Watanzania jitihada | Tanzanians [who are] diligent |
| Haitashindikana kumweza mwenyezi Mungu | It's not possible to praise the Lord |
| Inawezekana jaamani | It is possible people |
| Sote kwa pamoja | For us to go together |
| Tutashirikiana na ndugu nzetu tule nao | Let's work together as family and share a meal together |
| Aliyefariki dunia kwa ajili ya meli | S/he died in a boat accident |
| M.V. Bukoba kwenye Ziwa Victoria | M.V. Bukoba on Lake Victoria |
| Ili tuondoshe jamani katika harakati ya kuinua uchumi wa taifa letu | Come together people to make our national economy better |
| Taifa letu changa-eh. | Our nation is young [underdeveloped]. |

The song plays with two ideas: that Tanzanians should stand together and be hopeful that they can make the economy stronger. There is a brighter future ahead; it is possible. Yet death looms large as the singer expresses sadness at the loss of his mother in a ferry accident on Lake Victoria. The only reward may be that they can see God together. The opening word "haiwezekani" (it is not possible), however, has always struck me as ominous in that regard.

Collectively, the transitions discussed in this chapter reflect alterations occurring in people's relations to music and each other. They point to continued emphasis on valuing music as a commodity in relation to other people and global economic movements. They also point to weak-

Really?

High and low art (

nesses in improving on creativity of musical works. For instance, intellectual property rights restrict the potential of works to express people's interests in music and songs. And declines in musical education lead to less attention to imagination and expression within the arts. Could the future of music be an acceleration of commodity flows that ignore the importance of creativity within musical works? Might the significance of music as a social and cultural phenomenon be reduced solely to commodity flows in economies of music? While contemporary strategies continue to emphasize the economic relations of people to music, the cultural, emotional, and psychological attachments need to be addressed in order for music to become profitable. There is no work without commodity or commodity without work in contemporary music economies. The two ideas need to be supported and sustained for there to become increased opportunities in the transitions taking place within popular music.

Development debates have often failed to incorporate the importance of sustaining creativity and work in their discussions. The push for privatization and other neoliberal reforms focuses extensively on showing a need for something in the likeness of the West. Yet the changes associated with liberalization do not yield many benefits on the African continent, and have often led to the collapse of basic institutions and a rise in corruption (Ferguson 2006: 35). The push for people to attain something in the likeness of the West is no doubt a fallacy. Specific courses of action that development organizations take may only exacerbate problems in terms of understanding African peoples. Development, in other words, has helped to frame Africa in terms of powerlessness (poor, hungry, and illiterate) and helplessness without regarding people's own understanding of their social situations (Escobar 1995). Development may be trying too hard to save Africa without regarding people in different countries as intelligent and mindful of their own problems and, more important, their own solutions. They may not be looking for existing forms of creativity and innovation.

The Tanzanian music economy illustrates alternative forms of economic expansion that do not rely on models of development or foreign aid. True, the music economy would not have risen so dramatically without the insistence by foreign institutions that Tanzania privatize the media and allow for more open market practices. Yet the music economy may not have been as strong had multinationals or foreign businesses stepped in to establish a formal music industry that controlled the commodification of music. The success of radio, studio production, concert production, and the like is a product of people's creative practices and desires in forming an economy that is responsive to local issues and concerns. Illustrated in this ethnography is the success of the local music economy due in part to the structures provided across several political periods and through various cultural trends and movement.

Further, the creative practices illustrated in this ethnography undermine the notion that people in Tanzania sit around idly waiting for changes to come to them rather than creating strategies for bettering their lives. In May 2003, President Benjamin Mkapa spoke to a gathering of cabinet ministers, ambassadors, and members of the local business community in Dar es Salaam. According to reports on the event, Mkapa criticized the use of the term bongo. He stated that by using the term Bongoland instead of Tanzania, more youths were complacent in their activities, spending their days idly on the streets or waiting around for "miracles." In essence, he was arguing that the terms bongo and Bongoland had created a culture where people do not believe in work, but spend their days idly waiting for someone or something to help them.[8] Mkapa's administration pushed for neoliberal reforms, ushered in legislation aimed at appeasing international organizations, and entered into international agreements and partnerships. His critique of the term bongo came from his sense that too many people in the country, particularly youths, continued to believe that the government was going to do something for them instead of relying on their own knowledge to do something for themselves.

Attributing the country's problems to the use of the word bongo—instead of arguing that the country's problems resulted in the word—is an interesting tactic. Yet in this ethnography, the creative practices used by artists, producers, radio hosts, copyright officials, and many others show the dynamic use of resources that people employ to better their lives. These practices do not reflect a population waiting around for miracles. They emphasize the growing profitability of music and people's interests in finding ways to make a better living. As people engage with notions of profitability and commodification, there is a growing tendency to take advantage in any and all opportunities that become available. This is not just a result of deregulation but of an increased competition for resources and power that becomes emphasized, glorified, and sensationalized in the media, in conversations, and in people's everyday lives. The future success of music in Tanzania and other African countries depends on maintaining creativity within locally produced works that have cultural and economic benefits for local populations.

# Appendix A

## DESCRIPTIONS OF TANZANIAN GENRES OF MUSIC

In Tanzania, there are eight major genres of popular music: muziki wa injili (gospel music), muziki wa kwaya (choral music), muziki wa dansi (dance music), bongo flava or hip-hop (rap, ragga, and r&b), taarab (sung Swahili poetry), ngoma (traditional dance, drumming, and song), reggae, and mchiriku (electronic ngoma). Many other genres of music exist in Tanzania as well, such as brass band music (*tarumbeta*), performed at wedding ceremonies, particularly in Dar es Salaam, and military brass bands, used for political events and military affairs. A few steel pan groups also exist in public schools and other institutions, such as Jeshi la Kujenga Taifa (JKT, National Service Army). Finally, there are bands that perform at hotels and tourist attractions, usually playing cover songs or soft, slow versions of Tanzanian dansi hits. Here I provide explanations of the major genres of music in Tanzania, each of which plays an important part in Tanzania's music economy.

**Bongo flava** is a broad category that includes many internationally popular genres of music, such as rap, ragga, zouk, and r&b. Tanzanian youths use percussive beats of electronic studio productions—few artists use live bands—and rap in Swahili about issues they face in daily life. In the early period of Swahili-based rapping, most lyrics addressed social and political issues. A more current trend for rap, as well as r&b, is to sing about love, relationship, and sex, though a large portion of the population still discusses socially conscious issues. Many Tanzanian artists dislike the term bongo flava (also spelled bongo fleva), seeing it as a commercialized form of pop music. These groups prefer the term hip-hop, which they argue is a more authentic term for their music. Over two hundred rap groups and artists perform and record in Dar es Salaam, while hundreds more exist throughout the country. Thousands more, however, practice rap at school or at home, and compete with peers to decide who among them is the best rapper. For a history of rap in Tanzania, see Perullo 2007. Numerous publications have appeared since 2000 analyzing rap music in Tanzania. For a sample, see

Englert 2004; Haas and Gesthuizen 2000; Mangesho 2003; Ntarangwi 2009; Raab 2006; Remes 1998; Reuster-Jahn 2007; Saavedra 2006; and Suriano 2007. For video of bongo flava, see PURL A.1.

**Dansi** is a form of popular dance music that draws on Congolese rumba, Cuban son, traditional Tanzanian ngoma, and, historically, European ballroom dance. Dansi groups feature anywhere from ten to forty members depending on the number of backup musicians and dancers. The more classic dansi bands feature a horn section and a more relaxed dance beat. The contemporary dansi and Congolese-based groups use keyboards rather than horns and have a sound more akin to the Congolese rumba tradition. Instrumentation typically consists of a drummer (on a trap set), a conga or ngoma player, three guitarists (two lead and one rhythm, or vice versa), a bass player, a keyboardist, and several singers. The horn sections often include saxophones, trumpets, and, in rare cases, trombones. Many dansi bands have a mtindo (a style or dance) that identifies the band and acts as the band's musical foundation. For instance, DDC Orchestra Mlimani Park's mtindo is called *sikinde,* which is also the second name for the band. The term sikinde comes from a ngoma of the Zaramo people who live in and around Dar es Salaam. Dansi songs often address love and relationships, although many, especially songs from the 1960s and 1970s, discuss political issues or offer praise for the government. Most bands divide their songs into the "song" section, which is where the main lyrics are sung, and "*chemko,*" which is the faster, more danceable section (the chemko is also referred to by the Congolese term *sebene*). Audiences tend to sit or stand during the slow song section, soaking up the lyrics. Once the chemko starts, however, the dance floor fills. The guitars weave together, horn sections play call and response, and the drummers drive a steady, dance beat. Singers of the group often call out the names of people in the audience to show respect and, perhaps, earn extra tips. For more on dansi, see Askew 2002; Graebner 1997, 2000a, 2007; Perullo 2008b. For video of dansi, see PURL A.2, PURL A.3, and PURL A.4.

**Mchiriku** is derived from a traditional Zaramo ngoma. It preceded hiphop as a popular music among youth and is thought to have emerged in Dar es Salaam in the early 1970s. Often consisting of traditional drums, amplified voice, and keyboard, the music flows in continuous, repetitive cycles with lyrics that address social and political issues facing local populations. Mchiriku groups perform at weddings, small neighborhood gatherings, and naming or circumcision ceremonies. Even though the shows are exciting, energetic, and lively, the bawdy lyrics and erotic dancing have made the music a target of government censorship. In the 1970s and again in the mid-1990s, the government banned mchiriku for its "lewd lyrics and erotic dance style" (Graham 1994: 256;

Graebner 1999: 687). Nonetheless, the music and its musicians have persevered. Between 1997 and 2000, cassettes of mchiriku sold extremely well, and bands, such as Miami Beats, Mvita Group, and Night Star Musical Club, formed in Dar es Salaam. More recently, mchiriku has declined in status as bongo flava and hip-hop took over as a popular music among youths. Most groups lack managers, regular performance venues, or typical forms of publicity, and do not register, as bands are required to do, with the National Arts Council (BASATA). A group's name is only spread through word of mouth and a few signs that hang above the doors of members' homes. Still, their popularity emphasizes the importance of "electronic ngoma" among residents of Dar es Salaam. For video of mchiriku, see PURL A.5.

**Muziki wa Injili** is one of the more commercially successful genres in Tanzania, using Christian-influenced lyrics with a variety of popular music genres, including reggae, dansi, zouk, and taarab (Sanga 2007). The popularity of the genre owes to the growing influence of Christianity in the country, but also to the movement of religious music out of places of worship and into concert halls and evangelical meetings. Most performances are upbeat and lively, with electronic instruments, and the audience is often encouraged to participate in the performances. There is also attention to individual performers, whereas in kwaya music attention is paid more to an entire group. Many of the most popular performers in the genre are women, such as Bahati Bukuku and Rose Muhando, who perform in concert halls throughout Dar es Salaam. For more on muziki wa injili, see Sanga 2001, 2006a, 2007.

**Muziki wa Kwaya**, derived from the English word "choir," represents Christian choral groups that perform in churches and in competitions throughout Tanzania. There are many categories of music within the kwaya tradition, such as kwaya kuu (main choirs) and kwaya za uinjilisti (evangelical choirs) in the Lutheran church (Barz 2000; Sanga 2006b). Kwaya music began through missionary initiatives to "teach music to Africans" as early as the 1860s and prospered during colonialism as missionary schools and churches sought to convert and "civilize" local peoples (Coupland 1939: 355). Roman Catholics, Lutherans, and Anglicans were the dominant missionary religions in Tanzania, and each established a strong choral tradition within its churches. Missionaries taught locals both how to sing and how to teach others to sing, thereby allowing choral music to spread quickly throughout the country, even where missionaries had not evangelized. During the 1950s, kwaya alongside ngoma was a popular means to draw enthusiasm and support for the Tanganyika African National Union (TANU), the African independence organization. When Julius Nyerere, who was then head of TANU, traveled throughout the country gathering support, kwaya groups often greeted him. After independence, the government promoted nonreligious kwaya alongside vichikesho (comedy routines) and ngonjera (dramatic, recited poetry) to propagate the Arusha Declaration (Nyoni 1998). Schools and urban-based cultural troupes also established kwaya groups that sang political songs praising leaders and the party's religious and social ideologies. Over time, however, kwaya returned to a mainly religious music, though it remains important among a few secular groups such as Tanzanian One Theatre (TOT) Kwaya. Choirs typically meet several times a week to practice, and perform at least one service on Sunday. They also enter into large competitions with other kwaya groups, and occasionally record for television and radio stations. Most churches have an organ, piano, or synthesizer, and many use drums, either traditional or modern. A few churches even have bands to support kwaya groups. Although most churches rely on European religious songs translated into Swahili, others use songs written by local composers. For more on kwaya, see Barz 1997, 1998, 2000, 2003; Sanga 2006b. For video of muziki wa kwaya, see PURL A.6.

**Ngoma**, translated as dance, drumming, and song, either taken together or separately, is considered the traditional music of Tanzania. Most ngoma groups consist of a leader (who composes songs and directs a group in performance), drummers, instrumentalists, song leaders (who lead the main call of songs), and dancers (who also back up the singers). Currently, urban centers feature only a handful of ngoma groups that perform publicly for audiences, although there are numerous others that exist but rarely perform for events. In Dar es Salaam, there are currently sixty-one ngoma groups listed as active even though only five regularly perform. Elias Songoyi writes, "In a city like Dar es Salaam, the traditional community has ceased to exist.... The dances which were once most revered in the traditional community are no longer seen with the same attitude" (1988: 45). It is important to note that in rural areas and peri-urban areas of Dar es Salaam, ngoma music is still important and often performed nightly. It also influences musicians from a variety of musical genres and is still regarded as the basis of Tanzanian music. For more on ngoma, see Campbell 1983; Farrell 1980; Franken 1986; Gearhart 1998, 2000; Gunderson, 1999, 2000b; Hartwig 1969; Hill 2000, 2002; Martin 1991; Nyoni 1991; Pels, 2000; Ranger 1975; and Songoyi 1988. For video of ngoma, see PURL A.7.

**Reggae**: The father of Tanzanian reggae is Jah Kimbute, a 50-year-old Tanzanian with long dreadlocks usually covered by a tight, woven hat. Kimbute learned reggae in England while studying in college and began to play with groups there, followed by stints in Trinidad, Haiti, Europe, and Scandinavia. In 1981, he returned to Tanzania—a "repatriation," as he called it—and while working other jobs, he began to teach reggae music to other youth. At that time, as Kimbute says, "There was no reggae in Tanzania, they just knew about Bob Marley when he was dead in 1981. That was when people started to hear [about reggae]. But, by then, I was playing. So, I started to take some little gigs." In 1984, Kimbute formed his first official group, Roots and Culture, which continues today. In the late 1980s, he and his group performed at the Dar es Salaam YMCA, often for large audiences of freedom fighters from Namibia and South Africa. Local artists, such as Innocent Nganyangwa, Alex Kajumulo, and the late Justin Kalikawe, strengthened the reggae community by touring and releasing albums and videos. Still, local reggae receives very little airplay and is rarely featured live in Tanzania, much to the annoyance of local reggae artists. For more on the influence of Jamaican culture on youth in Tanzania, see Moyer 2005.

**Taarab**, also known as *mipasho* and *rusha roho,* is a form of sung Swahili poetry often divided into two forms, classical and modern. Classical taarab features an orchestra of instruments, such as the udi (plucked lute), fidla (violin), dumbaki (goblet drum), and daf (tambourine), and one or more vocalists who sing in either Arabic (taarabu ya kiarabu) or Swahili (taarab ya kiswahili). Classical taarab is most prominent in Zanzibar; no classical taarab groups perform in Dar es Salaam. Modern taarab, which is the most central form to this ethnography, occurs mainly in Dar es Salaam, Tanga, and Zanzibar, though it is popular in other parts of the country, particularly Dodoma, Mwanza, and Iringa. Only Dar es Salaam, however, can claim to have regular concerts by numerous groups, such as Muungano Cultural Troupe, Tanzanian One Theatre (TOT) Taarab, All Star Taarab, and Jahazi Modern Taarab. Taarab performances are well attended in Dar es Salaam, by women, some men, and members of the homosexual community, who are often allowed to dress and dance at taarab concerts in a way they cannot elsewhere. Many performances also have a play performed before the band starts, similar to a variety show–style. Modern taarab bands are organized similarly to dansi bands, with a bassist, drummer, one or more guitarists, and one or two keyboardists. Unlike dansi, however, taarab singers sit in a row in front of the band. One singer will rise to sing the song, which can be quite long and contain many verses, while the others remain seated and sing background vocals and the chorus. Throughout a song, the audience tips the singers, called *tuzo* in Swahili, to show appreciation for the singer's ability or choice of song. Although tipping occurs in performances of other genres, such as dansi and ngoma, it is expected at taarab concerts. For more on taarab, see Askew 2000, 2002; Daniels 1996; Fargion 1993, 2000; Graebner 1991, 1994a, 2007; Khatib 1992; Kirkegaard 1997, 1998; Knappert 1977, 1983; Lange 2002, 2008; Mgana 1991; and Robert 1991. For videos of taarab, see PURL A.8 and PURL A.9.

# Appendix B

The broadcast stations listed below are organized by the town or city where the station is located. The right-hand column identifies the market segment of a broadcast station and whether the station is authorized to broadcast at the national, regional, district, or community level. National authorization permits broadcasting to the entire country, whereas regional market segment is for one of the twenty-one administrative regions on mainland Tanzania. District refers to one of the ninety-eight administrative districts. The fees for application, licenses, and royalties vary depending on these market designations. A commercial television station that wants to broadcast for free (without a subscription) at the national level needs to pay a $1,000 application fee, a $4,000 initial license fee, and a $4,000 annual royalty. For radio stations, the national level designation costs the same for the application but half as much for the other costs, though the license only lasts for three years instead of five. At the district level, radio stations pay considerably less: the application fee is $20, the commercial license is $100, and the annual royalty is $200 for a three-year license. To renew any of these licenses costs the same as the initial license fee. In all these areas, non-commercial broadcasters, such as religious groups, pay half the fees assigned to commercial stations.

## RADIO STATIONS IN TANZANIA, 1994–2008

|   | DAR ES SALAAM | |
|---|---|---|
| 1 | Business Times FM | District |
| 2 | Classic FM | District |
| 3 | Clouds Entertainment Radio FM (CER) | National |
| 4 | East Africa FM | District |
| 5 | Magic FM | District |
| 6 | Morning Star FM | District |

| 7  | Praise Power Radio                 | District  |
|----|------------------------------------|-----------|
| 8  | PRT Radio Tanzania                 | Regional  |
| 9  | Radio Choice FM                    | District  |
| 10 | Radio East Africa FM               | National  |
| 11 | Radio Kheri Dar es Salaam (RKD)    | District  |
| 12 | Radio Maria                        | Regional  |
| 13 | Radio Mlimani FM                   | District  |
| 14 | Radio One                          | National  |
| 15 | Radio Quran                        | District  |
| 16 | Radio Sauti ya Qurran (defunct)    |           |
| 17 | Radio Sky FM                       | District  |
| 18 | Tanzania Broadcast Service         | District  |
| 19 | Radio Tumaini                      | Regional  |
| 20 | Radio Tumaini International         | Regional  |
| 21 | Radio Uhuru                        | Regional  |
| 22 | Times Radio FM                     | District  |
| 23 | Upendo FM Radio                    | District  |
| 24 | Wapo Radio                         | District  |

ARUSHA

| 25 | Orkonerei FM Radio    | Community |
|----|-----------------------|-----------|
| 26 | Radio 5 Arusha        | District  |
| 27 | Safina Radio FM       | District  |
| 28 | Sunrise FM Radio      | District  |
| 29 | Tanzanite Radio FM    | District  |
| 30 | Triple 'A' FM Radio   | District  |
| 31 | United Radio Services | District  |
| 32 | Radio 5 Arusha        | District  |

MWANZA

| 33 | Passion FM Ltd        | District  |
|----|-----------------------|-----------|
| 34 | Radio Free Africa     | National  |
| 35 | Radio Kiss FM         | Regional  |
| 36 | Radio Sauti FM Stereo | District  |
| 37 | Radio Sengerema       | Community |

MOROGORO

| 38 | Abood Radio    | District  |
|----|----------------|-----------|
| 39 | Radio Imaan FM | District  |
| 40 | Radio Ukweli   | District  |
|    |                | District  |

MOSHI

| 41 | Radio Kili FM         | District  |
|----|-----------------------|-----------|
| 42 | Radio Sauti ya Injili | Regional  |

IRINGA
| 43 | Country FM | District |
| 44 | Radio Ebony FM | District |

TABORA
| 45 | C.G. FM Radio | District |
| 46 | Voice of Tabora | District |

DODOMA
| 47 | Radio Mwangaza | District |

MUSOMA
| 48 | Victoria FM Radio | District |

MUSWA
| 49 | Sibuka FM Radio | District |

NGARA
| 50 | Radio Kwizera | Regional |

SHINYANGA
| 51 | Radio Faraja FM Stereo | District |

SONGEA
| 52 | Radio Maria | District |

SUMBAWANGA
| 53 | Chemchemi Radio Sumbawanga | District |

TELEVISION STATIONS IN TANZANIA, 1994–2008

DAR ES SALAAM
| 1 | Agape Television (ATV) | Regional |
| 2 | C2C Television | District |
| 3 | Channel Ten Television | National |
| 4 | CTN Television | District |
| 5 | Dar Es Salaam Television (DTV) | District |
| 6 | East Africa Television (EATV) | Regional |
| 7 | GTV (Tanzania) Limited | National |
| 8 | Independent Television (ITV) | National |
| 9 | Multichoice Tanzania Limited | National |
| 10 | Mussa Television Network | District |
| 11 | Pulse Television | District |
| 12 | Televisheni ya Taifa (TVT) | National |

MOROGORO
| 13 | Abood Television | District |
| 14 | Sokoine University of Agriculture Television (SUATV) | District |

| 15 | IRINGA<br>Iringa Municipal Council Television | District |
| 16 | KIOMBOI<br>Iramba District Council TV & Radio | District |
| 17 | MASASI<br>Masasi District Council Television | District |
| 18 | MBEYA<br>Mbeya City Council | District |
| 19 | MBOZI<br>Mbozi District Council Television | District |
| 20 | MWANZA<br>Star TV | National |
| 21 | NJOMBE<br>Njombe District Council Television | District |
| 22 | SONGEA<br>Songea Town Council Television | District |
| 23 | SUMBAWANGA<br>Sumbawanga Town Council Television | District |
| 24 | TABORA<br>C G TV Transmission Centre | District |
| 25 | TANGA<br>Tanga City Council | District |
| 26 | TUKUYU<br>Rungwe District Council Television | District |
| 27 | TUNDURU<br>Tunduru District Council Television | District |

# Appendix C

Below is a list of clubs in Dar es Salaam that have regularly scheduled live music. The days marked with an "X" indicate regularly scheduled weekly shows. Those marked with an "O" are those that occur on occasion. For instance, Diamond Jubilee is one of the largest performance spaces in the city, but concerts only occur there from time to time. Also, festivals, competitions, and album release concerts frequently occur but not on a regular basis, so there are often more events occurring than those marked below.

The majority of these clubs never advertise or make formal announcements about shows, and there are no newspapers or magazines that compile lists of upcoming events. The only way to hear about performances is through word of mouth or through banners posted in front of the clubs. The limited publicity for events made compiling this list more challenging, and I am indebted to James Nindi and Hamza Kalala for helping me to track down the information.

The list of clubs is organized by the three districts in Dar es Salaam: Kinondoni, Ilala, and Temeke.

|  | Tuesday | Wednesday | Thursday | Friday | Saturday | Sunday |
|---|---|---|---|---|---|---|
| KINONDONI |  |  |  |  |  |  |
| Ambassador Plaza |  |  |  |  | X |  |
| Anna Mwana Pub (Kimara) |  |  |  | X | X |  |
| Arcade Motel |  |  |  | X |  | X |
| Bahama Mama |  |  |  | X |  | X |
| Bahama Mama (Kimara) |  |  |  |  | X | X |
| Ben Night Club (Kinondoni) | X | X | X | X | X | X |
| CCM Mwinjuma (Mwanyamala) |  |  |  |  | X | X |

| | Tuesday | Wednesday | Thursday | Friday | Saturday | Sunday |
|---|---|---|---|---|---|---|
| Chagga Bite (Makumbusho) | | | | | X | X |
| Checkpoint | | | | | X | X |
| Chenzetemba (Kinondoni) | | | | | X | X |
| Cine Club (Mikocheni B) | | | | | X | X |
| Club Ambiance (Sinza) | | | | | X | X |
| Coco Beach (Oysterbay) | | | | | X | X |
| Dar Carnival (Mikocheni B) | | | | | X | X |
| DDC Magomeni (Kondoa-Magomeni) | | | | | X | X |
| DDC Mlimani Park (Survey) | | | | | X | X |
| FK Resort (Kimara) | | | | | X | X |
| FM Club | | | | X | | X |
| Friends Corner (Manzese) | | | | X | X | X |
| Golden Bridge (Mbezi Beach) | | | | | X | X |
| Habata Club (Kibamba) | | | | | X | X |
| Hunters Club (Kinondoni, Soko la Matx) | | | | | X | X |
| Kaba Kabana (formerly Wama Bar, Mwanyamala) | | | | | X | X |
| Kirimanjaro Bar (Magomeni Mapipa) | | | | | X | X |
| Landmark Hotel (Ubungo) | | | | | X | X |
| Leaders Club (Kinondoni Shamba) | | | | | | X |
| Legho Hotel | | | | | X | |
| Lion Hotel (Sinza) | | | | | X | X |
| Lunch Time Hotel (Manzese) | | | | | X | X |
| Maisha Club | X | X | X | X | X | X |
| Makumbusho (Kijitonyama) | | | | X | | X |

| | Tuesday | Wednesday | Thursday | Friday | Saturday | Sunday |
|---|---|---|---|---|---|---|
| Malaika (Mikocheni B) | | | | | X | X |
| Mambo Club (Ubungo Riverside) | X | X | X | X | X | X |
| Mango Garden (Kinondoni) | | X | | X | X | X |
| Maridadi Pub (Kinondoni Mkwajuni) | | | | | X | X |
| Masai Bar (Kinondoni) | | | | | X | X |
| Meeda Club (Sinza) | | | | | | |
| MK Bar | | X | | | X | X |
| Mlimani City (Mwenge) | | | | | | |
| Moshi Hotel (Manzese) | | | | X | X | X |
| Msasani Beach (Kawe) | | | | | X | X |
| Muafaka Bar (Mbezi Beach) | | | | | X | X |
| Mzalendo Pub (Makumbusho) | | | | | X | X |
| New Lango la Jiji (Magomeni) | | | | | X | X |
| New Msasani Club (Kawe) | | | | | X | |
| New Vijana Social Hall | | | | | | X |
| Nyama Chabesi (Tegeta) | | | | X | X | X |
| Nyumba ya Sanaa | | | | X | | |
| Open Air (Kawe) | | | | X | X | X |
| Platinum Disco (Mikocheni A) | | | | | | |
| Police Officers Mess (Oysterbay) | | | | X | | X |
| La Prima (Victoria) | | | | | X | X |
| Rainbow Hotel (Mbezi Beach) | | | | | X | X |
| Rambo Night Club (Manzese) | | | | | X | X |
| Riverside Bar (Ubungo) | | | | | | |
| Rovenna Pub (Kimara Baruti) | | | | | X | X |

|                              | Tuesday | Wednesday | Thursday | Friday | Saturday | Sunday |
|------------------------------|---------|-----------|----------|--------|----------|--------|
| San Sierro (Ubungo)          | X       | X         | X        |        | X        | X      |
| Santon Hotel (Manzese)       |         |           |          |        | X        | X      |
| Seacliff Hotel (Masaki)      |         |           |          |        | O        | O      |
| Silent Inn                   |         |           |          |        |          | X      |
| The Slipway                  |         |           |          | O      | O        | O      |
| Stereo Bar (Kinondoni)       |         |           |          |        | X        | X      |
| Sweeties (Oysterbay)         |         |           |          |        | X        | X      |
| Talk of the Town             |         |           |          |        | X        |        |
| Tiger Motel                  |         |           |          |        | X        | X      |
| Traventine Hotel (Magomeni)  |         |           |          |        | X        | X      |
| Triz Motel (Mbezi Beach)     |         |           |          |        | X        | X      |
| Ubungo Plaza (Ubungo)        |         |           |          |        | X        | X      |
| Usesi Club (Mabibo)          |         |           |          |        | X        | X      |
| Vatican Hotel (Sinza)        |         |           |          | X      | X        | X      |
| Vijana Social Hall (Kinondoni)|        |           |          |        | O        | O      |
|                              |         |           |          |        |          |        |
| ILALA                        |         |           |          |        |          |        |
| Africentre (Ilala)           |         |           |          | X      | X        | X      |
| Amana Social Hall (Ilala)    |         |           |          | X      | X        | X      |
| Annex Inn (Magomeni)         |         |           |          | X      | X        | X      |
| Blue Fish Pub (Kigamboni)    |         |           |          |        | X        | X      |
| CCM Hall (Kigamboni)         |         |           |          | X      | X        | X      |
| Check Point (Magomeni)       |         |           |          |        | X        | X      |
| Chemchem (Tabata)            |         |           |          |        | X        | X      |
| Club Billicanas (City Centre)| X       | X         | X        |        | X        | X      |
| Da West (Tabata)             |         |           |          |        | X        | X      |
| DDC Kariakoo (Kariakoo)      |         |           |          |        |          | X      |
| Diamond Jubilee (Ilala)      |         |           |          |        | X        | X      |

| | Tuesday | Wednesday | Thursday | Friday | Saturday | Sunday |
|---|---|---|---|---|---|---|
| Europa Pub | | | | | X | X |
| Highway Bar (Magomeni) | | | | X | X | X |
| Kakala (Kigamboni) | | | | | X | X |
| Kimboka Bar (Buguruni) | | | | | X | X |
| Kwazulu Natal (Tabata) | | | | | X | |
| Las Vegas Casino (Upanga) | | | | | O | O |
| Lindi View (Ilala) | | | | X | | |
| Madison Square | | | | | X | X |
| Mashujaa Night Park (Vingunguti) | | | | | X | X |
| Max Bar (Ilala) | | | | X | | X |
| Mazulia Bar | | | | X | X | X |
| Monie Club (Airport) | | | | | X | |
| Mrem's Bar (Buguruni) | | | | | X | X |
| New Jolly Club (Upanga) | | | | | O | O |
| Next Door (Tabata) | | | | X | X | X |
| Nyumba ya Sanaa/ Nyerere Cultural Centre (Ilala) | | | | O | X | X |
| Port View (Kurasini) | | | | | X | X |
| Ralway Club (Gerezani) | | | | | X | X |
| Rose Hill Pub (Segerea) | | | | | X | X |
| Ruhta Executive Centre (Tabata Segerea) | | | | | X | X |
| Rujewa (Vingunguti) | | | | | X | X |
| Salender Club (Ilala) | | | | X | X | X |
| Sembeti (Tabata Segerea) | | | | | X | X |
| Titanic (Vingunguti) | | | | | X | X |
| Wenge Pub (Ukonga) | | | | | X | X |
| Y2K | | | | X | X | X |
| **TEMEKE** | | | | | | |
| DDC Keko (Keko) | | | | | X | X |
| Equator Grill (Mtoni) | | | | | X | X |
| Gaddafi Pub (Yombo) | | | | X | X | X |

| | Tuesday | Wednesday | Thursday | Friday | Saturday | Sunday |
|---|---|---|---|---|---|---|
| Harbours Club (Kurasini) | | | | | X | X |
| Kata ya Kumi na Nne | | | | | X | X |
| Kilwa Road Pub (Temeke) | | | | | X | X |
| Kings Palace | | | | | | X |
| Kizota Bar | | | | | X | X |
| Luxury Pub (Temeke) | | | | | X | X |
| Masai Club (near national stadium) | | | | | X | X |
| Millenium [sic] Pub (Mbagala) | | | | | X | X |
| Pentagon (Kurasini) | | | | | X | X |
| Police Barracks (Ufundi) | | | | | X | X |
| PTA Hall (Temeke) | | | | | O | O |
| Supermini Bar | | | | | | X |
| TTC Club (Chang'ombe) | | | | | X | X |
| TTC Hall | | | | | | X |
| Vigae Classic (Mbagala) | | | | X | X | |
| Wonderful (Mtoni Kijichi) | | | | | X | |
| Zakheim Pub (Mbagala) | | | | | X | X |

# Appendix D

The following list presents one of the more impressive changes in the way music is being commodified in Tanzania. Most of the listed organizations formed in the early to mid-2000s when the arts became a more attractive means to earn an income. Promotion companies work in many areas of cultural production, promoting events and concerts or investing in the promotion of arts and other employment activities. Among many young and up-and-coming business entrepreneurs, there is a perception that organizing concerts or shows is both easy and profitable. Rarely is this true, however; most promotion companies break even or lose money on shows they promote.

ARUSHA

Aang Serian Peace Village
Concepts Elite Limited
Crown International Entertainment
Florida Promotion
G.S.M. Promotions
Heart to Heart Investment Ltd
J & J Promotion
Klub Afriko Cultural Orientation Centre
L.V.C. Holdings
Larra Le Maa Band and Arts Promotions
MAG Promotions and Entertainments
MC D. Promotion
Megatop Entertainment Promotion
Modern Linguistics Cultural Promotion Centre (Molac)
Motivation for Self-Employment strategies
Ricks Art Promotion
Sunset Entertainment and Promotions

Tanzania Direct Mineral
Watengwa Entertainment
Z.B. Promotions

## BAGAMOYO

'B'-KUBWA Entertainment
Hunters Entertainment
Naiza Theatre Resource Centre
Tanzania Social Theatre

## DAR ES SALAAM

03 World Theatre, Arts and Entertainment—WOTER
2 Eyez Production
Abas Chezn Temba Intertainment
Afcode Arts Promoters
Afri Cultural Promoters
African Beauty Management Agency
African Stars Entertainment
Afrika Kuza Arts Group
Afrika Sana
A.G.M. Promotion
Ahadi Productions
Air Arts Promotions
A.K. Productions
Al-Jazzirah Entertainment
All Arts Promoters
Ambassador Plaza (Hotel)
Amour Entertainment & Arts Promotion
A.M. Sound Promotion (Adolph Mbinga Sound)
A.M.W. Promotion
Apple Promotion
Awadh Arts Promotion
B & M Entertainment
B & S Promotion
B' Moran Promotion Group
B.P. Entertainment
Bahari Entertainment
Bell-Idda Restaurant Ltd.
Beta Musica C. Limited
The Biggs Promotions (T) Ltd

Black Warriors Entertainment (B.W.E.)
BMP Promotion
Bob Entertainments & Company
Bongo Splash Entertainment
Boy George Promotions
Candle Light Promotion
Capital Promoters International
Care Arts Promotion Tanzania
Carnival East Africa Ltd
Casino Entertainment
Cassy Promotions
Chabruma Art Promotion
Chama cha Wakuza Sanaa (Vinyago) Tanzania
Chama cha Wazazi cha Kuendeleza Wanafunzi—PSD
Che Chilala Promotion
Check Point Club & Promotion Centre
Chopsticks Limited—Arts Promotions
CK Promotion
Clouds Entertainment
Compass Communication
Com-Studio Art Promoters
Copa Cabana Entertainment Centre Ltd.
Craft & Tingatinga Arts Promotion Society
Crystal Work Promotion
Cudis Investment Limited
The CXC Holdings & Entertainment
Daglish Arts Promotion
Dandu Planet Africa
The Dar Boys Acrobatic Music and Art Group
Dar Metropolitan Promotions
Dar's Contemporary Artists Centre
Day Star Promotion Tanzania
Deiwaka Productions
Diamond Sound Electro-Entertainment Centre
Dimples Entertainment
Double 'K' & Bukavu Promotion
Dreams Promotions Group Limited
Dunia Company Ltd
Duo F.M. Musiconsultant Promotions
The East Africa Art Biennale
East African Movie Ltd

The East African Olduvai Award Trust
The East African Promotion
East Tourism Promoters Co. Ltd
Empty Soulz Production
Energy Art Promotions
Enrico Figueiredo Promotions
The Entertainment Network
Ericom Cultural Promotion
EXP. Momentum Promotions
Falcon Entertainment & Promotion Agency
FC-Full Talent Promotion
FM Productions Ltd.
Funika Promotions Co. Ltd
Gazeti Tafakari
Global Brotherhood of Light
Global Entertainment
Global Talent Search and Arts Promotion
Great Lakes Promotion
Great Venture Limited
The Heritage Group
Heritage Tanzania
Hisani Arts Promotion
HKM Promoters
Hollywood Promotion Company
Hollywood Bollywood Restaurant
Hotel Sea Cliff (Promotion)
Hoyce Production
Ilanda Digital Graphics Promota
Indian Raj Restaurant Ltd. & Arts Promotion
Inspirational Sounds Promotions
Interafrica Art Promotions
International Art Promotion
Ismail Yusuph
Jane Peter Mhina
Jaribu Promotion (Jambo Research & Information Bureau)
Jopa Promotion
Kabwie Art Promotion, Training and Production Centre
Kengele Cultural Promotion
Keza Arts Promotion
Khadija Collections
Khaki Production

Khash Entertainment and studio
Khashcas Promotions
Kibene Camp (Promotion)
Kim & The Boyz Promotion
The King Promoters
Kings International Promoters
Kizota in Promotion
Klub ya kuendeleza michezo na sanaa kwa Vijana
K.P. Promotion
Kwafujo Deejays
Kwetu Entertainment
Lake Zone Promotions
La Palace Entertainment Centre Ltd
Leisure Arts International
Leoz Promotion
Lete Mambo Arts Promotion
Lino International Agency
Lips Entertainment
Lohana Mahajan Community
Long Press Ltd
Look Promotions
Lugha na Utamaduni
Lukewarm promotion
Maasai Records & Entertainments
MAC 'D' Promotions
Mafasheni Entertainment
Magwa Arts Studio & Promotion
Mahogany 2000 Promotions
Mapacha Entertainment
Mapambano Arts Cultural and Study Centre
Mashamba Arts Promotion
Mawenzi Entertainment Promotion
Mbantu Production
Mbondo Cultural Institute
Mchabwede Sanaa Group
Men Entertainment
Miami FM Beauty Promoters
Migiringo Entertainment
Mimi Afrika Entertainment
Mionzi Entertainment
Mister & Miss University Committee Tanzania

M.J. Productions
M.J.S. Promotion
M.M. Entertainment
Moran Entertainment
Mpingo Arts Promotion
Msumari Promotion
Mtandao Arts Promotion
MTV Promotion
Mufindi Arts Promotion
Music Mayday Tanzania
Music Maestro & Supplies Ltd
Music World Entertainers
Musicmark
Mustapha Hassanali
Mzimba Art Promotion
New Africa Hotel (1993) Ltd.
The New Age Gospel Music Enterprise (NAGE)
New Super Mazuria
Next Level Incorporated
Ngana Culture Promotion
Ngara Promotion Art Group
Njalalikoko Research and Arts Promotion
N.J. Furniture Industry Co. Ltd
Nyawade Arts Promotion Group
Nyota Ensemble
OK's Promotion Agency
Omega Production
Opeum Addiktiv Produktiv (M.P.H.L)
Partners Relations Promotions (PR—Promotions)
Pink Coconut Entertainment
Premier Look International ( PLI)
Prime Time Promotions
Promo-Date Ltd.
Promoters & Developers International Ltd
Q. Losha Arts Promotion
Raha Leo Productions
Rain Bow Promotion
Red Promotions Incorporation
The Repataime Promotion
RM Promotions
Robinson Promotions

Royal Palm Hotel Dar es Salaam
Royal Palmodzi Promotions
Royal Productions and Entertainment
Ruaha Across Music & Culture Promotion
Rulu Arts Promoters
S. & H. Promotions
Sa Re Gama Bar & Restaurant (Arts Promotion)
Sakima Vijana
Sanaa Promotion
Sare Gama Arts Promotion
Scantan Entertainment
Scantanip Ltd.
Serious Entertainment Promotions
Sinai Arts and Cultural Entertainment
Six Manyara Arts Promotion
S.J. Arts Promotion
S.J. Entertainment
Sky Arts Promotion
Smooth Vibes
The Solfa Bureau
Sonafrique Limited
Strong Stage Promotions
Sun City Sound Promotion
Tafrija Entertainment & Investment Co. Ltd
Talk of the Town
Tamaduni Handicraft Promoters
Tan Vision 2000 Promotion
Tan Vision Limited
Tanrose Home Entertainment
Tanruss Investment Ltd.
Tanzania Arts Promotion (T.A.P)
Tanzania Black Art
Tanzania Breweries Ltd
Tanzania Cultural Ambassador
Tanzania Cultural Society
Tanzania Female Artists Network
Tanzania Female Artists Network (TAFANET)
Tanzania Gospel Music Promoters
Tanzania Music Project
Tanzania Sanaa Art & Culture Centre
Tanzania Sanaa Organisation—(TASO)

Taswira Arts Production
Teca Cultural Group Environmental Cleanliness Awareness
Tele Arts
Televisheni ya Taifa
T. Garden Arts Promoters
T.K. Arts Promotion
Tripple C. Investment Co.
Twiga Arts Promotions
The Twins Ladies Art Promotion
Uhuru Promotions
Umoja Inc. Promotion
Umoja Promotion
Universal Media Art Promotion
Ustaarabu wa Pwani
Utamaduni Institute Tanzania
Vijana Arts Promotion Centre
Volunteer Sanaa Promotion Unit
Wanaharakati Asilia wa Nang'oma
Wash Talent Promotion and Entertainment
Weusi Arts Production
White Sands Hotel
Young Men Promoters
Youth Welfare Trust Promotions
Z.K. Beauty Group Promotion

## DODOMA

Capital Music Culture Promoters
Chabela Salamu & Entertainment

## IRINGA

The Friendship Force of Iringa
Zabje Art Promotion,Njombe/Iringa

## KAHAMA

Asela Promotion
Igembe Sab'o Arts Group

## KIBAHA PWANI

Front Page Arts Promotion
J.M. Arts Promotion

Mnyalukolo Arts Promotion
Rogers Promotion

KIGOMA

Samina Arts Promotions

MBEYA

The Mbuzax Promotions
Ochio Entertainment
Sky FM Music & Culture Promotion

MTWARA

Asfa Promotion
Jojos Arts Entertainments
Kakakuona Arts Promotions
Paradise Group
Valentines Investments and Promotions

MOROGORO

Mtandao wa Wasanii Morogoro
Tanzania Arts Program
Vision 86 Artists Group Hall

MOSHI

Mt. Kilimanjaro African Culture Heritage Services
Viva Productions

MUSOMA

Mkurugenzi wa Mji
New Metro Merchandise
New space Entertainment
R & B Promotions
Wapendanao Group Promotion and Entertainments

MWANZA

Afri Kings Entertainment
DJ Engineer Promoter
Gees Vision
Hotco Arts Promoters

K.A.M. Arts Promotion
National Entertainment Centre
Nyanza Folklore Research
Rock Hill Promotion
Top Class
Valentino's Promotions

## SHINYANGA

Bukisa-Bukubata Kikundi cha Sanaa

## TABORA

Chifu Promotion
New Gwassa Arts Promotions

## TANGA

Amboni Culture & Guiding Promoters
Anak Arts Promoter
Five Brothers Promotion
Four Ways Hotel Promotions
Kishari Social Club & Sports
Park Lane
Susi Promoters
Tanga Cultural Heritage Limited
Tanga Film Makers Association

## TUNDUMA

Steven Saini Hayo

# Notes

## Preface

The opening quote from Remmy Ongala is from Graebner 1999: 685.

1. Paul Collier, Director of the Development Research Department, World Bank, Workshop on the Development of the Music Industry in Africa, sponsored by the World Bank and the Policy Sciences Center, Inc., Washington, D.C., June 20–21, 2001.

2. Frank Penna, Managing Director of the Policy Sciences, Inc., and the Development Grant Facility for Culture, Workshop on the Development of the Music Industry in Africa, sponsored by the World Bank and the Policy Sciences Center, Inc., Washington, D.C., June 20–21, 2001.

3. In 2007, there were sixteen record companies listed for the continent of Africa as members of the IFPI. The companies, listed by country, were as follows: South Africa (Sony BMG Music Entertainment Africa [Pty] Ltd., EMI Music South Africa [Pty] Ltd., Gallo Record Company, Universal South Africa), Nigeria (Kennis Communications Limited and Premier Records [Nigeria] Ltd.), Mozambique (Indico Music Lda and Vidisco Moçambique Lda), Malawi (A.A Mirza [Lords Best Collection]), Kenya (AI Records [Kenya] Ltd.), Egypt (ALAM EL PHAN, Mirage Records, Sono Cairo Audio & Video Co., Star), Zimbabwe (Zimbabwe Music Corporation), and Mauritius (I.K.S. Music & Vision Limited).

4. Funkazi Koroye-Crooks, *WIPO Meeting, Dar es Salaam, Tanzania,* April 3 and 5, 2001. For a discussion of WIPO's implementation of banderole in Africa, see An antipiracy program for Africa's music industry, *WIPO Magazine,* July–September 2002, 10–13.

5. The banderole program started in April 1992 in Ghana. The program met with immediate success because of the seizure of numerous illegal cassettes by various government agencies. See *Ghana Copyright News,* January 1991–December 1992, 4–5.

6. These numbers were established from two sources: one was information given to me by music distributors in Dar es Salaam, and the other was informal surveys done with cassette sellers in four Tanzanian cities, Iringa, Tanga, Arusha, and Dar es Salaam. In the surveys, I focused on asking how many recordings were sold in a given time period (day, week, and month), whether there were peak sales periods, and a general estimate of how many cassettes were sold in a year. There were then estimates made on the number of stores selling music in Tanzania.

7. For a comparative discussion of successful music industries in Africa, see Development Works, 2004, *Take Note! The (Re)naissance of the Music Industry in Sub-Saharan Africa*, paper prepared for The Global Alliance for Cultural Diversity Division of Arts and Cultural Enterprise, UNESCO, Paris.

## 1. Kumekucha

The meaning behind the title "Mjini Mipango" (In the City Is Planning) is that if you want to survive in the city, you need to have plans for making money.

1. The other songs that were recorded were "Barua Nyingi Nilizokutumia" (Many Letters I Sent to You), "Hayo Siyo Waliyokuambia" (That's Not What They Told You), and "Kipurepere."

2. All the names used in this opening narrative are pseudonyms with the exception of the band name Western Jazz.

3. Throughout this book, I use the term "Asian" and "Indian" interchangeably to refer to people of South Asian descent who migrated to Tanzania. James Brennan explains the reasons the term Asian is used in East Africa: "Many South Asians in East Africa employed the term 'Asian' instead of 'Indian' following India's 1947 partition in order to generate unity among Muslims and Hindus. 'Asian' was also a legal category that included Arabs and Indians in mainland British East Africa, and was titled 'Asiatic' until the mid-1940s" (2002: 1; see also Forster, Hitchcock, and Lyimo 2000: 76).

4. Tanzania ran into numerous problems after independence, losing aid from England and Germany (1966), encountering coups in Zanzibar (1967–1972), losing a large majority of Asian businesses (1969–1979), being forced to rebuild its transport and communication system after the breakup of the East African Community (1977), fighting in the Tanzania-Uganda War with Idi Amin, which involved heavy expenditures of manpower, finance, and equipment (1978–79), and suffering through the effects of an oil price increase (1979) and drought (1980–1982) (Bukuku 1993: 154).

5. Deo Ngonyani, letter to author, November 8, 1999.

6. Tanzania was the highest recipient of agricultural aid between 1991 and 2006. Not all of the World Bank projects and recommendations were failures, as discussed in the Independent Evaluation Group (IEG) report (2007). Yet considering the amount of loans that the country received, the results were far from impressive.

7. The impact these loans in particular and aid in general have on African countries has been a long-running debate in eastern Africa. Some economists argue that aid is itself the problem in African countries (Moyo 2009: 47), while others argue that there is still room for aid with significant reforms. President Julius Nyerere was against taking loans from international organizations, since lending agencies could influence the policies of recipient nations. In a 1972 speech, he said, "Charity—however well meaning—is no way out of the present appalling poverty in the world. The poverty of the underdeveloped world is as much a function of the world economic organization as it is of anything else" (1973: 375).

8. Mkumbwa Ally, Year of socialism, self-reliance in Tanzania, *Daily News,* January 1, 1990.

9. The Ministry of Culture was originally called the Ministry of National Culture and Youth (Wizara ya Mila na Vijana) when it was formed on December 10, 1962. It has undergone numerous name changes since independence (Askew 2002: 186).

10.  This quote is from the 1962 Tanzania National Assembly Official Records, cited in Mbuguni and Ruhumbika 1974: 277.

11.  The Ministry of Culture existed from 1962 to 1964 and from 1974 to 1980. In other years, cultural issues were subsumed under other ministries, which led to a significant loss of momentum for cultural initiatives. By the early 1990s, funding for culture diminished significantly before being revitalized again in the early 2000s.

12.  Properly written, Louis Mbughuni's name is spelled with an "h," but it is written as "Mbuguni" in the publication *Towards Ujamaa*. Mbughuni was Lecturer in the Department of Theatre Arts at the University of Dar es Salaam. Ruhumbika was Senior Lecturer in the Department of Literature at the University of Dar es Salaam at the time *Towards Ujamaa* was published.

13.  In its original formation, BASATA (Baraza la Sanaa la Taifa/ National Arts Council) focused on visual arts. Both BASATA and BAMUTA (Baraza la Muziki la Taifa/ National Music Council) were formed under the National Arts Council Act of 1974. Other departments were also formed in the 1970s, including the National Sports Council (Baraza la Michezo la Taifa), Department of National Archives, the Department of Museums (Makumbusho), the National Film Censorship Office, and the National Swahili Council (Baraza la Kiswahili la Taifa, BAKITA).

14.  Ministry of Education and Culture's 2001 policy document, Cultural Development Master Plan for Tanzania. The ministry is now known as the Ministry of Education and Vocational Training; the culture section was moved to the Ministry of Information, Culture, and Sports in 2006.

15.  Criticisms of foreign music are frequently aimed at bongo flava, though no references are ever made to this genre. For a recent discussion of promoting traditional ngoma music, see Tanzanian Parliament, Parliamentary debates, Twelfth meeting, session 33, July 28, 2008.

16.  See Tanzanian Parliament, Parliamentary debates, Fourth meeting, session 35, August 2, 2006, 62–63.

17.  The Swahili acronym MASHIBOTA stands for the Mashindano ya Bendi Bora Tanzania (Competition for the Best Tanzanian Band).

18.  BASATA is staffed by twenty-eight people: three in administration and finance, four in the performing arts section, three in arts and handcrafts, and four in music (the head, two assistants, and the secretary), with the remaining people serving as messengers, drivers, guards, and so on. Most of the senior staff are graduates of University of Dar es Salaam or the Bagamoyo College of Art.

19.  Ministry of Education and Culture, Cultural Development Master Plan for Tanzania, 2001.

20.  Chesi Mpilipili, BASATA ilichelewa kwa hili, lakini heri imefika! (BASATA was late with this, but we are happy it has arrived), *Raia Mwema*, July 16, 2008.

21.  Some of the articles in the *Mashindano!* collection that most relate to the genres being discussed in this collection include Askew 2000; Barz 2000; Graebner 2000a; Haas and Gesthuizen 2000; Hill 2000; Kezilahabi 2000; Lange 2000; and Nyoni 2000.

22.  Aloyse Menda, Miaka 45 ya uhuru; utandawazi umeleta ukoloni mpya ([After] 45 years of freedom; globalization brought a new colonialism), *Tanzania Daima*, December 8, 2006.

23.  Hafiz Juma, Have you seen my country? posted January 2, 2008, on the website conscious-revolution.blogspot.com.

24. Remarks by President Benjamin William Mkapa at the Launch of the Report of the World Commission on the Social Dimension of Globalisation, London, February 24, 2004.

25. Julio Godoy, 2007. Tanzania: Leaders at development summit reject neoliberalism, Interpress Service, November 29, 2007.

26. Presidential Parastatal Sector Reform Commission, www.psrctz.com. Last accessed November 2007.

27. Inaugural speech by the president of the United Republic of Tanzania, Jakaya Mrisho Kikwete, National Stadium, Dar es Salaam, December 21, 2005. Similar comments were given on December 30, 2005, by Kikwete on inaugurating the Fourth Phase Parliament of the United Republic of Tanzania, Parliament Buildings, Dodoma.

28. The project of privatizing DAWASA was supported by the British government and hailed as a model for bringing people out of poverty to meet the United Nations Millennium Development Goals. In fact, many reports stated that the DAWASA lease to City Water was going to become the model repeated in many other parts of the continent.

29. John Vidal, Flagship water privatisation fails in Tanzania: UK firm's contract cancelled amid row over supply, *Guardian,* May 25, 2005, www.guardian.co.uk/politics/2005/may/25/uk.world.

30. Hidaya, Vijana wakidumu hadi wanadumaa, vijana chipukizi tutasikilizwa na nani? (If youth fail to develop, who will listen to we who are younger?), *Raia,* August 13, 2008.

31. The majority of writing on economies of popular music, particularly in the context of African or developing countries, started to emerge in the late 1980s. For example, works that informed this research include Averill 1989, 1997; Barz 1998; Collins 1992; Farley and Blewett 1998; Feld 1994; Graebner 2004, 2007; Guilbault 1993; Kidula 2000; Malm and Wallis 1992; Manuel 1993; Meinjtes 2003; Negus 1996; Wallach 2008; Waterman 1990; White 2000, 2008. In African contexts, a few scholars were critical in looking at the production and consumption of music in earlier periods, including Coplan 1979, 1980, 1982, 1985, 1994; Nketia 1955; Racy 1977; Wallis and Malm 1984; and Waterman 1982, 1985. This ethnography has been greatly informed by the work of these scholars.

## 2. Shall We Mdundiko or Tango?

1. Francis Nicholas, Tribal dances as opposed to ballroom dances must be maintained at all costs, *Mambo Leo,* March 1954, 34.

2. The promotion of racial divisions in Tanganyika and Dar es Salaam emphasizes the prevalence of race in establishing political, social, and cultural barriers between populations. For more on the pre-independence history of race relations between populations, see Bertz 2008; Brennan and Burton 2007; Brennan 2002, 2006; and Iliffe 1979.

3. X. Kalale, Ukatili wa vijana wa Dar es Salaam (Cruelty of Dar es Salaam youth), *Mambo Leo,* September, no. 105 (1931): 173.

4. Mdundiko is a traditional dance of either the Zaramo or Wadangereko peoples. Both are culturally based in the Dar es Salaam region.

5. In writing about early taarab in Zanzibar, Laura Fair comments that two bands, Ikhwan Safaa and Nadi Shuub, competed against each by performing exact copies of Egyptian tunes heard from gramophones (2001b: 172). A similar process occurred in Dar

es Salaam, where early records were critical for many bands to learn techniques, styles, rhythms, and melodies of so-called modern popular music.

6. *Kwetu,* January 14, 1939: 16. The original advertisement, which was in Swahili, did not separate the speakers with quotation marks.

7. Recognizing Saad's popularity, Abdulkarim Hakim Khan and Gokaldes S. Rughani, local agents of HMV and Columbia, respectively, worked in Zanzibar to promote her music (Suleiman 1969: 87–88). According to Fair (2001a), however, the initial advertising budget for the 1928 recordings was only sixty-four rupees (around a hundred shillings).

8. Sahani za santuri za Kiswahili (Swahili gramophone records), *Mambo Leo,* no. 102 (June 1931): 109.

9. The GV series featured 250 double-sided 78 rpm discs that were issued by His Master's Voice between 1933 and 1958. The series drew from the catalogue of Gramophone and Victor record companies (thus the GV designation), and began emerging in Africa around 1933. These recordings were popular among musicians and music fans, and several early recordings feature Spanish renditions of songs. The recordings also appeared on radio. For more on the HMV GV series, see Fargion 2004.

10. These notes from Hugh Tracey can be found in the International Library of African Music (ILAM), Rhodes University, South Africa, code no. 28.5/15.1/RC28 and code no. 28.5/15.1/RC32. For a published account of this recording tour, see Tracey 1952.

11. Beni-ngoma had a hierarchical ranking system for officers based on European titles. This included the title Brigadier-General. Kidasi was part of the Arinoti ngoma group in Dar es Salaam in the 1920s before forming his own brass band (Ranger 1975: 95).

12. The company manufactured 4,000 radio receivers per month and approximately 50,000 per year in the 1960s. More information can be found in Tanzania's Ministry of Industries, Mineral Resources, and Power, *Tanzania trade and industry* 21–30 (1968): 29.

13. Several authors have noted the importance of Cuban music, particularly on GV records, in influencing African popular music (Gondola 1997: 206; Impey 1998: 416) and Tanzanian music (Graebner 2000b). John Storm Roberts writes, "CBS recordings by the great Cuban quarters and sextets of the 1930s were repressed in London, and circulated on 78s known and loved universally from Cameroun to Uganda by their prefix: GV.... The impact of the GV series was enormous, coming at the same time as the earliest available cheap guitars" (n.d.: back cover).

14. "La Paloma" was a popular Spanish song originating in Cuba sometime in the 1800s. Abdallah most likely heard the song from Latin American recordings. The friends in the group with Abdallah included Juma Ndehele, Abubakari Hoseni, Juma Kondo, Nzige, Mgembe, Daulinge, and later Kibwana Sefu and Juma Kilaza.

15. When Abdallah died in a car accident in Morogoro on November 19, 1965, the entire country mourned his loss. Abdul Wakil, the Minister of Information, Broadcasting, and Tourism, appeared on Radio Tanzania Dar es Salaam and said, "The death of Salum has brought a tremendous amount of anguish and sadness to all of Tanzania" (quoted in Mkabarah 1966: 56). Songs of mourning were written by bands, including Atomic Jazz in Tanga, Kilwa Jazz Band in Dar es Salaam, and Kiko Kids Jazz Band in Tabora. Abdallah in his short career became a legend of Tanzanian music, the nation's first great post-independence star, and he is regarded this way even today.

16. There were a few exceptions, such as several visits by Louis Armstrong's band to Africa. Armstrong's group toured Africa quite extensively during the 1950s and

1960s and typically performed "V.I.P." concerts for politicians and social leaders, and at general concerts for the public (Arvell Shaw, conversation with author, May 22, 2002, New York City). In Dar es Salaam, Armstrong performed at the Avalon Cinema in 1960, though only two Africans were reported to have been able to attend the show. Tickets may have been purchased by Asians and sold for a higher price to Europeans (Bertz 2008: 240).

17. Nyamwezi Jazz Band was asked to change its name by the government because Nyamwezi was the name of an ethnic group, and the government was trying to hinder tribalism to build a national identity. Moro Jazz Band later became Morogoro Jazz Band. A band called Atomic Jazz Band formed in Iringa in the late 1940s, though it is unclear if any of the same personnel performed in the Dar es Salaam band by the same name. There was also an Atomic Jazz Band in Tanga that formed in 1956.

18. Rama Athmani, Aretha Franklin, mnegro malkia wa soul (Aretha Franklin, black queen of soul), *Nyota Afrika,* June 1970: 18.

19. The Flaming Stars, *Nyota Afrika,* April 1966: 15.

20. Instruments were also difficult to purchase locally from the late 1970s onward due to the high costs of importing them. With the exception of a guitar factory in Moshi during the late 1960s and early 1970s, Western instruments that bands relied upon were hard to find in Tanzania (Malm and Wallis 1992: 116; Mytton 1976: 117).

21. *Utamaduni—Stahiki ya Tanzania: Mwalimu ahutubia mabolozi* (Culture—the Merits of Tanzania: Mwalimu addresses ambassadors), *Uhuru,* January 2, 1969: 1.

22. In a University of Dar es Salaam publication investigating ujamaa policies, the authors criticize the notion that ngoma is a statics tradition: "It is obvious that these *ngoma,* even in the parts of our society where they still form part of social life, are bound to change in rhythm with the changes taking place in the country" (Mbuguni and Ruhumbika 1974: 281).

23. Lawrence Mtawa, Ngoma zetu (Our *ngoma), Nchi Yetu,* no. 58 (November 1968): 22, 29.

24. Stephen Hill points out that the attention to forming a socialist vision of ngoma also brought a detachment of urban residents with their homeland communities, since the sound and lyrics of ngoma became more unified rather than distinctive and community-based (2007: 241).

25. Lawrence Mtawa, Ngoma zetu (Our *ngoma), Nchi Yetu,* no. 58 (November 1968): 22, 29.

26. Music Conservatoire of Tanzania, Ltd., was affiliated with the Institute of Adult Education, University College, Dar es Salaam. The government also formed the National Arts of Tanzania, Ltd., to promote traditional arts and crafts. See Markets: Bringing arts and commerce together, *Jenga* 9 (1971): 36–37.

27. Elias Songoyi provides a different analysis to ngoma in Dar es Salaam. He writes, "The rural people as they settled in the urban areas continued to practice their traditions and customs, to perform their traditional dances to sing their traditional songs and to play their traditional rhythms" (1988: 15). He then provides examples of different ethnic groups that lived together in the city and maintained their traditions.

28. Before independence, TANU leaders recognized the social importance of dansi and, during the 1950s, organized dansi concerts to draw supporters and financial contributions for TANU's independence movement. Werner Graebner states, "During the fight for independence dances were a good cover for clandestine meetings, and the

money made during the dances a welcome addition to party funds" (1997: 110; see also Askew 2002: 94).

29. Vijana Jazz Band was called TANU Youth League Jazz Band until 1971 and was under the *Umoja wa Vijana wa CCM.*

30. Mlimani Park moved under the DDC in 1982, but initially formed in 1979 under the Tanzania Transport and Taxi Services until its owners went bankrupt.

31. Lawrence Mtawa, Ulimwengu wa muziki Dar-Sengo, Oyee! (The world of music in Dar-Sengo Oyee!), *Nchi Yetu,* March 1968: 28–29.

32. John Esibi, Jamhuri Jazz Band wadondoaji Apollo (Jamhuri Jazz Band pick up Apollo), *Nyota Afrika,* April 1970: 11, 18.

33. O. Mohammed, The Comets tamashani (The Comets in concert), *Nyota Afrika,* October 5, 1970.

34. Lawrence Mtawa, Wanajeshi na muziki: Wataimba kienyeji (Soldiers and music: They will sing traditional [music]), *Nchi Yetu,* October 1968: 28–30.

35. This poem was printed in Swahili in the newspaper *Uhuru,* January 7, 1969: 4. The remaining seven verses name each of the musicians in the band and his specific musical skill.

36. NUTA became Juwata Jazz in 1977 and OTTU Jazz in 1991. It is now called Msondo Ngoma and is run as an independent band.

37. In an article on the Expo, however, Mwinshehe's name is not mentioned. The Tanzania Dance Company, featuring Morris Nyunyusa (Mzee Morris) and the Tanzania Police Band, are listed as performers at the June 15 exposition (see the 1970 issue of the Tanzanian publication *Jenga* 6: 30–35). Possibly, Mwinshehe was added later or featured with the other groups.

38. Tama Athmani, Morogoro Jazz Band: Washindi wa siku ya vijana Tanzania 1970 (Morogoro Jazz Band: Winners of Tanzanian youth day 1970), *Nyota Afrika,* June 1970: 18.

39. Aboud Jumbe was the president of Zanzibar from 1972 until 1984. Rashidi Mfaume Kawawa was the prime minister of Tanzania from 1972 until 1977.

40. See Erasto Malila and Potfary Ngilangwa, 'Acheni kuiga muziki wa kigeni'-Sadru (Stop imitating foreign music—Sadru), *Tumaini Hill,* November 2000; Abdi Sultane, Can't Tanzanian artists shine with local beats? *Sunday Observer,* April 22, 2001.

41. Half of the £40,000 cost to build the ACC was donated by the Greek national Mr. G. N. Arnautoglu, who was one of the Tanganyika's richest people (Bertz 2008: 245).

42. Dancing and the socializing were the more popular of the activities, and a variety of groups and bands performed at the ACC. Ned Bertz writes that the lack of commercially available films made the cinema less attractive than dancing and the bar. He also looked at the income statements for the ACC and found that "the bar almost always topped the revenue charts, usually by at least a two-to-one margin over the dance receipts, both of which were tens of times greater than the money generated from the cinema" (2008: 247n85).

43. Tanzania National Archives, Dar es Salaam, Tanzania, file Arnautoglu Community Centre, TNA 540/27/6. My thanks to Ned Bertz for providing me with notes on this file.

44. The advertisements for these clubs were in the *The Tanganyika Standard,* Saturday, June 24, 1950.

45. Along with running the clubs, the DDC also took over butcher shops, petrol stations, and a number of local buildings. Eventually, the corporation realized that it did not have the resources to run the butcher shops and ended its ownership of the shops in 1978. In 1992, the corporation privatized its petrol stations, but the DDC still controls the four clubs and numerous buildings in the city.

46. The literal translation of Sauti ya Dar es Salaam is the Voice of Dar es Salaam, but the station was known as the Dar es Salaam Broadcasting Station in English.

47. Radio Kenya formed in 1927 (and began its first regular service in 1928), Radio Hargeisa (Somalia) in 1943, Radio-AEF in 1946, and a private station in 1935 (both in the Republic of the Congo), private stations in Zaïre (Congo) in 1936, and Radio Lusaka (Zambia) in 1941. Other East African stations came much later, such as Radio Uganda in 1958, Malawi Broadcasting Corporation in 1964, Voice of the Revolution (Burundi) in 1960, and Radio Rwanda in 1962. Radio, such as the "General Overseas Service," could be heard in Dar es Salaam prior to 1956, and newspapers regularly posted timetables in the late 1940s and early 1950s.

48. The figure 210,000 comes from TBC estimates that 10 percent of the urban areas had radios and less than one in fifty in rural areas (Mytton 1976: 272). By 1973, the number of receivers reached 1,737,000, in part because of a radio manufacturing plant built by Philips in Arusha (Mytton 1976: 270).

49. J. Yinza and Maurus Sichalwe, Stesheni ya radio ya mjini Dar es Salaam Yaendelea Vyema (Dar es Salaam radio station going well), *Mambo Leo* 555 (1954): 36.

50. This information comes from several interviews with radio employees. Gaudens Makunja provided details on the cost of the licenses, as well as the exchange rate around 1959 or 1960, which was Tsh 7 for US$1.

51. Tanganyika, *Assembly debates,* Dar es Salaam, 1961, 117.

52. Wakil later became president of Zanzibar in 1985.

53. United Republic of Tanzania, *Parliamentary debates,* Dar es Salaam, 1964, 845–55.

54. Many foreign radio services also broadcast in Tanzania. Shortwave radio was common particular among missionary groups, who used them in remote areas of eastern Africa. Radio Cairo broadcast in East Africa and, during the 1940s and 1950s, had anti-British programming (Brennan 2010). All India Radio broadcast in Swahili, English, and Gujarati languages. In the 1980s, the Swahili broadcast was for one hour in the morning and one at night. The German radio service Deutsche Welle also broadcast Swahili programming throughout the week in the 1970s and 1980s (see *Swahili Language and Society: Notes-News* 5 [1988] and 6 [1989] for a list of programs).

55. The songs "Dada Yangu" was composed by Hassani Bitchuka.

56. Malm and Wallis (1992: 114) provide a table of the music and programming on RTD's three main radio services (National, Commercial, and External Service). For all of the programming on all of the services, 60 percent was speeches, 27 percent was Tanzanian music, 15 percent was African, and 16 percent was listed as "Anglo-American." The high percentage of speeches gives some sense as to the frustration that many people had with radio and the reason that the privatization of radio was embraced in the mid-1990s.

57. In 1967, 70 percent of the music on RTD's National Program was of East African origin and most was dansi, while on the commercial service only 39 percent was Tanzanian and 55 percent was Zairian (Magayane 1988: 290). The National Program also used

very little imported material: only an hour and a half was drawn from the BBC Swahili Service and Swahili report from the United Nations each week. RTD's English Service, however, relied mainly on imported programs.

58. The report appeared on TVT, the national television, which is now called TBC 1, in September 2007. The report is summarized on various websites, including blogs.rnw.nl/medianetwork.

### 3. Live in Bongoland

1. From a survey with local music fans conducted by the author in Dar es Salaam, 2001.

2. The exception to this in Tanzania is bongo flava and gospel music, which are more popular in the sale of albums than concert tickets. Popular bongo flava artists, for instance, sometimes play only a few shows per year to large audiences.

3. In October 2006, for instance, 1,500 people filled Diamond Jubilee to see the American rapper Jay Z (Shawn Carter) perform along with several local groups, including T.I.D. and Top Band.

4. All-Star Taarab formed in 1988 and consists mainly of family members, including Mzee Muchacho (Abrahman A. Khamis), who runs the group, and his wife, Latifa Khamis, who writes the song lyrics. The band consists of two keyboardists, a pre-programmed drum machine, a guitarist, a bassist, and at least seven singers.

5. Dance floors have routinely become spaces where gay men can publicly act out and project their desires. At non-taarab events, however, there are frequently people who criticize and insult those who display overt homosexuality. Despite comments made against homosexuality, however openly, Dar es Salaam appears more accepting of gay men performing at clubs than other areas of the country. This is only a possibility and not based on any firm evidence. For discussions of homosexuality in Tanzanian society, see Amory 1996, 1998.

6. Fred Ogot, Dudubaya needs psychiatric help, but BASATA is to blame, *Guardian,* February 10, 2004.

7. Rachel Makena, Dar court denies 'Dudubaya' bail, *Guardian,* September 29, 2004.

8. This quote appeared under the name Curtis on youngafrican.com in the Ya Tanzania Tupo/Buruduni/Dudubaya forum, accessed on September 9, 2004.

9. James Nindi, Dk. Remmy Ongala: Nikipona kiharusi nitafanya sherehe (Doctor Remmy Ongala: If I recover from my stroke I will celebrate), *Tanzania Leo,* October 30, 2000. See also Graebner 1997: 112; Stewart 1992: 26.

10. In November 2006, Wanaume split into two groups, Wanaume TMK and Wanaume Halisi.

11. The average daily paper sells around 30,000 copies per day or 150,000 per week, which equals what *Uwazi* sells with one issue. *Ujamaa* and *Kiu* sell around 120,000. From a 2002 interview with Charles Mateso, a newspaper editor based in Dar es Salaam.

12. The best example of a defamatory article written about Chocky and his father is: Choki [sic] adaiwa kutishia kumpiga baba yake! (It's claimed that Chocky threatens to beat his father), *Ijumaa,* July 5–11, 2002. This article was written the week after the original article about Chocky not supporting his father financially. Both turned out to be fabricated stories.

13. Other artists also compose songs that address problems with celebrity and gossip. Lady Jay Dee's "Rafiki wa Mashaka" (Uncertain Friends) addresses friends who slandered Lady Jay Dee to attain tabloid publicity.

14. *Tanzania Daima* is publishing again and is run by the opposition party CHADEMA.

15. Two unknown assailants attacked the managing editor and a staff person of *Mwanahalisi* in January 5, 2008, with machetes and acid. The attack occurred as a response to a series of articles that appeared in the newspaper. It was considered the first attack on journalists since privatization. Media Institute of Southern Africa, Newspaper Suspended for 'Seditious' Article—Security Forces Summon Editor for Questioning, press release, October 14, 2008.

16. Bongo Celebrity website, bongocelebrity.com/about/, accessed August 8, 2008.

17. Bob Muthusi, Heko dada, Nairobi nzima haitasahau midundo hiyo yenu (Congratulations sisters, all of Nairobi will not forget your music beats), *Nyota Afrika,* January 1969, 14.

## 4. The Submerged Body

1. During the 1840s, Ludwig Krapf and Reverend J. Rebmann found a "snow-capped mountain" (Mount Kilimanjaro) in their work among the Chagga. Krapf was also the first person to translate the New Testament into Swahili. See Ingham 1965: 88–89 and Marsh and Kingsnorth 1966: 52–53.

2. Form five is a grade after high school and before college. In Tanzania, forms one through four are equivalent to American high school, with forms five and six pre-college grades, followed by college.

3. For more on the use of African musicians in European ballroom dance, see Open air: fancy dress dance, *Dar-es-Salaam Times,* September 1, 1923; Anthony 1983; Baker 1931.

4. This quote comes from conversations with staff at the Amana Youth Centre in June 2005.

5. Rahid Masimbi, interview by James Nindi, Dar es Salaam, December 2002. I am indebted to Nindi for interviewing Masimbi on my behalf. See also Masimbi 1990.

6. Since the fire, the school has received considerable funding to rebuild, including a $30 million grant from Japan.

7. Madrasa schools are Islamic schools found in Africa that blend Qur'anic school education with Western pedagogy (Reed 2003: 184).

8. Given its strong presence in Tanzania, Norway is often held up as an example of a country with a far more formalized educational system where the national legislature requires that all areas of the country offer programs to train children in the arts. Norway supported arts programs in eastern Africa, and, in 2008, established a three-year contract with Dhow Countries Music Academy (DCMA) based in Stone Town, Zanzibar. The academy focuses on Zanzibar styles of popular music, such as taarab and *kidumbak.* While widely acknowledged as important endeavors, these types of support often emphasize the wide gulf that exists economically and socially between the arts in Tanzania and places like Norway.

9. John Damian Komba, *Kiu,* July 5–11, 2000.

10. Fatima Grace Bapumia, Interview with Banana Zorro: There is no future of music in Tanzania, www.theexpress.com/express%20375/picnews.htm.

11. Ministry of National Education, *Kitabu cha Elimu ya Watu Wazima* (Book of Adult Education) (Dar es Salaam: KIUTA, 1978).

12. Child Economic Activity and School Attendance Rates, October 7, 2005. www .dol.gov/ilab/media/reports/tda/tda2005/Tanzania.pdf

13. Information about the approved education expenditures required in the year ending June 30, 2010, were taken from the Parliament of Tanzania, Summary of Public Expenditure 2009/2010: Consolidated Fund services and supply votes; Vote 46: Ministry of Education and Vocational Training.

14. Kitime's father also recorded for Tanganyika Broadcast Corporation in the 1950s. Some of these recordings can be found on the *Original Music* LP "African Acoustic: Guitar Songs from Tanzania, Zambia, and Zaire," OMCD 023.

15. Gearhart (1998: 166) writes about joining and switching groups in traditional ngoma music competition, which has many parallels to Tanzania's popular music scene.

16. Other authors have discussed the movement of artists to different bands (Graebner 1994b: 361; Tsuruta 2000 and 2001). Tsuruta even did a survey among fifty-nine musicians in three publicly owned bands, Vijana Jazz, OTTU Jazz, and Mlimani Park Orchestra. He found the average length of stay in a band for these musicians was 3.4 years, while 60 percent stayed for less than two years (Tsuruta 2001: 142–43).

17. Tadasu Tsuruta writes about band expenses and salaries in his article about the profession of music in Tanzania. He explains that, before the 1990s, most publicly owned bands did not receive performance fees after concerts and were only paid a monthly salary. During the 1990s, bands renegotiated their payment schemes and started to earn a percentage of the net profit from certain or all of their performances (2001: 132).

18. The word "ngangari" was originally an idiophone and no exact translation exists in English. Yet the image portrayed by the word is that of a strong, unwavering person.

## 5. Radio Revolution

1. In July 1951, *Sauti ya Dar es Salaam* (the Voice of Dar es Salaam) went on the air. It became RTD in 1965 and TBC in 2006. On March 15, 1951, *Sauti ya Unguja* (the Voice of Unguja) began its broadcasts. After the union with mainland Tanzania, the station became *Sauti ya Tanzania Zanzibar* (the Voice of Zanzibar).

2. TVZ was operating on a trial basis in March 9, 1973, but was officially inaugurated on January 12, 1974 (Sturmer 1998: 295). Aside from the few in coastal towns such as Tanga and Bagamoyo who had antennae large enough to receive the station's signals, mainland Tanzanian residents could not watch TVZ. People who lived near the Kenyan border also had limited access to Kenyan programming (Tanzania Broadcasting Commission 2000: 6).

3. In "Dar TV video owners demi-gods" published in the *Daily News* on June 16, 1990, Muhidin Issa Michuzi writes that people who owned televisions and video players during the soccer World Cup became extremely popular; they taped and sold copies of games to Dar es Salaam residents. Malm and Wallis also emphasize the importance of televisions and VCRs in the late 1980s, used for showing videos in village shops, drinking places, and upper- and middle-class homes (Malm and Wallis 1992: 109).

4. Abdallah Yakuti, Editor says TV too expensive for mainland, *Daily News*, June 2, 1990.

5. Music videos have become a central part of the local music economy in Tanzania. Most artists who release songs for the radio also film videos for television. There are three varieties of music videos in Tanzania: those recorded at television stations and then broadcast; those recorded at concerts and then sold to the public; and the situational- or narrative-based videos that feature scripts, editing, and, typically, good production quality. Since 2004, there has been a proliferation of independent studios whose sole purpose is to produce these situational or narrative based videos. In the past few years, most television stations report that shows that feature these videos are their most popular form of programming.

6. There was one other radio station, *Redio Sauti ya Injili* (Radio Voice of the Gospel), run by the World Lutheran Federation, during the 1960s. Though based in Addis Ababa, the station had nine full-time staff members in Mwika, Tanzania, who produced programs in Swahili. These programs were aired on the TBC's national channel. In 1963, the Tanzanian government withdrew time for broadcasting religious programs on the national channel, arguing that churches have the opportunity to use the broadcasts of Radio Voice of the Gospel from Addis Ababa (Welbourn 1965: 190). Redio Sauti ya Injili returned to Tanzania's airwaves on a trial basis on November 27, 1994, and continues to broadcast in 2010.

7. Other radio stations could be heard in Tanzania even during the socialist period. Shortwave broadcasts of a variety of radio stations, including the Voice of America (VOA), the British Broadcasting Corporation (BBC), and the German Deutsche Welle, could be heard in many parts of the country. People who were close to the borders of other countries could also pick up the broadcasts of neighboring countries. For other broadcasts that could be heard in Tanzania, see chapter 2.

8. For a summary of the *Daily News* article, see www.misa.org/mediarelease/radiomainsource.html.

9. Steadman Group, Tanzania all media and products survey, Dar es Salaam, 2005.

10. Through interests of its members, the United Nations has pushed strongly to have African countries sign and ratify the United Nations Convention Against Corruption (UNCAC). Tanzania signed UNCAC on December 9, 2003, and ratified it on May 25, 2005. This convention illustrates, according to law professor John Hatchard, "the importance that the international community attaches towards ensuring states worldwide take appropriate steps to prevent and combat corruption" (2007: 4). Other institutions, such as the World Bank and the European Union, have also maintained that the control of corruption is a priority area that needs to be addressed in order to provide financial assistance to Tanzania.

11. MISA, African media barometer Tanzania, 2008, www.misa.org/programme/mediamonitoring/tanzania2008.pdf.

12. Under the Prevention and Combating of Corruption Act 2007, the president appoints the director general of PSSB, who then reports to the president on any corruption issues. See section 2.1.3 of the Ifahamu Sheria Mpya ya Kuzuia na Kupambana Na Rushwa Nchini Namba 11 ya Mwaka 2007 (Prevention and Combating of Corruption Act 2007).

13. Ibid 5.11. Julian Petley (1999: 143) notes that there are fifty pieces of legislation that affect the freedom of British media, which exceeds those in Tanzania.

14. The Tanzania Communications Regulatory Authority Act, 2003, section 5(a) and (b).

15.  The Broadcasting Services Act, 1993, section 13(c) and (d). These conditions are modeled on the Canadian Broadcasting Act. Section 3.d.i–ii of the Canadian Act states that broadcasting system should "serve to safeguard, enrich and strengthen the cultural, political, social and economic fabric of Canada," and "encourage the development of Canadian expression by providing a wide range of programming that reflects Canadian attitudes, opinions, ideas, values and artistic creativity, by displaying Canadian talent in entertainment programming and by offering information and analysis concerning Canada and other countries from a Canadian point of view."

16.  Part III, sections (a), (b), (d), and (g) of the Broadcasting Services (Content) Regulation 2005, Government Notice no. 430 published on December 23, 2005.

17.  Parliamentary Debates, June 30, 1964: 841. Quoted in Mytton 1976: 188–189.

18.  For stations, such as Clouds FM, this proved problematic. As Ruge Mutahaba told me, "The problem we had was the news. We were supposed to broadcast Radio Tanzania news. They gave us a hard time on that. Because we were not doing news—our idea was that we were not ready to do news. But they said, if you are not ready to do news, you have to take [the news] from Radio Tanzania [RTD]." Due to financial and staff limitations, Clouds FM could not carry their own news broadcasts and were therefore forced to carry the news from RTD.

19.  At the Broadcasting Commission, one of the offices has several televisions and a radio playing local broadcasts. When I went to visit, one person was monitoring everything at once while also sifting through a pile of paperwork. Though the office worker may have been able to detect certain errors in broadcasting, it would have been impossible to detect them all.

20.  Khatib was the Minister of State in the prime minister's office until January 2006, when he became the Minister of Information, Culture, and Sports.

21.  Tanzanian Parliament (Bunge la Tanzania), Fourteenth meeting, session 1, January 26, 1999.

22.  The survey was conducted by the author and James Nindi in many areas of Dar es Salaam including Kinondoni, Mikocheni, Kariakoo, Upanga, and City Centre. We received survey results from men and women of different ages and economic backgrounds. The surveys featured twenty two questions covering various media formats in the country, including radio and television. Though only a small population was surveyed, I later used this information in my interviews with musicians, broadcasters, and others to gain insight into radio broadcasting culture.

23.  James Mwakisyala, A man of the people, *East African,* November 27–December 3, 2000: 6, 10.

24.  Tanzanian musicians elbow out their Congolese rivals, *Business Times,* May 18, 2001.

25.  Miguel Suleyman, Tanzanian musicians in nostalgic bid to revive East African rhythms, *East African,* June 29–July 8, 1998: part 2, 4.

26.  Tanzanian musicians elbow out their Congolese rivals, *Daily News,* May 18, 2001.

27.  Abdi Sultane, Can't Tanzanian artists shine with local beats? *Sunday Observer,* April 22, 2001.

28.  For more information on the TOT and Muungano rivalry, see Lange 1995 and 2000.

29.  Jeff Leeds, The new deal: Band as brand, *New York Times,* November 8, 2007.

30.  Michuzi, Lady JD named Zain envoys, *Daily News,* September 13, 2008.

31.  Gadner [*sic*] Habash, *Baab Kubwa,* June-July 2008, 5.

32. In the United States, where payola was banned in 1960, strategies exist to push an artist's music on the airwaves. Since radio stations can no longer take money directly from record companies, they use middlemen. Record companies pay independent promoters, called "indies," who pay radio stations to play songs of artists owned by the record company. Sometimes referred to as "pay to play," this technique does not allow artists managed by small companies to become a part of mainstream radio, since they cannot afford to influence radio station playlists. It is only the artists with strong enough financial support that find their way onto mainstream radio.

33. Fumbuka Ng'wanakilala, Scramble for airwaves on, *Daily News,* November 25, 2000.

### 6. Analog, Digital . . . Knobs, Buttons

1. PREACH stands for Promote Righteous Environmental and Community Health. The workshops were also supported by PACT of Tanzania and the Madunia Foundation of Holland.

2. The Kilimanjaro Hotel has since been renovated and is now called the Kilimanjaro Hotel Kempinski Dar es Salaam.

3. *Hip Hop Conference,* Dar es Salaam, March 14, 2001.

4. Producer is a term used by Tanzanians to refer to the main engineer and technician during a recording session. Several terms can be used to refer to the producer including *produza, watayarishaji wa muziki,* or *mtengenezaji ala za muziki.* Interestingly, the linguist Deo Ngonyani also found that the term produza once meant someone who is a liar. Unlike producers in other countries, who tend to fund and design recording projects based on their knowledge of a group and the public's interest in music, producers in Tanzania only work in a studio. Along with recording the music, Tanzanian producers can also act as studio musicians, playing drums, guitar, keyboard, and so on for a band's song.

5. To give a sense of the responsibilities that producers have in Tanzania, Thomas Porcello writes that engineers must be able to "operate the control room equipment (in a visual field of knobs, switches, and lighted displays that resembles, at first glance, the complexity of an airplane cockpit): of knowing music theory and performance practice sufficiently to understand performers', arrangers', and producers' discussions; of being familiar enough with electrical flow to trouble-shoot the inevitable broken signal path or feedback loop; of possessing at least a rudimentary knowledge of acoustics in order to make informed judgments about how sounds will translate from one listening environment to the next; and of mastering the intricate processes of audio recording ranging from microphone (mic) selection and placement to 'building a mix' step-by-step from performances captured on tape or disk" (2004: 733)

6. P. Funk's birth name is Paul Matthysse. Juma Nature is also known as Sir Nature. His birth name is Juma Kassim Ally.

7. This quote is from a Tanzania Revenue Authority brochure, also published online at www.tanzania.go.tz/tra.html.

8. Madaktari wapata mafunzo ya udhibiti magonjwa Pemba (Doctors receive lessons on controlling illness on Pemba), *Mtanzania,* November 11, 2007.

9. Francis Godwin, Sita watimuliwa Njombe kwa tuhuma za kuchoma moto shule (Six expelled from Njombe after being suspected of setting fire to a school), *Majra,* June 11, 2007.

10. Markus Hororius, Afrika yetu ni vibwagizo vya ugaidi (Our Africa is haven for terrorists), 20 *Rai*, December 2007.

11. Wivu, uchawi waua 1,223: Arusha, Shinyanga, Dar zaongoza (Jealousy, witchcraft kills 1,223: Arusha, Shinyanga, Dar have the most), *Nipashe*, December 17, 2002.

## 7. Legend of the Pirates

1. Other companies that were under the Ministry of Information included AVI (Audio-Visual Institute), which is now TBC1, Radio Tanzania Dar es Salaam (now the TBC), Tanzania School of Journalism (TSJ), and SHIHATA (SHIrika la HAbari la TAnzania, the Tanzanian News Organization), which is now dissolved.

2. George Nyembela, TFC clears first hurdle, *Daily News*, December 10, 1984; TFC 1995: 6.

3. In response to Sindimba being a dance used in schools, L. A. Mbuguni and G. Ruhumbika write that when performed out of context, such as at schools, it "borders on obscenity" (1974: 276). The dance, which remains popular among ngoma troupes in Dar es Salaam, features erotic hip movements by men and women (Askew 2002: 210–11; Lange 1995: 44).

4. I am grateful to Remmy Ongala for graciously offering me a copy of the Polygram contract.

5. The quote of Fadili William's appears in Philly Karashani, Muziki wa Kiswahili kukabiliwa na giza? (Is music in Swahili confronted with darkness?), *Nyota Afrika*, November 1964.

6. Into the 1980s, there was a one-hour Sunday afternoon show beginning at 2:00 called *At My Request* that played foreign music in English. Listeners could request songs through submitting postcards to the station. Since the studio's collection of foreign music was limited, however, the radio staff would frequently read the postcard, ignore the request for the foreign song, and then play a local band instead.

7. During the 1960s, instruments, record players, and records could be purchased at the following stores in Dar es Salaam: Mahmoud Radio Service, African Mercantile Co. Ltd., Assanand and Sons, Gokaldas Sunderji Rughani Ltd., Souza Junior Dias (Radio) Ltd., and Twentsche Overseas Trading Co. Ltd. Other establishments in Tanganyika included the Tanga Emporium in Tanga, and Mamdani's Radio House in Mwanza. See *Owen's African and Middle East commerce and travel and international register* (London: Owen's Commerce & Travel Ltd., 1961). An advertisement also appeared in *Nyota Afrika*, March 1964, listing some of these companies.

8. For instance, Urafiki Jazz and Orchestra Vijana Jazz released records after the closing of the border. See the discography for 45 rpm records released in 1978 and 1980.

9. This advertisement appeared in the *Daily News*, December 12, 1984: 11.

10. A technical expert from the West German company *Metall Consult Industrieanlagenbau*, Bernhard Murra, arrived in Tanzania to inspect the facilities. He said that all disc cutting and pressing equipment had arrived and that four engineers from his firm were scheduled to supervise installation of the machinery in June. The factory was set to employ sixty people, sending several to Germany for six weeks of training on the "technology of sound recording and disc cutting equipment maintenance." Disc cutting starts August, *Daily News*, February 25, 1985; George Nyembela, TFC Clears First Hurdle. *Daily News*, December 10, 1984.

11. Many details about the history of the TFC come from an interview with Amari Bakari, formerly the accountant and acting general manager of the TFC. Although discussions with Bakari occurred on several occasions in 2000 and 2001, I conducted a formal interview with him on February 8, 2001, in Dar es Salaam, Tanzania.

12. In the 1960s, 45s were sold for only six or seven Tanzanian shillings, which was around US$1. LPs were thirty to fifty Tanzanian shillings.

13. This *Daily News* advertisement appeared on December 15, 1984: 10.

14. This case was argued in Nairobi at the High Court of Kenya in 1981, but the name of the defendant, judge, and civil case number are removed from the printed copy. AIT Records is also listed on the court order and therefore may have participated in the lawsuit. My thanks to Jwani Mwaikusa for providing me a copy of this case.

15. See Kitime 1998; Herald Tagama, Musical pirates in full song in Tanzania, *New African*, September 1997; Bob Karashani, Tanzania needs law update to fight piracy, *East African*, May 25–31, 1998; Mark Gleeson, Piracy rubbing out music industry in East Africa, *Variety*, June 22, 1988; Fred de Vries, The deadly music pirates, *New African*, May 1988; Steven Mwangi and Robert Otani, Beware, video pirates at large, *New African*, September 1997.

16. This quote is from an interview by Viktoria Stöger-Eising with Nyerere in Butiama, December 9, 1995. It was published in Stöger-Eising 2000: 121.

17. Muhidini Issa Michuzi, Authorities 'derail' copyright law, *Daily News*, November 2, 1994: 5.

18. Chandra Doshi is a pseudonym.

19. By the mid-1990s, other companies emerged to compete with the Big Five. One company was the result of another merger between F. K. Mitha and Sons, Burhani Impex, and Wananchi Stores, which was collectively referred to as F. K. Mitha. These companies merged with the Big Five in 1996.

20. Sharon Sauwa, Wamachinga Dar kuanzisha benki yao (Petty traders to open their own bank), *Alasiri,* October 22, 2008.

21. Elias Mhegera, Petty traders defy dubious eviction attempts, *Express*, January 21, 2010, Dar es Salaam.

22. See, for example, John Oywa, Princess Jully takes on pirates, *Daily Nation*, May 8, 1998.

23. Walusanga Ndaki, Music pirates still riding high in Tanzania, *Financial Times,* January 31–February 6, 2001.

24. Despite Zahoro's confidence that the act would benefit both distributors and musicians, Zahoro had misgivings about how it would assist him. As an older musician who led one of the more popular dansi bands, Kiko Kids Jazz Band, from 1952 until 1984, he was concerned that the new law would not protect his older recordings. Although he composed for Shikamoo Jazz, in his view his greatest days as a musician had already passed.

25. Highly paid American superstars can receive a 15 percent royalty. From this 15 percent, record companies take out a percentage to pay for the producer of an album, the costs of rerecording and packaging the album, and the costs of giving out free albums to radio stations and promoters. In the end, an artist or group can earn half the percentage of the original agreement (Krasilovsky and Shemel 1995).

26. The costs to produce cassettes in Tanzania are as follows: to make a cover (Tsh 100), buy a blank cassette in bulk (Tsh 200), and make a copy (Tsh 100) costs half the

price of the tape when it is sold to vendors at Tsh 800 (80 cents). Paying an artist a Tsh 150 royalty leaves a distributor with Tsh 250, which with contractual fees and shipping costs dwindles to around Tsh 150. For groups that can sell tens of thousand copies within the first few months of release, distributors can still make sizable profits. Further, once the tape is sold to vendors, GMC takes no further responsibility for the merchandise. They work as intermediaries between musicians and vendors in distributing cassettes throughout eastern Africa.

27. Draft document, United Republic of Tanzania, the copyright and neighboring rights (production and distribution of sound and audiovisual recordings) regulation, 2005. I am grateful to COSOTA for providing me with a copy of this document.

28. Details of this court case and others listed in this paragraph were provided to me by staff at COSOTA. I am grateful to them for showing me this and other cases related to current trends in popular music.

## 8. Everything Is Life

1. The stakeholders of these television stations include Ramish Patel, 6 percent; Shabir Abji, 20 percent; Shabir Dewji, 20 percent; Francesco Tramontano, 15 percent; Bud Kassum, 9 percent; Girish Chande, 10 percent; and Melton Ltd., 20 percent

2. This statement was made at the opening of the April 24, 2001, meeting entitled "Understanding and Enforcing Copyright in Tanzania," Dar es Salaam.

3. Ministry of Education and Culture's 2001 policy document, Cultural Development Master Plan for Tanzania.

4. This quote appeared on the Darhotwire website: www.darhotwire.com/bongo mdundo/news/2008/02/13/wengi_wamlilia_mjema.html, accessed on February 20, 2008.

5. Other people who have passed away in recent years include TX Moshi William, Freddy Benjamin, Justin Kalikawe, Nsimba Monimambo, Omar Kopa, Athuman Momba, Suleiman Mbembwe, Joseph Maina, Adbul Muhono, Adamu Bakari, Banza Mchafu, Jerry Nashoni, Mbuja Makonga Adios, Mulenga Kalonge, Ilunga Lubaba, Mbwana Cokks-Matimila, Tino Masinge, Chinyama Chianza, Mike Bilali, Bakari Mlanzi, Machaku Salum, Abel Batazali, Mohamed Mzee, Farahani Mzee, Francis Lubua, Mohamed Mwinyikondo, Juma Mrisho, Michael Vincent, Kyanda Songa, Dingituka Mulay, Joseph Mulenga, Batio Senga, Osi Senga, Asia Daruweshi, Rahma Shari, Nana Njige, Mohamed Shaweji, Mohamed Gotagota, Shaban Dogodogo, and, most recently, Mawazo Hunja (Shauri Mbele), Abou Semhando, and Remmy Ongala.

6. For instance, according to a medical study conducted in 2005, Dar es Salaam is reported to have some of the lowest suicide rates in the world (Mgaya et. al. 2008).

7. Comment on "Wengi wamlilia Mjema" (Many weep for Mjema), posted February 14, 2008, www.darhotwire.com/general/m_v.php?i=3022.

8. Mkapa declines the word 'bongo'!, www.darhotwire.com, May 5, 2003.

# References

## INTERVIEWS

All interviews were conducted face to face by the author in Dar es Salaam unless otherwise noted. Those interviews that were recorded have an "R" at the end of a reference and are available at the Archives of Traditional Music (ATM) at Indiana University, Bloomington, under the accession number 07-007-F/C/B. The majority of interviews were conducted in Kiswahili. The names are alphabetized by an individual's birth name. Any nicknames or common alternative spellings of the individual's names are placed in parentheses after the full name.

Ally, Waziri. June 17, 1999, April 30, 2001. R.
———. Personal communication. January 16, 2010.
Bakari, Amari. February 8, 2001.
Balisidya, Patrick. June 6, 1999. R.
Bangera, Monaliza. March 13, 2001.
Baraka, Asha. March 21, 2001.
Bitchuka, Hassani Rehani. June 17, 2005. R.
Bizman, Ntavyo. September 9, 2005. R.
Chavula, Serman. April 5, 2001.
Chenga, Norbert. October 12, 2000. R
Chidumule, Cosmas Tobias. October 30, 2000. R.
Chilala, Thomas. July 4, 2002. R.
Chocky, Ally. February 1, 2001, July 7, 2002, September 20, 2009. R.
Dede, Shabani (Shaaban) July 3, 2002. R.
Dilinga, John. July 2, 2002. R.
Dina, Ali. May 17, 2001.
Dola, Ahmed (Balozi Dola). November 11, 2000. R.
Enoch, Michael. November 3, 2000. R.
Graebner, Werner. December 29, 2000. R.
Gurumo, Muhidin. June 9, 2005. R.
Haniu, Jaffar. July 2, 2002. R.
Haroun, Inspekta. January 16, 2001. R.
Haule, Joseph (Professor Jay). Tanga, January 19, 2001. R.
Jamwaka, Ally Omary. May 30, 2001.

Karenga, Shem Ibrahim. July 4, 2002, and June 9, 2005. R.

Kari, Miikka Mwamba. December 6, 2000. R.

Kashamatubajike, Kanku Kelly. October 26, 2000. R.

Kasheba, Fred Ndala. October 16, 2000. R.

Kaswahili, Francis. July 15, 1999 and October 11, 2000. R.

Khamis, Abrahman. October 15, 2000.

Khamis, Ali Ahmed (Cool Para). November 3, 2000. R.

Kihwele, Lucy Tabasamu. March 5, 2001.

Kilosa, Boniface (Bonnie Luv). February 23, 2001. R.

Kimario, Joachim (Master Jay). November 29, 2000. R.

Kimbuteh, Jah. November 15, 2000. R.

Kinasha, Carola. March 28–29, 2001. R.

Kitime, John. June 14, 1999 and June 18, 2010. R.

Komba, John. February 6, 2001. R.

Kothari, Ramesh. June 11, 2001, July 10, 2005, and June 20, 2010.

Liochi, Abdallah. July 3, 2002. R.

Lipangile, Zainabu (Zay B). June 10, 2005. R.

Liundi, Taji. October 23, 2000, March 12, 2001, June 8, 2005. R.

Lubua, Francis (Nassir Lubua). October 10, 2000.

Luhala, Angelo. June 5, 1999. R.

Luhende, Samuel (Ngosha). November 3, 2000. R.

Maganga, Sebastian. October 14, 2000. R.

Mahingila, E. E. June 17, 1999. R.

Makunja, Gaudens. July 4, 2002. R.

Makwaia, Daudi. January 19, 2002. R.

Mangula, E. T. March 21, 2001.

Mapili, Kassim. June 15, 1999.

Mariki, Frederick (Mkoloni). June 13, 2005. R.

Mateso, Charles. August 28 and 31, 2002.

Mbenna, Paul (Mr. Paul). June 10, 2002.

Mbilinyi, Joseph (Mr. II/ Sugu). October 5, 1999, November 6, 2000, and July 12, 2005. R.

Mbunju, James. November 10, 2000. R.

Mbutu, Luizer (Luiza Mbuttu). May 15, 2001. R.

Menje, Sister Mary. November 4, 2000.

Mhutu, Charles. November 24, 2000. R.

Mjema, John. November 2, 2000. R.

Mkango, Yahaya Abeid (Professor). October 27, 2000. R.

Mngodo, Godfrey. February 22, 2001.

Mohamed, Jamal Jumbe (Jimmy Jamal). June 4, 2005. R.

Monimambo, Nsimba. January 10, 2001. R.

Moulanga, Kiti Omari Abdala (Q). October 9, 2000. R.

Mpango, Kikumbi Mwanza (Kiki, King). October 24, 2000, February 9, 2007, February 10, 2007. R.

Mponjika, Ramadhani (Rhymson). Phone Interview by author. May 23, 2004. R.

Mrisho, Juma. June 29, 1999. R.

Msindi, Suleiman (Afande Sele). June 13, 2005. R.

Mtetewaunga, Stephan Dominique. December 7, 2000. R.

Mulimba, Ruyembe C. November 28, 2000. R.
Mustapha, Rashid (Spider). November 2, 2000. R.
Mutahaba, Ruge. November 15, 2000. R.
Mwaikusa, Jwani Timothy. June 30, 1999. R.
Mwa-Mnyenyelwa, Mgurga. November 29, 2000. R.
Ndagala, Daniel. May 18, 2001. R.
Ngaiza, Anselim Tryphone (Soggy Doggy Anter). October 31, 2000. R.
Ongala, Ramadhani Mtolo (Remmy). October 19, 2000. R.
Paulsen, Rita. March 5, 2001.
Pentelakis, John Peter. June 18, 2005. R.
Ponera, Khalid. July 26,1999. R.
Said, Shakila. October 18, 2000. R.
Singo, Kibacha (KBC/ K-Singo). Phone interview by author. May 27, 2004. R.
Stone, Banza. December 8, 2000. R.
Sykes, Ally. June 7, 2005. R.
Tyabji, Rosa Constanza and Michel. January 10, 2001. R.
Tyabji, Rosa Costanza. Phone interview by author. June 6, 2003. R.
Wambura, Judith (Lady Jay Dee). February 26, 2001. R.
Waymark, Steven (Steve 2K). November 2, 2000. R.
Yessayah, Ambwene Allen (AY). June 4, 2005. R.
Zahoro, Salim. June 29, 1999. R.
Ziada, Rashidi (KR). November 9, 2000. R.

## ARCHIVES

Asian and Middle Eastern Collection, New York Public Library, New York.
East Africana section, University of Dar es Salaam Library, Dar es Salaam, Tanzania.
World Intellectual Property Organization Library, Geneva, Switzerland.

## PUBLISHED AND UNPUBLISHED MATERIALS

Abu-Lughod, Lila. 2005. *Dramas of nationhood: The politics of television in Egypt*. Chicago: University of Chicago Press.
Amabile, Teresa M. 1990. Within you, without you: The social psychology of creativity, and beyond. In *Theories of creativity*, ed. Mark A. Runco and Robert S. Albert, 61–91. Newbury Park, Calif.: Sage Publications.
Amory, Deborah P. 1996. Women in marriage on the East African Swahili speaking coast. Paper presented at the annual meeting of the African Studies Association, San Francisco.
———. 1998. Mashoga, mabasha, and magai: "Homosexuality" on the East African coast. In *Boy-wives and female husbands: Studies of African homosexualities*, ed. Stephen O. Murray and Will Roscoe, 67–87. New York: St. Martin's Press.
Anthony, David Henry, III. 1983. Culture and society in a town in transition: A people's history of Dar es Salaam, 1865–1939. Ph.D. diss., University of Wisconsin-Madison.
Appadurai, Arjun. 1986. Introduction: Commodities and the politics of value. *The social life of things: Commodities in cultural perspective*, ed. Arjun Appadurai, 3–63. New York: Cambridge University Press.

Ardener, Edwin. 1970. *Kingdom on Mount Cameroon: Documents for the history of Buea, 1844–1848.* West Cameroon: Government Press.

Arledge, Chris. 2009. Is copyright law stifling creativity? bighollywood.breitbart.com. Accessed August 1, 2009.

Arvidsson, Adam. 2005. Brands: A critical perspective. *Journal of Consumer Culture* 5 (2): 235–58.

Askew, Kelly M. 2000. Following in the tracks of *Beni:* The diffusion of the Tanga *taarab* tradition. In *Mashindano! Competitive music performance in East Africa,* ed. Frank Gunderson and Gregory F. Barz, 21–38. Dar es Salaam: Mkuki na Nyota.

———. 2002. *Performing the nation: Swahili music and cultural politics in Tanzania.* Chicago: University of Chicago Press.

———. 2006. Sung and unsung: Musical reflections on postsocialist Tanzania. *Africa* 76 (1): 15–43.

Attard, David. 1993. The fight against piracy. Paper presented at the Seminar on Copyright and Neighboring Rights for the Member States of the Gulf Cooperation Council, Abu Dhabi, United Arab Emirates, May 9–11.

Averill, Gage. 1989. Haitian dance bands, 1915–1970: Class, race, and authenticity. *Latin American Music Review* 10 (2): 203–35.

———. 1997. *A day for the hunter, a day for the prey: Popular music and power in Haiti.* Chicago: University of Chicago Press.

Baker, E. C. 1931. *Memorandum on the social conditions of Dar es Salaam, 4 June 1931.* University of London.

Ballanga, Andwele N. 1992. The National Dance Troupe as a case study. BA thesis, University of Dar es Salaam.

Baraza la Muziki la Taifa (BAMUTA). n.d. *Wanamuziki wetu: Kitabu cha Kwanza* [Our Musicians: The First Book]. Dar es Salaam: BAMUTA.

Barrett, David B., George T. Kurian, and Todd M. Johnson, eds. 2001. *World Christian encyclopedia: A comparative survey of churches and religions in the modern world.* Oxford: Oxford University Press.

Barz, Gregory Fredrick. 1997. The performance of religious and social identity: An ethnography of post-mission *Kwaya* music in Tanzania (East Africa). Ph.D. diss., Brown University.

———. 1998. Kwayas: They're singing jazz in the church. research.umbc.edu/eol/2/barz.

———. 2000. Politics of remembering: Performing history(-ies) in Youth *Kwaya* competitions in Dar es Salaam, Tanzania. In *Mashindano! Competitive music performance in East Africa,* ed. Frank Gunderson and Gregory F. Barz, 379–405. Dar es Salaam: Mkuki na Nyota.

———. 2003. *Performing religion: Negotiating past and present in Kwaya music of Tanzania.* Amsterdam: Rodopi.

Bauman, Richard, and Charles L. Briggs. 1990. Poetics and performance as critical perspectives on language and social life. *Annual Review of Anthropology* 19: 59–88.

Beck, Rose-Marie. 1992. Women are devils! A formal and stylistic analysis of Mwanameka. In *Sokomoko: Popular culture in East Africa,* ed. Werner Graebner, 115–32. Atlanta: Rodopi.

Belcher, Stephen P. 1999. *Epic traditions of Africa.* Bloomington: Indiana University Press.

Berger, Bennett M. 1971. *Looking for America: Essays on youth, suburbia, and other American obsessions*. Englewood Cliffs, N.J.: Prentice-Hall.

Bernstein, Arthur, Naoki Sekine, and Dick Weissman. 2007. *The global music industry: Three perspectives*. New York: Routledge.

Bertz, Ned O. 2008. Race, urban space, and nationalism in Indian Ocean world history: Schools, cinemas, and the Indian Diaspora in Tanzania, 1920–2000. Ph.D. diss., University of Iowa.

Bettig, Ronald V. 1996. *Copyrighting culture: The political economy of intellectual property*. Boulder, Colo.: Westview Press.

Bharati, Agehananda. 1972. *The Asians in East Africa: Jayhind and Uhuru*. Chicago: Nelson-Hall.

Bomani, Mark D. 2000. Foreword. *Tanzania Broadcasting Commission broadcasting directory*. Dar es Salaam: TBC.

Bourdieu, Pierre. 1998. The essence of neo-liberalism. *Le Monde Diplomatique*, December. mondediplo.com/1998/12/08bourdieu, accessed 2008.

Braudy, Leo. 2000. *The frenzy of renown: Fame and its history*. Bridgewater, N.J.: Replica Books.

Brennan, James R. 2002. Nation, race and urbanization in Dar es Salaam, Tanzania, 1916–1976. Ph.D. diss., Northwestern University.

———. 2006. Realizing civilization through patrilineal descent: The intellectual making of an African racial nationalism in Tanzania, 1920–1950. *Social Identities* 12 (4): 405–23.

———. 2010. Radio Cairo and the decolonization of East Africa, 1953–1964. In *Making a world after empire: The Bandung moment and its political afterlives*, ed. Christopher J. Lee, 173–95. Athens: Ohio University Press.

Brennan, James, and Andrew Burton. 2007. The emerging metropolis: A history of Dar es Salaam, circa 1862–2000. In *Dar es Salaam: The history of an emerging East African metropolis*, ed. Andrew Burton, James Brennan, and Yusuf Lawi, 13–75. London and Dar es Salaam: British Institute and Mkuki wa Nyota.

Brenneis, Donald. 1990. Musical imaginations: Comparative perspectives on music creativity. In *Theory of creativity*, ed. Mark A. Runco and Robert S. Albert, 170–89. Newbury Park, Calif.: Sage Publications.

Bridger, Susan, and Frances Pine. 1998. *Surviving post-socialism: Local strategies and regional responses in eastern Europe and the former Soviet Union*. Routledge studies of societies in transition 4. London: Routledge.

Bujra, Janet M. 2000. *Serving class: Masculinity and the feminisation of domestic service in Tanzania*. Edinburgh: Edinburgh University Press for the International African Institute, London.

Bukuku, Enos S. 1993. *The Tanzanian economy: Income distribution and economic growth*. Westport, Conn.: Praeger.

Bunten, Alexis Celeste. 2008. Sharing culture or selling out? Developing the commodified persona in the heritage industry. *American Ethnologist* 35 (3): 380–95.

Burawoy, Michael, Pavel Krotov, and Tatyana Lytkina. 2000. Involution and destitution in capitalist Russia. *Ethnography* 1 (1): 43–65.

Burton, Andrew. 2005. *African underclass: Urbanisation, crime and colonial order in Dar es Salaam 1919–61*. Athens: Ohio University Press.

Butler, Judith. 1990. *Gender trouble: Feminism and the subversion of identity.* New York: Routledge.

Caldwell, Melissa. 2008. Domesticating the French fry: McDonald's and consumerism in Moscow. *Journal of Consumer Culture* 4 (1): 5–25.

Campbell, Carol Ann A. 1983. Nyimbo za kiswahili: A socio-ethnomusicological study of a Swahili poetic form. Ph.D. diss., University of Washington.

Castile, George Pierre. 1996. The commodification of Indian identity. *American Anthropologist* 98 (4): 743–49.

Chachage, Seithy L. 2009. Ndani ya bongo: Utandawazi na migogoro ya utamaduni. Unpublished paper, Department of Sociology, University of Dar es Salaam.

Chasteen, John Charles. 2000. Black kings, blackface carnival, and nineteenth-century origins of the tango. In *Latin American Popular Culture,* ed. William H. Beezley and Linda A. Curcio-Nagy, 43–59. Wilmington, Del.: SR Books.

Chavula, Serman W. 1998. Current status of collective management of copyright in the southern Africa development community. Paper presented at the WIPO Technical Workshop on Collective Management of Copyright in the SADC Countries, Lusaka, Zambia, November 23–25.

Chilongo, Greenfield. 2003. The administration of reprographic rights and the establishment and role of reproduction rights organizations. Paper presented at the WIPO National Seminar on the Economic Importance of Copyright and Related Rights Protection, Kampala, Uganda, December 16–17.

Chiume, M.W. Kanyama. 1975. *Kwacha: An autobiography.* Nairobi: East African Publishing House.

Clark, Gracia. 1994. *Onions are my husband: Survival and accumulation by West African market women.* Chicago: University of Chicago Press.

Clarke, Simon. 2002. *Making ends meet in contemporary Russia: Secondary employment, subsidiary agriculture, and social networks.* Cheltenham: E. Elgar.

Cliggett, Lisa. 2005. *Grains from grass: Aging, gender, and famine in rural Africa.* Ithaca, N.Y.: Cornell University Press.

Coe, Cati, and Bonnie K. Nastasi. 2006. Stories and selves: Managing the self through problem solving in school. *Anthropology and Education Quarterly* 37 (2): 180–98.

Collins, John. 1992. *West African pop roots.* Philadelphia: Temple University Press.

———. 1993. The problem of oral copyright: The case of Ghana. In *Music and copyright,* ed. Simon Frith. Edinburgh: Edinburgh University Press.

Comaroff, Jean, and John L. Comaroff. 2001. Millennial capitalism: First thoughts on the second coming. In *Millennial capitalism and the culture of neoliberalism,* ed. Jean Comaroff and John L. Comaroff, 1–56. Durham, N.C.: Duke University Press.

Coplan, David. 1979. The African musician and the development of the Johannesburg entertainment industry: 1900–1960. *Journal of Southern African Studies* 5 (2): 134–64.

———. 1980. Marabi culture: Continuity and transformation in African music in Johannesburg, 1920–1940. *African Urban Studies* 6: 49–78.

———. 1982. The urbanization of African music: Some theoretical observations. *Popular Music* 2: 113–29.

———. 1985. *In township tonight! South Africa's black music city music and theatre.* New York: Longman.

———. 1994. *In the time of cannibals: The world music of South Africa's Basotho migrants.* Chicago: University of Chicago Press.

Coupland, Reginald. 1939. *The exploitation of East Africa: The slave trade and the scramble, 1856–1890.* London: Faber and Faber.

Crapanzano, Vincent. 2003. Reflections on hope as a category of social and psychological analysis. *Cultural Anthropology* 18 (1): 3–32.

Crowe, Barbara J. 2004. *Music and soulmaking: Toward a new theory of music therapy.* Lanham, Md.: Scarecrow Press.

Curtis, Debra. 2004. Commodities and sexual subjectivities: A look at capitalism and its desires. *Cultural Anthropology* 19 (1): 95–121.

Daniel, Yvonne. 1995. *Rumba: Dance and social change in contemporary Cuba.* Bloomington: Indiana University Press.

Daniels, Douglas Henry. 1996. Taarab clubs and Swahili music culture. *Social Identities* 2 (3): 413–38.

Danielson, Virginia. 1997. *The voice of Egypt: Umm Kulthum, Arabic song, and Egyptian society in the twentieth century.* Chicago: University of Chicago Press.

Davies, Bronwyn, and Rom Harré. 1990. Positioning: The discursive production of selves. *Journal of the Theory of Social Behavior* 20 (1): 43–63.

Development Economics Research Group on International Trade. 2001. Workshop on the development of the music industry in Africa. Washington, D.C.: The World Bank. siteresources.worldbank.org/INTCEERD/Resources/CWI_music_industry in _Africa_synopsis.pdf

Dikobe, Maude. 2003. Doing she own thing: Gender, performance, and subversion in Trinidad calypso. Ph.D. diss., University of California, Berkley.

Diouf, Mamadou. 2000. The Senegalese Murid trade diaspora and the making of a vernacular cosmopolitanism. *Public Culture* 12 (3): 679–702.

Downing, John, and Charles Husband. 2005. *Representing race: Racisms, ethnicities and media.* London: Sage Publications.

Durham, Deborah. 2004. Disappearing youth: Youth as a social shifter in Botswana. *American Ethnologist* 31 (4): 589–605.

Edmondson, Laura. 2007. *Performance and politics in Tanzania: The nation on stage.* Bloomington: Indiana University Press.

Englert, Birgit. 2004. Africa raps back: Reflections on hip hop from Tanzania and South Africa. In *Crossing borders: Interdisciplinary approaches to Africa,* ed. Anne Schröder, 77–79. Berlin: Lit Verlag.

Erlmann, Veit. 1996. *Nightsong: Performance, power, and practice in South Africa.* Chicago: University of Chicago Press.

Escobar, Arturo. 1995. *Encountering development: The making and unmaking of the third world.* Princeton, N.J.: Princeton University Press.

Ewens, Graeme. 1992. *Africa O-Ye!: A celebration of African music.* New York: Da Capo Press.

Fabian, Johannes. 1990. *Power and performance: Ethnographic explorations through proverbial wisdom and theater in Shaba, Zaire.* Madison: University of Wisconsin Press.

Fair, Laura. 2001a. Voice, authority, and memory: The Kiswahili recordings of Siti Binti Saadi. In *African words, African voices: Critical practices in oral history,* ed. Luise White, Stephan F. Miescher, and David William Coifen, 246–63. Bloomington: Indiana University Press.

———. 2001b. *Pastimes and politics: Culture, community, and identity in post-revolution Zanzibar, 1890–1945.* Athens: Ohio University Press.

Fardon, Richard, and Graham Furniss, eds. 2000. *African broadcast cultures: Radio in transition.* Oxford: J. Currey.

Fargion, Janet Topp. 1993. The role of women in Taarab in Zanzibar: An historical examination of a process of Africanisation. *The World of Music* 35 (2): 109–25.

———. 2000. Hot Kabisa! The Mpasho phenomenon and Taarab in Zanzibar. In *Mashindano! Competitive music performance in East Africa,* ed. Frank D. Gunderson and Gregory F. Barz, 39–53. Dar es Salaam: Mkuki na Nyota.

———. 2004. Liner notes for *Out of Cuba: Latin American music takes Africa by storm.* The British Library Sound Archive. Topic World Series, TSCD957.

Farley, Michael P., and Robert A. Blewett. 1998. Pocket money and Le Grand Maitre: The popular music industries of Kenya and Zaire contrasted. Paper presented at the annual meeting of the Society for Ethnomusicology, Bloomington, Indiana.

Farrell, Eileen Ruth. 1980. Ngoma ya Ushindani: Competitive song exchange and the subversion of hierarchy in a Swahili Muslim town on the Kenya coast. Ph.D. diss., Harvard University.

Feld, Steven. 1994. From schizophrenia to schismogenesis: On the discourses and commodification practices of 'world music' and 'world beat.' In *Music Groove: Essays and Dialogues,* ed. Charles Keil and Stephen Feld. Chicago: University of Chicago Press.

Ferguson, James. 2006. *Global shadows: Africa in the neoliberal world order.* Durham, N.C.: Duke University Press.

Finnegan, Ruth H. 2007. *The hidden musicians: Music-making in an English town.* Middletown, Conn.: Wesleyan University Press.

Florida, R. 2002. *The rise of the creative class: And how it's transforming work, leisure, community, and everyday life.* New York: Basic Books.

Forster, Peter G., Michael Hitchcock, and Francis F. Lyimo. 2000. *Race and ethnicity in East Africa.* New York: St. Martin's Press.

Foster, Robert J. 2002. *Materializing the nation: Commodities, consumption, and media in Papua New Guinea.* Bloomington: Indiana University Press.

———. 2007. The work of the new economy: Consumers, brands, and value creation. *Cultural Anthropology* 22 (4): 707–31.

Franken, Marjorie Ann. 1986. Anyone can dance: A survey and analysis of Swahili Ngoma, past and present. Ph.D. diss., University of California, Riverside.

Freedman, Des. 2008. *The politics of media policy.* Cambridge: Polity Press.

Freeman, Carla. 2007. The reputation of neoliberalism. *American Ethnologist* 34 (2): 252–67.

Friedson, Steven M. 1996. *Dancing prophets: Musical experience in Tumbuka healing.* Chicago: University of Chicago Press.

Frith, Simon. 2004. Towards an aesthetic of popular music. In *Music and identity.* Vol. 4 of *Popular music: Critical concepts in media and cultural studies,* ed. Simon Frith, 32–47. New York: Routledge.

Gearhart, Rebecca Kathleen. 1998. Ngoma memories: A history of competitive music and dance performance on the Kenya coast. Ph.D. diss., University of Florida.

———. 2000. Rama Maulidi: A competitive ritual Ngoma in Lamu. In *Mashindano! Competitive music performance in East Africa,* ed. Frank D. Gunderson and Gregory F. Barz, 347–65. Dar es Salaam: Mkuki na Nyota.

Geertz, Clifford. 1973. *The interpretation of cultures: Selected essays.* New York: Basic Books.

Geiger, Susan. 1997. *TANU women: Gender and culture in the making of Tanganyikan nationalism: 1955–1965.* Portsmouth, N.H.: Heinemann.

Gell, Alfred. 1986. Newcomers to the world of goods: Consumption among the Muria Gonds. In *The social life of things: Commodities in cultural perspective,* ed. Arjun Appadurai, 110–38. Cambridge: Cambridge University Press.

Geschiere, Peter. 1998. Globalization and the power of indeterminate meaning: Witchcraft and spirit cults in Africa and East Asia. *Development and Change* 29 (4):811–37.

Giddens, Anthony. 1991. *Modernity and self identity: Self and society in the late modern age.* Stanford: Stanford University Press.

Gilman, Lisa. 2009. *The dance of politics: Gender, performance, and democratization in Malawi.* Philadelphia: Temple University Press.

Ginsburg, Faye. 1997. 'From little things, big things grow': Indigenous media and cultural activism. In *Between resistance and revolution: Cultural politics and social protest,* ed. Richard G. Fox and Orin Starn, 118–44. New Brunswick, N.J.: Rutgers University Press.

Gluckman, Max. 1956. *Custom and conflict in Africa.* Oxford: Basil Blackwell.

Goldstein, Paul. 2003. *Copyright's highway: The law and lore of copyright from Gutenberg to the celestial jukebox.* New York: Hill and Wang.

Gondola, Charles Didier. 1997. *Villes miroirs: Migrations et identités urbaines à Brazzaville et Kinshasa, 1930–1970.* Paris: L'Harmattan.

Goode, William J. 1978. *The celebration of heroes: Prestige as a social control system.* Berkley: University of California Press.

Graebner, Werner. 1991. Tarabu Populäre musik am Indischen Ozean. In *Populäre musik in Afrika,* ed. Veit Erlmann, 181–201. Berlin: Museum für Völkerkunde.

———. 1994a. Swahili musical party: Islamic taarab music of East Africa. In *World music: The rough guide,* ed. Simon Broughton et al., 349–55. London: Rough Guides.

———. 1994b. Marashi ya Dar es Salaam: Dance with style; The flavour of Dar es Salaam. In *World music: The rough guide,* ed. Simon Broughton et al., 355–62. London: Rough Guides.

———. 1997. Whose music? The songs of Remmy Ongala and the Orchestra Super Matimila. In *Readings in African Popular Culture,* ed. Karin Barber, 110–17. Bloomington: Indiana University Press.

———. 1999. Tanzania—popular music and Tanzania/ Kenya—Taarab: The Swahili coastal sound. In *World music: The rough guide, vol. 1: Africa, Europe, and the Middle East,* ed. S. Broughton, M. Ellingham, and R. Trillo, 681–97. London: Rough Guides.

———. 2000a. Ngoma ya Ukae: Competitive social structure in Tanzanian dance music songs. In *Mashindano! Competitive music performance in East Africa,* ed. Frank D. Gunderson and Gregory F. Barz, 295–318. Dar es Salaam: Mkuki na Nyota.

———. 2000b. *Salum Abdallah and Cuban marimba: Ngoma Iko Huku.* CD liner notes. Todtnauberg, Germany: Dizim Records.

———. 2004. The interaction of Swahili taarab music and the record industry: A historical perspective (Tanzania). In *African media cultures: Transdisciplinary perspectives,* ed. Rose Marie Beck and Frank Wittmann, 171–92. Köln: Rüdiger Köppe Verlag.

———. 2007. The *ngoma* impulse: From club to nightclub in Dar es Salaam. In *Dar es Salaam: The history of an emerging East African metropolis*, ed. Andrew Burton, James Brennan, and Yusuf Lawi, 177–97. London and Dar es Salaam: British Institute and Mkuki wa Nyota.

Graham, Ronnie. 1992. *The world of African music*. Vol. 2 of *Stern's guide to contemporary African music*. London: Pluto Press.

———. 1994. Tanzanian new wave. In *World music: The rough guide*, ed. Simon Broughton, M. Ellingham, and R. Trillo, 356. London: Rough Guides.

Greene, Paul D., and Thomas Porcello. 2005. *Wired for sound: Engineering and technologies in sonic cultures*. Middletown, Conn.: Wesleyan University Press.

Greenhill, Romilly, and Irene Wekiya. 2004. *Turning off the taps: Donor conditionality and water privatisation in Dar es Salaam, Tanzania*. London: ActionAid International. www.actionaid.org.uk/_content/documents/TurningofftheTAps.pdf.

Gregory, Steven. 2007. *The devil behind the mirror: Globalization and politics in the Dominican Republic*. Berkeley: University of California Press.

Guilbault, Jocelyne. 1993. *Zouk: World music in the West Indies*. Chicago: University of Chicago Press.

———. 2007. *Governing sound: The cultural politics of Trinidad's Carnival musics*. Chicago: University of Chicago Press.

Gunderson, Frank. 1999. Musical labor associations in Sukumaland, Tanzania: History and practice. Ph.D. diss., Wesleyan University.

———. 2000a. 'Kifungua Kinywa,' or opening the contest with chai. In *Mashindano! Competitive music performance in East Africa*, ed. Frank D. Gunderson and Gregory F. Barz, 7–20. Dar es Salaam: Mkuki na Nyota.

———. 2000b. Witchcraft, witcraft, and musical warfare: The rise of the Bagiika-Bagaalu music competitions in Sukumaland, Tanzania. In *Mashindano! Competitive music performance in East Africa*, ed. Frank D. Gunderson and Gregory F. Barz, 407–19. Dar es Salaam: Mkuki na Nyota.

Gunderson, Frank, and Gregory F. Barz, eds. 2000. *Mashindano! Competitive music performance in East Africa*. Dar es Salaam: Mkuki na Nyota.

Guy, Nancy. 2003. Trafficking in Taiwan aboriginal voices. In *Handle with care: Ownership and control of ethnographic materials*, ed. Sjoerd R. Jaarsma. Pittsburgh: University of Pittsburgh Press.

Haas, Peter Jan, and Thomas Gesthuizen. 2000. Ndani ya Bongo: Kiswahili rap keeping it real. In *Mashindano! Competitive music performance in East Africa*, ed. Frank D. Gunderson and Gregory F. Barz, 279–94. Dar es Salaam: Mkuki na Nyota.

Hall, Stuart. 1999. A conversation with Stuart Hall. *Journal of the International Institute* 7 (1). Accessed quod.lib.umich.edu.

Hannerz, Ulf. 1990. Cosmopolitans and locals in world culture. In *Global Culture*, ed. Mike Featherstone, 237–52. London: Sage Publications.

Harrev, Flemming. 1989. Jambo Records and the promotion of popular music in East Africa: The story of Otto Larsen and East African Records, Ltd. 1952–1963. In *Perspectives on African music*, ed. Wolfgang Bender, 103–38. Bayreuth African Studies Series, Vol. 9. Bayreuth University: Eckhard Breitinger.

Hartwig, Gerald W. 1969. The historical and social role of Kerebe music. *Tanzania Notes and Records* 70: 41–56.

Hastings, Adrian. 1967. *Church and mission in modern Africa*. New York: Fordham University Press.

Hatchard, John. 2007. Review of the Prevention of Corruption Bill 2007 (Tanzania). Paper prepared for the donor community in Tanzania and the Parliament of Tanzania on the development of appropriate anti-corruption legislation.

Hebdige, Dick. 1979. *Subculture: The meaning of style*. London: Routledge.

Herrick, Allison Butler. 1968. *Area handbook for Tanzania*. Foreign Area Studies. Washington, D.C.: U.S. Government Printing Office.

Hill, Stephen. 2000. Mchezo umelala [The dance has slept]: Competition, modernity, and economics in Umatengo, Tanzania. In *Mashindano! Competitive music performance in East Africa*, ed. Frank Gunderson and Gregory Barz, 367–78. Dar es Salaam: Mkuki na Nyota.

———. 2002. Machini kubwa: Group dancing, politics, and modernity in Umatengo, Tanzania. Ph.D. diss., University of Illinois, Urbana-Champaign.

———. 2007. 'I am a partial person': The urban experience of rural music. In *Dar es Salaam: The history of an emerging East African metropolis*, ed. Andrew Burton, James Brennan, and Yusuf Lawi, 232–49. London and Dar es Salaam: British Institute and Mkuki wa Nyota.

Holm, Desiree Blankenburg, Kent Eriksson, and Jan Johanson. 1999. Creating value through mutual commitment to business network relationships. *Strategic Management Journal*, 20 (5): 467–86.

Horning, Susan Schmidt. 2004. Engineering the performance: Recording engineers, tacit knowledge and the art of controlling sound. Special issue, *Social Studies of Science* 34 (5): 703–31.

Ikoku, Emman U. 1980. *Self-reliance: Africa's survival*. Enugu, Nigeria: Fourth Dimension Publishers.

Iliffe, John. 1979. *A modern history of Tanganyika*. African Studies Series. Cambridge: University of Cambridge Press.

Impey, Angela Marguerite. 1998. Popular music in Africa. In *The Garland encyclopedia of world music: Africa*, ed. Ruth Stone, 415–37. New York: Garland Publishing.

Inda, Jonathan Xavier, and Renato Rosaldo. 2002. Introduction: A world in motion. In *Anthropology of globalization: A reader*, ed. Jonathan Xavier Inda and Renato Rosaldo, 1–34. Malden, Mass.: Blackwell.

Ingham, Kenneth. 1965. *A history of East Africa*. Rev. ed. New York: Praeger.

Ishumi, Abel. G.M. 1984. *The urban jobless in eastern Africa: A study of the unemployed population in the growing urban centres, with special reference to Tanzania*. Uppsala, Sweden: Scandinavian Institute of African Studies.

Ivaska, Andrew M. 2002. Anti-mini militants meet modern misses. Urban style, gender and the politics of national culture in 1960s Dar es Salaam, Tanzania. *Gender and History* 14 (3): 584–607.

———. 2003. Negotiating "culture" in a cosmopolitan capital: Urban style and the Tanzanian state in colonial and postcolonial Dar es Salaam. Ph.D. diss., University of Michigan.

Jaszi, Peter. 1992. On the author effect: Contemporary copyright and collective creativity. *Cardozo Arts and Entertainment Law Journal* 10: 293–320.

Joireman, Sandra Fullerton. 2001. Inherited legal systems and effective rule of law: Africa and the colonial legacy. *Journal of Modern African Studies* 39 (4): 571–96.

Jorgensen, Estelle R. 1997. *In search of music education.* Urbana: University of Illinois Press.

Kabalimu, Joseph Mwombeki Alfred. 1996. Development of an information support system for radio services in Tanzania. M.S. thesis, University of Dar es Salaam.

Katz, Mark. 2004. *Capturing sound: How technology has changed music.* Berkeley: University of California Press.

Kayinga, Joseph V. 1996. Problems facing youth artistic groups in Tanzania. Ph.D. diss., Northwestern University.

Kezilahabi, E. 2000. Competitive Dance and Social Identity: Converging Histories of Southwest Tanzania. In *Mashindano! Competitive music performance in East Africa,* ed. Frank Gunderson and Gregory Barz, 177–97. Dar es Salaam: Mkuki na Nyota.

Khatib, Muhammed Seif. 1992. *Taarab Zanzibar.* Dar es Salaam: Tanzania Publishing House.

Kidula, Jean. 2000. The impact of the Christian music industry in shaping theological and musical trends in Kenya. *Worship Leader* 43 (1): 4–11.

Kilimwiko, Lawrence. 2000. Greasing the newsgate: Journalists on the take. *The Tanzania Journalist* 1 (1): 3–8.

King, Kenneth. 1996. *Jua kali Kenya: Change & development in an informal economy, 1970–95.* Athens: Ohio University Press.

Kirkegaard, Annemette. 1997. Indledning ved offentligt forsvar af ph.d.-afhandlingen Taarab na Muziki wa densi [Introduction to the defense of the Ph.D. dissertation Taarab na Muziki]. *Musik & Forskning* 22: 21–31.

———. 1998. Om populærmusikkens rolle i de Afrikanske byer; med eksempler fra Dar es Salaam og Zanzibar Town [Popular music in African towns, including examples from Dar es Salaam and Zanzibar City]. *Musik & Forskning* 23: 126–58.

Kitime, John. 1998. Piracy of video and audio cassettes in Tanzania. Paper presented at the Intellectual Property Rights Workshop at the Zanzibar International Film Festival, July 14–16.

———. n.d. The story behind the Tanzania Copyright Act no. 61 of 1966.

de Kloet, Jeroen. 2001. Red sonic trajectories: Popular music and youth in urban China. Ph.D. diss., University of Amsterdam.

Knappert, Jan. 1977. Swahili Tarabu songs. *Afrika und Übersee* 60 (1/2): 116–55.

———. 1983. Swahili songs with double entendre. *Afrika und Übersee* 66 (1): 67–76.

Knowlson, T. Sharper. 1918. *Originality: A popular study of the creative mind.* Philadelphia and London: J. B. Lippincott.

Komba, D., H. S. Mosha, and K. M. Osaki. 2000. The impact of corruption on the quality of education in Tanzania. In *Quality of education in Tanzania: Issues and experiences,* ed. Justinian C.J. Galabawa, Fikeni E.M.K. Senkoro, and A.F. Lwaitama, 154–67. Dar es Salaam: Faculty of Education, University of Dar es Salaam.

Kongolo, Tshimanga. 1999. Does the Congo's copyright and neighboring rights law conflict with the TRIPS agreement? *Journal of World Intellectual Property* 2 (2): 311–27.

Koroye-Crooks, Funkazi. 1999. Enforcement of copyright in national law and the TRIPS agreement. Paper presented at the WIPO Roving Seminars on Copyright and Neighboring Rights, Dar es Salaam, Tanzania, October 11–13.

Krasilovsky, M. William, and Sidney Shemel. 1995. *This business of music.* New York: Billboard Books.

Kubik, Gerhard. 1981. Neo-traditional popular music in East Africa since 1945. In *Popular music I: Folk or popular? Distinctions, influences, continuities,* ed. Richard Middleton and David Horn. Cambridge: Cambridge University Press.

Lange, Siri. 1995. *From nation-building to popular culture: The modernization of performance in Tanzania.* Bergen, Norway: Chr. Michelsen Institute.

———. 2000. Muungano and TOT: Rivals on the urban cultural scene. In *Mashindano! Competitive music performance in East Africa,* ed. Frank Gunderson and Gregory Barz, 67–85. Dar es Salaam: Mkuki na Nyota.

———. 2002. Multipartyism, rivalry, and Taarab in Dar es Salaam. In *Playing with identities in contemporary music in Africa,* ed. Mai Palmberg and Annemette Kirkegaard, 165–80. Uppsala, Sweden: Nordiska Afrikainstitutet.

———. 2008. Muungano cultural troupe: Entertaining the urban masses of Dar es Salaam. In *African Theatre: Companies,* ed. James Gibbs. Oxford: James Currey.

Lave, Jean. 1982. A comparative approach to education forms and learning processes. *Anthropology and Education Quarterly* 13 (2): 181–87.

Leander, Kevin M. 2004. "They took out the wrong context": Uses of time space in the practice of positioning. *Ethos* 32 (2): 188–213.

Lefebvre, Henri. 1991. *The production of space.* Trans. Donald Nicholson-Smith. Cambridge, Mass.: Blackwell.

———. 2008. *The critique of everyday life, volume 1.* Trans. John Moore. London: Verso.

Lema, Eliesha, Marjorie J Mbilinyi, and Rakesh Rajani. 2004. *Nyerere on education: Selected essays and speeches, 1954–1998.* Dar es Salaam: HakiElimu.

Leslie, John Arthur Kingsley. 1963. *A survey of Dar es Salaam.* New York: Oxford University Press.

Lewinson, Anne. 2003. Imagining the metropolis, globalizing the nation: Dar es salaam and national culture in Tanzanian cartoons. *City and Society.* 15 (1): 9–30.

Lobo, Lois. 2000. *They came to Africa: 200 years of the Asian presence in Tanzania.* Dar es Salaam: Sustainable Village.

Lovering, Timothy John. 2002. Authority and identity: Malawian soldiers in Britain's colonial army, 1891–1964. Ph.D. diss., University of Stirling

Lugalla, Joe L.P. 1995. *Crisis, urbanization, and urban poverty in Tanzania: A study of urban poverty and survival politics.* Lanham, Md.: University Press of America.

———. 1997. Development, change, and poverty in the informal sector during the era of structural adjustments in Tanzania. *Canadian Journal of African Studies / Revue Canadienne des Études Africaines* 31 (3): 424–51.

Magayane, Bakilana C.M. 1988. The role of mass media in promoting socialist consciousness among Tanzanian workers and peasants: A case study of radio Tanzania Dar es Salaam. Master's thesis, University of Dar es Salaam.

Mahon, Maureen. 2000. The visible evidence of cultural producers. *Annual Review of Anthropology* 29: 467–692.

Malm, Krister, and Roger Wallis. 1992. *Media policy and music activity.* New York: Routledge.

Mangesho, Peter. 2003. Global cultural trends: The case of hip-hop music in Dar es Salaam. Master's thesis, University of Dar es Salaam.

Manuel, Peter. 1993. *Cassette culture: Popular music and technology in north India.* Chicago: University of Chicago Press.

Marsh, Zoe, and George W. Kingsnorth. 1966. *An introduction to the history of East Africa,* 3rd ed. Cambridge: Cambridge University Press.

Martin, Phyllis. 1995. *Leisure and society in colonial Brazzaville.* New York: Cambridge University Press.

Martin, Stephen. 1980. Music in urban East Africa: A study of the development of urban jazz in Dar es Salaam. Ph.D. diss., University of Washington.

———. 1991. Brass bands and the *Beni* phenomenon in urban East Africa. *Journal of the International Library of African Music* 7 (1): 72–81.

Masimbi, Rashid. 1990. Chuo cha Sanaa: A bridge between two countries: Achievements and drawbacks. *Musiikin Suunta* 12 (4): 5–10, 14.

Mbega, Daniel. 2001. Ukiritimba wa Redio Tanzania Uliathiri Maendeleo ya Muziki wa Tanzania. Unpublished paper.

Mbembe, Achille, and Sarah Nuttall. 2004. Writing the world from an African metropolis. *Public Culture* 16 (3): 347–72.

Mbunga, Stephen. 1968. Music reform in Tanzania. *AFER (African Ecclesiastical Review)* 10 (1): 47–54.

Mbuguni, L.A., and Gabriel Ruhumbika. 1974. TANU and national culture. In *Towards Ujumaa: Twenty years of Tanu leadership,* ed. Gabriel Ruhumbika, 275–87. Kampala: East African Literature Bureau.

McCann, Anthony T. 2002. Beyond the commons: The expansion of the Irish Music Rights Organisation, the elimination of uncertainty, and the politics of enclosure. Ph.D. diss., University of Limerick.

Meinjtes, Louise. 2003. *Sound of Africa!: Making music Zulu in a south African studio.* Durham, N.C.: Duke University Press.

———. 2005. Reach 'Overseas': South African sound engineers, technology, and tradition. In *Wired for sound: Engineering and technologies of sonic cultures,* ed. Paul D. Greene and Thomas Porcello. Middletown, Conn.: Wesleyan University Press.

Mekacha, Rugatiri. 1992. Are women devils? The portrayal of women in Tanzanian popular music. In *Sokomoko: Popular Culture in East Africa,* ed. Werner Graebner, 99–113. Atlanta: Rodopi.

Merriam, Alan P. 1964. *The anthropology of music.* Evanston: Northwestern University Press.

Mesaki, Simeon. 1994. Witch-killing in Sukumaland. In *Witchcraft in contemporary Tanzania,* ed. Ray Abrahams, 47–60. Cambridge: University of Cambridge.

Meyer, Birgit. 1998. The power of money: Politics, occult forces, and pentecostalism in Ghana. *African Studies Review* 41 (3): 15–37.

Mgana, Issa. 1991. *Jukwaa La Taarab Zanzibar.* Helsinki: Mradi wa Mediafrica.

Mgandu, John. 1987. Music in institutions of higher learning in Tanzania. Master's thesis, University of Dar es Salaam.

Mgaya, Edward, Method R. Kazaura, Anne Outwater, and Lina Kinabo. 2008. Suicide in the Dar es Salaam region, Tanzania, 2005. *Journal of Forensic and Legal Medicine* 15 (3): 172–76.

Mkabarah, Jumaa R.R. 1966. *Mwanamuziki wa Tanzania: Salum Abdallah.* Dar es Salaam, Tanzania: Taasisi ya Uchunguzi wa Kiswahili, Chuo Kikuu cha Dar es Salaam.

Moore, Sally Falk. 1978. *Law as process. An anthropological approach.* London: Routledge and K. Paul.

Moyer, Eileen. 2003. In the shadow of the Sheraton: Imagining localities in global spaces in Dar es Salaam, Tanzania. Ph.D. diss., University of Amsterdam.

———. 2005. Street-corner justice in the name of Jah: Imperatives for peace among Dar es Salaam street youth. *Africa Today* 51 (3): 30–58.

Moyo, Dambisa. 2009. *Dead aid: Why aid is not working and how there is a better way for Africa.* New York: Farrar, Straus and Giroux.

Moyse-Bartlett, Lieutenant-Colonel H. 1956. *The king's African rifles: A study in the military history of East and Central Africa, 1890–1945.* Aldershot: Gale & Polden.

Munishi, Gaspar K. 2000. Quality of education and the national policy management context in Tanzania. In *Quality of Education in Tanzania,* ed. Justinian C.J. Galabawa, Fikeni E.M. K. Senkoro and A. F. Lwaitama, 21–31. Dar es Salaam, Tanzania: University of Dar es Salaam.

Mwakikagile, Godfrey. 2006. *Life in Tanganyika in the fifties: My reflections and narratives from the white settler community and others: With photos.* [Grand Rapids, Mich.]: Continental Press.

Mytton, Graham. 1976. The role of the mass media in nation building in Tanzania. Ph.D. diss., University of Manchester.

Nash, June. 2007. Consuming interests: Water, rum, and Coca-Cola from ritual propitiation to corporate expropriation in highland Chiapas. *Cultural Anthropology* 22 (4): 621–39.

Negus, Keith. 1996. *Popular music in theory: An introduction.* Hanover, N.H.: University Press of New England.

Ngahyoma, John. 2001. Taarab yateka soko la muziki [*Taarab* captures music market]. *Kitangoma* 1 (1): 54–55.

Niranjana, Tejaswini. 2006. *Mobilizing India: Women, music, and migration between India and Trinidad.* Durham, N.C.: Duke University Press.

Nketia, J. H. Kwabena. 1955. The gramophone and contemporary African music in the gold coast. *Proceedings* 5: 191–201.

———. n.d. *Report on the establishment of an institute of musicology and related studies in Dar es Salaam.* Dar es Salaam, Tanzania: East Africana Collection.

———. 1973. The musician in Akan society. In *The traditional artisan African societies,* ed. W. L. d'Azevedo. Bloomington: Indiana University Press.

———. 1990. Contextual strategies of inquiry and systematization. *Ethnomusicology* 34 (1): 75–97.

Ntarangwi, Mwenda. 2009. *East African hip hop: Youth culture and globalization.* Urbana: University of Illinois Press.

Ntiro, S. J. 1975. Traditional arts in the post-independence era. *Tanzania Notes and Records* 76: 113–18.

Nyerere, Julius K. 1967. *Freedom and unity, uhuru na umoja: A selection from writings and speeches, 1952–1965.* London: Oxford University Press.

———. 1971. *Ujamaa: Essays on socialism.* New York: Oxford University Press.

———. 1973. *Freedom and development, uhuru na maendeleo: A selection from writings and speeches, 1968–1973.* Dar es Salaam, Tanzania: Oxford University Press.

Nyoni, Frowin Paul. 1991. *Lindeku: A multifunctional form of African music in Umatengo.* Master's thesis, University of Dar es Salaam.

———. 1998. Conformity and change: Tanzanian plural theatre and social-political changes. Ph.D. diss., University of Leeds.

———. 2000. The social significance of *Mganda-wa Kinkahi* dance contests among the Wamatengo. In *Mashindano! Competitive music performance in East Africa*, ed. Frank Gunderson and Gregory Barz, 233–53. Dar es Salaam, Tanzania: Mkuki na Nyota.

Ojaide, Tanure. 2001. Poetry, performance, and art: Udje dance songs of Nigeria's Urhobo people. *Research in African Literatures* 32 (2): 44–75.

Okpewho, Isidore.1992. *African oral literature: Backgrounds, character, and continuity.* Bloomington: Indiana University Press.

Oliver, R. A. 1952. *The missionary factor in East Africa.* London: Longmans, Green and Co.

Ong, Aihwa. 2006. *Neoliberalism as exception: Mutations in citizenship and sovereignty.* Durham, N.C.: Duke University Press.

Ortner, Sherry B. 1995. Resistance and the problem of ethnographic refusal. *Comparative studies in society and history* 37 (1): 173–93.

Osaki, K. M. 2000. Curriculum and quality. In *Quality of education in Tanzania: Issues and experiences,* ed. J.C.J. Galabawa, F.E.M.K. Senkoro, and A. F. Lwaitama, 225–50. Dar es Salaam: Faculty of Education, University of Dar es Salaam.

Otieno, Nahashaona, A.O. 2000. The impact of primary school management on quality in Tanzanian mainland. In *Quality of education in Tanzania,* ed. J.C.J. Galabawa, F.E.M.K. Senkoro, and A.F. Lwaitama, 33–60. Dar es Salaam: Faculty of Education, University of Dar es Salaam.

Ottenberg, Simon. 1996. *Seeing with music: The lives of 3 blind African musicians.* Seattle: University of Washington Press.

Oyegoke, Lekan. 1994. "Sade's testimony": A new genre of autobiography in African folklore. Research in African Literatures 25 (3): 131–40.

Patico, Jennifer. 2005. To be happy in a Mercedes: Tropes of value and ambivalent visions of marketization. *American Ethnologist* 32 (3): 479–96.

Pels, Peter. 2000. Kizungu rhythms: Luguru Christianity as Ngoma. In *Mashindano! Competitive music performance in East Africa,* ed. Frank Gunderson and Gregory Barz, 101–42. Dar es Salaam: Mkuki na Nyota.

Perullo, Alex. 2001. *The music business in Tanzania: Copyright law, contracts, and collective management organizations* (English and Swahili). Dar es Salaam: American Embassy.

———. 2003. 'The life that I live': Popular music, Agency, and Urban Society in Dar es Salaam, Tanzania. Ph.D. diss., Indiana University.

———. 2005. Hooligans and heroes: Youth identity and rap music in Dar es Salaam, Tanzania. *Africa Today* 51 (4): 74–101.

———. 2007. "Here's a little something local": An early history of hip hop in Dar es Salaam, Tanzania, 1984–1997. In *Dar es Salaam: The history of an emerging East African metropolis,* ed. Andrew Burton, James Brennan, and Yusuf Lawi. London and Dar es Salaam: British Institute and Mkuki wa Nyota.

———. 2008a. Morning 'till night, cradle to the grave: Laura Boulton, recorded sound, and meaning in Angolan music. *Resound* 26 (1/2 and 3/4): 1–15.

———. 2008b. Rumba in the city of peace: Migration and the cultural commodity of Congolese music in Dar es Salaam, 1968–1985. *Ethnomusicology* 52 (2): 296–324.

———. 2008c. Conceptions of song: Ownership, rights, and African copyright law. *The Garland Handbook of African Music*, 2nd ed., ed. Ruth M. Stone. London and New York: Routledge.

———. 2009. Generations of sound: Popular music and performance in Dar es Salaam, Tanzania. *Ethnomusicology Video for Instruction and Analysis (EVIA) Digital Archive*, Indiana University, Bloomington, and the University of Michigan, Ann Arbor.

Peters, Michael. 1999. Neoliberalism. In *Encyclopaedia of philosophy of education*. London: Routledge.

Petley, Julian. 1999. The regulation of media content. In *The media in Britain: Current debates and developments*, ed. Jane C. Stokes and Anna Reading, 143–57. New York: St. Martin's Press.

Pitcher, M. Anne, and Kelly M. Askew. 2006. African socialisms and postsocialisms. *Africa* 76 (1): 1–14.

Porcello, Thomas. 1998. 'Tails out': Social phenomenology and the ethnographic representation of technology in music-making. *Ethnomusicology* 42 (3): 485–510.

———. 2004. Speaking of sound: Language and the professionalization of sound-recording engineers. Special issue, *Social Studies of Science* 34 (5): 733–58.

Prestholdt, Jeremy. 2008. *Domesticating the world: African consumerism and the genealogies of globalization*. The California world history library 6. Berkeley: University of California Press.

Raab, Klaus. 2006. Rapping the nation. Die aneignung von hiphop in Tanzania (Musikethnologie 6). Berlin: LIT.

Racy, Ali Jihad. 1977. The impact of commercial recording on the musical life of Egypt, 1904–1932. *Essays in Arts and Sciences* 6 (1): 58–94.

———. 1978. Arabian music and the effects of commercial recording. *World of Music* 20 (1): 47–58.

Ramirez, Rafael. 1999. Value co-production: Intellectual origins and implications for practice and research. *Strategic Management Journal* 20 (1): 49–65.

Ranger, Terence. 1975. *Dance and society in Eastern Africa 1890–1970: The Beni Ngoma*. London: Heinemann.

———. 1996. Postscript: Colonial and postcolonial identities. In *Postcolonial Identities in Africa*. ed. Richard Werbner and Terence Ranger, 271–81. London: Zed Books.

Reed, Daniel B. 2003. *Dan Ge performance: Masks and music in contemporary Côte d'Ivoire*. Bloomington: Indiana University Press.

Reichl, Karl. 2000. *The oral epic: Performance and music*. Intercultural music studies, 12. Berlin: VWB, Verlag für Wissenschaft und Bildung.

Remes, Pieter Walter. 1998. "Karibu geto langu/Welcome to my ghetto": Urban youth, popular culture and language in 1990s Tanzania. Ph.D. diss., Northwestern University.

Reuster-Jahn, Uta. 2007. Let's go party! Discourse and self-portrayal in the Bongo Fleva-song 'Mikasi.' *Swahili Forum* 14: 225–44.

Rizzo, Matteo. 2002. Being taken for a ride: Privitisation of the Dar es Salaam transport system 1983–1998. *Journal of Modern African Studies* 40 (1): 133–57.

Robert, Shaaban. 1991. *Wasifu wa Siti binti Saad*. Dar es Salaam: Mkuki wa Nyota.

Roberts, John Storm. n.d. *The Tanzania sound*. LP liner notes. Tivoli, N.Y.: Original Music OMA 106.

Rothenbuhler, Eric W. 2005. The church of the cult of the individual. In *Media anthropology*, ed. Eric W. Rothenbuhler and Mihai Coman, 91–100. Thousand Oaks, Calif.: Sage Publications.

Saavedra Casco, Jose Arturo. 2006. The language of the young people: Rap, urban culture and protest in Tanzania. *Journal of Asian and African Studies* 41 (3): 229–48.

Said, Mohamed. 1998. *The life and times of Abdulwahid Sykes (1924–1968): The untold story of the Muslim struggle against British colonialism in Tanganyika*. London: Minerva Press.

Sanders, Todd. 2001. Save our skins: Structural adjustment, morality, and the occult in Tanzania. In *Magical interpretations, material realities: Modernity, witchcraft and the occult in postcolonial Africa*, ed. Henrietta L. Moore and Todd Sanders, 160–83. London: Routledge.

———. 2003a. Invisible hands and visible goods: Revealed and concealed economies in millennial Tanzania. In *Transparency and Conspiracy: Ethnographies of Suspicion in the New World Order*, ed. Harry G. West and Todd Sanders, 148–74. Durham, N.C.: Duke University Press.

———. 2003b. Reconsidering witchcraft: Postcolonial Africa and analytic (un)certainties. *American Anthropologist* 105 (2): 338–52.

Sanga, Imani. 2001. Construction of Gender and Gender Roles in Religious Choirs in Dar es Salaam. Master's thesis, University of Dar es Salaam.

———. 2006a. Muziki wa injili: The temporal and spatial aesthetics of popular church music in Dar es Salaam, Tanzania 1980s-2005. Ph.D. diss., University of KwaZulu-Natal.

———. 2006b. Composition processes in popular church music in Dar es Salaam, Tanzania. *Ethnomusicology Forum* 15 (2): 247–71.

———. 2007. Gender in church music: Dynamics of gendered space in *Muziki wa Injili* in Dar es Salaam, Tanzania. *Journal of Popular Music Studies* 19 (1): 59–91.

Scheper-Hughes, Nancy. 2000. The global traffic in human organs. *Current Anthropology* 41 (2): 191–224.

Scott, James C. 1985. *Weapons of the weak: Everyday forms of peasant resistance*. New Haven, Conn.: Yale University Press.

Seago, Alex. 1987. East African popular music. *African Music: Journal of the International Library of African Music*. 6 (4): 176–77.

Seeger, Anthony. 1987. *Why Suya sing: A musical anthropology of an Amazonian people*. Cambridge: Cambridge University Press.

———. 1991. Singing other people's songs. *Cultural Survival Quarterly* (Summer): 36–39.

———. 1992. Ethnomusicology and music law. *Ethnomusicology* 36 (3): 345–60.

———. 2006. Who got left out of the property grab again? Oral traditions, indigenous rights, and valuable old knowledge? In *Code: Collaborative ownership and the digital economy* ed. Rishab Aiyer Ghosh. Cambridge, Mass.: MIT Press.

Sell, Susan K. 2003. *Private power, public law: The globalization of intellectual property rights*. Cambridge: Cambridge University Press.

Shivji, Issa G. 2006. *Let the people speak: Tanzania down the road to neo-liberalism*. Codesria book series. Dakar, Sénégal: Codesria.

Shule, Vicensia. 2009. The mop. In *Tell me, friends: Contemporary stores and plays of Tanzania*, ed. Lilian Osaki and Lisa Maria B. Noudehou. Dar es Salaam, Tanzania: Mkuki na Nyota.

Skinner, Ryan. 2009. *Artistiya:* Popular music and personhood in postcolonial Bamako, Mali. Ph.D. diss., Columbia University.

Small, Christopher. 1998. *Musicking: The meaning of performance and listening.* Middletown, Conn.: Wesleyan University Press.

Soja, Edward W. 1989. *Postmodern geographies: The reassertion of space in critical social theory.* London: Verso.

Songoyi, Elias Manandi. 1988. Commercialization and its impact on traditional dances. Norway, Trondheim: Rådet for folkemusikk og folkedans.

Sorokobi, Yves. 2001. Attacks on the press 2000: Africa analysis. Committee to Protect Journalists. March 19, cpj.org/.

Spitulnik, Debra. 1997. The social circulation of media discourse and the mediation of communities. *Journal of Linguistic Anthropology* 6 (2): 161–87.

Springer, Jennifer Thorington. 2008. "Roll it gal": Alison Hinds, female empowerment, and calypso. *Meridians: Feminism, Race, Transnationalism.* 8 (1): 93–129.

Stark, David. 1989. Coexisting organizational forms in Hungary's emerging mixed economy. In *Remaking the economic institutions of socialism: China and Eastern Europe,* ed. Victor Nee and David Stark, 137–68. Stanford, Calif.: Stanford University Press.

———. 1997. Recombinant property in East European capitalism. In *Restructuring networks in post-socialism: Legacies, linkages, and localities,* ed. Gernot Grabher and David Stark, 35–69. Oxford: Oxford University Press.

Stewart, Gary. 1992. *Breakout: Profiles in African rhythm.* Chicago: University of Chicago Press.

Stöger-Eising, Viktoria. 2000. "Ujamaa" revisited: Indigenous and European influences in Nyerere's social and political thought. *Africa* 70 (1): 118–43.

Stone, Ruth M. 1982. *Let the inside be sweet: The interpretation of music event among the Kpelle of Liberia.* Bloomington: Indiana University Press.

Sturmer, Martin. 1998. *The media history of Tanzania.* Ndanda: Ndanda Mission Press.

Suleiman, A. A. 1969. The Swahili singing star Siti binti Saad and the *Tarab* tradition in Zanzibar. *Swahili* 39: 87–90.

Suriano, Maria. 2007. 'Mimi ni msanii, kioo cha jamii.' Urban youth culture in Tanzania as seen through Bongo Flavour and hip-hop. *Swahili Forum* 14: 207–23.

Tanzania African National Union (TANU). 1967. *The Arusha declaration and TANU's policy on socialism and self-reliance.* Dar es Salaam: The Publicity Section, TANU.

Tanzania Broadcasting Commission (TBC). 2000. *Broadcasting directory 2000.* Dar es Salaam: TBC.

Tanzania Film Company (TFC). 1995. *Corporate plan: 1995–1999.* Dar es Salaam: TFC.

Taylor, Charles. 1985. *Human agency and language.* Cambridge: Cambridge University Press.

Théberge, Paul. 1997. *Any sound you can imagine: Making music/consuming technology.* Hanover, N.H.: University Press of New England.

Thomas, Nicholas. 1997. Nations' endings: From citizenship to shipping? In *Narratives of nation in the South Pacific,* ed. T. Otto and N. Thomas, 211–19. Amsterdam: Harwood Academic Publishers.

Tracey, Hugh Travers. 1952. Recording tour in Tanganyika by a team of the African Music Society. *Tanganyika Notes and Records* 32: 43–49.

Tripp, Aili Mari. 1997. *Changing the rules: The politics of liberalization and the urban informal economy in Tanzania.* Berkeley: University of California Press.

Tsing, Anna Lowenhaupt. 2005. *Friction: An ethnography of global connection.* Princeton, N.J.: Princeton University Press.

Tsuruta, Tadasu. 2000. The development process of dance bands in urban Tanzania—in connection with changes in socioeconomic and political circumstances from the colonial period to the 1980s. *Nilo-Ethiopian Studies* 5–6: 9–24.

———. 2001. Music as a profession: Dance band musicians in Dar es Salaam and their urban networks. In *Cultures sonores d'Afrique* II, ed. Junzo Kawada and Kenichi Tsukada, 127–47. Hiroshima: Hiroshima City University.

United Nations Development Programme (UNDP). 2007. *Tanzanian millennium development goals.* www.tz.undp.org/mdgs_goa12.html. Accessed August 8, 2008.

United Republic of Tanzania. 1993. *Broadcasting services act, 1993.* Dar es Salaam: Government Printer.

———. 1999a. *Tanzania's third phase government fight against corruption: A brief on achievements and challenges 1995–1999.* Dar es Salaam: Government Printer.

———. 1999b. *The copyright and neighboring rights act, 1999.* Dar es Salaam: Government Printer.

———. 2000. *Regulations: The copyright and neighboring rights act, 2000.* Dar es Salaam: Government Printer.

Van Zyl Slabbert, Frederik, Charles Malan, Hendrik Marais, Johan Olivier, and Rory Riordan. 1994. Youth in the new South Africa: Towards policy formulation: Main report of the Co-operative Research Programme: South African Youth. Pretoria: HSRC Publishers.

Wallach, Jeremy. 2008. *Modern noise, fluid genres: Popular music in Indonesia, 1997–2001.* Madison: University of Wisconsin Press.

Wallis, Roger, and Krister Malm. 1984. *Big sounds from small peoples: The music industry in small countries.* Sociology of music, No. 2. New York: Pendragon.

Ward, Gertrude. 1899. *Letters from East Africa 1895–1897.* London: Universities' Mission to Central Africa.

Waterman, Christopher Alan. 1982. "I'm a leader, not a boss": Popular music and social identity in Ibaden, Nigeria. *Ethnomusicology* 26 (1): 59–72.

———. 1985. Juju. In *The Western impact on world music: Change, adaptation, and survival,* ed. Bruno Nettl, 87–90. New York: Schirmer Books.

———. 1990. *Jùjú: A social history and ethnography of an African popular music.* Chicago studies in ethnomusicology. Chicago: University of Chicago Press.

———. 2002. Big man, black president, masked one: Models of the celebrity self in Yoruba popular music in Nigeria. In *Playing with identities in contemporary music in Africa,* ed. Mai Palmberg and Annemette Kirkegaard, 19–34. Uppsala, Sweden: Nordiska Afrikainstitutet.

Weidmann, W. 1955. A short history of the Klub Dar-es-Salâam. *Tanganyika Notes and Records* 41: 59–61.

Weiss, Brad. 2004. Introduction: Contentious futures: Past and present. In *Producing African futures: Ritual and reproduction in a neoliberal age,* ed. Brad Weiss, 1–20. Leiden: Brill.

———. 2009. *Sweet Dreams and Hip Hop Barbershops: Global Fantasy in Urban Tanzania.* Bloomington: Indiana University Press.

Welbourn, Frederick Burkewood. 1965. *East African Christian*. London: Oxford University Press.

West, Harry G. 2005. *Kupilikula*. Chicago: University of Chicago Press.

———. 2007. *Ethnographic sorcery*. Chicago: University of Chicago Press.

White, Bob Whitman. 2000. *Soukouss* or sell-out? Congolese popular dance music as cultural commodity. In *Commodities and globalization: Anthropological perspectives*, ed. Angelique Haugerud, M. Priscilla Stone, and Peter D. Little, 33–58. Lanham, Md.: Rowman and Littlefield.

———. 2008. *Rumba rules: The politics of dance music in Mobutu's Zaire*. Durham, N.C.: Duke University Press.

Widner, Jennifer A. 2001. *Building the rule of law*. New York: W.W. Norton.

Wilk, Richard. 2006. Bottled water: The pure commodity in the age of branding. *Journal of Consumer Culture* 6 (3): 303–25.

Williams, James Alan. 2006. Phantom power: Recording studio history, practice, and mythology. Ph.D. diss., Brown University.

Wilson, Margaret. 2001. Designs of deception: Concepts of consciousness, spirituality and survival in Capoeira Angola in Salvador, Brazil. *Anthropology of Consciousness* 12 (1): 19–36.

Wizara ya Elimu na Utamaduni. 1999. *Sera ya utamaduni* (Cultural Policy). Dar es Salaam, Tanzania: Jamhuri ya Muunngano wa Tanzania.

World Bank Independent Evaluation Group. 2007. *World Bank Assistance to Agriculture in Sub-Saharan Africa*. Washington, D.C.: World Bank.

World Intellectual Property Organization. 2001. *Intellectual property profile of the least developed countries*. WIPO publication, no. 486. Geneva, Switzerland: World Intellectual Property Organization.

Wright, Susan. 1998. The politicization of 'culture.' *Anthropology Today* 14 (1): 7–15.

Zaloom, Caitlin. 2004. The productive life of risk. *Cultural Anthropology* 19 (3): 365–91.

# Discography

The following represents a select list of artists, albums, and distribution companies discussed in this ethnography. Many of the materials below are part of a collection I gathered during my research and are deposited in the Archives of Traditional Music, Indiana University, Bloomington, under the accession number 07-007-F/C/B. I am grateful to Ramesh Kothari, James Nindi, Werner Graebner, Kelly Askew, Mathew Lavoie, and Tim Clifford (kentanzavinyl.com) for assisting me in locating other materials. In identifying the 78 rpm discs listed below, I used the matrix number etched into the record. (Labels can often peel off, rendering other numbers less useful.)

CT= cassette; CD=compact disc; LP=long-playing record

African Stars Band. *African Stars Band*. African Stars Entertainment. Dar es Salaam, 2000. CT.
———. *Chuki Binafsi*. African Stars Entertainment (ASET03021). 2002. CT.
———. *Fainali Uzeeni*. African Stars Entertainment. Dar es Salaam, 2001. CT.
———. *Jirani*. African Stars Entertainment. Dar es Salaam, 2003. CT.
———. *Mtaa wa Kwanza*. African Stars Entertainment (ASET2008). 2008. CD.
———. *Mtu Pesa*. African Stars Entertainment (ASET07041). 2004. CD.
———. *Mwana Dar es Salaam*. African Stars Entertainment (AS008-009). 2009. CD.
———. *Password*. African Stars Entertainment (ASET2006). 2006. CD.
———. *Safari 2005*. African Stars Entertainment (ASET05082). 2005. CD.
———. *Ukubwa Jiwe*. FKW and African Stars Entertainment (ASET 04031). 2001. CT.
Afro 70 (Patrick Balisidya). "Nakupenda Kama Lulu" and "Kabla Hujafa." Moto Moto (Moto 7-904). 1974. 45 rpm disc.
———. "Pembenyi Moto" and "Ndugu Samora." Afrousa (Afro 7-1). 1975. 45 rpm disc.
———. "Pesa/Angelina." Saba Saba (Saba 7-207). 1973. 45 rpm disc.
———. "Safari Ya Nairobi/Kufaulu." Saba Saba (Saba 7-178). 1973. 45 rpm disc.
———. "Shangwe/Florence." *Saba Saba* (Saba 7-219). 1973. 45 rpm disc.
———. "Unavyo Fikiria/Mwenzangu Nakupenda." Saba Saba (Saba 7-208). 1974. 45 rpm disc.
All Stars Modern Taarab. *Vol. 7: Kilio Changu*. Dar es Salaam, 1996. CT.
———. *Vol. 11: Tiba ya Jiji*. Dar es Salaam, 1999. CD.
———. *Vol. 13: Mtu Mzima Dawa*. F.K. Mitha & Sons. Dar es Salaam, 2000. CT.

Al-Watan Musical Club (led by Subeti Salim Saidi). "Ee, baba Pakistani/Napenda ueleze kisi." Gallotone (XYZ 6080/88). 78 rpm disc.

———. "Sida imezidi/Heri unambie siku maalumu." Gallotone (XYZ 6067/87). 78 rpm disc.

Amberson, .Bom. "Nahawandi." Gallotone (XYZ 6040). 1950. 78 rpm disc.

———. "Sika, No. 1/Nahawand, no. 2" Gallotone. XYZ 6069/6089). 1950. 78 rpm disc.

Askari wa King's African Rifles ya Sita. "Mwakambeya (Wimbo-Kingoni)." Columbia (W-63432). April 1930. 78 rpm disc.

———. "Mangala Sivema (Ngoma-Kihehe)." Columbia (W-63436). April 1930. 78 rpm disc.

———. "Nitapige Hodi (Wimbo-Kingoni)." Columbia (W-63438). April 1930. 78 rpm disc.

———. "Kofia (Wimbo-Kiswahili)." Columbia (W-63450). April 1930. 78 rpm disc.

A.S.P.Y.L. (Culture). *Njoo Mpenzi Njoo.* TFC. 1976. 45 rpm disc.

Atomic Jazz Band (John Kijiko). "Atomic Tumetimia/Hata Mkisema Sana." Polydor (POL 7-024), 1969. 45 rpm disc.

———. "Christina/Waubani." Kwetu (RTRS 1026), 1976. 45 rpm disc.

———. "Dunia Ina Tabu/Dada Tabiya Zako Mbaya." Saba Saba (Saba 7-39), 1971. 45 rpm disc.

———. "Maimouna/Umeona Mwanangu." Kwetu (RTRS 1027). 1976. 45 rpm disc.

———. "Mapenzi Ya Matatizo/Kifo Cha Ngala." Africa (AFR 7-31). 1973. 45 rpm disc.

———. "Mpenzi Joisi/Mpenzi Selina." Saba Saba (Saba 7-38). 1971. 45 rpm disc.

———. "Shemeji Usimpigedada/Mpenzi Stela." Saba Saba (Saba 7-36). 1971. 45 rpm disc.

———. "Usitamani Kitu/Fika Uwone Mwenyewe." Polydor (POL 7-005). 1968. 45 rpm disc.

Bahati Bukuku. *Nani Aitikise Dunia, Vol. 2.* GMC (GK-5 301). CT.

———. *Nimesamehewa Dhambi, Siyo Majaribu, Vol. 3.* GMC (Kw 0710293). CT.

———. *Yashinde Mapito, vol. 1.* GMC Wasanii Promoters Ltd. c2009. CT.

Balesa Kakere and The Revolutions. "Dunia (Part 1)/Dunia (Part 11)." TFC (SP-003). 1985. 45 rpm disc.

Banana Zorro. *Banana.* GMC Wasanii Promoters Ltd. Smooth Vibes. CD.

———. *Subra.* GMC (AP -060518). CT.

Beta Musica. *Caterpillar.* GMC. Dar es Salaam, 2000. CT.

Bizman. *Ningekuwa Kwetu.* GMC Wasanii Promoters Ltd. 2005. CD.

Black Star Musical Club. "Amana/Ukuu." Philips (HL 7-259). 45 rpm disc.

———. "Enyi Wana Adamu/Mnazi Mkinda." Philips ( HL 7-240). 45 rpm disc.

———. "Salamu/Ulimi." Philips (HL 7-261). 45 rpm disc.

Black Star Musical Club/Lucky Star Musical Club. *Nyota: Classic Taarab from Tanga.* GlobeStyle Records (CDORBD 044). 1989. LP.

Black Warriors. *Bubu Ataka Kusema.* CBS Ken-Tanza (KTLP 002/4). LP.

———. "Najuta, part 1/Najuta, part 2." Ken-Tanza (KT 023). 45 rpm disc.

———. "Nawashukuru Wazazi Wangu, part 1/Nawashukuru Wazazi Wangu, part 2." Ken-Tanza (KT 008). 45 rpm disc.

Butiama Jazz Band. "Mwayango Mwayango/Kila Siku Silali." Africa (AFR 7-1002). 1976. 45 rpm disc.

———. "Mwayango Mwayango/Nilikuya Nikuone." Africa (AFR 7-1004), 1976. 45 rpm disc.

———. "Rebeca/Rose Mpenzi." Africa (AFR 7-1003). 1976. 45 rpm disc.

Bwagajuga, Mohomedi A. "Nimepiga pegi mbili, tatu/Dar es Salaam usiende." Gallotone (XYZ 6091/6093). 1950. 78 rpm disc.

———. "Pole, Mama Kitwana/Ukiwa Wangu." Gallotone (XYZ 6085/6092). 1950. 78 rpm disc.

Chipukizi Rumba, (led by Abdala Ibrahimu). "Hayo ni Maradhi/Brasho Dawa Ya Shaba." Trek (XYZ 5175/75). 1950. 78 rpm disc.

Chocho, J. "Dima Dima/Halo-Halo." Kwetu (RTRS 1007). 1976. 45 rpm disc.

Chu-Chu Sound. *Hodi Hodi Tanzania.* FKW. Dar es Salaam, 2001. CT.

———. *Kombora Ndani na Nje ya Jiji.* FKW. Dar es Salaam, 2000. CT.

———. *Mkataa Pema.* FKW. Dar es Salaam, 2002. CT.

———. *Zimamoto Ndani na Nje ya Jiji.* FKW. Dar es Salaam. CT.

Cool James. *Mtoto wa Dandu, Karubandika.* GMC (323). 2001. CT.

———. *Rafiki Yangu.* GMC. CT.

———. *The Very Best, Mtoto wa Dandu, Sina Makosa.* GMC (322). 2001. CT.

Cuban Marimba Band (led by Salum Abdallah). "Beberu/Ndio Hali Ya Duniya." Philips (HL 7-30). 45 rpm disc.

———. *Ngoma Iko Huko: Vintage Tanzanian Dance Music, 1955–1965.* Dizim Records (Dizim 4701). 2000. CD.

———. "Salam Kwa Jumla/Wanawake Wa Tanzania." Philips (HL 7-29). 45 rpm disc.

———. "Shirikisho-Chechembo/Wetu Katutoka." Philips (HL 7-80). 45 rpm disc.

Cuban Marimba Band (led Juma Kilaza). "Kifo cha Bavon Marrie/Pesa Sabuni ya Roho." Saba Saba (SABA 7-164). 45 rpm disc.

———. "Kuja Kwangu Sitaki/Marry." Saba Saba (Saba 7-146). 1972. 45 rpm disc.

———. "U.W.T./Betty." Saba Saba (SABA 7-133). 45 rpm disc.

Dar es Salaam Jazz Band (led by Shabani Abdullah). "Chama nikiingiya." Gallotone (XYZ 6066). 78 rpm disc.

———. "Hayo siyakweli/Nimepata mpenzi mtoto, mdogo, mzuri simwachi." Gallotone (XYZ 6012/16). 78 rpm disc.

———. "Kutwa nasbinda kwako/Bustani mzuri." Gallotone (XYZ 6013/14). 78 rpm disc.

———. "Kwa jinsi nina-vyokupenda." Gallotone (XYZ 6015). 78 rpm disc.

———. "Nani Aliyemtia Bure." Trek (XYZ 6017). 78 rpm disc.

Dar-es-Salaam Swingers (led by Ally Sykes). "Chaupele Mpenzi/Chineno." Trek (XYZ 5062/6011). 78 rpm disc.

Dar International (led by Marijani Rajab). *Vol. 1: Pesa Sabuni ya Roho.* Ahadi (MSK CAS 515). CT.

———. *Vol. 2: Masudi.* Ahadi (MSK CAS 516). CT.

———. *Vol. 3: Mwanameka.* Ahadi (MSK CAS 517). CT.

———. *Vol. 4: Paulina.* Ahadi (MSK CAS 518). CT.

———. *Vol. 5: Kifo ya Rufaa.* Ahadi (MSK CAS 519). CT.

———. *Vol. 6: Carolina.* Ahadi (MSK CAS 520). CT.

———. *Vol. 7: Zuwena.* Ahadi (MSK CAS 521). CT.

———. *Vol. 8: Pendo.* Ahadi (MSK CAS 522). CT.

DDC Mlimani Park Orchestra. *Full Squad.* GMC. c2005. CD.

———. *Kauli Mali.* Mamu et al: Dar es Salaam, 1997. CT.

———. *Maneno Maneno.* GMC Wasanii Promoters Ltd. (GB-4, 198). 2004. CD.

———. *Mdomo Huponza Kichwa.* FK Mitha Ltd (Twalib). 1996. CT.

———. *Mtoto wa Mitaani.* FK Mitha et al. [Big Seven]. 1998. CT.

———. *Nachechemea.* FKW (006). 2000. CT.

———. *Onyo.* GMC. c2002. CT.

———. *Overtime.* F.K. Mitha et al. [Big Seven]: Dar es Salaam, 1998. CT.

———. *Sikinde.* Africassette (AC9402). 1994. CD.

———. *Sungi.* Popular African Music (PAM403). 1994. CD.

———. *Ubaya.* FK Mitha Ltd. (Twalib). CT.

Diamond Stars Band. *Kumbukumbu.* M.J. Production. GMC (317). 2001. CT.

Dolasoul (Balozi Dola). *Balozi Wetu/Wenu.* GMC Series. 2000. CT.

———. *Ubalozini.* GMC. 2001. CT.

Double M Sound. *Kilio cha Yatima.* GMC. 2002. CD.

———. *Kiu ya Mapenzi.* GMC. 2002. CD.

Dudubaya. *Amri Kumi za Mungu.* FKW. 2002. CT.

———. *Ni Saa ya Kufa Kwangu.* FKW. 2001. CT.

East African Melody Modern Taarab. *Mkoko Unalika Maua.* F.K. Mitha & Sons. 2000. CT.

———. *Taxi Bubu.* FKW. 2001. CT.

Egyptian Musical Club (led by Bom Anderson). "Baadina/Leshishi." Gallotone (XYZ 6041/42). 78 rpm disc.

———. "Hijaz bashraf/Sika no.2." Gallotone (XYZ 6035). 1951. 78 rpm disc.

———. "Mahaba jamani yanania-tile/Silali Mchana Sili." Gallotone (XYZ 5084/6078). 1950. 78 rpm disc.

———. "Pumzi, Mhibu, Sipumui Sawa Pemba Ina Siri." Gallotone (XYZ 6070/71). 1950, 78 rpm disc.

———. "Sheikh Salim's Song/Bom song." Gallotone (XYZ 6036/37). 1950. 78 rpm disc.

Extra Bongo Next Level. *Bullet Proof.* GMC (GB275). 2004. CT.

———. *Kujinafasi.* GMC. 2003. CD.

FM Academia. *The Dream Team.* Musicland FTP-786. Dar es Salaam, 1999. CT.

———. *Dunia Kigeugeu/Wazee wa Mjini.* Ujamaa Records (UR005). 2007. CT.

FM Musica Academia. *Adija.* FKW. 2000. CT.

———. *New Look.* FKW. 2000. CT.

———. *Sitoweza.* FKW. 2000. CT.

Gangwe Mobb. *Nje/Ndani.* GMC Wasanii, 2003. CT.

———. *Simulizi la Ufasaba.* GMC. 2001. CD.

Haroun, Inspector. *Pamba Nyepesi.* GMC Wasanii. CT.

In Afrika Band. *Indege.* GMC. 2002. CD.

Jahazi Modern Taarab. *V.I.P.* GMC Wasanii Promoters Ltd., 2008. CT.

———. *Wana Nakshi Nakshi.* GMC Wasanii Promoters Ltd. (TR 07080). CT.

Jamhuri Jazz Band. "Kiboko/Twamuomba Mola." Philips (PK 7-9046). 1969. 45 rpm disc.

———. "Magdalena/Pesa Sina Mfukoni." Philips (PK 7-9091). 1971. 45 rpm disc.

———. "Mwenge/Marafiki Zangu." Philips (PK 7-9051). 1969. 45 rpm disc.

———. "Nafikiria Kurudi Shamba/Fikeni Jamhuri." Philips (PK 7-9069). 1970. 45 rpm disc.

———. "Shingo ya Upanga/Kipande Cha Papa." Philips (PK 7-9070). 1970. 45 rpm disc.

———. "Simba Mwituni/Wasiwasi Ondoa." Philips (PK 7-9072). 1970. 45 rpm disc.

———. "Susana/Sophia Amerika." Philips (PK 7-9092). 1971. 45 rpm disc.

———. *Vol. 1–4.* Dar es Salaam Music and Sport. Dar es Salaam. CT.
JKT Jazz. "TANU na AFRO (Muungano wa Vyamo)/Wazazi." Kwetu(RTRS1003). 1976. 45 rpm disc.
JKT Taarab. *Kali za Taarab (JKT Remixes).* GMC. 2002. CD.
———. *Vol. 7: Shangingi Kachuna Buzi.* F.K. Mitha et al. [Big Seven]. 1998.CT.
———. *Vol. 8: Mpishi.* Mamu et al. [Big Five]. 1998. CT.
Juma Nature. *Ubin-Adam Kazi.* GMC Wasanii Promoters Ltd., P. Funk, and Bongo Records. 2005. CD.
———. *Zote History.* GMC Wasanii Promoters Ltd. and Bongo Records. 2006. CD.
Juwata Jazz. *Kauka ni kuvae.* FK Mitha et al. [Big Five]. 1994. CT.
———. *Mpenzi Zarina.* F.K. Mitha & Sons. Dar es Salaam. CT.
Kalala, Hamza, and Bantu Group. *Manamba.* 2000. CT.
———. *Tutabanana Hapa Hapa.* GMC (GMC 330). 2001. CT.
———. *Vol. 7 Kisimbago Kaabhuka.* CT.
Kalikawe, Justin. *Duniani, part 2,* 1996. CT.
———. *Upatanisho,* 1996. CT.
———. *Usimdhurau.* Mamu Store. Dar es Salaam, 1997. CT.
———. *Mtizamo.* GMC: Dar es Salaam, 2002. CT.
Kasheba, Ndala. *Best of. . . .* Dar es Salaam Music and Sport. Dar es Salaam. CT.
———. *Vol. 1: Duku Duku.* Dar es Salaam Music and Sport. Dar es Salaam. CT.
———. *Yellow Card.* Limitless Sky Records, 2002. CD.
Kilimanjaro Band. *Gere.* Kilimanjaro Band. Dar es Salaam, 2004. CD.
———. *Kata-Kata.* Kilimanjaro Band. 1989. CT.
———. *Kinyaunyau.* Kilimanjaro Band. Dar es Salaam, 2000. CD.
———. *Maua.* FM Music Bank. Dar es Salaam, 1997. CT.
Kilwa Jazz. "Malaika/Jeni Nateseka." Saba Saba (Saba 7-203). 1973. 45 rpm disc.
———. "Niku Onyeshapo Pesa/Uwache Kuruka." Saba Saba (Saba 7-204). 1973. 45 rpm disc.
———. *Wawili Wawili.* FKW. CD.
———. *Vol. 1–Vol. 3.* Dar es Salaam Music and Sport. Dar es Salaam, 2000. CT.
Kimbuteh, Jah. *True Democracy 2000–2010.* Roots and Kulture Production. 2000. CT.
Kinasha, Carola. *Maono.* 2008. CD.
King Crazy GK. *Nitakupa Nini?* GMC. 2002. CT.
King Kiki Masantula. *Jivereko.* Dar es Salaam Music and Sport. 1999. CT.
———. *Kamanyola Bila Jasho.* King Kiki. Dar es Salaam, 2002. CT.
———. *Kamanyoia Masantula.* King Kiki Release, 2005. CD.
———. *Raisi Jakaya M Kikwete.* 13S Planet (PLANET006). 2008. CD.
———. *Sababu ya Nini.* Dar es Salaam Music and Sport. 2000. CT.
Lady Jay Dee (Judith Wambura). *Binti.* GMC/Smooth Vibes. 2003. CT.
———. *Machozi.* GMC. 2001. CT.
———. *Moto.* GMC. 2005. CT.
———. *Shukruni.* GMC. 2007. CT.
———. *Ya 5.* GMC. 2009. CT.
Lucky Star Taarab. "Kupe/Nakupenda." Polydor (POL 7-096). 1972. 45 rpm disc.
———. "Macho Yanacheka/Mwiba wa Mahaba." Saba Saba (SABA 7-75). 45 rpm disc.
Mabaga Fresh. *Utatanishi.* Musicland, 2001. CT.
Makwaia, Daudi. *Western Jazz Academia.* GMC. 2002. CT.

Mangwair. *a.k.a. Mimi.* GMC Wasanii Promoters Ltd. (GR-4, 142). CD.

MB Dog. *Si Uliniambia.* GMC Wasanii (RP-060413). 2006. CT.

———. *Dar Itawaka Moto.* GMC Wasanii. 2008. CT.

Mchinga Sound Band. *Kisiki cha Mpingo.* GMC. CT.

Micky Sound Band. *Kinate.* Micky Sound Band. Dar es Salaam, 2002.

Mjema, John. *Mimi Sio Mwizi.* GMC. 2001. CT.

MK Group with Kasongo Mpinda Clayton. *Kibela.* Dar es Salaam Music and Sport. CT.

Morogoro Jazz Band. "Kifo cha Karume/Mitindo Yetu." Polydor (POL 7-099). 1972. 45 rpm disc.

———. "Mapenzi Shuleni?/Nirudie Mama." Polydor (POL 7-146). 1973. 45 rpm disc.

———. "Mapenzi Yanitesa/Dr. Kleruu." Polydor (POL 7-098). 1972. 45 rpm disc.

———. "Zima Moto/Sululu ya Moro." Polydor (POL 7-081). 1972. 45 rpm disc.

Mr. Ebbo. *Fahari Yako.* GMC. 2002. CT.

———. *Niwe wa wewe.* Bang Bit Records. CT.

Mr. Nice. *Bahati.* FKW, F.K Mitha &Sons, Kings Brothers Wananchi Stores (FKW 247). CT.

———. *Bwana Shamba.* FKW, F.K Mitha &Sons, Kings Brothers Wananchi Stores (FKW 417). CT.

———. *Mama.* FKW, F.K Mitha &Sons, Kings Brothers Wananchi Stores (FKW 082). CT.

———. *Rafiki* FKW, F.K Mitha &Sons, Kings Brothers Wananchi Stores (FKW 127). CT.

Mrisho Mpoto. *Mjomba/Nikipata Nauli.* Global Limited (2C). CT.

Mr. II/II Proud/Sugu. *Itikadi.* Global Sounds, Mamu Stores, Congo Corridor Store (GMC). 2002. CD.

———. *Millenia.* GMC (Master J Producer). 2000. CT.

———. *Muziki na Maisha.* Global Sounds, Mamu Stores, Congo Corridor Store (GMC). 2001. CT.

———. *Na Mimi.* 1995. CT.

———. *Ndani ya Bongo.* FM Music Bank. 1996. CT.

———. *Niite Mr. II.* FM Music Bank. 1998. CT.

———. *Nje ya Bongo.* Mr. II. 1999. CT.

———. *Sugu.* Social Misfit (SME0055). 2004. CT.

Msondo Ngoma Music Band. *Kaza Moyo.* FKW. 2005. CD

———. *The Best Of Msondo Ngoma.* Ujamaa Records (UR004). CD.

Mugarula, L M. "Choma Moto/Sungura." TFC (2008). 1976. 45 rpm disc.

Muungano Cultural Troupe. *Vol. 13: Mtambaji Katambiwa.* FK Mitha et al. 1998. CT.

———. *Vol. 18: Mambo Bado.* GMC. 2000. CT.

———. *Vol. 19: Sanamu la Michelini.* GMC. 2000.

———. *Vol. 20: Eti Mambo ya Fesha.* GMC. Dar es Salaam, 2001. CT.

———. *Vol. 21: Kishata Mtaa.* GMC Wasanii Promoters Ltd.. 2005. CT.

Mwinshehe, Mbaraka. *Masimango: Best of Tanzania 1969–1972.* Dizim Records, dizim 4702. CD, 2000. CT.

———. *Ukumbusho, Vol. 1: Nisalimie Wanazaire.* Polydor (POLP 536). 1983. CT.

———. *Ukumbusho, Vol. 2: Urafiki Mwisho wa Mwezi.* Polydor (POLP 537). 1983. CT.

———. *Ukumbusho, Vol. 3: Nirudie Mama.* Polydor (POLP 542). 1983. CT.

———. *Ukumbusho, Vol. 4: Bibi wa Watu.* Polydor (POLP 550). 1985. CT.

———. *Ukumbusho, Vol. 5: Matamko ya Viongozi Wetu.* Polydor (POLP 553). 1986. CT.

———. *Ukumbusho, Vol. 6: Kifo cha Pesa.* Polydor (POLP 564). 1987. CT.

———. *Ukumbusho, Vol. 7: Penzi Lako Hatari.* Polydor (POLP 566). 1988. CT.

Ndala Kasheba. *Best of Ndala Kasheba, vol. 1.* Dar es Salaam Music and Sport. 1999. CT

———. *Bingwa: Kesi ya Khanga pt. 1.* CT.

———. *Yellow Card.* Africa Nature Ltd. Limitless Sky Records. 2002. CD .

Nuta Jazz Band. "Amina/Bwana Mwizi." African Beat (AB 7-5069). 1969. 45 rpm disc.

———. "Dada Mwajuma/Dunia Ya Leo Mbaya." Philips (PK 7-9173). 1973. 45 rpm disc.

———. "Mpenzi Nakupenda/Kipenzi Moshi." African Beat (AB 7-5066). 1969. 45 rpm disc.

———. "Mpenzi Ninakukanya/Instrumental no.2." Philips (PK 7-9157). 1973. 45 rpm disc.

———. "Ninapo Kuona/Gomiyangu." African Beat (AB 7-5076). 1969. 45 rpm disc.

———. "Punguza Chenga Zako/Kisomo Cha Watu Wazima." Uhuru Stars (US 7-27). 1975. 45 rpm disc.

Orchestra Safari Trippers. "Nenda Shule Rosa/Arusi." Saba Saba (Saba 7-152). 1973. 45 rpm disc.

Orchestra Super Volcano/Super Volcano/Super Volcano Jazz Band. "Angela Rudi Makwenu, part 1/Angela Rudi Makwenu part 2." Polydor (POL 520). 1974. 45pm disc.

———. "Fulu Ilagala/Walisema." Polydor (POL 7-266). 1974. 45pm disc.

———. "Harusi Imevunjika/Unaulizwa." Polydor (POL 7-268). 1974. 45pm disc.

———. "Masika No. 2/Masika Zole-Zole." Polydor (POL 7-265). 1974. 45pm disc.

———. "Utanikondesha Maria/Mama Chakula Bora." Polydor (POL 189). 1973. 45pm disc.

Ongala, Remmy and (Orchestra) Super Matimila. *Kifo.* GMC. Dar es Salaam, 2000. CT.

———. *Kilio Cha Samaki.* GMC. Dar es Salaam, 2000 [1993]. CT.

———. "Maisha." TFC (SP 002). 45 rpm disc.

———. *Mambo.* Real World, CDRW 22. 1991. CT.

———. *Mbele kwa Mbele.* GMC. Dar es Salaam, 2002 CT.

———. *Nalilia Mwana.* WOMAD, WOMAD010. 1988. CT.

———. *On Stage With.* Ahadi (Kenya). AHDLP 6007. 1988. CT.

———. *Sema.* WOMAD SELECT, WS 002. 1996. CD.

———. *Songs for the Poor Man.* Real World, CDRW 06. 1989. CD.

Orchestra BIMA Lee. *Mbele kwa Mbele.* GMC. 2002. CT.

———. "Ombi Pts 1 & 2." Lima 5. 45 rpm disc.

Orchestra Fauvette. *Nono na Kaleme.* Dar es Salaam Music and Sport. Dar es Salaam. CT.

Orchestre Makassy. "Obasani Part I/Obasani Part II." Kwetu (RTRS1038). 45 rpm disc.

Orchestre Safari Sound. 1984. *Dunia Msongamano.* Tanzania Film Company (TFCLP 001). 1984. LP.

OTTU Jazz Band. *Demokrasia ya Mapenzi.* F.K. Mitha & Sons, 2000. CT.

———. *Gangamala.* F.K. Mitha & Sons et al. [Big Seven]. 1998. CT.

———. *Kimanzichana.* 1998. CT.

———. *Piga Ua, Talaka Utatota.* Ujamaa Records (UR002). 2005. CT.

———. *Rabana.* FKW. Dar es Salaam, 2001. CT.

Prince Dully Sykes. *Historia ya Kweli.* GMC. 2002. CT.

Professor Jay. *Aluta Continua.* GMC Wasanii Promoters Ltd. 2007. CT.

———. *J.O.S.E.P.H.* GMC Wasanii Promoters Ltd. (GR-5, 365). 2006. CD .

————. *Machozi, Jasho, na Damu.* FKW. Dar es Salaam, 2001. CT.

————. *Mapinduzi Halisi.* GMC Wasanii. 2003. CT.

Rhythms Experts Band (led by Joseph Silasi). "Lukas Ana Wasi Wasi." Trek (XYZ 5242). 78 rpm disc.

————. "Mapenzi Yakwetu Sisi/Luka Nipe Nafasi Bwana." Trek (XYZ 5243/6102). 78 rpm disc.

Rose Muhando. *Jipange Sawa Sawa.* GMC (Kw 0801317). CT.

————. *Uwe Macho.* GMC Wasanii Promoters Ltd. 2005. CD.

————. *Zawadi ya Christmas.* GMC (Kw 0610138). CD.

Saad, Siti Binti. "Ashee Regea, part 1/Ashea Reagea, part 2." Columbia (EO-2001). June 1939. 78 rpm disc.

————. "Manzowea Namapenzi, part 1/Manzowea Namapenzi, part 2." Columbia (EO-2006). June 1939. 78 rpm disc.

————. "Ya Laiti, part 1/Ya Laiti, part 2." Columbia (EO-2002). June 1939. 78 rpm disc.

Safari Trippers Band (led by Marijani Rajab). *Georgina.* Dar es Salaam Music and Sport. Dar es Salaam. CT.

————. *Rosa (Nenda Shule).* Dar es Salaam Music and Sport. Dar es Salaam. CT.

Saida Entertainment. *Vol. 1: Kanichambua kama Karanga.* FMP C-092. FM Music Bank. Dar es Salaam, 2001. CT.

————. *Vol. 2: Mapenzi Kizunguzungu.* Tape 102. FM Music Bank. Dar es Salaam, 2002. CT.

Salum's Brass Band (led by Salum Seliman). "Marafiki/Hawana Kazi Makarani." Trek (XYZ 5083/6063). 78 rpm disc.

————. "Mahava Matamu/Sayadana Khalifa na Malikiia." Trek (XYZ 6059/6060). 78 rpm disc.

————. "Shukurani/Twakukumbuka." Trek (XYZ 6061/62). 78 rpm disc.

Sele, Afande. *Darubuni Kali.* GMC Wasanii (GR-4, 056). 2004. CD.

Shakila. *Vol. 2: Kali za Taarab.* GMC. Dar es Salaam, 2001. CD.

Shikamoo Jazz Band. *Vol. 1: Chela Chela.* RetroTan. CD.

————. *Vol. 2: Wazee wa Safari.* RetroTan, RC 005. CD.

Stone Musica. *Chini ya Ulinzi.* GMC. 2002. CT.

Sykes, Ally. "Nakupenda Ricky/Tabu." Jambo. 78 rpm disc.

————. "Pene Lango [sic]/Nakupenda." From Jambo Film "Nyimbo za Ki-Sasa." Jambo (EA-244). 78 rpm disc.

————. "Wangu Ricky/Mpenzi Teckla." From Jambo Film "Nyimbo za Ki-Sasa." Jambo. 78 rpm disc.

Tabora Jazz Band. "Dada Helena/Kaka Tulia." Saba Saba (SABA 7-180). 45 rpm disc.

————. "Mpenzi Sofia/Sakina Umeni Shida." Saba Saba (SABA 7-162). 45 rpm disc.

————. *Tucheze Segere.* FKW. CT.

Tanzania One Theatre Band. *Vol. 1: Achimenengule: Mtaji wa Masikini.* TOT 567. CT.

Tanzania One Theatre Kwaya. *Mgeni, TOT Plus 10th Anniversary.* TOT 575. Super Shine Ltd. Zanzibar, 2002. CT.

————. *Nyimbo za Maombolezo ya Mwalimu J.K. Nyerere.* TOT 532. Dar es Salaam, 1999. CT.

————. *Vol. 3: Tuombe.* Space Recordings Ltd., Mamu Stores, Down Town, and Galaxy. Dar es Salaam, 1993. CT.

Tanzania One Theatre Taarab. *Vol. 22: Mambo Iko Huku.* TOT (561). 1999. CT.

————. *Vol. 23: Zoba.* Dar es Salaam, 1999. CT.

————. *Vol. 24: Mtie Kamba Mumeo.* TOT (563). 2000. CT.

————. *Vol. 25: New* Milenia *2000 Y2K.* TOT (565). 2000. CT.

————. *Vol. 26: Kinyan Gunya.* TOT (566). 2001. CT.

————. *Vol. 33: Nnalijua Jiji.* Super Shine Ltd. Zanzibar. CD.

TatuNane. *Bongoland.* Amanda Music (MC AMA 9504). 1995. CD.

————. *Tanzanian Beat (World Music Library).* King Record Co. (KICC 5221). 1997. CD.

Tuff Gong Music (Reggae Boy's [*sic*]). *Vol. 1: Ikisu Kyonangike.* GMC. Dar es Salaam, 2001. CT.

Urafiki Jazz Band. "CCM/Jembe na Panga." Moto Moto (1013). 1978. 45 rpm disc.

————. "Rukia Hukusikia/Sumu ya Mapenzi." Kwetu (RTRS1022). 1976. 45 rpm disc.

————. *Vol. 1: Liptoyo Wabaya.* FKW. Dar es Salaam, 2001. CT.

————. *Vol. 2: Jembe na Panga.* FKW. Dar es Salaam, 2001. CT.

————. *Vol. 3: Kwa Mjomba.* FKW. Dar es Salaam, 2001. CT.

Various Artists. *Tudumishe Utamaduni na . . . Siasa Yetu.* Azimio (AZLP-001). LP.

————. *Tanzania Hit Parade 88.* Ahadi (AHDLP 6005). 1988. LP.

————. *Dada Kidawa.* Original Music (OMCD032). 1995. LP.

————. *Muziki wa Dansi.* Africassette (AC 9403). 1995. CD.

————. *The Tanzania Sound.* Original Music (OMCD 018). LP.

————. *Asabuhi, Coulds FM.* GMC. Dar es Salaam, 2000. CD.

————. *Madongo Shoka.* Bongo Records. GMC. Dar es Salaam, 2002. CD.

————. *Ujumbe na Ladha.* MJ Records. GMC. Dar es Salaam, 2002. CD.

————. *Vol. 1: Bongo Explosion.* FKW. Dar es Salaam, 2002. CD.

————. *Vol. 1: Bongo Hottest Flava.* GMC. Dar es Salaam, 2002. CD.

————. *Tanzania Instruments: Tanganyika 1950.* SWP Records (SWP022). 2003. CD.

————. *Tanzania Vocals: Tanganyika 1950.* SWP Records (SWP023). 2003. CD.

————. *Bongo Flava: Swahili Rap from Tanzania.* Out Here Records (OH003). 2004.

————. *Out of Cuba: Latin American Music Takes Africa by Storm.* Topic Records (TSCD927). 2004. CD.

————. *Vol. 1–Vol. 8: Bingwa za Bongo.* GMC Wasanii Promtoers Ltd. 2004–2005.

————. *Zanzibara, Vol. 3: Ujamaa.* Buda Musique (860142). 2007. CD.

————. *Poetry and Languid Charm: Swahili Music from Tanzania and Kenya from the 1920s to the 1950s.* Topic Records (TSCD936). 2007. CD.

————. *Zanzibara, Vol. 5: Hot in Dar.* Buda Musique (860184). 2009. CD.

Vijana Jazz Band. "Hasira Hasara part1/Hasira Hasara part 2." Polydor (Pol 462). 1980. 45 rpm disc.

————. *Mary Maria.* Ahadi (AHDLP 6004). 1986. CT.

————. "Ngoma/Lela." Moto Moto Dynamite (TNT7). 1978. 45 rpm disc.

————. "Pili Nihurumie/Zuhura Naondoka." Moto Moto (Moto 7-928). 1976. 45 rpm disc.

————. "Shangazi/Gwe Manetu Fii." Moto Moto (Moto 7-923). 1975. 45 rpm disc.

————. "Stella Mwenye Fikara Nzuri part 1/Stella Mwenye Fikara Nzuri part 2." Polydor (Pol 462). 1980. 45 rpm disc.

————. "Urijani Mwema/Koka Koka." Moto Moto (Moto 7-922). 1975. 45 rpm disc.

Vijana Jazz Orchestra. *Mzinga.* Mamu Store et al. [Big Five] (C 4860). CT.

————. *Ogopa Tapeli.* F.K. Mitha et al. [Big Seven]. CT.

————. *Pambamoto.* F.K. Mitha et al. [Big Seven]. 1997. CT.

————. *Vol. 3: Mwanamke Salo.* F.K. Mitha et al. [Big Seven]. 1997. CT.

————. *Zilipendwa Vol. and Vol. 2.* Dar es Salaam Music and Sport. Dar es Salaam, 1999. CT.

Vijana wa Mbeya. "Siwezi kuiacha rumba/Mtoto mzuri simwachi." *Gallotone* (XYZ4895/XYZ4896). 1950. 78 rpm disc.

Wagosi wa Kaya. *Nyeti.* GMC Wasanii (GR-5, 413). CT.

————. *Ripoti Kamili.* GMC. MJ Productions. N.D. CT.

————. *Ukweli Mtupu.* GMC. Dar es Salaam, 2002. CT.

Wanaume (TMK). *Kutoka Kiumeni.* GMC Wasanii (GR-4 222). 2002. CT.

Western Jazz Band. [See Table 7.1 for a list of 45 rpm discs.]

————. *Rosa.* Dar es Salaam Music and Sport. Dar es Salaam. CT.

Zay B. *Mama Afrika.* GMC. Dar es Salaam, 2002. CT.

# Index

Page numbers in *italics* refer to illustrations.
Page numbers followed by a *t* refer to tables.

**Alex Perullo** is Associate Professor of Ethnomusicology and African Studies at Bryant University. His research interests include popular music, migration, youth and urban society, and intellectual property rights in eastern and central Africa. He has published articles in *Africa Today, Popular Music and Society, Ethnomusicology,* and several edited volumes. He is also co-editor of the EVIA Digital Archive and founder of the Tanzania Education Resource Network (TERN).